Trade Policy in Developing Countrie

Trade Policy in Developing Countries is an analysis aimed at academics, graduate students, and professional, policy-oriented economists. It is the first work in the field to examine trade policy in an integrated theoretical framework based on optimizing dynamic models that pay careful attention to the structural features of developing country economies. Following a thorough critique of the debate on inward- vs. outward-oriented trade regimes, Buffie explores the main issues of concern to less developed countries in the areas of optimal commercial policy, trade liberalization, and direct foreign investment. In addition to many new and important results, the book contains systematic reviews of the empirical evidence and three expositional chapters that show the reader how to use the technical machinery of economic theory to construct and manipulate multisector dynamic general equilibrium models.

Edward F. Buffie is Professor of Economics at Indiana University. He previously taught at the University of Pennsylvania and Vanderbilt University. Professor Buffie has written extensively on trade and macroeconomic policies in less developed countries, publishing his research in diverse scholarly journals such as *International Economic Review, Journal of Economic Dynamics and Control, Economica, Journal of International Economics, Journal of Monetary Economics, Oxford Economic Papers, Journal of Development Economics, European Economic Review*, and *Journal of Public Economics*. He was an associate editor of the *Journal of Development Economics* from 1990 to 1995 and has served as a consultant to The World Bank, the Inter-American Development Bank, and the United States Agency for International Development.

Trade Policy in Developing Countries

EDWARD F. BUFFIE
Indiana University

CAMBRIDGE
UNIVERSITY PRESS

CAMBRIDGE
UNIVERSITY PRESS

32 Avenue of the Americas, New York NY 10013-2473, USA

Cambridge University Press is part of the University of Cambridge.

It furthers the University's mission by disseminating knowledge in the pursuit of education, learning and research at the highest international levels of excellence.

www.cambridge.org
Information on this title: www.cambridge.org/9780521004268

© Edward F. Buffie 2001

First published 2001

A catalogue record for this publication is available from the British Library

Library of Congress Cataloguing in Publication data

Buffie, Edward F.
  Trade policy in developing counries / Edward F. Buffie.
    p. cm.
  Includes bibliographical references and index.
  ISBN 0-521-78223-6
    1. Development countries—Commercial policy—Econometric models.
    2. Free trade—Developing countries—Econometric models.
    3. Investments, Foreign—Developing countries—Econometric models.
    I. Title.

  HF1413.B83   2001
  382′.3′091724   dc21   00-063071

ISBN 978-0-521-78223-4 Hardback
ISBN 978-0-521-00426-8 Paperback

Contents

CHAPTER 1

Introduction

Indeed, the association between higher growth rates and an export-promotion strategy had already been established before the present project began, although additional evidence has since confirmed the results. . . . It seemed neither necessary nor desirable to cover that ground again. (Krueger, 1983, p. 6)

That a liberal is preferable to a restrictive trade regime is now generally accepted, and a substantial body of empirical research carried out over the last 20 years supports this conclusion. (Michaely, Papageorgiou, and Choksi, 1991, p. 1)

The question of the wisdom of an outward-oriented (export-promoting) strategy may be considered to have been settled. (Bhagwati, 1987, p. 257)

[O]ne must resist succumbing to the oversimplifications and generalizations that have too frequently plagued the debates in the sphere of trade strategy . . . what seems to emerge from this survey is a need for a fresh review of fairly major proportions . . . of experience and knowledge of the interaction between trade and other policies and their joint effects upon industrialization and development. Such a review would be particularly valuable if it avoided prejudgements about the relative efficacy of specific trade and other policies in general; and instead explored the specific circumstances in which particular policies, instruments, and policy mixes were less or more effective. (Helleiner, 1990, pp. 880, 894)

The mainstream view is that . . . policy should be directed toward eliminating barriers to trade. There is also an increasing body of literature supporting the opposite point of view. . . . The best summary so far is that the debate is inconclusive: an a priori case for either an open or closed trade policy can never be fully proved . . . this Scotch verdict also applies to the empirical evidence on the relationship between openness and growth. (Shapiro and Taylor, 1990, p. 870)

Neat certainties have a very limited truth. (Robertson Davies, *The Merry Heart*, p. 281)

The last ten years have seen profound changes in the conduct of trade policy in the Third World. After following highly protectionist policies

1

from the end of WWII until 1990, many less developed countries (LDCs) have eliminated quotas and sharply reduced tariffs. Effective rates of protection above 200%, which were common in earlier decades, are now comparatively rare. But while protection is less extreme, it is by no means dead. Trade policy still retains a strong import-substituting bias in much of Sub-Saharan Africa and South Asia. Even in regions where liberalization has progressed much further, one does not have to search very long to find countries that subject imported consumer goods to tariffs of 30% plus a variety of hidden trade taxes.[1]

None of this has escaped the attention of neoclassical economists who believe in the sanctity of free trade. The prevalence of import-substituting industrialization has provoked no less than five major studies aimed at convincing policy makers their countries would fare better under a more outward, export-oriented trade strategy.[2] These studies have demonstrated successfully that there is no sound economic justification for tariffs and quotas that allow domestic prices to be two or three times higher than prices in world markets. But despite a general consensus that some reduction in trade barriers is desirable, the debate on trade policy remains contentious, at times acrimonious. Critics of the World Bank charge that its ill-conceived programs of trade liberalization are inflicting de-industrialization in Sub-Saharan Africa,[3] structuralist economists continue to argue that moderate protection may be beneficial, and the most recent large-scale study of LDC trade policy casts doubt on the objectivity and robustness of the conclusions trumpeted in earlier studies: ". . . to suggest that there is a universal trade policy prescription that will generate improved economic performance for all is to ignore too much recent experience" (Helleiner, 1994, p. 32).[4] Clearly, not

---

[1] In the Dominican Republic, the average tariff on consumer imports was 28% in the mid-nineties. Foreign exchange commissions, consular legalization fees, charges for "services rendered by the port authorities," and selective consumption taxes (that fall only on imports), however, push the effective tariff up to 97%. Various hidden trade taxes are also significant in Brazil, Colombia, and El Salvador. See *Trade Policy Review* (World Trade Organization) for the details.
[2] See Little, Scitovsky, and Scott (1970), Balassa and Associates (1971), Krueger (1978) and Bhagwati (1978), Krueger et al. (1982), and Michaely, Papageorgiou, and Choksi (1991).
[3] See, for example, Stein (1992), Cornia van der Hoeven and Mkandawire (1992), and Stewart (1994).
[4] The World Institute for Development Economics Research (WIDER) commissioned a new study to provide a "balanced and independent review" of LDC experiences with trade policy and industrialization in the seventies and eighties (Helleiner, 1994).

everyone concedes that proponents of an export-oriented strategy have a monopoly on the truth, or even a commanding market share. The debate is not closed.

This book analyzes the main issues of concern to LDCs in the areas of commercial policy, trade liberalization, and direct foreign investment in an integrated theoretical framework. Is there really a need for this given all the work that has been done on the pure theory of international trade and all that has been written about trade policy in developing countries? I believe there is. Students of development economics will find much that is useful and relevant in existing trade theory. They may also, however, doubt the value of time spent studying the factor–price equalization theorem or grow weary after a while of laboring through models more appropriate for Canada than Bangladesh or Costa Rica. The trade and development literature, on the other hand, is conspicuously lacking in formal theory and rigorous analysis. This criticism applies with special force to the heart of the literature: the major studies of LDC trade policy are long on advocacy and assertion but distressingly short on clean analytical and empirical results.

In what follows the reader will encounter many optimizing dynamic general equilibrium models. The emphasis on dynamics is unusual in a book devoted to trade policy. It is essential, however, to a theory-based analysis of trade policy in developing countries. Policy makers in LDCs wish to know *inter alia* how large the short-run costs of liberalization are relative to its long-run benefits, what underemployment and underinvestment imply for the optimal export subsidy and the optimal tariffs on consumer goods, intermediate inputs and capital goods, the extent to which lack of credibility may undermine reforms that would otherwise work well, whether foreign investment displaces or is complementary to domestic investment, and how different trade taxes affect real wages and the distribution of income in the short vs. long run. The analysis of these and other issues requires an intertemporal framework that pays careful attention to sectoral interactions and the structural features of production. Consequently, most of the analysis in the book is based on dynamic general equilibrium models of varying complexity. I am trying to sell not only a particular set of conclusions but also a general approach to the analysis of policy issues.

Calibration techniques are an important part of the approach. The analysis of optimizing dynamic models is inherently demanding because current economic actions both depend on and influence the economy's future path. In two- or three-sector dynamic models this can produce complicated interactions and dense, tortuous algebra. It often proves useful, therefore, to supplement theory with numerical solutions that cover a wide range of potentially relevant cases. Sometimes the numerical solutions will argue strongly in favor of a particular outcome. At the very least, they can help narrow the zone of disagreement; that is, if the model is judged acceptable, then all interested parties can agree that policy x is desirable when parameter z lies between 0 and .75.

1.1   Overview of the Book

The main body of the book consists of five chapters on different aspects of trade policy and three expositional chapters on duality theory and solution techniques in continuous-time dynamic models. The expositional chapters do not pretend to be comprehensive. My objective is rather to show the reader how to use the technical machinery of economic theory to build and solve interesting general equilibrium models. In my view, we do a bad job of this in economics. For some reason, many of the tools widely used in the application of theory have not yet found their way into graduate textbooks. The texts on dynamics are especially deficient in this regard. The solution for the perfect foresight path in dynamic general equilibrium models typically requires solutions from a pseudostatic variant of the model that relates the paths of endogenous variables to the paths of the variables that form the dynamic system. Strangely, most texts do not discuss this or provide a clear statement of the condition for saddlepoint stability in higher dimensional models, and none explains how to solve for the transition path when a policy or shock is temporary instead of permanent. Nor is it easy to learn the relevant techniques from the journals. The journals are full of cryptic statements of the type "Using standard solution techniques, we obtain . . ." or "It is straightforward to show that . . ." But for the uninitiated (e.g., graduate students), nothing is "straightforward" and solution techniques are not "standard."

The expositional chapters are introduced when needed. Since duality theory is used throughout the text, it is covered in Chapter 2. The material on dynamics appears later, in Chapters 4 and 7. The rationale for this organizational structure is that it is probably most efficient to study the solution techniques just before the chapters which utilize the techniques intensively. Nothing, however, prevents those who have a robust appetite for mathematics from reading Chapters 4 and 7 immediately after Chapter 2 – the three "Tools and Tricks of the Trade" chapters are a self-contained unit.

I begin the analysis of trade policy proper in Chapter 3 with a critique of the debate on the merits of inward- vs. outward-oriented trade regimes. The central message of the critique is that there is a considerable imbalance in the literature between what is asserted and what is actually known. If defenders of protection are too quick to dismiss the policy prescriptions of neoclassical economics, it is equally true that proponents of export promotion have repeatedly made claims far stronger than either theory or empirical evidence can support. It can be said with some assurance that extreme protectionist policies are economically harmful. But the case for free trade is not airtight, and there is no general theoretical presumption that the market failures common in LDCs favor an export-oriented rather than an import-substituting trade strategy. At present, far more is known about the consequences of bad trade policy than about the makeup of optimal trade policy.

This latter conclusion serves as the motivation for Chapter 5. Guidelines for optimal commercial policy should be based on the results obtained from optimizing dynamic models that occupy the middle ground between toy models that leave out too much and CGE black boxes that include too much and rely on ad hoc behavioral assumptions. I try to make some progress in this direction by developing a model that incorporates export, import-competing, and nontradables production, capital accumulation in all three sectors, imports of intermediate inputs, consumer goods, and capital goods, and a realistic government budget constraint. The allocation of resources at the initial free trade equilibrium is distorted by underemployment and underinvestment, and the task of the social planner is to choose the three import tariffs, the export subsidy, and the value added tax to maximize social welfare subject to the constraint that revenues cover the cost of export subsidies and other government expenditures.

The results provide something for everyone. Advocates of *sensible* import-substituting policies will be happy with the conclusion that an escalated structure of protection (i.e., higher tariffs on consumer goods than on intermediate inputs and capital goods) is more effective in stimulating capital accumulation and reducing underemployment than export promotion. But moderately high levels of protection are optimal only when combined with substantial export subsidies in the primary sector. If primary export subsidies are not feasible because of political or administrative constraints, the optimal effective rate of protection is quite low (10–30%). Moreover, in many cases, the direction of trade changes and the former import-substituting sector becomes a net exporter of manufactured goods. Overall, therefore, the results support a mixed ISEP strategy – either import substitution plus export promotion or import substitution then export promotion.

The finding that most countries would be better off had they opted for a moderate ISEP strategy does not necessarily justify calls for aggressive trade liberalization. When contemplating cuts in protection, the government has to be sure it can handle any adverse effects on employment and the balance of payments, and that the long-run gains from liberalization suffice to compensate for losses suffered during the adjustment process. Chapters 6 and 8 deal with these issues. Chapter 6 focuses mainly on the problem of transitory unemployment. This is not a subject that lends itself to sharply defined conclusions because much depends on the nature of technology, private sector expectations, the speed of adjustment in the labor market, and the other policies that comprise the reform program. Several themes emerge, however, from the analysis: (i) different types of liberalization programs would be expected to have different *qualitative* effects on labor demand and unemployment; (ii) weak credibility exacerbates the problem of transitory unemployment; and (iii) in some cases the losses from transitory unemployment are relatively large and the optimal tariff cut stops well short of the *ex ante* optimal tariff.

The credibility problem shows up in Chapter 6 because fears that liberalization may not last affect labor mobility and the duration of transitory unemployment. Chapter 8 investigates two other aspects of the problem. The first part of the chapter develops Guillermo Calvo's crucial insight that expectations of a policy reversal distort intertemporal choice by creating an incentive to consume more in the near term while imports are temporarily cheap. Employing a mix of theory and numerical methods, I analyze how large the losses from the intertemporal distortion are relative to the gains from trade and the implications of this for the optimal tariff cut. The second part of the chapter seeks explanations for the key stylized fact that many liberalization programs have been abandoned in the face of unexpectedly large balance of payments deficits. One explanation for the policy reversals is simply that the government lacks the foreign exchange reserves to support the liberalization attempt. A second, equally straightforward explanation holds that persistent payments deficits stem from the failure to properly coordinate fiscal policy and trade reform. These explanations may be correct in many cases, but they are not the only possible explanations. The analysis in Chapter 8 shows that the causal links connecting credibility, payments deficits, and fiscal adjustment are subtle and bidirectional when the government's reputation has been damaged by past failures. It may not be easy therefore to judge whether private sector pessimism or incompatible policies are the source of failure: reform programs that are fundamentally sound may fail merely because they are expected to fail.

Chapter 9 takes up the question of what LDCs have to gain from direct foreign investment. I first analyze how foreign investment affects welfare and the dynamics of domestic capital accumulation and under-employment in the simplest case where foreign firms use the same technology as domestic firms and are not subject to any special regulations. This is followed by analysis of more complicated cases involving technology transfer, joint ventures and minimum export requirements. It turns out that a lot depends on the details of the overall package, including the sector in which foreign firms invest. The prospects for a welfare gain are best when foreign investment generates favorable technological spillovers and the government imposes minimum export and local equity requirements. Even then, however, it is risky to allow foreign firms to compete with domestic firms in the home manufactures market. This type of foreign investment often reduces the *aggregate* capital stock (i.e., it crowds out domestic capital more than one-for-one) and worsens underemployment in the long run. Thus, the results do not support the current trend toward laissez faire policies. In a second-best environment characterized by underemployment and underinvestment, it does not make sense to drop performance requirements and let foreign firms invest in any sector they like.

Chapters 2–9 contain many models and many results. They also leave a lot of territory unexplored. In some chapters, the analysis ignores important policies; in others, it is restricted to models that are appropriate for region A of the Third World but not regions B, C, and D. The concluding chapter elaborates on this and the closely related subject of promising directions for future research.

CHAPTER 2

Tools and Tricks of the Trade, Part I: Duality Theory

Many policy issues in development economics cannot be addressed in a rigorous manner without building models that allow for considerable structural detail. Depending on the issue, it may be important to distinguish between agriculture and industry, between importable, exportable, and nontraded goods, between employment in high-wage vs. low-wage sectors, between domestically produced and imported capital goods, or between private and parastatal production. Unfortunately, there is a basic problem with the generally laudable strategy of including all relevant structural detail in a model: the more complicated the economic interactions, the messier the analysis and the more difficult it is to derive clean, insightful results. This is why duality theory should be part of the policy-oriented development economist's tool kit. Duality theory provides the model builder with functions based on the solutions to various static optimization problems. The functions summarize in a compact manner how demand and supply depend on preferences, technology, and optimizing behavior on the part of competitive, price-taking firms and consumers. This enables multisector general equilibrium models to be specified and manipulated with comparative ease as it is not necessary to explicitly solve the optimization problems that govern private agents' behavior. When duality theory is used to characterize demand and supply responses, general comparative statics results can be derived directly by exploiting the properties of the relevant maximum or minimum value functions.

2.1   Duality Theory and Supply

I start by discussing the duality functions that describe production and supply. The exposition will be heuristic, with an emphasis on how to apply duality theory for the purpose of constructing and manipulating models. Readers who desire a more in-depth treatment of the subject should consult Blackorby, Primont, and Russel (1978); Diewert (1978); McFadden (1978); Chambers (1988); and Cornes (1992).

8

2.1.1   The Cost Function

Let $\mathbf{x} = (x_1, \ldots x_n)$ be a vector of inputs, $\mathbf{w} = (w_1, \ldots w_n)$ an associated vector of factor prices, Q output, and $f(\mathbf{x})$ an increasing, continuous, quasi-concave production function. The cost function is the solution to the problem of choosing inputs so as to minimize the cost of producing a given level of output:

$$C(\mathbf{w}, Q) = \underset{\{\mathbf{x}\}}{\text{Min}}\{\mathbf{wx}\mid\ f(\mathbf{x}) \geq Q, \quad \mathbf{x} \geq 0\}. \tag{1}$$

Since more inputs have to be purchased to produce more output, C is increasing in Q. It is also increasing, homogeneous of degree one, and concave in $\mathbf{w}$. Linear homogeneity follows from the observation that replacing $\mathbf{w}$ in (1) by $\lambda\mathbf{w}$ does not alter the optimal input choices. The concavity property falls out directly from a comparison of the true cost function and the cost function for Leontief technology. In the case of Leontief technology, C is a linear function of factor prices because the inputs x_i are fixed. Hence, if any substitution is possible, costs increase less than linearly when factor prices rise. This argument underlies the convexity/concavity properties of other duality functions – the general implication of substitution is that minimum value functions are concave in prices and maximum value functions are convex.

The structure of the optimization problem in (1) suggests a dual relationship between the cost function and the production function that appears in the constraint set. This conjecture is correct when technology is convex [i.e., $f(\mathbf{x})$ is quasi-concave] as the underlying production function can be recovered from the cost function. The procedure for doing so is straightforward. A continuous quasi-concave production function has convex isoquants. Every input vector on an isoquant is thus an optimal choice for some set of factor prices. By holding output constant and varying $\mathbf{w}$, the entire isoquant can be reconstructed from the cost function.

There is one slightly tricky aspect to the dual nature of cost and production functions. While the two functions embody the same information about technology, they need not bear a family resemblance. Functions that *do* possess this property are said to be self-dual. For example, the Cobb–Douglas production function

$$Q = x_1^b x_2^{1-b}$$

generates the similar-looking cost function

$$C(\mathbf{w}, Q) = kw_1^b w_2^{1-b} Q,$$

where $k \equiv b^{-b} (1 - b)^{b-1}$. Many of the other functional forms commonly used to represent technology are self-dual (e.g., Leontief and Constant Elasticity of Substitution (CES) functions). There are some exceptions, however. Translog functions, in particular, are not self-dual. A translog cost function can be generated from some well-behaved convex technology, but not from a translog production function.

2.1.1.1   INPUT DEMANDS AND FACTOR SUBSTITUTION PATTERNS

The cost function associated with a quasi-concave production function may have kinks or flat segments that preclude differential comparative statics analysis. Under the slightly stronger assumption that the production function is strictly quasi-concave, these curvature problems disappear. Strict quasi-concavity guarantees that the optimal input vector is unique and the cost function continuously differentiable. Moreover, the optimal input choices can be pulled out of the cost function in a single easy step. Recall from the envelope theorem that the adjustment of optimal input demands may be ignored when calculating the impact on the maximand $\mathbf{wx}$ of small changes in w_i – to a first-order effect, $\mathbf{w}\partial\mathbf{x}/\partial w_i = 0$. Thus,

$$C_i \equiv \partial C / \partial w_i = x_i(\mathbf{w}, Q).\tag{2}$$

The above result, that C_i yields the factor demand x_i, is known as *Shephard's lemma*.

I mentioned earlier that the duality of cost and production functions means that the firm's isoquant map can be reconstructed from its cost function. It should be possible, therefore, to describe the scope for substitution between inputs in terms of the cost function. There are several ways of doing this. The most direct is to assume C is twice differentiable and then define the conditional factor demand elasticities[1]

$$\eta_{ij} \equiv \frac{\partial x_i}{\partial w_j} \frac{w_j}{x_i} = \frac{C_{ij} w_j}{C_i}.\tag{3}$$

The conditional elasticities are subject to certain adding-up constraints. Since C is homogeneous of degree one in $\mathbf{w}$, its partial derivatives are homogeneous of degree zero.[2] Thus $C_i(\mathbf{w}, Q) = C_i(\alpha\mathbf{w}, Q)$, implying that for each input the own- and cross-price elasticities sum to zero:

---

[1] The *conditional* factor demand elasticity is defined for a given level of output.
[2] Functions that are homogeneous of degree k have partial derivatives that are homogeneous of degree $k - 1$.

$$\sum_{j=1}^{n} C_{ij}w_j = 0 \quad \Rightarrow \quad \sum_{j=1}^{n} C_{ij}w_j/C_i = \sum_{j=1}^{n} \eta_{ij} = 0, \qquad i = 1, \ldots n. \qquad (4)$$

Theory does not restrict the sign of η_{ij}, $i \neq j$, when there are more than two inputs. The own-price elasticity η_{ii}, however, cannot be positive. Since C is concave in $\mathbf{w}$, $[C_{ij}]$ is a symmetric, negative, semidefinite matrix having nonpositive elements on the diagonal. The own-price elasticity is of the same sign as C_{ii}, so $\eta_{ii} \leq 0$.

The second method of characterizing the curvature of isoquants relates the cost function to the Allen–Uzawa (AU) partial elasticities of substitution (Allen, 1938; Uzawa, 1962). The AU partial elasticity of substitution between factors i and j is defined as

$$\sigma_{ij} = \frac{C_{ij}C}{C_i C_j}.$$

The cost share for factor j, $\theta_j \equiv w_j x_j/C = w_j C_j/C$, links σ_{ij} and η_{ij}:[3]

$$\eta_{ij} \equiv \frac{C_{ij}w_j}{C_i} = \left(\frac{C_{ij}C}{C_i C_j} \right) \frac{w_j C_j}{C} = \sigma_{ij}\theta_j. \qquad (5)$$

From (5) and the adding-up constraint (4),

$$\sum_{j=1}^{n} \sigma_{ij}\theta_j = 0, \qquad i = 1, \ldots n. \qquad (6)$$

Furthermore, it is easily established from concavity of the cost function and the definition of the partial elasticities of substitution that $[\sigma_{ij}]$ is a

---

[3] The AU elasticity of substitution is often criticized as a nonintuitive elasticity that adds little or no information to that already contained in the conditional cross-price elasticity of demand (Chambers, 1988, p. 95; Blackorby and Russel, 1989). Blackorby and Russel argue, in addition, that it is not a natural measure of curvature faithful to Hicks' original concept of the elasticity of substitution.

Both of these criticisms strike me as superficial. The intuition for the AU elasticity is that it generalizes the decomposition of the cross-price elasticity for the two-input case to the case of many inputs. When there are just two inputs, the conditional cross-price elasticity η_{ij} can be expressed as the product of the cost share θ_j and the elasticity of substitution σ. In the general many-input case, σ_{ij} assumes the role of σ. The AU partial elasticity cannot be equated with a single substitution parameter (assuming there is more than one) in the underlying production function. It depends instead on all of the substitution parameters and cost shares that affect the degree to which an increase in w_j causes substitution toward or away from x_i. See the intuitive explanation given in example #2 at the end of the chapter.

symmetric, negative semidefinite matrix. This provides a number of additional, useful restrictions: $\sigma_{ii} \leq 0$, $\sigma_{ij} = \sigma_{ji}$ (by symmetry of $[\sigma_{ij}]$), and $\sigma_{ii}\sigma_{jj} \geq \sigma_{ij}^2$ (own-substitution effects are generally stronger than cross-substitution effects).[4]

Using the formula connecting the cost function to the AU partial elasticities, it is easy to shift from a general representation of technology to a particular production function. For a standard CES production function, $\sigma_{ij} = \sigma$, $i \neq j$, with $\sigma_{ij} = 1$ and $\sigma_{ij} = 0$ defining Cobb–Douglas and Leontief technology, respectively. More complicated, nested production functions can be defined by setting appropriate restrictions on subsets of the σ_{ij}. This is often the way to make precise an otherwise vague hypothesis about technology. Consider, for example, the claim, common in the development literature, that production at levels close to full-capacity output requires an adequate supply of foreign exchange because it is much more difficult to substitute between imported inputs and primary factors than between different primary factors. This suggests the production function $Q = F[V(K, L), Z]$, in which capital K and labor L produce value added V, which is then combined with imported intermediates Z to generate output. The particular separable form of the pro-

Blackorby and Russels' objection, that the AU elasticity of substitution does not subscribe to Hicks' definition of the elasticity of substitution, can be dealt with by taking "of substitution" out of the name for σ_{ij}. It certainly does not mean that the AU elasticity is not a useful measure of curvature. The AU elasticity is, to use Chambers' (p. 94) terminology, a one-factor–one-price elasticity of substitution that seeks only to measure the impact of a change in w_j on the demand for input x_i. The *Morishima elasticity of substitution* and the *shadow elasticity of substitution* provide suitable measures of how the input ratio x_i/x_j responds to a change in the relative price w_i/w_j (see Chambers, 1988, pp. 32–36, 93–100). But when production requires more than two inputs, these substitution elasticities may classify x_i and x_j as substitutes when an increase in w_j lowers the demand for x_i. Since all of the proposed elasticities of substitution have "shortcomings," the appropriate elasticity depends on the question one is interested in answering. Chambers has it right when he concludes (pp. 99–100): "The fact that differing elasticities do not give the same results when stratifying inputs into complements and substitutes does not mean that there is something inherently wrong with any of them. Rather, it highlights the difficulties ... with defining a meaningful measure of substitution relationships in the many-input case. The reader should bear in mind that each measures quite different, although related, phenomena. Thus, it seems apparent that applied production analysts might have occasion to be interested in all three concepts."

[4] A number of other restrictions can be derived from the signs of the principal minors of $[\sigma_{ij}]$. It is difficult, however, to give a clear intuitive interpretation of these restrictions.

duction function implies that the marginal rate of substitution between K and L is independent of Z. The corresponding restrictions on the AU partial elasticities of substitution are that σ_{KL} is independent of the price of intermediates and that $\sigma_{KZ} = \sigma_{LZ} = \sigma_{VZ}$.[5] If domestic production depends mainly on the availability of imported inputs, σ_{VZ} is positive but small in absolute terms and relative to σ_{KL}.

2.1.1.2   THE COST FUNCTION UNDER CONSTANT RETURNS TO SCALE

When there are constant returns to scale the technology used to produce one level of output can be replicated at any other level of output. Costs are minimized by finding the least costly way of producing one unit of output and then adjusting the scale of operations appropriately to meet the output target. Total costs are thus the product of output and the unit cost function $h(\mathbf{w})$:[6]

$$C = h(\mathbf{w})Q. \tag{7}$$

One other implication of constant returns technology is worth emphasizing. Perfectly competitive firms equate price P to marginal cost. Because $h(\mathbf{w})$ in (7) is both the marginal and average cost of production, $P = h(\mathbf{w})$ is equivalent to a zero-profit condition; firms in a competitive industry do not earn any pure economic profits.

2.1.2   The Revenue or GNP Function

The revenue or gross national product (GNP) function is the solution to the problem of choosing the output vector $\mathbf{Q} = (Q_1, \dots Q_m)$ so as to maximize the value of sales at the price vector $\mathbf{P} = (P_1, \dots P_m)$ subject

---

[5] Assume that the aggregator function $V(K, L)$ is homothetic and let P_z, w, and r denote, respectively, the price of the imported input, the wage, and the capital rental. $F[\cdot]$ is then weakly homothetically separable and the associated cost function is separable in P_z, (w, r) and output Q. Separability allows the cost function to be written as $C[P_z, c(w, r), Q]$, where $c(\cdot)$ is the exact price index for the composite input V and has all the properties of a cost function. Since $\sigma_{LZ} = \sigma_{KZ} = C_{21}C/C_2C_1$, capital and the imported input are AU substitutes to the same degree as labor and the imported input.

[6] Under constant returns to scale, $f(\alpha\mathbf{x}) = \alpha Q$. Set $\alpha = 1/Q$, define $\mathbf{x}^* = \mathbf{x}/Q$, and rewrite the minimization problem in (1) as

$$C(\mathbf{w}, Q) = \underset{\{\mathbf{x}^*\}}{\text{Min}}\{Q\mathbf{w}\mathbf{x}^* \mid f(\mathbf{x}^*) \geq 1, \quad \mathbf{x}^* \geq 0\}$$
$$= Q\underset{\{\mathbf{x}^*\}}{\text{Min}}\{\mathbf{w}\mathbf{x}^* \mid f(\mathbf{x}^*) \geq 1, \quad \mathbf{x}^* \geq 0\} = Qh(\mathbf{w}).$$

to the constraints imposed by the m production functions $f^j(\mathbf{x}^j)$ and available factor supplies $\mathbf{X} = (X_1, \ldots X_n)$. Assuming that all output fetches a positive price, we can set $Q_j = f^j(\mathbf{x}^j)$ to eliminate the constraints involving the production functions and state the maximization problem in terms of choosing the optimal allocation of inputs (x_i^j) across sectors:

$$R(\mathbf{P}, \mathbf{X}) = \underset{\{\mathbf{x}^j\}}{\text{Max}} \left\{ \sum_{j=1}^{m} P_j f^j(\mathbf{x}^j) \; \middle| \; \sum_{j=1}^{m} x_i^j \le X_i, i = 1, \ldots n \right\}. \tag{8}$$

It is readily shown that R is increasing and concave in $\mathbf{X}$, and increasing, homogeneous of degree one, and convex in $\mathbf{P}$.[7]

As laid out in (8), the revenue function is the solution to a planning problem. But if there are no production distortions (i.e., no externalities, no factor price rigidities, etc.), the input choices of competitive profit-maximizing firms coincide with those of the planner. The revenue function then summarizes how GNP depends on prices and factor endowments in a decentralized market economy. Furthermore, differentiation of R with respect to $\mathbf{P}$ and $\mathbf{X}$ yields results that are easy to interpret and behaviorally useful. After exploiting the envelope theorem, we have

$$R_j \equiv \partial R / \partial P_j = f^j[\mathbf{x}^j(\mathbf{P}, \mathbf{X})] = Q_j(\mathbf{P}, \mathbf{X}), \tag{9}$$

$$\partial R / \partial X_i = w_i, \tag{10}$$

since the Lagrange multiplier on the ith resource constraint in (8) equals w_i when the planner and the competitive economy solve the same maximization problem. The first result is *Hotelling's lemma*: R_j returns the general equilibrium supply function for good j. The second says that w_i measures the increase in GNP brought about by a small increase in the supply of factor i.

When $R(\mathbf{P}, \mathbf{X})$ is twice differentiable, general equilibrium elasticities defining the responses of supply and factor prices to goods prices and factor endowments can be determined from (9) and (10). The properties of the revenue function (concave in $\mathbf{X}$, linearly homogeneous and convex in $\mathbf{P}$) enable some structure to be placed on these elasticities.

---

[7] Concavity in $\mathbf{X}$ reflects the assumption of convex technology. R is homogeneous of degree one in $\mathbf{P}$ because a doubling of all output prices does not alter optimal input choices. R is also convex in $\mathbf{P}$ since revenues increase more than linearly if it is possible to substitute in production toward goods whose relative prices have increased.

2.1.2.1 MODIFYING THE REVENUE FUNCTION TO ALLOW FOR DISTORTIONS

With slight modifications, the revenue function can accomodate a variety of production distortions, although it loses some of its more useful properties in the process. I discuss below the modifications required by three types of production distortions that are potentially relevant to LDCs.

1. *Open unemployment caused by a rigid real wage.* Let X_1 be labor and suppose w_1 is fixed above its market clearing level. In this case the revenue function retains the same form, and (9) and (10) remain valid. However, since X_1 is now an endogenous variable, R_j and R_{X_i} measure the impact on GNP for a given level of employment. The total impact on output includes any associated changes in labor demand. For example, an increase in X_2 raises GNP by the amount

$$\frac{dR}{dX_2} = w_2 + \frac{w_1 dX_1}{dX_2}.$$

If w_1 is exogenous and one is content with a very general solution, $R_{X_1} = w_1$ can be solved for dX_1/dX_2; otherwise, the change in employment has to be determined elsewhere in the model.

2. *The labor market is distorted by a sectoral wage gap.* To simplify notation, I separate out labor from the input list. L and L_1 denote, respectively, the total supply of labor and employment in sector one; v_1 is the wage in sector one and v the wage in sectors $2, \ldots m$.

   This case is handled easily by imposing the artificial constraint that labor input in sector one equal L_1 in the maximization problem in (8):

$$R(\mathbf{P}, \mathbf{X}, L, L_1) = \underset{\{L_j, \mathbf{x}^j\}}{\text{Max}} \left\{ P_1 f^1(L_1, \mathbf{x}^1) + \sum_{j=2}^{m} P_j f^j(L_j, \mathbf{x}^j) \right|$$

$$\sum_{j=2}^{m} L_j \leq L - L_1, \quad \sum_{j=1}^{m} x_i^j \leq X_i, \quad i = 2, \ldots n \right\}. \tag{11}$$

To evaluate the impact on GNP of an increase in L_1, note that higher employment in sector one comes at the expense of employment in sectors 2–m. Thus, $\partial R / \partial L_1 = v_1 - v$ – a small increase in L_1 raises GNP by the amount of the existing sectoral wage gap. With respect to the other terms, as before, $R_j = Q_j$, $R_{X_i} = w_i$, and $R_L = v$, but the corresponding total derivatives include the gains/losses arising from induced changes in sector one employment [e.g., $dR/dX_2 = w_2 + (v_1 - v)dL_1/dX_2$]. When v_1 is exogenous, $R_L = v$ and $R_{L_1} = v_1 - v$ yield solutions for v and L_1 as a function of $\mathbf{P}, \mathbf{X}$, and L.

3. *External economies at the level of industry output.* Let industry one
consist of s identical firms, and suppose aggregate output in the industry creates a favorable externality that enters multiplicatively in the
production function of individual firms in the industry, i.e.,

$$q_k = g(Q_1)f^1(\mathbf{x}_k^1), \qquad k = 1, \ldots s. \tag{12}$$

Aggregating across identical firms and assuming constant returns to
scale gives[8]

$$Q_1 = g(Q_1)f^1(\mathbf{x}^1). \tag{13}$$

Since individual firms view Q_1 as parametric, the solution to the
problem

$$\underset{\{\mathbf{x}^j\}}{\text{Max}}\left\{ P_1 g(Q_1)f^1(\mathbf{x}^1) + \sum_{j=2}^{m} P_j f^j(\mathbf{x}^j) \right|$$
$$\left. \sum_{j=1}^{m} x_i^j \le X_i, i = 2, \ldots n \right\} \tag{14}$$

yields the revenue function $R[P_1 g(Q_1), P_2, \ldots P_m, \mathbf{X}]$, which differs
from the standard revenue function only in P_1 being multiplied by
$g(Q_1)$. The solution for Q_1 implicit in

$$Q_1 = g(Q_1)R_1[P_1 g(Q_1), P_2, \ldots P_m, \mathbf{X}] \tag{15}$$

pins down the total derivatives

$$dR/dP_j = Q_j + P_1 Q_1 (g'/g) dQ_1/dP_j,$$
$$dR/dX_i = w_i + P_1 Q_1 (g'/g) dQ_1/dX_i.$$

2.2   Duality Theory, Welfare, and Demand

We now turn our attention to consumers and the duality functions that
describe the interdependence of demand patterns, welfare, prices, income,
and preferences. In what follows, $\mathbf{x} = (x_1, \ldots x_n)$ and $\mathbf{P} = (P_1, \ldots P_n)$ refer
to the consumption bundle and its associated price vector; M is money

[8] Under constant returns to scale, $sf^1(\mathbf{x}_k^1) = f^1(s\mathbf{x}_k^1) = f(\mathbf{x}^1)$. If there are decreasing returns to scale, the industry production function differs from the individual
firm's production function. Since $f^1(s\mathbf{x}_k^1) = s^b f(\mathbf{x}_k^1)$ $(b < 1)$, summing across firms
gives $sf^1(\mathbf{x}_k^1) = s^{1-b}f^1(s\mathbf{x}^1) = h(\mathbf{x}^1)$ [where $h(\mathbf{x}^1) = s^{1-b}f(\mathbf{x}^1)$].

income; and $u(\mathbf{x})$ is an increasing, continuous, strictly quasi-concave utility function.[9]

2.2.1 The Indirect Utility Function

The indirect utility function is the solution to the ordinary utility maximization problem of choosing $\mathbf{x}$ to reach the highest indifference curve subject to the constraint that expenditure not exceed money income:

$$V(\mathbf{P}, M) = \underset{\{\mathbf{x}\}}{\text{Max}}\{u(\mathbf{x})| \mathbf{Px} \le M, \mathbf{x} \ge 0\}. \tag{16}$$

V is strictly increasing in M (assuming no satiation), decreasing and convex in $\mathbf{P}$, and homogeneous of degree one in $\mathbf{P}$ and M.[10] Given the assumption that $u(\mathbf{x})$ is strictly quasi-concave, there is a one-to-one mapping between points on utility contours in price and quantity space. The direct and indirect utility functions are therefore alternative, fully equivalent representations of preferences. In passing, it should be mentioned that the indirect utility function is well defined even if no restrictions are placed on $u(\mathbf{x})$. But if duality is given up, there is no assurance that the indirect utility function derives from a coherent, sensible preference ordering (i.e., an ordering that satisfies the axioms of reflexivity, completeness, transitivity, and continuity).

Since the optimal consumption bundle varies with prices and income, the consumer's Marshallian demand functions are buried in the indirect utility function. These can be retrieved via *Roy's identity*, which states that

$$x_i = -V_i/V_M, \tag{17}$$

where $V_i \equiv \partial V/\partial P_i$ and $V_M \equiv \partial V/\partial M$. To prove the identity, define α to be the Lagrange multiplier attached to the budget constraint and note from the envelope theorem that $V_i = -\alpha x_i$ and $V_M = \alpha$.

Roy's identity is especially useful in dynamic models. When private agents solve intertemporal optimization problems, M is a choice variable (i.e., M is total consumption spending) and the marginal utility of consumption, V_M, shows up in a first-order condition. As a result, when

---

[9] Strict quasi-concavity is assumed to ensure that the optimal consumption bundle is unique.

[10] V is homogeneous of degree one in P and M because a doubling of all prices and money income leaves the budget constraint unchanged. To prove the convexity property, simply note that indifference curves are convex in price space whenever consumers substitute between goods in response to a change in relative prices.

one analyzes the impact of some shock, awkward-looking terms appear involving the second derivatives of $V(\mathbf{P}, M)$. Roy's identity provides the link between these terms and the fundamental parameters that describe preferences. Logarithmic differentiation of both sides of (17) produces

$$\mu_i = -\frac{V_{MM} M}{V_M}\left(\frac{V_{iM}}{V_{MM} x_i}+1\right), \tag{18}$$

where $\mu_i \equiv (\partial x_i/\partial M)\,(M/x_i)$, the income elasticity of demand for good i. I have written the solution in this form because often it is necessary to work with a cardinal specification of utility in which the marginal utility of consumption is decreasing ($V_{MM} < 0$) and $-V_{MM}M/V_M$, the elasticity of the marginal utility of income, is positive and well defined. (An ordinal ranking of utility does not restrict the sign of V_{MM}.) In dynamic models this elasticity plays a pivotal role in determining the path of consumption over time. The larger the elasticity, the more concave the utility function, and, *ceteris paribus*, the smoother the optimal path of consumption. For this reason, the reciprocal elasticity, $\tau \equiv -V_M/V_{MM}M$, is called the *intertemporal elasticity of substitution*. Accordingly, when employing a cardinal utility function, I shall write (18) as

$$\frac{V_{iM}}{V_{MM} x_i} = \mu_i \tau - 1. \tag{18'}$$

2.2.2   *The Expenditure Function*

In the maximization problem associated with the indirect utility function the consumer arranges his purchases to achieve the highest level of utility consistent with his budget constraint. The expenditure function is found by solving the converse optimization problem. The consumption bundle is chosen so as to minimize expenditure subject to the constraint that utility exceed a certain level:

$$E(\mathbf{P}, u^\circ) = \underset{\{\mathbf{x}\}}{\text{Min}}\{\mathbf{Px}|\ \ u(\mathbf{x}) \geq u^\circ, \mathbf{x} \geq 0\}. \tag{19}$$

The minimization problem in (19) is isomorphic to (1) underlying the cost function: $\mathbf{P}$ replaces $\mathbf{w}$, $u(\mathbf{x})$ replaces the production function $f(\mathbf{x})$, and u^o replaces Q. All of the results for the cost function carry over therefore to the expenditure function. E is increasing in u, and increasing, homogeneous of degree one, and concave in $\mathbf{P}$. Shephard's lemma now supplies us with compensated demand functions:

$$E_i \equiv \partial E/\partial P_i = x_i(\mathbf{P}, u) \equiv D^i(\mathbf{P}, u). \tag{20}$$

The compensated elasticities $\varepsilon_j^i = (\partial D^i/\partial P_j)(P_j/D^i)$ are subject to the same restrictions as the conditional factor price elasticities, and the partial elasticities of substitution are defined in exactly the same way ($\sigma_{ij} = E_{ij}E/E_iE_j$). Income elasticities of demand and marginal propensities to consume can also be recovered since, at fixed prices, changes in utility are tied to changes in money income. For $M = E(\mathbf{P}, u)$ in the Marshallian demand function, consumers have the minimum amount of income needed to reach the utility level u. Thus,

$$E_i(\mathbf{P}, u) \equiv x_i[\mathbf{P}, E(\mathbf{P}, u)]. \tag{21}$$

Differentiating both sides with respect to u gives $E_{iu} = (\partial x_i/\partial M)E_u$, from which we obtain expressions for the income elasticity of demand μ_i and the marginal propensity to consume c_i:

$$\mu_i \equiv \frac{\partial x_i}{\partial M}\frac{M}{x_i} = \frac{E_{iu}E}{E_u E_i}, \tag{22}$$

$$c_i \equiv P_i \frac{\partial x_i}{\partial M} = \frac{P_i E_{iu}}{E_u}. \tag{23}$$

2.2.2.1 HOMOTHETIC PREFERENCES, AGGREGATION, AND WELFARE

When preferences are homothetic the curvature of every utility contour is the same and the expenditure function takes the multiplicative form[11]

$$E(\mathbf{P}, u) = \varphi(u)e(\mathbf{P}). \tag{24}$$

It is easy to confirm that $\mu_i = 1$ and that $x_i/x_j = e_i/e_j$. Intuitively, since indifference curves are radial replicas of one another, the ratio in which any two goods are consumed is independent of the level of utility; this implies that the consumer's Engel curves are linear, or, equivalently, that all income elasticities of demand equal unity.

For the most part I will abstract from distributional effects, which are difficult to sign empirically and usually irrelevant to the insights I wish to convey. The special significance of homothetic preferences in this regard is that they provide a rigorous justification for models that employ the simplifying device of a representative consumer. If we assume that consumers have identical homothetic preferences, then the distribution

---

[11] In the case of constant returns to scale, Q appeared in the cost function where $\varphi(u)$ appears in (24). $\varphi(u)$ equals u only if the marginal utility of consumption is constant. With diminishing marginal utility of consumption, φ is convex.

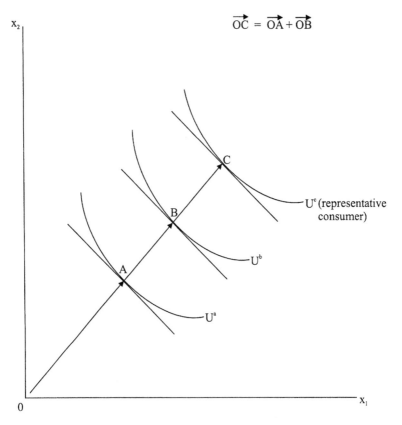

Figure 2.1. Homothetic preferences and aggregation.

of income does not affect demand patterns because whoever spends a dollar spends it in exactly the same way. This is transparent in the two-good, two-person case illustrated in Figure 2.1. Since the rich and the poor share the same linear Engel curve, aggregate demand for each good is independent of how close point A is to point B. It is legitimate, therefore, to pretend as if spending choices are made by a representative consumer who receives all income generated in the economy.

An alternative approach developed by Gorman (1953) permits aggregation while allowing income elasticities to differ from unity and for limited heterogeneity of preferences. The Gorman polar form assumes preferences such that

$$V(\mathbf{P}, M^j) = A(\mathbf{P})M^j + B^j(\mathbf{P}). \tag{25}$$

For this indirect utility function, Roy's identity gives

$$x_i^j = \frac{M^j \, \partial A / \partial P_i + \partial B^j / \partial P_i}{A} = a(\mathbf{P})M^j + b^j(\mathbf{P}) \tag{26}$$

as individual j's demand for good i. The intercept b^j differs across individuals, so preferences are not identical and income elasticities of demand need not equal unity. But since Engel curves are linear and parallel, income responses are identical [$\partial x_i / \partial M^j = a(\mathbf{P}), \forall j$]; consequently, the distribution of income does not affect demand patterns as long as all individuals consume positive amounts of all goods.

I assume identical homothetic preferences even though aggregation is possible under weaker restrictions. The cost of imposing homotheticity is that all income elasticities of demand have to be set equal to unity. In the highly aggregated models I construct this is a fairly minor cost. When a model allows for consumption of only two or three goods, each good should be interpreted as proxying for a bundle of many other goods. If there is no reason to think that any bundle is comprised predominantly of necessities or luxuries, little is lost in assuming unitary income elasticities of demand.

While aggregation of individual demand functions can be justified under the assumption of identical homothetic preferences, it is problematic to take the representative consumer's indirect utility function [or u in his expenditure function $E(\mathbf{P}, u)$] as a measure of welfare. The utility contours of the representative agent correctly reflect the qualitative outcome for Pareto-improving or Pareto-worsening changes. But in other situations there is no getting around the need to make explicit interpersonal utility comparisons – to decide on an appropriate way to aggregate u^a and u^b in Figure 2.1. Because most economists are loath to make such comparisons, it is common practice to describe the welfare outcome in terms of whether the hypothetical representative agent is better or worse off. This rough welfare criterion sweeps distributional issues under the rug to focus on changes in GNP adjusted for the impact of distortions on allocative efficiency. The movement from a lower to a higher utility contour by the representative agent shows only that it is possible to redistribute the economy's aggregate consumption bundle in a manner that makes everyone better off, not that everyone actually is better off or that welfare has improved in some overall sense. Short of reaching a consensus on the appropriate social welfare function, the best way of handling this problem is to pay attention to the more important distributional effects when evaluating the welfare statements made by representative agent models. At the level of aggregation assumed in the models of later chapters, this pretty much amounts to keeping track of what happens to real wages and the distribution of employment between low- and high-wage sectors.

2.2.3   *The Indirect Utility Function and the Expenditure Function for the CES–CRRA Utility Function*

In the identity $u \equiv V(\mathbf{P}, M)$, V is increasing and monotone in M. It can be "inverted" therefore to obtain $M = E(\mathbf{P}, u)$, the expenditure function. Because it is easy to move from the indirect utility function to the expenditure function, and vice versa, it is also easy to compute compensated and uncompensated elasticities of demand. I demonstrate how this is done in the case of a constant relative risk aversion (CRRA) utility function where individual consumption goods define a CES index of aggregate consumption. The CES–CRRA specification is quite flexible and allows for varying degrees of intratemporal and intertemporal substitution. I will use it extensively in subsequent chapters.

Consider the utility function

$$u = \begin{cases} \dfrac{\left[\left(\sum_{i=1}^{n}(k_i x_i^{\rho})^{1/\rho}\right)\right]^{1-\phi}}{1-\phi}, & \rho \neq 0, \phi \neq 1 \\[3ex] \ln\left[\sum_{i=1}^{n}(k_i x_i^{\rho})^{1/\rho}\right], & \phi = 1, \rho \neq 0 \\[3ex] \dfrac{\left[\sum_{i=1}^{n} k_i \ln x_i\right]^{1-\phi}}{1-\phi}, & \rho = 0, \phi \neq 1 \end{cases} \tag{27}$$

where k_i, ρ, and ϕ are constants. The expression enclosed in square brackets is a CES index of aggregate consumption in which the elasticity of substitution between any two goods x_i and x_j is $\beta = (1 - \rho)^{-1}$. At the outer tier of the utility function, the parameter ϕ measures the elasticity of the marginal utility of aggregate consumption. (If we define J to be the CES index of aggregate consumption, then $u = J^{1-\phi}/1 - \phi$ and $-u'' J/u' = \phi$.)

To solve for the expenditure function, form the Lagrangian

$$\mathcal{L} = \sum_{i=1}^{n} P_i x_i + \alpha \left\{ [u(1-\phi)]^{1/1-\phi} - \left(\sum_{i=1}^{n} k_i x_i^{\rho}\right)^{1/\rho} \right\}. \tag{28}$$

The first-order conditions are

$$\alpha\left(\sum_{i=1}^{n}k_i x_i^{\rho}\right)^{(1-\rho)/\rho} k_i x_i^{\rho-1} = P_i, \qquad i=1,\dots,n. \tag{29}$$

$$\left(\sum_{i=1}^{n}k_i x_i^{\rho}\right)^{1/\rho} = [u(1-\phi)]^{1/1-\phi}. \tag{30}$$

Multiply both sides in (29) by x_i and sum over the n conditions. This gives

$$\alpha\left(\sum_{i=1}^{n}k_i x_i^{\rho}\right)^{(1-\rho)/\rho}\sum_{i=1}^{n}k_i x_i^{\rho} = \sum_{i=1}^{n}P_i x_i,$$

or

$$\alpha\left(\sum_{i=1}^{n}k_i x_i^{\rho}\right)^{(1-\rho)/\rho} = \frac{E}{\sum_{i=1}^{n}k_i x_i^{\rho}}. \tag{31}$$

Substituting (31) into (29), we have

$$\frac{Ek_i}{\sum_{i=1}^{n}k_i x_i^{\rho}} = P_i x_i^{1-\rho}. \tag{32}$$

Recall that $\beta = (1-\rho)^{-1}$ and note from (30) that $\sum_{i=1}^{n}k_i x_i^{\rho} = [u(1-\phi)]^{\rho/(1-\phi)}$. Thus (32) may be written as

$$P_i x_i = k_i^{\beta} P_i^{1-\beta} E^{\beta} [u(1-\phi)]^{-\rho\beta/(1-\phi)}, \qquad i=1,\dots,n, \tag{32'}$$

from which we obtain the expenditure function

$$E(\mathbf{P},u) = [u(1-\phi)]^{1/1-\phi}\left(\sum_{i=1}^{n}k_i^{\beta}P_i^{1-\beta}\right)^{1/(1-\beta)}. \tag{33}$$

Solving for u produces the indirect utility function

$$V(\mathbf{P},E) = \frac{E^{1-\phi}\left(\sum_{i=1}^{n}k_i^{\beta}P_i^{1-\beta}\right)^{(1-\phi)/(\beta-1)}}{1-\phi}. \tag{34}$$

I assumed homothetic preferences in (27). The expenditure function therefore is of the general form stated in (24) and the indirect utility function factors into $V(\mathbf{P},\,E) = f(E)g(\mathbf{P})$. Observe also that the CES–CRRA functions in (27), (33), and (34) are self-dual.

With the expenditure and indirect utility functions in hand, it is a straightforward business to derive the compensated and uncompensated demand elasticities. Roy's identity and (34) give the solutions for the uncompensated demand functions,

$$x_i(\mathbf{P}, E) = \frac{k_i^\beta P_i^{-\beta} E}{\sum_{i=1}^n k_i^\beta P_i^{1-\beta}}, \tag{35}$$

while Shephard's lemma and (33) generate

$$D^i(\mathbf{P}, u) = [u(1-\phi)]^{1/1-\phi} \left(\sum_{i=1}^n k_i^\beta P_i^{1-\beta} \right)^{\beta/(1-\beta)} k_i^\beta P_i^{-\beta} \tag{36}$$

for the compensated demands. The own-price and cross-price uncompensated and compensated elasticities are thus

$$\delta_i \equiv -\frac{\partial x_i}{\partial P_i}\frac{P_i}{x_i} = \beta \left(1 - \frac{k_i^\beta P_i^{1-\beta}}{\sum_{i=1}^n k_i^\beta P_i^{1-\beta}} \right) + \frac{k_i^\beta P_i^{1-\beta}}{\sum_{i=1}^n k_i^\beta P_i^{1-\beta}}, \tag{37}$$

$$\delta_j^i \equiv -\frac{\partial x_i}{\partial P_j}\frac{P_j}{x_i} = \frac{k_j^\beta P_j^{1-\beta}}{\sum_{i=1}^n k_i^\beta P_i^{1-\beta}}(\beta-1), \quad i \neq j, \tag{38}$$

$$\varepsilon_i \equiv -\frac{\partial D^i}{\partial P_i}\frac{P_i}{D^i} = \beta \left(1 - \frac{k_i^\beta P_i^{1-\beta}}{\sum_{i=1}^n k_i^\beta P_i^{1-\beta}} \right), \tag{39}$$

$$\varepsilon_j^i \equiv -\frac{\partial D^i}{\partial Pj}\frac{P_j}{D^i} = \frac{k_j^\beta P_j^{1-\beta}}{\sum_{i=1}^n k_i^\beta P_i^{1-\beta}}\beta, \quad i \neq j. \tag{40}$$

Fortunately, the ugly terms involving k_i are just expenditure shares. From (35),

$$\gamma_i \equiv \frac{P_i x_i}{E} = \frac{k_i^\beta P_i^{1-\beta}}{\sum_{i=1}^n k_i^\beta P_i^{1-\beta}}, \tag{41}$$

so we can express the elasticities in (37)–(40) more compactly as

$$\delta_i = \beta(1-\gamma_i) + \gamma_i, \tag{37'}$$

$$\delta_j^i = (\beta-1)\gamma_j, \quad i \neq j, \tag{38'}$$

$$\varepsilon_i = \beta(1-\gamma_i), \tag{39'}$$

$$\varepsilon_j^i = \beta\gamma_j, \qquad i \neq j. \tag{40'}$$

For a given j, the ε_j^i are positive and equal. The δ_j^i are also equal and may be positive or negative, depending on whether $\beta \lessgtr 1$. These results reflect some simple accounting and the symmetry of the CES–CRRA utility function. Since each good enters the utility function in exactly the same way, the cross-price effects take the form of a proportionate increase or decrease in $x_1, x_2, \ldots x_{j-1}, x_{j+1}, \ldots x_n$. The sign of the uncompensated cross-price elasticity hinges on that of $\beta - 1$ because when $\beta > 1$ an increase in P_j *reduces* the expenditure share of good j, freeing up money to be spent on other goods. In the special case of Cobb–Douglas preferences ($\beta = 1$), expenditure shares are fixed and the price increase affects only the demand for good x_j.

2.3 Examples[12]

#1. Consider a small open economy that produces an export good and an import good. The world market price of each good equals unity and imports are subject to a tariff t. Production in each sector requires capital and labor. Both factors are in fixed supply and are intersectorally mobile. There is full employment and technology exhibits constant returns to scale.

The government permits foreign investment, so part of the capital stock is owned by foreign firms. Let K^f denote the foreign-owned capital stock and K^d the domestically owned capital stock. If the earnings of foreign capital are untaxed, the economy's budget constraint reads

$$E(P_m, u) = R(P_m, K^d + K^f) + t[D^m(P_m, u)$$
$$- R_m(P_m, K^d + K^f)] - rK^f, \tag{42}$$

where $P_m = 1 + t$ is the domestic price of the imported good, u is utility, r is the capital rental, and $R_m \equiv \partial R/\partial P_m$ is the domestic supply function for the importable good. The fixed price of the export good and the fixed supply of labor have been suppressed in $E(\cdot)$, $R(\cdot)$, $R_m(\cdot)$, and $D^m(\cdot)$. The second term on the right side represents tariff revenues, which are assumed to be rebated to the private sector in a lump-sum fashion.

Goods and factor prices are linked via the zero-profit conditions

---

[12] Example #1 is based on Brecher and Diaz Alejandro (1977) and Buffie (1985).

$$1 + t = C^m(w, r), \tag{43}$$

$$1 = C^x(w, r), \tag{44}$$

where C^i is the *unit* cost function (not total costs) in sector i and w is the wage. Note that as long as the tariff is fixed, w and r are constant.

a. Show that when the government allows some additional foreign capital into the country domestic welfare rises or falls depending on whether the import sector is relatively labor- or capital-intensive. (Hint: Make use of the fact that $R_{mK} = R_{Km} = \partial r / \partial P_m$.)
b. Suppose now that the import sector is protected by a quota instead of a tariff. The quota fixes the volume of imports at Z. Under a quota, the economy's budget constraint becomes

$$E(P_m, u) = R(P_m, K^d + K^f) + (P_m - 1)Z - rK^f, \tag{43'}$$

where $(P_m - 1)Z$ reflects the rents accruing to holders of import licenses. The domestic price of the import good adjusts to clear the market:

$$D^m(P_m, u) = R(P_m, K^d + K^f) + Z. \tag{45}$$

Show that an inflow of foreign capital is always welfare-improving. Why is the outcome so different when protection takes the form of a quota instead of a tariff?

Solution

a. Differentiate the budget constraint with respect to K^f and u. After choosing units so that $E_u = 1$ and making use of (10) ($R_K = r$), (23), and Shephard's lemma, we get

$$\left(1 - \frac{c_m t}{1 + t}\right) du = -t R_{mK} dK^f, \tag{46}$$

where c_m denotes the marginal propensity to consume the imported good.

Equation (46) indicates that domestic welfare falls or rises depending on whether the capital inflow raises or lowers production of the importable good. The intuitive explanation for this result is that the tariff distorts the initial equilibrium by depressing consumption of the imported good and attracting too many resources into import-competing production. If the capital inflow increases production of the importable, it exacerbates the misallocation of resources and thereby lowers domestic welfare. Put differently, if any part of the capital inflow finds its way into the import sector, domestic welfare falls because foreign capital gets paid too much – more than its social marginal product.

Intuition suggests that the capital inflow is likely to increase importables production if the import sector is relatively capital-intensive. To confirm this, note that $R_{mK} = R_{Km} = \partial r/\partial P_m$. The solution for r is

$$\partial r/\partial P_m = \frac{Q_m}{L_m(k_m - k_x)}, \tag{47}$$

where k_i is the capital–labor ratio in sector i and L_m and Q_m are employment and output in sector m. [In deriving (47), Shephard's lemma was used to replace C_w^i and C_r^i with employment and the capital stock per unit of output in sector i.] Substituting for R_{mK} in (46) now produces the conclusion that du/dK^f is of the same sign as $k_x - k_m$.

b. Differentiation of (43′) with respect to P_m, u, and K^f yields

$$du = -K^f dr = -K^f R_{Km} dP_m, \tag{48}$$

since $R_m + Z - E_m = Q_m + Z - D^m = 0$. The last step follows from the fact that r depends only on P_m (not also on $K^d + K^f$). Consequently, $dr = (dr/dP_m)dP_m = R_{Km}dP_m$.

Now solve (45) for P_m as a function of u and K^f. The general form of the solution is

$$P_m = h(u, K^f),$$

where $h_1 > 0$ and h_2 is of the same sign as $-R_{mK}$. Substituting for dP_m in (48) gives

$$\frac{du}{dK^f} \text{ sign of } \frac{K^f(R_{Km})^2}{1 + K^f R_{Km} h_1} > 0. \tag{49}$$

When $R_{Km} < 0$, stability of the goods market requires $1 + K^f R_{Km} h_1 > 0$. (When an increase in P_m lowers r, payments to foreign capital decline and national income rises. If this income effect is too strong, a rise in P_m increases excess demand for the importable.) Hence, the capital inflow is always welfare-improving.

Under a quota, the capital inflow does not alter the trade distortion because the import volume is fixed. With the trade distortion invariant to the capital inflow, the impact on welfare depends solely on whether payments to inframarginal units of foreign capital fall or rise. Payments always fall because, not surprisingly, a greater supply of capital always lowers the capital rental: if the import sector is capital-(labor-) intensive, the capital inflow raises (lowers) the supply of good m and the induced fall (rise) in P_m causes r to decline.

#2. Consider the production function $Q = F[Z, V(K, L)]$ in which $V(\cdot)$ is a composite input generated from the services of capital K and labor L, and Z is some third input. Show that when $F[\cdot]$ and $V(\cdot)$ are linearly homogeneous CES functions

$$\sigma_{KL} = \sigma_2 + (\sigma_2 - \sigma_1)\frac{\theta_Z}{1 - \theta_Z},$$

where θ_Z is the cost share of Z, σ_2 is the elasticity of substitution between capital and labor in the production of V, and σ_1 is the elasticity of substitution between Z and V.

Solution

Let P_z, w, and r denote the price of input Z, the wage and the capital rental. Since the production function is separable between K and L on the one hand and Z on the other, the unit cost function is

$$C(P_z, w, r) = C[P_z, c(w, r)],$$

where $c(w, r)$ is a subcost function for the composite input V. Thus

$$C_r = C_2[P_z, c(w, r)]c_r(w, r),$$

$$C_w = C_2[P_z, c(w, r)]c_w(w, r),$$

and

$$\sigma_{KL} \equiv \frac{C_{rw}C}{C_r C_w} = \frac{C_{22}C}{C_2^2} + \frac{c_{rw}C}{C_2 c_r c_w}. \tag{50}$$

Rewrite this as

$$\sigma_{KL} = \frac{C_{22}C}{C_2^2} + \frac{c_{rw}c}{c_r c_w}\frac{C}{C_2 c}. \tag{50'}$$

Note that $C_2 c/C = \theta_V$, the cost share of the composite input V, and that[13]

---

[13] The formula for the Allen–Uzawa partial elasticity of substitution also applies to the subcost function $c(w, r)$. This provides the expression for σ_2.

$$\sigma_{VV} = \frac{C_{22}C}{C_2^2} \quad \text{and} \quad \sigma_2 = \frac{C_{rw}C}{C_r C_w}.$$

The adding-up condition on the partial elasticities of substitution implies $\theta_V \sigma_{VV} = -\sigma_1 \theta_Z$, so

$$\sigma_{KL} = \frac{\sigma_2 - \sigma_1 \theta_Z}{\theta_V},$$

or

$$\sigma_{KL} = \sigma_2 + (\sigma_2 - \sigma_1)\frac{\theta_Z}{1 - \theta_Z} \tag{51}$$

as $\theta_V = 1 - \theta_Z$.

The expression for the Allen–Uzawa partial elasticity in (51) agrees with intuition. Both σ_1 and σ_2 enter into σ_{KL} because an increase in the wage induces substitution not only between capital and labor but also between V and Z. The overall substitution effect consists of the direct substitution effect captured by σ_2 plus an adjustment to reflect substitution between V and Z. The magnitude of the latter adjustment depends on $\sigma_2 - \sigma_1$ and the relative importance of Z as measured by the ratio of its cost share to the cost share of V.[14]

---

[14] Observe that when $\sigma_1 = 0$ equation (51) gives $\sigma_{KL} = \sigma_2(1 - \theta_Z)^{-1}$. Blackorby and Russel (1989) find it disturbing that $\sigma_{KL} \neq \sigma_2$ in this case. The term $(1 - \theta_Z)^{-1}$, however, simply acts as a conversion factor in the decomposition of the conditional cross-price elasticity η_{KL}. Recall that $\eta_{KL} = \theta_L \sigma_{KL}$; hence $\eta_{KL} = \theta_{VL}\sigma_2$, where $\theta_{VL} = \theta_L/(1 - \theta_Z)$. This more natural decomposition says that the conditional cross-price elasticity depends on σ_2 and the cost share of labor in the *production of the composite input V*.

CHAPTER 3

The Trade Policy Debate

In this chapter I try to provide a balanced, dispassionate critique of the various arguments that have been advanced for export promotion and against protection.[1] The chapter begins with a brief overview of LDC trade policy that introduces some basic concepts and discusses the main features of import-substituting industrialization (ISI). Following this, Section 3.2 examines at length the argument that the first-best remedy for most types of market failure is to combine free trade with an appropriate tax or subsidy. The argument is powerful but subject to the qualifications that the most direct tax/subsidy intervention (i) not involve greater administrative costs than the comparable trade tax, and (ii) not adversely affect the strategic environment in which policy makers operate. If these qualifications matter, trade taxes may have a place in the optimal policy package.

The second half of the chapter deals with more specific aspects of the policy debate. Section 3.3.1 appraises the infant industry argument, the oldest and most common defense of protection. In Section 3.3.2, I discuss the nature of factor market distortions in LDCs and the claim that ISI exacerbates the underemployment problem. Sections 3.3.3 and 3.3.4 examine the theory and empirical evidence bearing on the connection between trade policy, production and prices in oligopolistic markets, scale economies, and productivity growth.

3.1   A Quick Overview of LDC Trade Policy

The distinguishing characteristic of trade policy in countries pursuing ISI is that consumer goods are subject to much higher tariffs and more restrictive quotas than imports of intermediate inputs and capital equipment. Because the price of intermediates affects industry costs, there is no simple formula relating trade taxes to the sectoral pattern of output.

---

[1] Excellent surveys of the literature and different aspects of the policy debate may be found in Bliss (1989), Helleiner (1990, 1994), and Rodrik (1992a, 1992b, 1995). The earlier surveys of Diaz Alejandro (1975) and Bhagwati and Srinivasan (1979) also repay careful reading.

30

Output may not increase, for example, in all highly protected industries. The only reliable way to determine the impact of the tariff structure on the allocation of resources is to solve the appropriate general equilibrium model (Bhagwati and Srinivasan, 1973; Bruno, 1973). Not surprisingly, most empirical studies have shied away from this difficult task, assessing the bias of the trade regime instead by comparing effective rates of protection (ERP) across sectors. The ERP is defined as

$$\text{ERP} = \frac{\text{VA}_d - \text{VA}_w}{\text{VA}_w}, \tag{1}$$

where VA_d and VA_w stand for value added at domestic and world market prices. In words, the ERP measures the percentage increase in value added, or payments to primary factors of production, made possible by the structure of protection. To link the change in value added to the industry's cost structure and the tariffs on final goods and intermediates, t_f and t_z, set world market prices equal to unity and assume that domestic and imported consumer goods are perfect substitutes. Since the industry then sells its output Q at the price $1 + t_f$ and pays $1 + t_z$ to purchase imported intermediates Z,

$$\text{VA}_w = Q - Z \quad \text{and} \quad \text{VA}_d = (1+t_f)Q - (1+t_z)Z.$$

Substituting these expressions into (1) and defining $\theta_z \equiv (1 + t_z)Z/(1 + t_f)Q$ to be the cost share of imported intermediates [by definition, total revenue, $(1 + t_f)Q$, equals total costs] produces

$$\text{ERP} = \frac{t_f - t_z\theta_z(1+t_f)/(1+t_z)}{1 - \theta_z(1+t_f)/(1+t_z)},$$
$$\Rightarrow \text{ERP} \gtreqless t_f \quad as \quad t_f \gtreqless t_z. \tag{1'}$$

The ERP for an export industry is computed in the same manner, but with the export subsidy s replacing t_f.

Under the escalated structure of protection characteristic of ISI, $t_f > t_z$. The percentage increase in value added exceeds t_f because the protected industry benefits from a lower real price of imported intermediates. For protected industries that rely heavily on imported inputs, the ERP will therefore be much greater than the tariff on competing consumer goods. For example, when $t_f = .50$, $t_z = .20$, and $\theta_z = .50$, the ERP is 100%, double the value of t_f. As should be evident from Table 3.1, this example is not unrealistic. In the heyday of ISI, ERPs far above 100% were not at all unusual.

A few countries in East Asia and elsewhere combined high levels of

Table 3.1. *Average effective rate of protection for manufacturing.*

Argentina, 1969	111
Brazil, 1963	184
Chile, 1967	175
Colombia, 1969	19
Indonesia, 1971	119
Ivory Coast, 1973	41
Pakistan, 1970–71	200
South Korea, 1968	−1
Thailand, 1973	27
Tunisia, 1972	250
Uruguay, 1965	384

Source: Krueger (1981b).

protection with vigorous export promotion measures. In general, however, ISI was associated with a strong bias against export production. The ERP for exports of agricultural goods and other primary products was sometimes negative, owing to export taxes or tariffs on imported inputs. Exporters of manufactured goods were usually accorded more favorable treatment, often receiving modest subsidies and the right to import intermediates and machinery at duty-free prices. But these measures rarely sufficed to restore neutrality to the trade regime. Until very recently, ERPs were invariably much higher in the import sector than the export sector.

High levels of protection were (and still are) more often the product of quotas than tariffs. This feature of ISI is disturbing, for while protection may be defensible there are no intellectually respectable arguments for quotas. Quotas generate a set of implicit tariffs equal to the difference between domestic and world market prices. Implicit tariffs, however, are less transparent than explicit tariffs, and they vary whenever changes in internal or external conditions alter the demand for imports. More importantly, quotas increase the costs of protection by (i) depriving the government of revenues,[2] (ii) creating incentives for private agents to squander resources in competing for the rents that import licenses confer,[3] and (iii) allowing firms in concentrated industries to engage in

[2] Welfare declines if the loss of tariff revenues requires other distortionary taxes to be set at higher levels.
[3] The revenue loss and efficiency costs of rent-seeking behavior can be avoided if the government auctions import licenses. This is rarely done in practice.

oligopolistic pricing.[4] Despite all of these drawbacks, policy makers have relied more heavily on quotas than tariffs. In fact, a number of the more ardent practioners of ISI automatically banned imports of any good produced by domestic firms (Bhagwati and Srinivasan, 1979, pp. 12–13; Krueger, 1983, p. 49).

The prevalence of quotas is *prima facie* evidence that ISI was seldom guided by a sensible, coherent economic strategy (Krugman, 1993). Case studies buttress this claim (Meier, 1990). Typically, tariffs and quotas were applied in a slapdash manner to foster infant industries and promote industrialization, to raise revenues, to remedy payments deficits, and to protect special interests. The resulting chaotic structure of protection exhibited tremendous variance within and across sectors. In 1971, the ERP in Indonesia ranged from –19% to 5400% (Krueger, 1983, p. 34). In Brazil, the mean ERP in 1963 was 75% and the standard deviation 242% (Krueger, 1978, p. 114).

The costs of indiscriminate, undisciplined protectionist policies became increasingly clear over time. Experience, along with the trenchant criticisms marshalled against ISI policies in the influential works of Balassa (1971) and Little, Scitovsky, and Scott (1970), brought about a change of outlook in policy circles and frequent attempts at trade reform. Many of these attempts were merely tidying-up operations that rendered the structure of protection more coherent but did not significantly reduce the bias in favor of import substitution (Bhagwati, 1978). Since the mid-eighties, however, trade liberalization has carried the day. As part of sweeping, market-oriented reforms, trade barriers have been dramatically reduced in much of East Asia and Central and South America. Today high levels of protection are confined mainly to Sub-Saharan Africa and South Asia (India, Pakistan, and Sri Lanka).[5]

There is no doubt that protectionist policies in the past were extreme and economically harmful. What is still unclear is exactly where trade policy should head: toward moderate protection, balanced incentives for import-substitution and export production, or completely free trade? The answer to this question ultimately requires that one make a judgement about the set of policy instruments at the government's disposal and their efficacy in ameliorating important market failures. The next three sections address various aspects of this issue. In Chapter 5, I

---

[4] Quotas have this disadvantage when domestic goods and imports are perfect substitutes. There is no significant difference between tariffs and quotas when imports and domestic goods are imperfect substitutes. See Section 3.3.3.2.
[5] India has liberalized imports of intermediate inputs and capital goods, but high tariffs and restrictive quotas are still in place for consumer imports.

attempt to go further by developing a dynamic general equilibrium model that incorporates much of the structural detail required for quantitative policy analysis.

3.2   The Argument that Free Trade Is First-Best

If a country is too small to affect world market prices, perfect competition prevails everywhere, all markets clear, and there are no externalities, we have as a trivial corollary of the First Welfare Theorem that the free trade equilibrium is Pareto-efficient. Furthermore, if lump-sum transfers are feasible, the Second Welfare Theorem tells us that every Pareto-efficient allocation is sustainable as a free trade equilibrium. More intuitively, free trade is optimal in the world assumed by the two welfare theorems because it satisfies the basic marginal conditions for efficient resource allocation. Trade provides the country with an alternative "technology" for converting exportable goods into importable goods. An efficient pattern of expenditure requires that each consumer's marginal rate of substitution (MRS) between any two traded goods x and y equal the rate at which x can be converted into y through trade as given by the relative world market price P^*. For the condition MRS $= P^*$ to be satisfied, consumers must face world market prices. Similarly, efficiency in production calls for equal marginal rates of transformation through trade and domestic production. With perfect competition and no externalities, the behavior of profit-maximizing firms ensures that the marginal rate of transformation (MRT) on the economy's production possibility frontier equals the domestic relative price of good x. Hence, if domestic prices equal world market prices, the second condition for efficient resource allocation, MRT $= P^*$, is also satisfied.

3.2.1   The Principle of Targeting

The First Welfare Theorem invokes a number of heroic assumptions which guarantee that the laissez faire equilibrium is Pareto-efficient. If these assumptions are relaxed, the laissez faire equilibrium is suboptimal and trade taxes may be welfare-improving. This is not enough, however, to justify interventionist trade policy. When markets operate imperfectly, the Principle of Targeting states that the first-best solution is to combine free trade with an appropriate tax or subsidy that directly offsets the source of market failure.[6] Trade taxes are not first-best unless

---

[6] The classic pieces are Johnson (1965) and Bhagwati (1971). See Dixit and Norman (1980, chapter 6) for a duality-based analysis.

trade itself is the cause of market failure (e.g., the country is large enough to affect its terms of trade).

The easiest way to understand the Principle of Targeting is to work through an example.[7] To keep the general equilibrium framework simple, suppose the country in question is small in world markets and produces just two traded goods, an export good and an importable manufactured good. In the manufacturing sector there are economies of scale external to the firm but internal to the industry. The external effect appears as the multiplicative term $g(Q_m)$ in each firm's production function, where Q_m is aggregate output. As explained in Section 2.1.2, for this type of externality the revenue function takes the form $R[g(Q_m)P_m, P_x, S]$ and aggregate domestic production of manufactured goods is

$$Q_m = g(Q_m)R_1[g(Q_m)P_m, P_x, S], \tag{2}$$

where P_i is the price of good i and S is a vector of fixed factor supplies. Since a general equilibrium model without money determines only relative prices, we may designate one good the numeraire. In this and subsequent sections, I make the export good the numeraire and set all world market prices equal to unity. Suppressing the export price and employing the same notation as in Chapter 2, the budget constraint of the representative agent reads

$$E(1+t,u) = R[g(Q_m)(1+t),S]$$
$$+ t\{D^m(1+t,u) - g(Q_m)R_1[g(Q_m)(1+t),S]\}. \tag{3}$$

The expenditure function $E(\cdot)$ relates total spending on the two goods to the tariff t and welfare u. On the right side of the equality sign, the second term represents either a lump-sum rebate of tariff revenues or a lump-sum tax levied to pay for an import subsidy.

The relationship between welfare and the tariff can be obtained directly from the budget constraint. Setting $E_u = 1$ and recalling that $(1+t)D_2^m = c_m$, the marginal propensity to consume the manufactured good, we have from (3)

$$\left(1 - \frac{tc_m}{1+t}\right)\frac{du}{dt} = R_1 g' dQ_m/dt$$
$$+ t[D_1^m - gg'R_{11}(1+t)dQ_m/dt - g^2 R_{11}], \tag{4}$$

which simplifies to

---

[7] The example is based on Corden (1974, pp. 18–20).

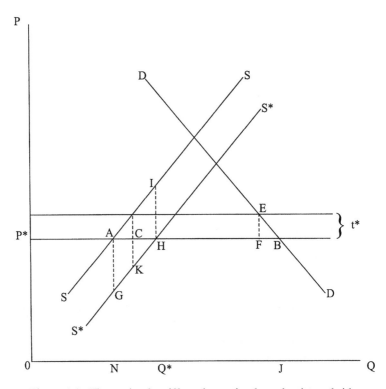

Figure 3.1. The optimal tariff vs. the optimal production subsidy.

$$\frac{du}{dt} = R_1 g' \frac{dQ_m}{dt} > 0 \qquad\qquad (4')$$

when evaluated at $t = 0$. The imposition of a small tariff starting from a position of free trade is thus welfare-improving; this can be seen in Figure 3.1. SS is the perceived marginal cost schedule of private firms, S^*S^* is the social marginal cost schedule, and DD is the demand curve.[8] Under free trade, consumption is OJ and domestic production is ON. At point B the value consumers attach to an additional unit of the manufactured good just equals the world price. Due to the externality, however, the marginal social cost of production is less than the price of imports. An infinitesimally small tariff is welfare-improving since the gain from

---

[8] SS and S*S* are upward sloping under the assumption that a fixed factor in sector m creates diminishing returns.

replacing imports by domestic production is the first-order magnitude *AG* while the loss from the distortion of consumption patterns is second-order small (i.e., consumption remains approximately equal to its optimal level *OJ*).

As the tariff increases manufacturing output moves closer to the optimal point *H*, where the marginal social cost of production equals the world market price. But once the tariff ceases to be small it also creates a byproduct distortion: consumers allocate their purchases so that MRS = 1 + t, violating the efficiency condition MRS = 1. In Figure 3.1 the loss on the last unit of forgone consumption equals the vertical distance between the demand curve and the world price. The optimal tariff *t** balances at the margin the benefits of higher manufacturing output against the costs of driving consumption further away from its free-trade level. This is the value of t for which $du/dt = 0$ in (4):

$$t^* = \frac{R_1 g' dQ_m/dt}{gg' R_{11}(1+t)dQ_m/dt + g^2 R_{11} - D_1^m}. \tag{5}$$

To express *t** in terms of elasticities describing the responses of demand and supply, define $\chi \equiv g' Q_m/g$ and $\varepsilon \equiv -D_1^m(1+t)/D^m$ to be the elasticity of the external effect and the compensated own-price elasticity of demand for manufactures. Also note from (2) that the general equilibrium own-price supply elasticity in the manufacturing sector is

$$\eta \equiv \frac{dQ_m}{dP_m}\frac{P_m}{Q_m} = \frac{gR_{11}(1+t)/R_1}{1 - \chi[1 + gR_{11}(1+t)/R_1]}.$$

Making use of the expressions for η, χ, and ε allows the solution in (5) to be rewritten as

$$t^* = \frac{\chi\eta}{\eta(1+\chi) + \varepsilon D^m/Q_m}. \tag{5'}$$

Since the severity of the byproduct consumption distortion depends on the price responsiveness of demand, *t** is smaller the larger ε is. For the optimal tariff shown in Figure 3.1 the benefits of greater productive efficiency sum to *AGKC* and the total cost of the consumption distortion is *EFB*.

While a tariff that is not too large succeeds in raising welfare, protection is not the first-best intervention. A production subsidy of *IH* = $\chi/(1-\chi)$ brings output to the socially optimal level *Q** without distorting consumption patterns. The cost of settling for the second-best solution associated with *t** is *CKH* + *EFB*.

3.2.2   *Limitations of the Principle of Targeting*

3.2.2.1   ADMINISTRATIVE COSTS

In demonstrating that a production subsidy is superior to a tariff for dealing with a production externality, I implicitly assumed that the subsidy could be financed by a lump-sum tax. This suggests an obvious objection to first-best solutions that prescribe some type of corrective subsidy. In practice, lump-sum taxes are not available, so the production subsidy will have to be financed by some distortionary tax. But when the costs of the accompanying distortionary tax are taken into account, it is no longer obvious that a production subsidy cum tax dominates a tariff. Both policies improve allocative efficiency by increasing output in the manufacturing sector, and both create byproduct distortions.

This defense of protection is plausible but incorrect. A tariff is equivalent to an equal rate production subsidy and consumption tax on the importable good. The tax component of the tariff, however, raises more revenue than needed to pay for the production subsidy. Simply unbundling the tariff allows the production subsidy to be paired with a smaller consumption tax. A tariff is inferior to an appropriate tax/subsidy policy, therefore, even if a consumption tax on the importable good is the only possible source of revenue.

Given the possibility of unbundling, a tariff cannot be the first-best intervention unless it entails fewer administrative costs than the alternative of intervening directly at the source of the distortion. This rationale for protection would not seem especially convincing when the comparison is between a tariff and some other tax. I argue shortly, however, that in LDCs the unregulated market tends to generate too little employment in the high-wage industrial sector and too little investment overall. The Principle of Targeting demands wage and investment subsidies to correct these distortions. The first-best policy package would thus require the deployment of resources both to collect taxes and to disburse subsidies to firms at various sites.[9] A tariff, by contrast, raises revenue and disburses subsidies in a single step at a central location (the port). Moreover, because they can be implemented without information supplied by individual firms, tariffs are less vulnerable than subsidies to problems of fraud.[10]

---

[9] Corden (1974, pp. 64–66) and Rodrik (1992a, p. 312) emphasize that administrative costs are a serious barrier to the implementation of first-best policies.

[10] For example, a government intent on using a wage subsidy to combat underemployment may have to incur considerable costs in verifying the employment

Underemployment and the Optimal Tariff vs. the Optimal Employment Subsidy

A tariff saves on administrative costs but distorts consumer choice more than the alternative subsidy cum tax intervention. While the nature of this tradeoff is inevitably case-specific, the example in this section suggests it will usually be a close call as to which intervention is first-best. The reason is that the costs of the consumption distortion tend to be small. Consequently, for believable differences in administrative costs, the optimal tariff is often nearly as good as or superior to the competing tax/subsidy package that preserves free trade.

To fix ideas, suppose a minimum wage law exists but cannot be enforced outside the import-competing manufacturing sector. L_m workers are employed in the import sector at the wage w_m.[11] All other workers take jobs in the informal/export sector where competitive forces drive the wage down to the level that equates labor supply and labor demand. The sectoral wage gap mirrors an equal gap in the marginal product of labor. Thus, the labor market is distorted by too little employment in the high-wage manufacturing sector.

The government can tackle the distortion either by imposing a tariff t or by taxing consumption of manufactures at the rate b and using the proceeds to pay firms a subsidy s per employee. In the case of a tariff, the budget constraints of the private agent and the government are

$$E(1+t,u) = R(1+t,L_m)+T, \tag{6}$$

$$T = t[D^m(1+t,u)-Q_m], \tag{7}$$

where revenues are rebated to the public as lump-sum transfers T. When the employment subsidy and consumption tax are the policy instruments, equations (6) and (7) get replaced by

$$E(1+b,u) = R(L_m)+sL_m, \tag{8}$$

$$bD^m(1+b,u) = sL_m + h(b)D^m(1+b,u)+g(s)L_m. \tag{9}$$

figures that firms report. If the government does not verify employment figures, distortionary taxes will be higher than needed to finance the true corrective wage subsidy. In effect, some distortionary taxes will be levied to finance a transfer to firms.

[11] It might make more sense to have w_m adjust with prices to preserve the existing level of utility workers enjoy. I assume w_m is fixed to focus on administrative costs and abstract from the complications that arise when the labor market distortion is endogenous. (That case will be analyzed in Section 3.2.2.2.)

The terms hD^m and gL_m capture collection and disbursement costs. The evidence for developed countries indicates that the ratio of collection costs to revenues is insensitive to the tax base (implying that D^m should enter multiplicatively) but increasing in the tax rate (enforcement is more difficult at higher rates).[12] Since the same probably holds true for disbursement costs, I assume $h(b)$ and $g(s)$ to be increasing and possibly convex: $h', g' > 0, h'', g'' \geq 0$.

Labor is the only mobile factor, and technology and preferences are described by CES production functions and a CES–CRRA utility function. The complete model consists of either (6)–(7) or (8)–(9); the two production functions

$$Q_m = \left[a_1 + a_2 L_m^{(\sigma^m-1)/\sigma^m} \right]^{\sigma^m/(\sigma^m-1)}, \tag{10}$$

$$Q_x = \left[a_3 + a_4 L_x^{(\sigma^x-1)/\sigma^x} \right]^{\sigma^x/(\sigma^x-1)}; \tag{11}$$

the full-employment condition

$$L_m + L_x = L; \tag{12}$$

the sectoral labor demands

$$L_m = a_2^{\sigma^m} Q_m \left(\frac{w_m - s}{1+t} \right)^{-\sigma^m}, \tag{13}$$

$$L_x = a_4^{\sigma^x} Q_x w_x^{-\sigma^x}; \tag{14}$$

the collection and disbursement cost functions

$$h(b) = c_1 b + c_2 b^2/2, \tag{15}$$

$$g(s) = c_3 s + c_4 s^2/2; \tag{16}$$

and the indirect utility function

$$V(1+t+b,E) = \frac{E^{1-\phi} \left[1 + k^\beta (1+b+t)^{1-\beta} \right]^{(1-\phi)/(\beta-1)}}{1-\phi}, \qquad \phi \neq 1, \tag{17}$$

where L is the fixed supply of labor; σ^i is the elasticity of substitution between labor and the fixed factor in sector i; ϕ is the elasticity of the marginal utility of consumption; β is the elasticity of substitution

[12] See Agha and Haughton (1996).

between the importable and exportable goods; and a_1–a_4, c_1–c_4, and k are constants.

The general form of the optimal policy rules can be derived by following the same procedure as in Section 3.2.1. Note first that $\partial R/\partial L_m = w_m - s - w_x$ and that $(\partial Q_m/\partial L_m)(L_m/Q_m) = \theta_L^m$, the cost share of labor in sector m. Equations (8)–(9) then give

$$E_u\left(1 - \frac{b-h}{1+b}\gamma\right)du = (w_m - s - g - w_x)dL_m - g'L_m ds$$

$$- D^m\left(h' + \frac{b-h}{1+b}\varepsilon\right)db, \tag{18}$$

while (6) and (7) yield

$$E_u\left(1 - \frac{t}{1+t}\gamma\right)\frac{du}{dt} = \left(\frac{1}{1+t} - \psi\right)\theta_L^m Q_m\Omega - \frac{t}{1+t}D^m\varepsilon, \tag{19}$$

where $\psi \equiv w_x/w_m$, γ is the consumption share of good m (the same as the marginal propensity to consume good m when preferences are homothetic), and $\Omega > 0$ is the elasticity of labor demand with respect to the product wage in sector m. The optimal tariff thus satisfies

$$t^* = \frac{(1-\psi)\theta_L^m\Omega}{\psi\theta_L^m\Omega + \varepsilon D^m/Q_m}. \tag{20}$$

This solution is similar in form to (5′). For $\varepsilon > 0$, the by-product distortion of consumption patterns places the social optimum out of reach – i.e., $t^* < \psi/(1 - \psi)$.

A bit more effort is required to derive the optimal employment subsidy and consumption tax. From (9),

$$db = \left[D^m\left(1 - h' - \frac{b-h}{1+b}\varepsilon\right)\right]^{-1}$$

$$\left[L_m\left(1 + g' + \frac{s+g}{w_m - s}\Omega\right)ds - \frac{(b-h)\gamma E_u}{(1+b)}du\right]. \tag{21}$$

Substituting this into (18) and setting du/ds equal to zero produces

$$\frac{(w_m - s - g - w_x)\Omega}{w_m - s} = g' + \left(h' + \frac{b-h}{1+b}\varepsilon\right)\left[1 + \frac{(w_m - w_x)\Omega}{w_m - s}\right]. \tag{22}$$

Equations (9) and (22) jointly define the optimal policy rules for s and b.

A. Calibration of the Model

To calibrate the model, we have to find values for the distribution parameters (a_1–a_4 and k), the parameters of the collection and disbursement cost functions (c_1–c_4), and factor endowments (L) that are consistent with the structure assumed for the economy at the initial free trade equilibrium. For the CES production functions and the CES–CRRA utility function,

$$\gamma = \frac{k^\beta (1+b+t)^{1-\beta}}{1+k^\beta (1+b+t)^{1-\beta}},$$

$$\theta_L^m = a_2^{\sigma^m} \left(\frac{w_m - s}{1+t} \right)^{1-\sigma^m},$$

$$\theta_L^x = a_4^{\sigma^x} w_x^{1-\sigma^x},$$

$$\Omega = \sigma^m / (1-\theta_L^m),$$

$$\varepsilon = \beta(1-\gamma).$$

Choose labor units so that w_m equals one and let an o subscript refer to the value of a variable at the initial free trade equilibrium where $b = s = t = 0$. Since $w_m = 1$, the initial value of w_x determines the severity of the labor market distortion. The values assigned to w_{xo}, θ_{Lo}^i, and γ_o thus fix the values of a_2, a_4, and k:

$$a_2 = \left(\theta_{L_o}^m \right)^{1/\sigma^m},$$

$$a_4 = \left(\theta_{L_o}^x w_{xo}^{\sigma^x - 1} \right)^{1/\sigma^x},$$

$$k = \left(\frac{\gamma_o}{1-\gamma_o} \right)^{1/\beta}.$$

The other two distribution parameters in the production functions depend on the share of value added produced initially by the manufacturing sector; call this VA_m. By definition,

$$VA_m = \frac{Q_{mo}}{Q_{mo} + Q_{xo}},$$

so

$$Q_{mo} = \frac{\mathrm{VA_m}}{1 - \mathrm{VA_m}} Q_{xo}.$$

Without loss of generality, we can set Q_{xo} equal to 100.[13] The above and

$$L_{mo} = \theta_{L_o}^m Q_{mo}$$

$$L_{xo} = \theta_{L_o}^x Q_{xo} / w_{xo}$$

then determine Q_{mo} and L_{io} as a function of the values chosen for $\mathrm{VA_m}$, θ_{Lo}^i, and w_{xo}. Once the values for L_{io} are in hand, the solutions for a_1, a_3, and the total labor force L fall out from the two production functions and the full-employment condition:

$$a_1 = Q_{mo}^{(\sigma^m - 1)/\sigma^m} - a_2 L_{mo}^{(\sigma^m - 1)/\sigma^m},$$

$$a_3 = Q_{xo}^{(\sigma^x - 1)/\sigma^x} - a_4 L_{xo}^{(\sigma^x - 1)/\sigma^x},$$

$$L = L_{mo} + L_{xo}.$$

Finally, the only way to pin down c_1–c_4 is to take a deep breath and make guesses for the curvature of $h(b)$ and $g(s)$ and the size of collection/disbursement costs at particular values of s and b. I assume (i) that collection costs are f percent of revenues and disbursement costs are r percent of subsidies at $s = b = .10$, and (ii) that $c_1 = zf$ and $c_3 = zr$, where $0 \leq z \leq 1$. This implies

$$c_2 = 20f(1-z) \quad \text{and} \quad c_4 = 20r(1-z).$$

The model is now complete. After making use of the expressions for $\gamma, \theta_L^i, \Omega, \varepsilon, a_1$–$a_4, c_1$–$c_4, k$, and L, the computer solves (10)–(14) and either (6), (7), and (20) or (8), (9), and (22) for Q_i, L_i, w_x, E, and either T and t or b and s. Since free trade is the common starting point for the two policy interventions, the appropriate measure of the welfare gain is the *compensating variation* CV. This is calculated as the amount of extra income that raises welfare at the initial free trade equilibrium to the level associated with the optimum; that is,

$$\mathrm{CV} = \frac{E_2 - E_o}{E_o} \times 100,$$

---

[13] The value of Q_{xo} fixes the absolute size of the economy but is otherwise irrelevant. This reflects the assumption of constant returns to scale.

where

$$E_o = Q_{mo} + Q_{xo},$$

$$E_2 = [V*(1-\phi)]^{1/1-\phi}(1+k^\beta)^{1/(1-\beta)},$$

and $V*$ is utility at the optimum.

B. Numerical Solutions
The numerical solutions cover the cases where

$$\begin{array}{lll}
\sigma^m = .75; & \sigma^x = .50; & w_{xo} = .50, .67; \\
\gamma_o = .30; & \text{VA}_{mo} = .15; & \beta = .15, .25, .50; \\
z = 0, 1; & f = r = .03, .05, .075, .10; \\
\theta^m_{Lo} = .30 \text{ and } \theta^x_{Lo} = .40; & \theta^m_{Lo} = \theta^x_{Lo} = .45.
\end{array}$$

These values are consistent with the findings in the empirical literature, a full review of which will be supplied in Chapter 5. The only observation I wish to make here is that a certain amount of judgement is involved in choosing parameter values that do not exaggerate the costs of the trade and labor market distortions. One needs to be alert, in particular, to the implications of assigning realistic values to γ and VA_m and letting the export sector play the role of the "rest of the economy." This may prejudice the solutions by equating a tariff with an unrealistically large change in the relative price of the import good. Simple two-sector trade models do not allow for the fact that a tariff drives up the price of non-tradables when goods are substitutes in consumption and/or production.[14] The induced increase in the price of nontraded goods limits the decrease in imports and thereby reduces the loss from the trade distortion. If a nontradables sector is added to the present model, for example, the solution in (19) changes to

$$E_u\left(1 - \frac{t}{1+t}\gamma_m\right)\frac{du}{dt}$$
$$= \left(\frac{1}{1+t} - \psi\right)\frac{\theta^m_L}{1 - \theta^m_L}Q_m\sigma^m - \frac{t}{1+t}D^m\beta(1 - \gamma_m - \gamma_n\lambda), \qquad (19')$$

where λ is the elasticity of P_n with respect to P_m. The increase in P_n does not alter the production distortion, but it does lower the loss from the consumption distortion.[15] Furthermore, since nontradables account for

---

[14] I regard this as the normal case. In theory, however, importables and nontradables could be complements instead of substitutes.
[15] In equation (19), $\Omega = \sigma^m/(1 - \theta^m_L)$ and $\varepsilon = \beta(1 - \gamma_m)$.

40–50% of GDP, the reduction in the consumption distortion is significant when the supply response is not so elastic as to hold λ below .30.
For $\gamma_m = .25$ and $\lambda_n = .50$, the loss from the consumption distortion is the
same when $\beta = .30$ in the two-sector model as it is when $\beta = .50$ and $\lambda =$
.60 in the three-sector model.[16] β should be set below its true value therefore to the extent that the two-sector model overstates how much a tariff
increases the relative price of importables to consumers.[17] This is the
rationale in this and later chapters for examining the outcome when β
takes a very low value like .15.

Turn now to Tables 3.2 and 3.3. The entries show the solutions for the
optimal values of t, s, b, and the welfare gains achieved by operating at
the optimum. In Table 3.2 the cost shares for labor are $\theta_{Lo}^m = .30$ and θ_{Lo}^x
= .40, while in Table 3.3 both shares are initially .45. The base run assumes
that collection/disbursement costs are linear ($z = 1$) and that the wage in
manufacturing is initially 50% higher than the wage in the export sector
($w_{xo} = .67$). These parameters take different values in the second and
third panels of the tables.

A brief inspection of the solutions reveals that the tariff fares best
when β is small and w_{xo} and θ_{Lo}^m are large. This is to be expected. A tariff
is, to repeat, an equal rate consumption tax and production subsidy. The
surplus revenue rebated to the public, and the portion of the production
subsidy that falls on the nonlabor input, are pointless transfers paid for
by a distortionary consumption tax. *Ceteris paribus*, therefore, the tariff
is less efficient the more elastic is demand and the larger the cost share
of the nonlabor input. Moreover, these costs assume more importance
when a large sectoral wage gap calls for a strong policy intervention. The
bluntness of the tariff is thus more of a handicap when the labor market
is more distorted ($w_{xo} = .50$ vs. $w_{xo} = .67$).

Getting down to brass tacks, can administrative costs restore
respectability to protection? Regrettably, the answer seems to be yes. Not
much is known about the magnitude of administrative costs, but there
is some evidence that collections costs for consumption taxes are 4–5
percentage points higher than for tariffs (World Development Report,
1988). If these numbers can be trusted, *and* if disbursement costs are

[16] This value for λ is not implausible. Assume the nontraded good is also produced by labor and a fixed factor. λ then equals .55 when $\sigma^m = 0.75$, $\sigma^n = \sigma^x = .5$,
$\gamma_m = .30$, $VA_m = .15$, $\psi = .50$, $\theta_L^m = .30$, $\theta_L^x = .40$, $\theta_L^n = .45$, and $h = .25$. Dropping σ^n
to zero raises λ to .74.

[17] A similar adjustment should be made to σ^m when an increase in the price of
nontradables weakens the impact of the tariff on domestic production in the
import sector. No adjustment is required in the current model because w_m is fixed
and labor is the only mobile factor of production.

Table 3.2. *The optimal tariff vs. the optimal wage subsidy plus consumption tax when there are administrative costs and the cost share of labor is initially 30% in the import sector and 40% in the export sector.*

	Base run					
	Optimal tariff		Optimal wage subsidy			
β	t	CV	s	b	CV	f, r
.15	.240	.176	.240	.051	.190	.03
			.204	.043	.133	.05
			.157	.033	.076	.075
			.107	.022	.034	.10
.25	.185	.137	.237	.051	.187	.03
			.201	.043	.131	.05
			.155	.032	.075	.075
			.105	.022	.034	.10
.50	.117	.088	.230	.049	.181	.03
			.195	.041	.127	.05
			.149	.031	.072	.075
			.102	.021	.032	.10

$w_{xo} = .50$

	Optimal tariff		Optimal wage subsidy			
β	t	CV	s	b	CV	f, r
.15	.437	.455	.399	.109	.595	.03
			.362	.096	.471	.05
			.313	.081	.336	.075
			.261	.066	.225	.10
.25	.324	.347	.393	.107	.583	.03
			.356	.095	.462	.05
			.308	.080	.330	.075
			.257	.065	.220	.10
.50	.195	.217	.378	.102	.556	.03
			.342	.090	.440	.05
			.295	.076	.315	.075
			.246	.062	.210	.10

$z = 0$

	Optimal tariff		Optimal wage subsidy			
β	t	CV	s	b	CV	f, r
.15	.240	.176	.187	.037	.171	.03
			.149	.029	.133	.05
			.119	.023	.104	.075
			.099	.019	.085	.10
.25	.185	.137	.185	.037	.169	.03
			.148	.029	.132	.05
			.118	.023	.103	.075
			.098	.018	.085	.10
.50	.117	.088	.181	.036	.166	.03
			.146	.028	.130	.05
			.117	.022	.102	.075
			.097	.018	.084	.10

Table 3.3. *The optimal tariff vs. the optimal wage subsidy plus consumption tax when there are administrative costs and the cost share of labor is initially 45% in both sectors.*

	Base run					
	Optimal tariff		Optimal wage subsidy			
β	t	CV	s	b	CV	f, r
.15	.291	.410	.234	.080	.376	.03
			.206	.070	.286	.05
			.170	.057	.190	.075
			.132	.044	.113	.10
.25	.248	.350	.230	.079	.370	.03
			.202	.069	.281	.05
			.167	.056	.187	.075
			.130	.043	.111	.10
.50	.179	.255	.222	.076	.355	.03
			.195	.066	.269	.05
			.160	.054	.179	.075
			.125	.042	.107	.10

$w_{xo} = .50$

	Optimal tariff		Optimal wage subsidy			
β	t	CV	s	b	CV	f, r
.15	.563	1.123	.386	.175	1.161	.03
			.355	.158	.960	.05
			.316	.137	.735	.075
			.275	.117	.543	.10
.25	.466	.940	.378	.170	1.132	.03
			.348	.154	.936	.05
			.310	.134	.718	.075
			.270	.114	.530	.10
.50	.322	.622	.360	.160	1.066	.03
			.331	.145	.881	.05
			.294	.126	.676	.075
			.256	.107	.499	.10

$z = 0$

	Optimal tariff		Optimal wage subsidy			
β	t	CV	s	b	CV	f, r
.15	.291	.410	.185	.059	.333	.03
			.151	.047	.265	.05
			.123	.037	.211	.075
			.103	.031	.175	.10
.25	.248	.350	.183	.058	.329	.03
			.150	.046	.262	.05
			.122	.037	.209	.075
			.103	.030	.174	.10
.50	.179	.255	.178	.057	.320	.03
			.146	.045	.257	.05
			.120	.036	.206	.075
			.101	.030	.171	.10

similarly large, then tariffs are often first-best or nearly first-best.[18] This is the case in the base runs in both tables when $\beta = .15, .25$. For $\beta = .50$ or $w_{xo} = .50$, the tariff does not gain the upper hand until administrative costs claim 7–10% of revenues/disbursements.[19] But notice that for $f = .05$ the optimal tariff picks up 50–99% of the gain delivered by the optimal employment subsidy, and that the absolute difference in the CVs never amounts to more than .22% of initial income. The reward for getting all the way to the optimum is just a bit of extra pocket change.[20]

3.2.2.2 ENDOGENOUS VS. EXOGENOUS DISTORTIONS

Administrative costs provide one potential justification for employing tariffs instead of more complex tax/subsidy schemes. A second, more speculative defense of protection is based on the distinction between exogenous and endogenous distortions. Consider in this connection two equally plausible stories as to why the wage in the manufacturing sector

[18] Clarette and Whalley (1987) compare the marginal welfare costs of a tariff on consumer imports and a consumption tax on the importable in a seven-sector CGE model calibrated to a 1978 dataset for the Philippines. After finding that the marginal welfare costs of the tariff are much higher, they conclude that differences in administrative costs are unlikely to justify protection. The results are not strong enough, however, to support this conclusion. The model does not incorporate administrative costs or any distortion in the import-competing sector that could be lessened by a tariff. Consequently, the welfare costs of the tariff include both the distortion of consumer choice and the misallocation of resources in production. This bias is made worse by the assumption of a high degree of substitutability in production and consumption (production and utility functions are Cobb–Douglas, and capital and labor are intersectorally mobile) and the presence of other taxes (on exports and imported producer goods) at the initial equilibrium that imply that the consumption tax is welfare-improving until it exceeds 15%.
[19] It is important to remember that the chosen example is not favorable to protection. Since the cost share of labor is small, 55–70% of the production subsidy conferred by the tariff is wasted on the fixed factor. It will become clear in Chapter 5, however, that the optimal tariff is larger in models that allow for both underemployment and underinvestment. In such models, the entire production subsidy component of the tariff works to offset distortions in factor markets. I conjecture that in this case administrative costs of just 1–3% would make the tariff first-best.
[20] I have restricted the analysis to the cases where the government chooses either a tariff or a wage subsidy plus consumption tax. The gains would be larger (though probably not much larger) if all three instruments were chosen optimally.

typically exceeds its market-clearing level. In the first we again have a minimum wage law that is enforced only in the manufacturing sector. Since the manufacturing wage is exogenous, the comparison of alternative policies is a cut and dried affair: the Principle of Targeting informs us that if tariffs are just as costly to administer as other policies the first-best intervention is a wage subsidy (plus tax).

Now suppose instead that high wages in manufacturing reflect the power of unions operating in the formal sector. For simplicity, assume workers in manufacturing are represented by a single monopolistic union and that labor is the only mobile factor of production. Union membership is $M > L_m$, and members who fail to obtain a job in manufacturing settle for lower paying work in the primary export sector. Workers have identical homothetic preferences represented by the CES–CRRA indirect utility function

$$V(P_m + b, w_i) = \frac{w_i^{1-\phi}\left[1 + k^\beta(P_m + b)^{1-\beta}\right]^{(1-\phi)/(\beta-1)}}{1-\phi}$$
$$= v(P_m + b)w_i^{1-\phi}, \qquad \phi \neq 1, \ i = m, x, \tag{23}$$

where $P_m = 1 + t$, the tariff-inclusive price received by producers, and all other variables are defined as before. The union sets the wage to maximize expected utility of its representative member,

$$U = v(P_m + b)\left[\frac{L_m}{M}w_m^{1-\phi} + \left(1 - \frac{L_m}{M}\right)w_x^{1-\phi}\right], \tag{24}$$

subject to the labor demand schedule

$$L_m = G\left(\frac{w_m - s}{P_m}\right). \tag{25}$$

The optimal wage satisfies the first-order condition

$$G'\left(\frac{w_m - s}{P_m}\right) = -\frac{(1-\phi)G[(w_m - s)/P_m]w_m^{-\phi}P_m}{w_m^{1-\phi} - w_x^{1-\phi}}. \tag{26}$$

The solution to the union's optimization problem is depicted in Figure 3.2. The U_o contour shows different combinations of w_m and L_m consistent with the same level of expected utility. It is convex in the neighborhood of the optimal wage.

The crucial difference between this and the previous case where w_m was fixed by a minimum wage law is that the distortion is no longer an

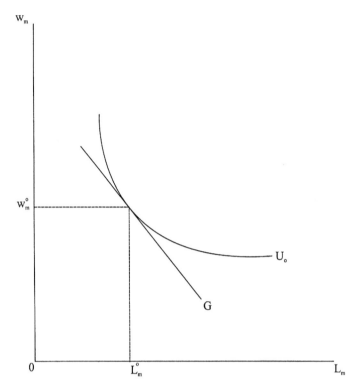

Figure 3.2. The wage chosen by an optimizing union.

easy, immobile target: when the government alters one of its policy instruments, the union will also adjust its wage demand. The first-order condition (26) yields

$$\left[2\Omega \frac{w_m}{w_m - s}(1-\phi) + \phi(1-\phi) - (1-\psi^{1-\phi})\alpha\Omega\left(\frac{w_m}{w_m - s}\right)^2 \right]\hat{w}_m$$

$$= \Omega\left[1 - \phi + (1-\psi^{1-\phi})\frac{w_m}{w_m - s}(1-\alpha) \right]\hat{P}_m - \Omega\frac{w_m}{w_m - s}$$

$$\left[1 - \phi - (1-\psi^{1-\phi})\frac{w_m}{w_m - s}\alpha \right]\frac{ds}{w_m} - \Omega\frac{w_m}{w_m - s}\psi^{1-\phi}(1-\phi)\hat{w}_x, \quad (27)$$

where a circumflex ($\hat{}$) denotes the percentage change in a variable ($\hat{x} = dx/x$) and $\alpha \equiv -G''[(w_m - s)/P_m]G'$ is the elasticity of the slope of the manufacturing sector labor demand schedule. (As before, $\psi \equiv w_x/w_m < 1$ and $\Omega > 0$ is the elasticity of labor demand with respect to the product wage.) Note from the first-order condition that

$$\Omega(1 - \psi^{1-\phi}) = (1 - \phi)\frac{w_m - s}{w_m}, \qquad \phi \neq 1. \tag{26'}$$

This allows the solution in (27) to be expressed more simply as

$$\hat{w}_m = \frac{\Omega - \alpha}{F}\frac{ds}{w_m} + \frac{\Omega + 1 - \alpha}{F}\frac{w_m - s}{w_m}\hat{P}_m + \frac{\Omega\psi^{1-\phi}}{F}\hat{w}_x, \tag{27'}$$

where $F \equiv \Omega\psi^{1-\phi} + \Omega + 1 - \alpha - s/w_m$ is positive by the second-order condition. Conveniently, the union wage demand is independent of the tax b. The above solution reflects therefore the response of w_m to tariffs and to a wage subsidy financed by a consumption tax on the manufactured good.

Since dw_m/ds, $\hat{w}_m/\hat{P}_m < 1$, both policy instruments increase employment in manufacturing and may be used to secure a welfare improvement. A wage subsidy is more effective, however, in stimulating labor demand. For a given value of w_m, an increase in the wage subsidy of $ds = (w_m - s)\hat{P}_m$ reduces real labor costs by the same amount as a tariff that increases the domestic price of manufactures by $\hat{P}_m$. Making this comparison in (27') shows that protection provokes a larger increase in union wage demands than the comparable wage subsidy. In fact, a wage subsidy may even reduce w_m. This happens when the labor demand schedule becomes enough flatter in slope as it shifts to the right. The result seems odd, but it is not confined to exotic production functions. For CES technology,

$$\Omega = \sigma/\theta_K \quad \text{and} \quad \alpha = \frac{\sigma(1 + \theta_L) + \theta_K - \theta_L}{\theta_K},$$

where $\theta_K = 1 - \theta_L$ (the cost share of the fixed factor). Substituting these expressions into (27') produces

$$\hat{w}_m = \frac{\theta_L(1 - \sigma) - \theta_K}{\sigma + \theta_K[\phi(1 - s/w_m) - 1] + \theta_L(1 - \sigma)}\frac{ds}{w_m}$$

$$+ \frac{\theta_L(1 - \sigma)}{\sigma + \theta_K[\phi(1 - s/w_m) - 1] + \theta_L(1 - \sigma)}\frac{w_m - s}{w_m}\hat{P}_m$$

$$+ \frac{\sigma\psi^{1-\phi}}{\sigma + \theta_K[\phi(1 - s/w_m) - 1] + \theta_L(1 - \sigma)}\hat{w}_x. \tag{27''}$$

Ignoring general equilibrium effects (i.e., $\hat{w}_x$), a wage subsidy induces the union to *moderate* its wage demand provided only that $\sigma > 1 - \theta_K/\theta_L$. For a tariff to accomplish the same, it is necessary that σ exceed unity.

In view of these results it should come as no surprise that the optimal wage subsidy plus consumption tax generates a greater welfare gain than the optimal tariff. Not only does a tariff impose an overly large consumption tax that generates surplus revenue and subsidizes other inputs in the manufacturing sector besides labor, it also reduces real wage costs less than the comparable wage subsidy.[21] As usual, the policy that operates directly on the relevant margin is superior to protection.

No damage has been done so far to the Principle of Targeting. However, if the strategic environment differs depending on the government's choice of policy instrument, the first-best policy's strength may also be its weakness. To see this, consider the case where lump-sum taxes are possible and the government aims for the socially optimal level of employment L_m^2 in Figure 3.3 by setting the subsidy s so that the cost of labor is the same for firms in the manufacturing and primary export sectors. Because it is so direct, the wage subsidy may reveal to the union the government's policy rule of setting $s = w_m - w_x$. But if the union catches on to the government's policy rule, its maximization problem becomes

$$\underset{\{w_m\}}{\text{Max}} \frac{G(w_x/P_m)}{M} w_m^{1-\phi} + \left[1 - \frac{G(w_x/P_m)}{M}\right] w_x^{1-\phi},$$

which does not have a solution. The first-best policy is infeasible because it presents the union with a vertical labor demand schedule that eliminates the tradeoff between wage demands and employment.[22]

Under the more realistic assumption that revenues have to be raised by distortionary taxes, a wage subsidy is feasible but still suffers from the drawback of making the union more aggressive in its wage demands. In Figure 3.4, point A again represents the wage and level of employment when the union solves the maximization problem defined by (24) and (25). Point A is not the equilibrium, however, if the introduction of the wage subsidy enables the union to learn the government's policy rule.[23] In this latter case, point B is the equilibrium since the union realizes that

---

[21] I am ignoring here the impact of changes in w_x, which is clearly an induced, second-round effect.

[22] I have assumed in Figure 3.3 that the union recognizes the government's policy rule only after the economy reaches L_2. If the union becomes aware of the policy rule at some earlier point, the L^d schedule turns vertical somewhere to the left of L_m^2.

[23] The analysis here and in Section 3.4 parallels Calmfors (1984).

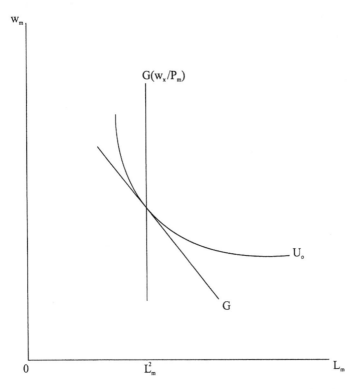

Figure 3.3. Infeasibility of a wage subsidy when the union knows the government's policy rule.

the wage–employment tradeoff is governed by the steeper schedule $G_1 G_1$, along which higher wage costs for firms are partly offset by higher subsidies. And because the distortionary tax is higher and employment lower at B compared to A, the optimal subsidy does not always dominate the optimal tariff. The policy that intervenes directly at the source of the distortion is not necessarily first-best when it also aggravates the distortion. The essence of the problem is the *Lucas Critique* (Lucas, 1976): equation (27′) is not a reduced form the government can manipulate through a wage subsidy *rule*.

Comparisons of the Optimal Tariff and the Optimal Employment Subsidy

I have provided a rough, intuitive sketch of the idea that indirect interventions which conceal the government's underlying policy rule *may* be superior to direct interventions based on transparent policy rules. It is a

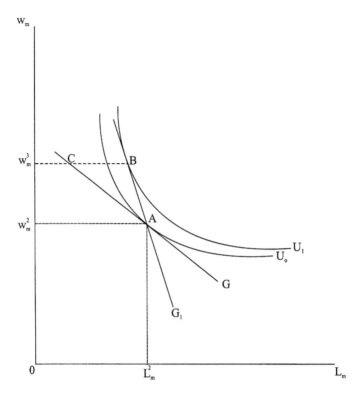

Figure 3.4. The impact of a wage subsidy when the union knows the government's policy rule and the subsidy is financed by a distortionary tax.

long way from this to a solid justification for protection. The traditional policy ranking holds up if the byproduct distortions stemming from protection prove more costly than the adverse strategic effects associated with operating directly on the relevant margin. Moreover, one can always take issue with the premise that the public is unable to detect the policy rule associated with more indirect interventions (i.e., that the Lucas Critique applies asymmetrically). In fact, there is not even agreement in the literature about which policy rule is more transparent. The impact on union wage demands has been used both by critics of protection (Krugman, 1993, p. 134) and by those sceptical of first-best solutions (Rodrik, 1992a). The possbility that the point applies with equal force to both policy interventions has been ignored.

To clarify matters, I compute the welfare gains produced by the optimal tariff and the optimal wage subsidy for the Nash case and for the cases where one of the two players is a Stackelberg leader. This enables the two policies to be ranked for all possible leadership/follower patterns. One can determine, for example, whether the normal policy ranking is reversed when the union views tariffs as parametric but behaves as a Stackelberg leader in the event the government gives out a wage subsidy.

The model is the same as in the preceding section, except the wage is chosen by the union and the government budget constraint is

$$bD^m(1+t+b,u)+t[D^m(1+t+b,u)-Q_m]=S+sL_m. \tag{28}$$

There are no administrative costs, and expenditures now include fixed purchases of the export good S as well as the employment subsidy sL_m. The spending requirement S is introduced to obtain a quantitatively accurate comparison of the costs of the byproduct distortions that accompany the tariff and the employment subsidy. Prior spending commitments matter because, when S is positive at the initial free trade equilibrium, so also is the distortionary consumption tax b. A wage subsidy aggravates the existing distortion as it requires a further increase in the tax. A tariff does likewise, but the extra revenues it brings into government coffers can be used to reduce the consumption tax. This lessens but does not eliminate the disadvantage the tariff faces as the less direct policy intervention. Although a tariff allows the explicit consumption tax to be reduced, the total consumption tax, $b + t$, is always higher because the implicit production subsidy tQ_m costs more than the comparable wage subsidy.

The easiest cases are those in which the union behaves passively. Consider first the Nash solution. In this case, the union treats b, s, and t as fixed when solving the optimization problem in (24)–(25) and the government treats w_m as fixed when choosing b and either t or s to maximize social welfare. The wage is determined by (26) while the optimal tariff and the optimal employment subsidy satisfy

$$(\text{tariff}) \quad \frac{(b+t)\varepsilon}{1+b+t}[1+(1-\psi)\theta_L^m\Omega]=\left(1-\psi-\frac{t}{1+t}\right)\theta_L^m\Omega, \tag{29}$$

$$(\text{subsidy}) \quad \frac{b\varepsilon}{1+b}\left[1+(1-\psi)\Omega\frac{w_m}{w_m-s}\right]=(1-\psi-s/w_m)\Omega\frac{w_m}{w_m-s}, \tag{30}$$

with b adjusting to meet the government budget constraint (28).

The solutions are almost identical in form when the government is a Stackelberg leader. All that changes is the perceived impact of the policy instrument on labor demand in the manufacturing sector. In the Nash case, this is given simply by Ω because the government views w_m as parametric when choosing t and s. But when the government leads it recognizes that t and s affect w_m directly and through induced variations in w_x. The impact on labor demand is calculated therefore from (13), (27″), and the market clearing solution for $\hat{w}_x$. This works out to

$$\frac{\hat{L}_m}{\hat{P}_m} = \frac{\sigma^x[\sigma^m + \theta_K^m(\phi-1)]}{\sigma^x\theta_K^m Z/\sigma^m + \sigma^m\theta_K^x\psi^{1-\phi}L_m/L_x}, \tag{31}$$

$$w_m\frac{\hat{L}_m}{ds} = \frac{\sigma^x(\sigma^m + \theta_K^m\phi)}{\sigma^x\theta_K^m Z(1-s/w_m)/\sigma^m + \sigma^m\theta_K^x\psi^{1-\phi}L_m/L_x}, \tag{32}$$

where $Z \equiv \sigma^m + \theta_K^m(\phi-1) + \theta_L^m(1-\sigma^m)$. These expressions replace Ω in (29) and $\Omega w_m/(w_m - s)$ in (30); everything else stays the same.

In the last and most difficult case, the government is passive and the union is a Stackelberg leader. Equations (28)–(30) again define the government reaction function, but now the union takes account of how its choice of w_m conditions government policy by solving the problem[24]

$$\underset{\{w_m\}}{\text{Max}}\,MU = v[1+b(w_m)+t(w_m)]\left\{G\left[\frac{w_m - s(w_m)}{1+t(w_m)}\right]w_m^{1-\phi}\right.$$
$$\left.+\left\{M - G\left[\frac{w_m - s(w_m)}{1+t(w_m)}\right]\right\}w_x^{1-\phi}\right\}. \tag{33}$$

This leads to

$$\text{(tariff)}\quad G' = -\frac{1+t}{\left(1-\frac{t'w_m}{1+t}\right)(w_m^{1-\phi} - w_x^{1-\phi})}\left\{L_m(1-\phi)w_m^{-\phi}\right.$$
$$\left.+\frac{v'(t'+b')}{v}[L_m w_m^{1-\phi} + (M-L_m)w_x^{1-\phi}]\right\}, \tag{34}$$

---

[24] The standard practice in the literature is to assume that the union does not take account of subtle general equilibrium effects when choosing w_m. I assume therefore that the union views u and w_x as exogenous when solving its maximization problem.

$$\text{(subsidy)} \quad G' = -\left[(1-s')(w_m^{1-\phi} - w_x^{1-\phi})\right]^{-1}\left\{L_m(1-\phi)w_w^{-\phi}\right.$$

$$\left. + \frac{v'b'}{v}\left[L_m w_m^{1-\phi} + (M-L_m)w_x^{1-\phi}\right]\right\}, \tag{35}$$

where t', b', and s' are obtained by solving (28)–(30) for s, b, and t as a function of w_m. Note that (34)–(35) collapse to (26) when $t' = b' = s' = 0$.

A.   Numerical Solutions

The numerical solutions in Tables 3.4 and 3.5 were computed using the same values for initial cost shares, elasticities of substitution, and initial consumption and production shares as in Section 3.2.2.1. In the runs where the union is a Stackelberg leader, union membership is twice the initial level of employment in manufacturing ($M = 2L_{mo}$). At the initial free trade equilibrium, $b_o = .15$ and $w_{mo} = 1$. Normalizing w_{mo} at unity implies from (26') that

$$w_{xo} = \left(1 + \frac{\phi - 1}{\Omega}\right)^{1/(1-\phi)}, \quad \phi \neq 1.$$

The solutions confirm that the critical issue is whether the strategic environment is invariant to the choice of policy instrument. When it is, comparisons are confined to the same panel and the Principle of Targeting picks out the best policy intervention each and every time. The employment subsidy always wins, and usually by a large margin: in 26 of 36 cases the welfare gain produced by the optimal subsidy is 1.7–5 times larger than the gain produced by the optimal tariff; and in the case where $\beta = .50$, $\phi = 2$, and the union is a Stackelberg leader, the imposition of a tariff actually proves harmful.[25]

The superiority of the subsidy reflects not only a smaller distortion of consumption choice but also a favorable or less adverse impact on union wage demands. In the Nash solutions and those where the government is a Stackelberg leader, the optimal subsidy *reduces* w_m or increases it by less than 1%. The optimal tariff, on the other hand, pushes up the wage by 1–10%. Both policies provoke a sharp increase in the wage when the union is a Stackelberg leader, but the optimal subsidy always lowers the product wage more [$w_m - s < w_m/(1 + t)$]. These results and the

---

[25] The "optimal" tariff is harmful because the government fails to realize that the union will raise the wage when the tariff increases. If the government understood this, it would recognize that the true optimal tariff is zero.

Table 3.4. *The optimal tariff vs. the optimal wage subsidy when the cost share of labor is initially 30% in the import sector and 40% in the export sector.*

					Nash Solution				
		Tariff				Wage subsidy			
β	t	b	w_m	CV	s	b	w_m	CV	ϕ
.15	.556	−.035	1.062	.43	.327	.252	.899	.74	2
	.352	.023	1.040	.21	.285	.223	.977	.35	4
.25	.416	.010	1.047	.31	.319	.248	.901	.71	2
	.266	.054	1.031	.14	.275	.220	.977	.32	4
.50	.228	.073	1.027	.13	.297	.240	.908	.63	2
	.138	.100	1.016	.05	.249	.213	.979	.27	4

					Union is a Stackelberg Leader				
		Tariff				Wage subsidy			
β	t	b	w_m	CV	s	b	w_m	CV	ϕ
.15	.838	−.136	1.377	.15	1.788	.665	2.426	.36	2
	.437	−.008	1.132	.15	.878	.372	1.591	.25	4
.25	.567	−.045	1.266	.04	1.405	.547	2.071	.26	2
	.315	.036	1.096	.08	.763	.341	1.496	.19	4
.50	.285	.052	1.156	−.09	.978	.417	1.700	.10	2
	.157	.093	1.052	≈0	.588	.295	1.362	.09	4

					Government is a Stackelberg Leader				
		Tariff				Wage subsidy			
β	t	b	w_m	CV	s	b	w_m	CV	ϕ
.15	.520	−.026	1.058	.44	.329	.252	.898	.74	2
	.330	.030	1.038	.21	.286	.223	.977	.35	4
.25	.380	.020	1.043	.31	.321	.250	.901	.71	2
	.243	.061	1.028	.14	.276	.221	.977	.32	4
.50	.198	.081	1.023	.13	.302	.243	.906	.63	2
	.116	.107	1.014	.05	.252	.214	.979	.27	4

preceding theoretical analysis point to the same conclusion: there is a strong presumption, bordering on certainty, that the optimal subsidy dominates the optimal tariff whenever the two policies compete in the same strategic environment. For those seeking to justify protection, all that remains therefore is the argument that an employment subsidy

Table 3.5. *The optimal tariff vs. the optimal wage subsidy when the cost share of labor is initially 45% in both sectors.*

					Nash Solution				
		Tariff				Wage subsidy			
β	t	b	w_m	CV	s	b	w_m	CV	ϕ
.15	.559	−.004	1.100	.70	.317	.295	.966	.97	2
	.366	.034	1.065	.36	.268	.254	1.010	.48	4
.25	.458	.022	1.083	.55	.306	.290	.966	.92	2
	.305	.053	1.055	.28	.257	.250	1.009	.45	4
.50	.300	.065	1.055	.31	.281	.277	.967	.80	2
	.201	.086	1.036	.14	.231	.239	1.007	.37	4

					Union is a Stackelberg Leader				
		Tariff				Wage subsidy			
β	t	b	w_m	CV	s	b	w_m	CV	ϕ
.15	1.021	−.147	1.547	.24	1.609	.839	2.329	.41	2
	.519	−.012	1.213	.25	.778	.448	1.540	.34	4
.25	.726	−.064	1.396	.09	1.251	.675	1.987	.27	2
	.404	.020	1.165	.16	.673	.405	1.453	.26	4
.50	.413	.027	1.241	−.10	.855	.498	1.640	.05	2
	.247	.070	1.104	.03	.513	.342	1.329	.12	4

					Government is a Stackelberg Leader				
		Tariff				Wage subsidy			
β	t	b	w_m	CV	s	b	w_m	CV	ϕ
.15	.519	.002	1.093	.70	.317	.295	.956	.97	2
	.343	.039	1.061	.36	.267	.254	1.010	.48	4
.25	.414	.029	1.075	.55	.307	.290	.966	.92	2
	.277	.059	1.050	.28	.257	.249	1.009	.45	4
.50	.257	.073	1.048	.32	.282	.278	.967	.80	2
	.171	.093	1.031	.15	.230	.239	1.007	.37	4

changes the strategic environment for the worse. Accepting the argument on its own terms, suppose the government cedes its position as Stackelberg leader to the union when it intervenes with an employment subsidy instead of a tariff. In Table 3.5, where the cost share of labor in manufacturing is high (for an LDC), the tariff then wins in every case, but the difference in the welfare gain is imperceptible for $\phi = 4$. When θ_L^m takes the more normal value of .30 (Table 3.4), each policy claims three narrow victories. *Asymmetric* strategic effects make tariffs competitive with employment subsidies, the most direct policy intervention; however, they do not *decisively* override the Principle of Targeting unless the cost share of labor is high *and* the wage gap is large ($\phi = 2$, $\sigma^m = .75$, and $\theta_{Lo}^m = .45$ imply $w_{mo}/w_{xo} = 1.73$).

Further Considerations
Before making too much of the results in Tables 3.4 and 3.5, two more points have to be weighed carefully. First, the Principle of Targeting remains valid if we simply add the qualification that the government precommit to the subsidy s^* associated with point A in Figure 3.4. If the union believed the government declaration, it would prefer w_m^2 to w_m^3, making point A the equilibrium.

The problem with this remedy is that the government's commitment to provide a subsidy no larger than s^* is not time-consistent. While the union and the government disagree about whether B is preferable to A, both prefer B to C. This gives the union an incentive to test the government's resolve. By keeping the wage at w_m^3 instead of w_m^2, the union puts pressure on the government to reverse its announced policy and provide the larger subsidy that shifts the equilibrium from C to B. Whether A or B is the equilibrium thus depends in large measure on the government's reputation. If the government is "soft," the union knows it can win the battle of nerves quickly and judges it worthwhile to tolerate the short-run losses from low employment at C to make B the permanent equilibrium rather than A.[26]

Finally, it is important to note that the possibility the economy will end up at the inferior equilibrium B establishes only that a tariff may be superior to an employment subsidy, not that a tariff is the first-best policy. For a tariff to be first-best, it must dominate all other policy interventions. This brings out a difficulty in discerning the operational implications of endogenous distortions. As we move down the policy continuum, at what point do we reach the dividing line where policy interventions are "indirect" and the union no longer assumes the position of Stackelberg leader? In the traditional policy ranking an employment subsidy is first-best, a production subsidy is second-best, and a tariff is third-best. I have shown that an employment subsidy may be less effective than a tariff because it

---

[26] Even if the union is wrong and the government turns out to be tough, the losses suffered from time spent at C have to be taken into account when comparing the welfare effects of a tariff and a wage subsidy.

is an overly blunt intervention that apprises the union of the rule guiding government policy. It does not automatically follow from this, however, that a tariff and an employment subsidy switch positions in the policy ranking. If a production subsidy also possesses the virtue of being indirect, a tariff moves up only one place, from third- to second-best.[27]

3.2.3 Is Free Trade Always First-Best?

Taking stock, how solid is the argument that free trade is always part of the first-best policy package? No special problems arise when market imperfections are exogenous and the appropriate intervention is a corrective tax. But for the distortions of greatest concern in LDCs, under-investment and underemployment, these are strong qualifications. According to the Principle of Targeting, wage and capital subsidies should be used to remedy underinvestment and underemployment, with the subsidies being financed by the least distortionary set of taxes. The implementation of such large, complicated tax/subsidy schemes would undoubtedly involve much greater administrative costs than the imposition of an export tax or a tariff. Furthermore, the power unions command in parts of Latin America and Sub-Saharan Africa casts doubt on the efficacy of wage subsidies for ameliorating underemployment. Sophisticated unions that think in strategic terms may appropriate much of the wage subsidy. This is what happens in the middle panels of Tables 3.4 and 3.5. Firms see their net labor costs decrease by only 20–30% of the wage subsidy when the union is a Stackelberg leader in the policy game played with the government.

The bottom line is that theory does not come down so strongly in favor of free trade as is commonly supposed (e.g., Dixit and Norman, 1980); clearly, the question of whether protection may be justified on normative grounds cannot be satisfactorily answered until we learn more about the behavior of unions and the extent to which administrative costs matter for the comparison of different tax/subsidy interventions. Given the lack of empirical evidence capable of resolving the ambiguous implications of theory, perhaps the best motivation for examining trade policy is a positive one: in practice, governments have made exten-

---

[27] In the present model, a tariff is equivalent to a production subsidy because surplus revenues are used to lower the consumption tax b. [To see this, note that when $s = 0$ the budget constraint in (28) is $(b + t) D^m = S + tQ_m$. t can be interpreted as a production subsidy and $b + t$ as the total consumption tax.] If some part of tariff revenues were rebated to the public, then a tariff would result in a higher consumption tax than the comparable production subsidy.

sive use of quotas and trade taxes, and it is important to know how these interventions have affected allocative efficiency, growth, and the distribution of income. Indeed, this, rather than the precise ranking of trade taxes vis à vis other potential policy interventions, has always been the main focus of the debate on alternative trade strategies.

3.3   Import Substitution vs. Export Promotion: The Main Elements of the Debate

3.3.1   The Infant Industry Argument

The infant industry argument was first formulated by Mill and still provides the most popular rationale for protection among policy makers (Havrylyshyn, 1990, p. 2). The argument rests on the notion that firms may become more efficient as they gain experience through the act of production. This is represented in Figure 3.5 by the two supply curves SS and S'S'. SS is the supply schedule during the infancy phase when the industry is unable to compete at world market prices. If imports are subject to a tariff of, say, OA − 1, domestic firms initially produce OB. As the industry matures, the supply curve shifts downward and output increases steadily. When the supply schedule reaches S'S' the potential for learning is exhausted, the tariff is removed, and domestic production settles at OF. Since the fully mature industry generates producer surplus equal to S'1J, economic welfare is higher than at the initial free trade equilibrium. If the present value of the benefits reaped after the industry is mature exceed the present value losses suffered during the infancy phase, protection yields an overall welfare gain; it will have been worthwhile to nurture the ugly duckling into a swan.

The main shortcoming of the infant industry argument is that it lacks an effective rebuttal to the Principle of Targeting. If the industry truly has good long-term prospects and credit markets operate efficiently, firms should be able to borrow to cover the losses they incur during the learning phase. In point of fact, private credit markets may not operate efficiently and firms may be denied the loans they need.[28] But this implies

[28] Flam and Staiger (1991) argue that infant industry protection may be justified when credit markets are plagued by adverse selection problems. Due to the adverse selection problem (high-risk firms are most likely to apply for loans), banks have to charge a loan rate above the safe rate to compensate for losses from default. The safest firms therefore do not apply for a loan. (Expected profits for the firm are increasing in project risk.) Since all firms have the same expected costs and are seeking finance for socially profitable projects, the market equilibrium is distorted by too little entry. A tariff induces some low-risk firms to enter (i.e., apply for a loan) and is thus welfare-improving.

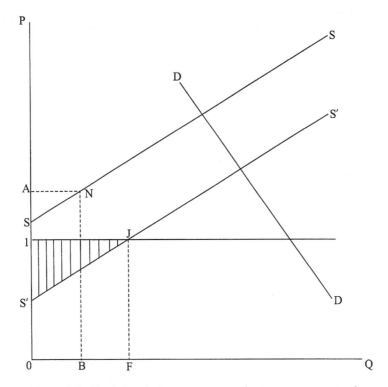

Figure 3.5. The infant industry argument for temporary protection.

only that the government should supply credit through a development bank, not that a tariff should be levied to make the industry profitable while it is inefficient. In contrast to some of the market imperfections examined earlier, it is difficult to argue that intervening at the source of the distortion by granting a loan entails greater administrative costs than imposing a temporary tariff.

The Principle of Targeting shows that while protection may be welfare-improving it is not the best way to promote infant industries. A much more powerful criticism of the infant industry argument, put forward by Matsuyama (1990) and Tornell (1991), asserts that protection may be counterproductive, inhibiting the very technological progress that is supposed to serve as its justification. Suppose that development loans and other superior policy interventions are not feasible for some reason and that the government has an uncanny knack for picking winners – for distinguishing true infant industries from those that have no realistic chance of becoming internationally competitive. These strong assumptions are still not enough to guarantee that protection will be welfare-improving. It is necessary to assume as well that technological progress occurs automatically through learning-by-doing. The consensus among those scholars who have looked into the issue carefully, however, is that technological progress depends very much on the effort firms put out, that is, on investments made to improve technological capability (Bell, Ross-Larsen, and Westphal, 1984; Pack, 1992). This is important, for if a firm has the latitude to affect the level of productive efficiency, it can also affect the amount of protection it receives. Returning to Figure 3.5, the firm may know, for example, that the tariff will be maintained as long as the supply curve is SS because once production has commenced the government would be unwilling to tolerate the temporarily high unemployment that would result if protection were eliminated. In this situation, the firm will choose to remain an infant if the profits realized with protection and inferior technology are greater than the net profits associated with superior technology, free trade, and adulthood. The government, of course, may announce that protection is temporary in an effort to spur firms to invest in better technology. But since the government prefers protection to free trade when firms operate at point N on SS, the announcement is not credible if the government has the reputation of being "soft." The soft government's inability to solve the time consistency problem thus transforms a potential winner (a healthy infant) into a loser (an infant who fails to grow up). As in our earlier analysis of the use of a wage subsidy to lessen underemployment, the strategic environment changes adversely at the same time as the policy is introduced, thereby undermining its effectiveness.

3.3.1.1   THE EMPIRICAL EVIDENCE

The empirical evidence bearing on the infant industry argument is limited and indirect. It is not clear that anything meaningful can be inferred from the fact that many industries have remained dependent on protection for a very long time. Governments adopt protectionist policies for a variety of reasons; a proper test of the infant industry argument would therefore have to isolate those industries where infant industry considerations were the primary motivation for protection.[29] Related to this last point, some industries that policy makers targeted as promising in Brazil, S. Korea, and Taiwan *did* develop rapidly with the

---

[29] This is a problem with the test of the infant industry argument in Krueger and Tuncer (1982). In addition, it is not clear whether their conclusions are consistent with the data. The rate of productivity growth appears to be highest in moderately protected industries (Havrylyshyn, 1990, pp. 17–18).

aid of protection and became efficient exporters in a short period of time (Bell, Ross-Larson, and Westphal, 1984).

Despite the absence of hard evidence to the contrary and the existence of some success stories, I am highly sceptical of the idea that promotion of infant industries should carry much weight in the formulation of trade policy. At the operational level, a quite basic problem is the paucity of data needed to identify promising infant industries: there is virtually no empirical information available about learning curves in either developed or developing countries (Pack, 1992, pp. 38–39). And even if the requisite information becomes available some day, to successfully execute an infant industry policy the government must overcome a potential time consistency problem by convincing the private sector that protection will be strictly temporary. The governments of S. Korea and Taiwan were able to precommit effectively to temporary protection (Lee, 1997; Pack, 1988, p. 339), but it is obvious that this feat would be more difficult to replicate in many other LDCs where policy makers have a long history of imposing tariffs and quotas to shelter domestic firms from foreign competition.

3.3.2   Factor Market Distortions

While all sorts of factor market distortions are potentially relevant to the design of optimal trade policy, I shall focus on those that cause the price of labor in the industrial sector to be too high and the overall level of investment in the economy to be too low. For several reasons, I feel this emphasis is appropriate. First, capital and labor market distortions are weighty in that they affect major allocative decisions; as such, they are capable of justifying protection or export promotion on an extensive scale, not just for a few industries having special characteristics. Second, the problems of underemployment and underinvestment have long been major concerns of development economists. They remain so today, not least because the aftermath of the debt crisis has turned out to be a "lost generation of development." Third, in the trade debate itself, both critics of protection and its defenders concur that labor market distortions merit special attention in the design of optimal policy (e.g., Little, Scitovsky, and Scott, 1970, pp. 13, 15; Krueger, 1983, p. 11; Rodrik, 1992a, p. 310). The massive NBER study of trade and employment in developing countries (Krueger et al., 1981b), for example, was undertaken solely to improve our understanding of how different trade strategies affect aggregate labor demand and underemployment.

After discussing what theory and empirical studies have to say about the nature of capital and labor market distortions in LDCs, I present the case for the conventional view that ISI exacerbates the underemployment problem. For the most part, this is background material. In Chapter 5, I will construct an optimizing, dynamic, multisector model to analyze rigorously how trade policy affects capital accumulation, real wages, welfare, and underemployment.

3.3.2.1   UNEMPLOYMENT, UNDEREMPLOYMENT, AND THE FORMAL SECTOR WAGE PREMIUM

Workers in the formal industrial sector are often paid substantially higher wages than workers in other sectors. In much of Latin America, the Caribbean, and Sub-Saharan Africa, minimum wage laws and/or unions keep the industrial sector wage above its market clearing level. Institutional factors, however, are not the only possible explanation for the wage differential. Purely economic forces may also generate a two-tiered labor market. In a development context, the central hypothesis of efficiency wage models is that firms obtain certain benefits by paying a wage higher than needed to recruit labor from agriculture or the urban informal sector. The benefits may take the form of workers exerting greater effort on the job, a lower quit rate, or greater success in recruiting a high-quality workforce. Firms determine the optimal wage by balancing these benefits against the direct costs of a higher wage bill; the wage differential thus arises naturally from profit-maximizing behavior.

The extent to which high wages in the formal industrial sector distort the allocation of labor depends on how much of the wage differential can be explained by differences in human capital characteristics and workplace conditions. Almost all empirical studies reach the conclusion that after controlling for these factors there remains a significant wage premium. The size of the estimated premium varies considerably, ranging from a modest 20–30% to 100–150%.[30]

In a pioneering paper, Harris and Todaro (1970) argued that persistent open unemployment would emerge as workers migrated out of rural areas to search for high-paying jobs in the industrial sector. In the simplest variant of their model, workers are risk-neutral and the probability of obtaining employment in the industrial sector equals the ratio

[30] See Merrick (1976), Porter, Blitzer, and Curtis (1986), Mazumdar (1984), Alderman and Kozul (1989), Fields (1990), Gindling (1991), Marcouiller, Ruiz de Castilla, and Woodruff (1993), and de Melo and Roland-Holst (1994). In many of the countries studied in the NBER project, social insurance payments and other charges increased the cost of labor in the formal sector by 20–30% (Krueger, 1983, p. 149).

of jobs J to the urban labor force L_u. Under the assumption of risk neutrality, migration continues until the sure wage to be had in agriculture, w_a, equals expected earnings in the city, $w_f J/L_u$, where w_f is the wage paid in the formal sector. This implies an equilibrium unemployment rate in the city of $1 - w_a/w_f$, which is far too high. More realistic variants of the model, however, produce more sensible results. If it is possible to conduct a limited search for high-paying work in industry while holding down a job in the urban informal sector, the predicted unemployment rate is much lower since most migrants probably prefer this to the alternative of full-time search permitted by full-time unemployment. Because it is easier to search for a formal sector job when residing in the city, in equilibrium the wage in the urban informal sector should be less than the agricultural wage.

The data have not been kind to the Harris–Todaro model. The findings from a large body of empirical research do not support the critical assumption that those who are unemployed or working in the informal sector stand a better chance of landing a job in the formal sector: (i) vacancies in the formal sector are filled mainly by recruiting workers directly from rural areas and by relying on the family connections of existing employees and supervisors; (ii) irrespective of whether they settle in the formal or informal sector, most migrants arrive with a job already in hand; (iii) 60–80% of the workers in the formal sector have been employed there since their first job; (iv) many of those employed in the informal sector report that they expect to stay there and are not searching for work in the formal sector; (v) circular migration is common in some countries (i.e., migrants regularly alternate between working in the city and the countryside); (vi) most migrants working in the informal sector report that their standard of living and real income are higher than before, not lower, as should be the case if migration improves the prospects of moving on to a high-paying job in the formal sector.[31]

All of this suggests that search activity is of limited importance and that, net of migration costs, labor earns roughly the same wage in rural areas and the urban informal sector. What is more difficult to judge is whether persistent involuntary unemployment is a major problem. In earlier periods one could discount this possibility by appealing to empirical studies supportive of the "luxury unemployment" hypothesis: labor force surveys from the sixties and the seventies revealed that the unemployed were predominantly young, relatively well-educated dependents from families with above-average incomes (Udall and Sinclair, 1982;

---

[31] See Mazumdar (1976, 1989), Gregory (1986, pp. 151–166), and Williamson (1990).

Berry and Sabot, 1984). Much of this remains true today, but unemployment rates in urban areas and for the young have risen to levels which seriously weaken the presumption that most unemployment is of a quasivoluntary nature (Turnham, 1993). Be that as it may, I shall follow the common practice of treating open unemployment as a "short-term," cyclical problem.

3.3.2.2   CAPITAL MARKET DISTORTIONS

Private agents accumulate capital until the after-tax return equals their own rate of time preference, whereas intertemporal efficiency calls for the pre-tax return on capital to equal the social time preference rate. Taxation alone, therefore, is enough to cause underinvestment. In addition, the private time preference rate will exceed the social time preference rate if individuals would be willing to enter into a social contract that required everyone to save more. This is an example of the prisoner's dilemma, or what Sen calls the "isolation paradox." Following Sen (1967), consider a representative individual who attaches the values 1, γ, β, and α, respectively, to his own consumption, the consumption of his heirs, the consumption of others, and the consumption of others' heirs. If the benefits from saving accrue entirely to one's own heirs, the optimal plan for each individual acting in isolation is to save up to the point where the return on capital r equals $1/\gamma$. However, if $1/\beta > \gamma/\alpha$, an agreement on the part of all to save a little more would raise everyone's welfare. To see why, add up the gains and losses to oneself of participating in the agreement. From the envelope theorem, the small bit of extra saving I contribute does not cause a net change in my own welfare. On the other hand, when my contemporaries forego one more unit of consumption, I value their loss at β and the benefit for their heirs at $r\alpha = \alpha/\gamma$. Thus, if $1/\beta > \gamma/\alpha$, the additional saving done by others makes me better off. A Pareto-improving social contract is possible because each individual gains when he *and* everyone else save more.

The condition $1/\beta > \gamma/\alpha$ says that I place a greater value on my own consumption relative to that of my contemporaries than I do on the consumption of my heirs relative to the consumption of others' heirs. Adopting this perspective, Sen regards the condition as plausible because it captures "the personal nature of egoism" (p. 118). An alternative, more flattering interpretation is that, due to a general concern for the welfare of future generations, people are more evenhanded in valuing the consumption of their own and others' heirs (i.e., it is easier to love humanity in the abstract). On this view, there is a public good aspect to economic development (Baumol, 1965, p. 37), with the implication that the social time preference rate "must be administratively determined as a matter of public policy [because] the market cannot express the 'collective' demand for investment to benefit the future" (Feldstein, 1964, pp. 362, 365).

3.3.2.3 PROTECTION, REAL WAGES, AND UNDEREMPLOYMENT: THE CONVENTIONAL WISDOM

Available empirical evidence strongly suggests that exportable activities, in a developing country contemplating trade liberalization, would be more labor intensive than importable activities (see NBER, 1981–3). Hence liberalization should lead to increased demand for labor, and thus for increased wages and a higher share of labor in aggregate income ... relaxation of protection would tend to promote agriculture and, in relative terms discourage manufacturing: this, we have seen in chapter 7, has indeed been most often the case. Thus, by promoting the low-wage sector and relatively contracting the high-wage sector, liberalization should contribute to the intersectoral equalization of wages. (Michaely, Papageorgiou, and Choksi, 1991, p. 105)

Krueger (1978b) has further convincing data that export activities are much more intensive in unskilled labor than the industries based on import substitution. . . . Hence, the unemployed seem more likely to be soaked up with an outward-looking policy, and the consequences for income distribution seem more favorable when LDCs exploit their comparative advantage rather than resisting it. (McKinnon, 1979, p. 450)

Elimination of the bias in favor of capital-intensive import substitutes moves the economy onto a more labor-intensive development path, raising unskilled wages. (Summers and Pritchett, 1993, p. 385)

The pursuit of industrialization has also aggravated the problem of unemployment, and thus further contributed to inequalities in the distribution of income ... the methods used to encourage industrialization, in particular the policy of protection, have tended to favor, within the industrial sector, profits over wages, and to create a bias against the employment of labour. They have discouraged traditional export industries, such as the textile industry, which are usually labour intensive. Protection has also discouraged the use of labour by enabling the exchange rate to be overvalued, thus making it possible to allow capital equipment to be imported cheaply, either by having low duties on such imports, or by remitting them. (Little, Scitovsky, and Scott, 1970, p. 8)

Likewise, alteration of the trade strategy could have resulted in sizable increases in the demand for unskilled labour, even in the presence of inappropriate relative prices for use of factors of production. . . . Moreover, the income distribution implications of the findings seem to accord fairly well with the proposition that inward-oriented trade strategies and measures which increased incentives for using capital-intensive techniques probably contributed to a less equal income distribution than might otherwise have been observed. (Krueger, 1981a, pp. 299–300)

Conventional wisdom holds that ISI lowers overall demand for labor in the economy and thereby worsens both the distribution of income and the underemployment problem. The OECD and NBER studies emphasized two channels through which protection reduces aggregate labor demand. First, an escalated structure of protection makes capital cheap relative to labor by appreciating the real exchange rate. The argument is not spelled out in detail; presumably, wages rise more than the price of capital goods when tariffs on consumer imports pull up the general price level.[32] If this occurs, the higher relative cost of labor induces firms in all sectors to adopt more capital-intensive technology. The second channel is a general equilibrium one connected with the impact of protection on the composition of output. The findings of the NBER study on trade and employment in Table 3.6 confirm that LDCs have a comparative advantage in exporting labor-intensive goods. Since most of the ratios in Table 3.6 are well above unity, it seems sensible to conclude that, on balance, the reallocation of resources associated with protection weakens labor demand: expansion in the highly capital-intensive import sector is not likely to generate enough employment to absorb all of the workers released by the labor-intensive export sector. Pursuing this theme, Krueger (1981a, pp. 297–298) presents calculations of how much labor demand would increase if protection were lowered and resources were shifted from the import to the export sector.

The logic underpinning this critique is a bit elusive. If we introduce a

---

[32] Krueger emphasizes the connection between protection and the real exchange rate (1983, pp. 121, 142, 145). An overvalued exchange rate, however, reduces the prices for both importable consumer goods and imported machinery. Since the nominal wage usually moves with the general price level and imported machinery is only part of total capital costs, it is not clear that overvaluation raises the cost of labor relative to the cost of capital. An increase in the relative cost of labor is most likely when quantitative controls are used to support the importation of capital goods at a low preferential exchange. But even in this case one has to analyze carefully how import rationing affects the price of nontraded goods before reaching any conclusions about whether protection reduces the relative cost of capital.

Table 3.6. *Ratio of labor per unit of value added in the export sector to labor per unit of value added in the import-competing sector.**

| | HOS Exports | | | |
	Manufactures not PCB	PCB manufactures	Total	NRB exports
Argentina, 1963	—	—	1.24	—
1973	—	—	1.30	—
Brazil, 1970	—	—	2.07	2.02
Chile, 1966–68	1.50	—	.80	—
Colombia, 1973	—	—	1.88	—
Indonesia, 1971	1.58	—	2.09	—
Ivory Coast, 1972				
modern sector	—	—	1.35	2.28
total	—	—	1.16	9.04
Pakistan, 1969–70	1.23	1.69	1.42	—
S. Korea, 1968	—	—	1.00	—
Thailand, 1973	3.20	1.58	2.07	—
Tunisia, 1971	2.08	.79	1.28	3.31
Uruguay, 1968	—	—	1.53	1.45

* A dash indicates that no data are available. HOS exports are Heckscher-Ohlin-Samuelson exports (i.e., manufactured exports), and NRB exports are natural-resource–based exports. Primary-commodity–based (PCB) manufactures are separated out from total HOS exports.
Source: Krueger (1981b).

fixed sectoral wage gap $w_m = \lambda w_x$ ($\lambda > 1$) in the traditional 2×2 trade model, the zero-profit conditions in the import and export sectors read

$$P_m = C^m(\lambda w_x, r), \tag{36}$$

$$1 = C^x(w_x, r), \tag{37}$$

where C^i is the unit cost function and r is the capital rental. Solving for w_x and r yields

$$\hat{w}_x = -\frac{\theta_K^x}{\theta_L^x - \theta_L^m}\hat{P}_m, \tag{38}$$

$$\hat{r} = \frac{\theta_L^x}{\theta_L^x - \theta_L^m}\hat{P}_m. \tag{39}$$

If the capital–labor ratio in the import sector exceeds that in the export sector by a sufficient margin, then $\theta_L^x > \theta_L^m$, $\hat{w}_m = \hat{w}_x < 0$, and $\hat{r} > \hat{P}_m > 0$.[33] Apart from the qualification that physical and value intensity rankings agree in sign, these are the familiar corollaries of the Stolper–Samuelson theorem: a tariff unambiguously reduces the real wage and unambiguously increases the real capital rental when import production is relatively capital-intensive. Observe also, however, that underemployment decreases (more jobs are created in the high-wage manufacturing sector) and that the fall in the real wage is tied up with a higher cost of capital and firms switching to more labor-intensive technology. Evidently then, the notion that protection depresses labor demand by encouraging firms to utilize more capital-intensive techniques of production involves an appeal to dynamic effects: when an escalated structure of protection lowers the relative price of imported machinery, an increase in the supply of capital holds down the cost of capital services (r) relative to the wage. But this points to confusion of a different sort. Normally, factors are gross complements in the sense that greater usage of one input increases the marginal productivity of other inputs (Rader, 1968). An increase in the supply of capital and a shift toward more capital-intensive technology would therefore be expected to increase labor demand and push up the real wage. This mechanism operates with a delay since it takes time to produce new capital goods. Expansion of the capital goods industry, however, is likely to put upward pressure on wages in the short and medium run (the construction sector tends to be labor-intensive). Thus, many new elements enter the picture when capital accumulation is endogenous. In the optimizing model of Chapter 5, an escalated structure of protection always *increases* the real wage in the informal sector and always reduces the sectoral wage gap in the long run. Moreover, the real wage often rises immediately and stays above its previous level on the entire transition path to the new long-run equilibrium.

3.3.3   Scale Economies and Procompetitive Effects

We have assumed so far that goods markets are perfectly competitive and that production in all sectors is subject to constant or decreasing returns to scale. These assumptions may be appropriate for agriculture, construction, services, and transportation, but they are harder to justify for the manufacturing sector. In some manufacturing industries the minimum efficient plant size is large and a handful of firms supply most of the market. Firms in such industries are likely to be oligopolists oper-

---

[33] Let k_i denote K_i/L_i. Then $\theta_L^x > \theta_L^m$ iff $k_m/k_x > \lambda$.

ating on the downward sloping portion of their average cost schedule. Critics of ISI invariably assert that this strengthens the case for trade reform on the grounds that (i) lower trade barriers should limit the ability of oligopolistic firms to exercise market power, and (ii) when entry and exit are possible, the industry will reorganize to permit more intensive exploitation of scale economies: if import penetration beats down domestic prices, entrepreneurs will no longer earn a normal rate of return; some firms will have to exit the industry so that those that remain can produce a higher level of output at lower unit costs.[34]

These claims are incautious. The relationship between protection, domestic supply, and efficiency in oligopolistic industries is far from straightforward. Much depends on the form of protection, the characteristics of demand, the nature of technology inside and outside the industry, and whether the industry is closed or open to entry. To illustrate the diversity of potential outcomes, I shall formulate a general equilibrium version of the model in Buffie and Spiller (1986).

3.3.3.1 A SIMPLE GENERAL EQUILIBRIUM MODEL OF PROTECTION AND IMPERFECT COMPETITION

Consider an industry that consists of N firms who are sheltered from foreign competition by an import quota. The firms are identical and produce a single homogeneous good that is a perfect substitute for imports Z. In equilibrium each firm produces the same level of output q. Thus, the manufactures market clears when

$$D^m(P,u) = Nq + Z. \tag{40}$$

Solving for P gives the industry's inverse demand function:

$$P = P(S,u),$$

where

$$P_1 = -P/D^m \varepsilon,$$

$$P_2 = c_m/D^m \varepsilon,$$

c_i is the marginal propensity to consume good i, and $S \equiv Nq + Z$, the total supply of manufactured goods.

Labor is the only factor of production. Firms incur a fixed cost of B

---

[34] See, for example, Little, Scitovsky, and Scott (1970, p. 98), Corden (1974, chapter 8), Krueger (1991), Dornbusch (1992, pp. 75–76), and Krugman (1993).

units of labor and hire $g(q)$ workers to produce current output. Firm profits are therefore $P(S, u)q - wg(q) - B$. Under Cournot–Nash competition, the first- and second-order conditions for profit maximization are

$$P_1(Nq + Z, u)q + P(Nq + Z, u) - wg'(q) = 0,   \tag{41}$$

$$P_{11}q + 2P_1 - wg'' < 0.   \tag{42}$$

In the export sector technology exhibits constant or decreasing returns to scale

$$Q_x = H(L_x),   H' > 0, H'' \le 0,   \tag{43}$$

and perfectly competitive firms hire labor up to the point where its marginal product equals the wage w:

$$H'(L_x) = w.   \tag{44}$$

The wage adjusts to equate labor demand and the fixed supply of labor L. Since the import sector generates $N[g(q) + B]$ jobs, full employment requires

$$N[g(q) + B] + L_x = L.   \tag{45}$$

If there are barriers to entry, N is fixed and firms in the quota-protected sector earn supranormal profits. The model is then closed by the representative agent's budget constraint

$$E(P, u) = PNq + Q_x + tZ,   \tag{46}$$

where $t \equiv P - 1$, the implicit tariff associated with the quota.

When entry cannot be prevented, profits in the protected sector are not inflated by rents. Firms enter or exit the industry until price equals average cost:

$$P = \frac{wg(q) + B}{q} \equiv G(q).   \tag{47}$$

The first-order condition (41) and the above zero-profit condition define a symmetric Chamberlinian equilibrium: each firm's perceived demand curve is tangent to its average cost schedule, implying $G' < 0$ – economies of scale exist at the equilibrium level of output.

Before fixing on either the no-entry or free-entry equilibrium, it will be helpful to undertake some preliminary manipulations. From (43)–(46),

$$du = N(P - wg')dq + [Pq - w(g + B)]dN - tdZ. \tag{48}$$

The second term on the right side drops out as profits are zero in a free-entry equilibrium. Entry and exit affect welfare therefore only insofar as they affect output per firm in the industry. Note also from the first-order condition (41) that $P - wg' = Pq = \theta P/\varepsilon N$, where $\theta \equiv Nq/S$, the market share of domestic firms. Thus,

$$du = \frac{\theta P}{\varepsilon} dq + tdZ. \tag{48'}$$

Since the import volume is exogenous under a quota, the gain from reducing the trade distortion is simply tdZ. In a competitive industry this measures the entire welfare gain. But when oligopolists in the protected industry keep price above marginal cost, variations in firm output q also affect welfare. If a loosening of the import quota leads to an increase in q, the distortion caused by oligopoly pricing is lessened and the welfare gain is larger than when firms are perfect competitors. This is the beneficial procompetitive effect that advocates of liberalization have in mind.

The answer to the critical question of how firm output responds is buried in the first-order condition (41). After using (45) to pin down the adjustment in the market clearing wage, (41) yields

$$\left[1 + N + \frac{P_{11}qN}{P_1} + \frac{N(g')^2 H''}{P_1} - \frac{wg''}{P_1} \right] dq = -\frac{P_2 + qP_{12}}{P_1} du$$

$$- \left(1 + \frac{P_{11}q}{P_1} \right) dZ - \left[1 + \frac{P_{11}q}{P_1} + \frac{g'H''(g + B)}{P_1} \right] dN. \tag{49}$$

No Entry

A larger quota reduces profits in the import sector by driving down the domestic price P.[35] Nevertheless, output may increase in the protected manufacturing industry. When there are barriers to entry, all that matters is how the increase in the quota affects firms' perceived marginal revenue. If the inverse demand curve is convex ($P_{11} > 0$) or takes on a flatter slope as welfare rises ($P_{12} > 0$), firms may raise output in response to a perceived flattening of their marginal revenue schedule. To obtain sharper results, let $F \equiv -P_{11}S/P_1$ and $\varepsilon^* \equiv \varepsilon N/\theta$ denote, respectively, the elasticity of the slope of the inverse demand function and the individual

---

[35] The empirical estimates in all five country studies in the World Bank project on "Industrial Competition, Productivity and Their Relation to Trade Regimes" support the "import discipline" hypothesis (Roberts and Tybout, 1996)

firm's perceived elasticity of demand. Setting $dN = 0$ and solving (48′) and (49) for u and q then gives

$$\frac{du}{dZ} = \frac{t\varepsilon Y + \theta(1+t)(F\theta/N - 1)}{\varepsilon Y - \theta c_m(1+qP_{12}/P_2)}, \tag{50}$$

$$\frac{dq}{dZ} = \frac{F\theta}{N} - 1 + \frac{c_m}{1+t}(1+qP_{12}/P_2)\frac{t\varepsilon Y + \theta(1+t)(F\theta/N-1)}{\varepsilon Y - \theta c_m(1+qP_{12}/P_2)}, \tag{51}$$

where

$$Y \equiv 1 + N - F\theta - wg''/P_1 + H''(g')^2 N/P_1 > 0.^{36}$$

Clearly, a variety of outcomes is possible, depending on the properties of the demand schedule, the restrictiveness of the quota, and the number of firms in the industry. Suppose, for instance, that the elasticity of demand for industry output (ε) is constant. With isoelastic demand, $F = (1 + \varepsilon)/\varepsilon$ and $qP_{12}/P_2 = (\varepsilon - 1)/\varepsilon^*$. It follows from (51) that

$$\varepsilon^* - \varepsilon < 1$$

is sufficient for output per firm to increase and hence for welfare to rise more than in the perfectly competitive case.[37] This condition is always satisfied when domestic firms operate a perfect cartel and initially supply the entire market ($\varepsilon^* = \varepsilon$ for $N = \theta = 1$).

Consider next the outcome when demand is linear. Setting $F = P_{12} = 0$ in (50) and (51) immediately establishes that q falls and that $du/dZ < t$, the welfare gain in the competitive case. More importantly, the anticompetitive effect may be so strong that liberalization ends up lowering welfare. With constant marginal costs in both sectors ($g'' = H'' = 0$),

$$\frac{du}{dZ} \gtreqless 0 \quad \text{as} \quad \frac{t\varepsilon^*}{1+t} \gtreqless \frac{N}{1+N}.$$

[36] The second-order condition requires that Y be positive. The term $\varepsilon Y - \theta c_m(1 + qP_{12}/P_2)$ is positive under the assumption that "multiplier" effects are not destabilizing (i.e., that $q \uparrow \rightarrow u \uparrow \rightarrow$ demand $\uparrow \rightarrow q \uparrow$ is consistent with stability).
[37] The condition $\varepsilon^* - \varepsilon \gtreqless 1$ determines the impact on output in partial equilibrium models where domestic and foreign firms engage in Cournot competition and home and export markets are segmented (Brander, 1981). In this setting, $\varepsilon^* - \varepsilon > 1$ is usually assumed so that reaction curves slope downward (i.e., firm outputs are strategic substitutes).

The gain from reducing the trade distortion increases with t while the loss from the anti-competitive effect is greatest when ε^* is small and N is large. (The markup of price over marginal cost and the reduction in domestic output are then large.) If $t > N$, the gain from lowering the trade distortion is always great enough to ensure a welfare improvement ($\varepsilon^* > 1$). But this requires the implicit tariff to be extremely high – 100% at a minimum. For smaller values of t, welfare losses may occur when ε^* is well above unity and the markup of price over marginal cost is not abnormally large. With $N = 4$ and $t = .5$, for example, welfare declines when $\varepsilon^* < 2.4$.

Free Entry
The free entry/exit variant of the model contains one extra equation, (47), and one additional endogenous variable, N, the number of firms in the industry. From (45) and (47),

$$\left[q + \frac{H''(g+B)^2}{P_1 q}\right] dN = -\left[N - 1 + Ng'\frac{H''(g+B)^2}{P_1 q}\right] dq - \frac{P_1}{P_2} du - dZ. \tag{52}$$

Substituting for dN in (49) gives

$$dq = \frac{c_m}{\Delta}\left[\frac{H''(g+B)^2}{1+t}(1/\varepsilon^* + qP_{12}/P_2) - \frac{q^2}{D^m}(F\theta/N + qP_{12}/P_2)\right] du$$

$$+ \frac{H''(g+B)^2}{\Delta}(F\theta/N - 1/\varepsilon^*)dZ, \tag{53}$$

where

$$\Delta \equiv P_1 q^2 (2 - F\theta/N - wg''P_1)$$

$$+ H''(Pq/w)^2\left[2 - wg''/P_1 - \frac{F\theta}{\varepsilon^*} - \frac{1}{\varepsilon^*}(1 - N/\varepsilon^*)\right] < 0.^{38}$$

---

[38] $\Delta < 0$ under the stability assumption that entry does not raise firm profits. In the linear and isoelastic cases in (53a) and (53b), Δ is always negative. This can be confirmed directly in the isoelastic case after noting that the first term is positive by the second-order condition. In the linear case, the result can be established from this and the fact that since $\varepsilon^* > 1$ the term $(1/\varepsilon^*)(1 - N/\varepsilon^*)$ is either negative or smaller than unity.

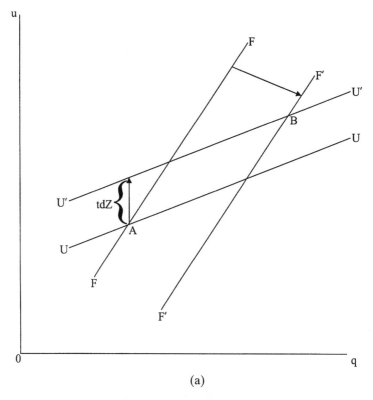

Figure 3.6. (a) The impact of increasing the import quota when demand is isoelastic.

Equation (53) shows the combinations of q, u, and Z that are consistent with the first-order and zero-profit conditions after taking account of entry into or exit from the manufacturing sector. In the cases of linear and isoelastic demand:

$$\text{(linear)} \quad dq = \frac{H''(g+B)^2}{\Delta\varepsilon^*}\left(\frac{c_m}{1+t}du - dZ\right), \qquad (53a)$$

$$\text{(isoelastic)} \quad dq = \frac{\theta}{\Delta N}\left\{\left[\frac{H''(g+B)^2}{1+t} - \frac{2q^2}{D^m\varepsilon}\right]c_m\,du\right.$$
$$\left. + H''(g+B)^2\,dZ\right\}. \qquad (53b)$$

Figures 3.6a and b depict the solutions to equations (48′) and (53). The upward sloping UU schedule represents the positive relationship in

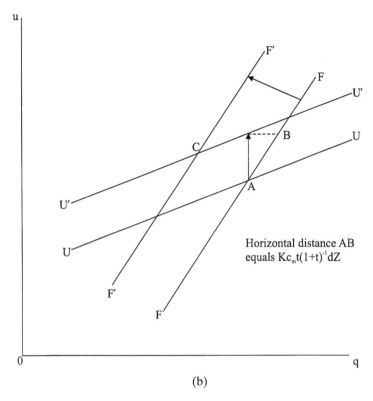

(b)

Figure 3.6. (b) The impact of increasing the import quota when demand is linear.

(48′) between output per firm and welfare, while the FF schedule is based on either (53a) or (53b). Under the assumption that u and q do not feed back on one another in a destabilizing fashion, FF is more steeply sloped than UU.

Loosening the import quota shifts the UU schedule vertically upward by the amount tdZ. In the case of isoelastic demand, FF shifts to the right (for $H'' < 0$). Output per firm increases and the welfare gain from reducing the trade distortion is augmented by a pro-competitive effect.

When demand is linear FF shifts leftward to F′F′ in Figure 3.6b. Moreover, q must be lower at the new equilibrium C.[39] Observe that the

---

[39] In many models with free entry and either Cournot competition or monopolistic competition, adjustment occurs entirely through exit/entry with output per firm remaining constant (e.g., Helpman and Krugman, 1985; Horstmann and Markusen, 1986). This conclusion requires (i) that general equilibrium interac-

movement up the FF schedule from A to B increases q by the amount $Kc_m t(1 + t)^{-1}dZ$, where $K \equiv H''(g + B)^2\theta/\Delta N$. This is smaller than KdZ, the leftward shift of the schedule, whenever labor demand in the export sector is not perfectly elastic ($H'' < 0$). Thus, irrespective of whether the industry is closed or open to entry, with linear demand output falls and welfare rises less than in the competitive case.

3.3.3.2   OTHER SCENARIOS

While quota liberalization seems a risky venture, in our model there is a different type of liberalization program that is sure to deliver a pro-competitive effect. As shown in Figure 3.7, if the quota is replaced by a less protective tariff, the representative firm in the industry increases output because it perceives its marginal revenue schedule to be flat up to the demand curve.[40] This result, however, is not altogether robust. If imports and domestic goods are imperfect rather than perfect substitutes, switching from a quota to a less protective tariff does not return the economy to a setting of perfect competition where firms equate price to marginal cost, and the analysis and range of outcomes is then similar to that in the preceding section.[41] In general, it is hard to make a case that liberalization is likely to improve competitive performance in protected industries, or even to argue with much conviction for the weaker proposition that the distortion from oligopoly pricing will not worsen to the point of lowering welfare.[42]

tions do not alter industry costs, and (ii) either that demand is linear or that changes in the tariff/quota do not change welfare by distorting consumer choice (as for small changes in the neighborhood of free trade). To see this in the current model, set $H'' = 0$ and assume $t \simeq 0$. Since the FF schedule is vertical when demand is linear, shifts in the UU schedule do not affect q. In the case of isoelastic demand, FF is still positively sloped, but neither FF nor UU shifts if $H'' = 0$ and the implicit tariff is imperceptibly small.

[40] This result is essentially a restatement of the classic Bhagwati (1965) result on the nonequivalence of tariffs and quotas. Nor does it differ substantively from Muller and Rawana's (1990) conclusion that tariff cuts increase firm output when a perfectly elastic supply of imports forces domestic oligopolists to limit price.

[41] See Horstmann and Markusen (1986). Under imperfect substitutability, a great deal depends on how a cut in the tariff and the reduction in demand affect the slope of the inverse demand schedule.

[42] I have analyzed only a few of many possible cases, but the wider literature on pro-competitive effects repeatedly echoes this theme (Markusen and Venables, 1988). The conclusions are sensitive to whether markets are segmented or unified (when domestic firms can export), to whether entry/exit is possible, to factor intensity rankings and the degree of substitutability between inputs used by

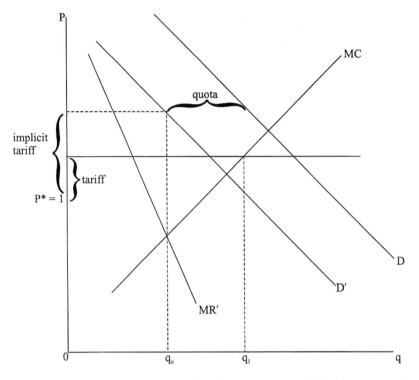

Figure 3.7. The impact of replacing a quota with a less protective tariff.

3.3.3.3 THE EMPIRICAL EVIDENCE

When attempting to judge the potential importance of pro-competitive effects, we would like to know how widespread internal increasing returns to scale are in the manufacturing sector and how firm output responds to trade reform. The first piece of information sheds light on the market structure of the manufacturing sector since perfect competition is incompatible with internal increasing returns. (Either perfect or imperfect competition is possible, of course, under constant or decreasing returns to scale.) The second bears directly on the question of whether liberalization lessens or aggravates the distortion caused by

imperfectly competitive industries and the rest of the economy (Flam and Helpman, 1987; Brown, 1991), and to how entry/exit affects the variety of differentiated products (Hertel, 1994).

oligopoly pricing. As we have just seen, pro-competitive effects are tied to higher output per firm regardless of whether economies of scale do or do not exist at the plant level.

The evidence on the relationship between unit costs and plant size in LDCs is limited and inconclusive.[43] Although economies of scale appear to be present over the range of output relevant to LDCs in cement, steel, metal products, chemicals, and automobiles (Teitel, 1975), engineering data suggest that scale elasticities are very modest (<1.05) in most industries (Tybout and Westbrook, 1996). Nor have microeconometric studies uncovered any evidence of extensive scale economies in manufacturing. James Tybout and various coauthors (Roberts and Tybout, 1990; Tybout, de Melo and Corbo, 1991; Westbrook and Tybout, 1993; Tybout and Westbrook, 1995) have subjected plant-level data from the manufacturing sectors in Mexico, Chile, and Colombia to a wide battery of tests. In the great majority of tests and industries the estimated scale economies are small and consistent with the null hypothesis of constant returns.[44] Unfortunately, the tests are only capable of detecting scale economies generated by decreasing marginal costs. The findings do not rule out the possibility that scale economies may arise from other sources, for example, spreading fixed costs over a larger level of output.

On the more important issue of how trade reform alters average plant size, numerous simulation studies have argued that strong pro-competitive effects may boost the efficiency gains from liberalization from less than 1% of GDP to 2–10%. These numbers are impressive, but they merely illustrate the properties built into the models underlying the simulations. The models typically assume both very large scale elasticities and demand functions and pricing behavior for firms that guarantee large increases in output in oligopolistic industries following liberalization.[45] Neither theory nor empirical studies, however, justify the assumption that output increases in oligopolistic industries. Roberts and Tybout (1990), Tybout, de Melo, and Corbo (1991), and Tybout and Westbrook (1995) found that in Chile, Colombia, and Mexico average plant size

[43] See Berry (1992). It is difficult, *inter alia*, to disentangle economies of scale, size, and scope.

[44] Srivastava's (1996, pp. 114–124) estimates for India also do not show any evidence of significant departures from constant returns to scale. His estimates of the scale parameter (based on a panel dataset for private corporations in the manufacturing sector) in 16 industries range from .88 to 1.07. In eight industries the scale parameter lies between .97 and 1.03; there is support for modest increasing returns in only two cases (cotton textiles and jute textiles).

[45] See Tybout (1993) and Tybout and Westbrook (1996) for surveys of the literature.

decreased in almost all import-competing industries that underwent liberalization. It can be objected that no firm conclusions should be drawn on the basis of just three studies.[46] Conceding this, it remains true that there is virtually no empirical evidence that liberalization generates significant pro-competitive effects.

3.3.4   Productivity Growth

The last important element in the debate concerns the impact of trade policy on productivity growth. We have already touched on this issue at a couple of different points. Under a successful infant industry policy, productivity gains materialize as firms that are uncompetitive in the short run become efficient through experience. There is also a connection between trade policy and productivity when import competition affects exploitation of scale economies in oligopolistic industries. The emphasis in this part of the debate, however, has been mainly on productivity gains generated by improvements in X-efficiency, the relief of import bottlenecks, technology transfer, and research and development. I examine each of these linkages in the following subsections and then critique the vast empirical literature that investigates the relationship between growth and the orientation of the trade regime.

3.3.4.1   PROTECTION, X-EFFICIENCY, AND THE QUIET LIFE

ISI is often criticized for reducing the pressures on firms to achieve maximum technical efficiency (or X-efficiency).[47] According to the usual story, costs could be lowered and profits increased if firm owners put more effort into running their enterprises efficiently. If survival of the enterprise were at stake, owners would almost surely undertake the hard work required to move closer to best-practice technology. But thanks to protection they can choose instead to enjoy comfortable profits while leading a slow-paced, quiet life of leisure. In short, protection lowers productivity by allowing entrepreneurs to be lazy.

This argument has been evaluated by Martin (1978). Suppose labor L is the only variable input and productivity varies with the effort G the firm's owner devotes to the dreary business of achieving technical efficiency:

---

[46] Dutz's (1996) estimates for Morocco also suggest that import penetration has a strong adverse effect on firm output. [A 1% increase in imports is associated with a 1.51% reduction in firm output evaluated at the sample means (p. 152).]
[47] See, for example, Keesing (1967), Balassa (1988), and Roemer and Radelet (1991).

$$Q = \phi(G)f(L), \qquad \phi', f' > 0, \phi'', f'' < 0. \tag{54}$$

More effort brings more profits π but also cuts into the time available for leisure, $T - G$. This is the basic tradeoff the owner contemplates when solving the problem

$$\operatorname*{Max}_{\{G,L\}} U(\pi, T - G) \tag{55}$$

subject to

$$\pi = (1+t)\phi(G)f(L) - wL, \tag{56}$$

where $U(\cdot)$ is increasing and strictly concave. The first-order conditions governing the optimal choices for G and L require that the marginal value product of labor be equated to the wage

$$(1+t)\phi(G)f'(L) = w, \tag{57}$$

and that the return on effort equal the marginal rate of substitution between profits and leisure:

$$(1+t)f(L)\phi'(G) = \frac{U_2(\pi, T-G)}{U_1(\pi, T-G)}. \tag{58}$$

Brief inspection of (58) reveals that the impact of a higher tariff on owner effort is ambiguous owing to conflicting income and substitution effects. Assuming leisure is a normal good, the increase in profits tends to lower effort. However, a higher tariff also raises the return to effort, directly by increasing the price the firm can charge and indirectly by making it profitable to expand employment. (The larger the scale of output, the greater the absolute return to any increase in productivity ϕ'.)[48] The nature of preferences and technology determines whether this latter substitution effect is stronger than the income effect. But even if the income effect dominates, it follows only that protection lowers productivity in the import sector, not that the overall level of productivity in the economy falls. When protection is increased firms in the import sector hire more labor, bidding up the wage. The increase in the wage reduces profits and the return to effort for firms in the export sector. If firm owners everywhere are of the same character type, productivity *rises*

---

[48] A similar effect operates in Rodrik (1988). Protection may improve productivity because the marginal benefit of devoting time and resources to achieving a cost reduction is greater when the firm's market share (or scale of output) is larger.

in the export sector as the income effect again dominates the substitution effect. Clearly, partial and general equilibrium analysis may give different answers as to the impact of protection on economywide productivity (Martin, 1978, pp. 277–280; Rodrik, 1992c, p. 158).

There is yet another, more basic problem with the argument: settling the general equilibrium repercussions and the opposing income and substitution effects in favor of the claim that ISI weakens the incentives to achieve technical efficiency does not produce the desired conclusion that the costs of protection are greater than normal. Quite the contrary – they will be less! Suppose, for example, that protection lowers effort in the import sector while leaving it unchanged in the export sector. Ignoring distributional effects, pretend agents *qua* consumers are identical so that overall welfare is $u = V(1 + t, E) + \psi(T - G)$, where the indirect utility function $V(\cdot)$ measures utility from goods consumption. Letting η denote the general equilibrium own-price elasticity of supply in the import sector, the welfare loss from raising the tariff is

$$\frac{du}{dt} = -\frac{t(D^m \varepsilon + Q_m \eta)}{1 + tc_x}. \tag{59}$$

Since firm owners in the import sector internalize all the costs of their decision to lower effort, there are no direct welfare effects associated with variations in effort and hence the loss from protection is given by the usual formula (Martin, 1978, p. 281).[49] But while the formula is the same, η will be smaller when effort declines. The welfare cost of protection is smaller because domestic supply in the import sector is less elastic.

3.3.4.2 IMPORT BOTTLENECKS

An escalated structure of protection discriminates against export production and encourages imports of intermediate inputs and capital goods. It is widely believed that as a consequence import-substitution–based

---

[49] The principal-agent version of the X-efficiency argument developed by Vousden and Campbell (1994) is not flawed in this way. In their model, the owner of the firm does not know the cost type and cannot observe the effort exerted by the manager. The principal–agent problem gives rise to an intrafirm distortion when the optimal payment schedule offered by the owner to induce the manager to reveal his cost type results in effort and output being below their full information levels. Unfortunately, it is not clear whether protection worsens this distortion. Much depends on the nature of technology; strong restrictions have to be placed on the cost function to ensure that protection induces greater managerial slack.

growth must eventually run out of steam. After the easy phase of import substitution in consumer products is complete, the economy is left with a weakened export sector that is unable to pay for the imported inputs essential to ongoing, rapid expansion in the industrial sector (Krueger, 1983, pp. 8, 47–48). A shift toward more export-oriented policies is then required to break the import bottleneck and revive growth.

This story makes some sense in a partial equilibrium setting, but it falls completely apart once all relevant general equilibrium effects are brought within view. The story is erroneous because, as Dani Rodrik observes (1992c, p. 158), it "mixes up microeconomics and macroeconomics." There is a fallacy of concreteness involved in focusing on the fact that exports earn dollars and imports use them up. As should be evident from the saving-investment identity

$$\text{Current Account Surplus} = S - I + T - G,$$

balance of payments problems arise either from fiscal deficits or an imbalance between domestic saving and investment. Apart from periods marked by major policy shifts, the connection between these variables and the orientation of the trade regime is tenuous; in practice, persistent balance of payments problems invariably reflect loose fiscal policies (Easterly and Schmidt-Hebbel, 1994, pp. 24, 60–63). Seeking a line consistent with the saving–investment identity, one could recast the story in the preceding paragraph in terms of deeper import-substitution reducing tariff revenues and increasing the fiscal deficit. But the resulting balance of payments difficulties will obviously not be resolved by switching to a more export-oriented trade strategy (which may make matters even worse by further raising the fiscal deficit). If growth is held back by import rationing, fiscal policy, not trade policy, is in need of reform.

3.3.4.3   TECHNOLOGY TRANSFER AND TRADE

Most advocates of export promotion contend that trade promotes the transfer of technology from developed to less developed countries. Although this proposition is difficult to prove formally, it exercises a certain appeal in discussions carried on at the level of intelligent conjecture. There is, after all, a direct, mechanical link between trade and technology when exports supply the foreign exchange needed to import improved technology embodied in new capital goods (World Bank, 1993, chapter 6). More generally, it seems plausible that, having more contact with the outside world, firms in outward-oriented economies would be more likely to learn of new products and technologies developed abroad. In support of this view one can point to documented cases of customers in developed countries furnishing valuable technical information to their LDC suppliers.[50]

One part of this argument may be dismissed immediately. Foreign exchange for the import of machinery embodying technological improvements will *not* be more readily available under an export-oriented than an import-substituting trade regime. To claim otherwise is to again confuse microeconomics and macroeconomics; import bottlenecks and balance of payments problems are macroeconomic phenomena.

The other channel through which export orientation might facilitate the transfer of technology – greater contact with the outside world – undoubtedly operates to some extent. Its implications for policy, however, depend on additional considerations. It is not clear that a large export sector is essential to the the acquisition of foreign know-how. The high-performance East Asian economies successfully encouraged the acquisition of foreign technology through direct foreign investment, licensing, and other mechanisms while protecting many domestic markets (World Bank, 1993, chapter 6). Perhaps therefore policies to promote technology transfer and commercial policy should be treated as essentially separate policies. The main qualification to this view comes from the case studies mentioned earlier which show that sometimes foreign customers pass on valuable information to their LDC suppliers. But this and other export-linked, informal mechanisms of technology transfer do not justify policy intervention unless either the government possesses better information than private agents about the prospects of gaining knowledge through exporting, or the acquisition of knowledge by firms in one sector spills over to benefit firms in other sectors.

3.3.4.4 ENDOGENOUS GROWTH MODELS OF TRADE AND RESEARCH AND DEVELOPMENT

Modern trade theory has allocated a lot of human capital to analysis of the relationship between trade and technological advances stemming from research and development (R + D hereafter). The literature on this subject is *potentially* relevant to developing countries. The reason for the qualifier "potentially" is that it is not easy in most LDCs to find something that looks like an R + D sector (Bardhan, 1995, p. 2988). But surface appearances may be deceiving: perhaps firms conduct R + D in-house in an informal way that is not visible to casual observation.

---

[50] See Pack and Page (1994). They also note the potentially important point that there appear to be fewer proprietary restrictions on knowledge in older industries with labor-intensive technology, where LDCs are likely to have a comparative advantage.

Following Grossman and Helpman (1991) and Feenstra (1996), suppose final goods are produced by labor L and a mix of intermediate inputs Z_i:

$$Q_j = L_j^{\alpha} \sum_{i=1}^{n} Z_{ij}^{\sigma}, \qquad j = 1, \dots m. \tag{60}$$

The cost function for each intermediate is the same. Since the Z_i enter (60) symmetrically, it turns out in general equilibrium that $Z_{ij} = Z_j, \forall\ i$, and that aggregate purchases of intermediates are $X_j = nZ_j$. Making use of this result, we can rewrite (60) as

$$Q_j = n^{1-\sigma} L_j^{\alpha} X_j^{\sigma}. \tag{60'}$$

Holding total resource use constant, output increases when firms have access to a wider range of specialized intermediate inputs. The term $n^{1-\sigma}$ thus measures the productivity gain from pure economies of specialization (Ethier, 1982).

New types of intermediates are supplied on a regular basis by the R + D sector.[51] The labor cost of developing a new product is wb/K, where w is the wage, b is a constant, and K is the stock of general knowledge capital. General knowledge is a public good that grows with cumulative R + D experience. The latter is assumed to be proportional to the variety of intermediate inputs in existence. Hence, labor costs equal wb/n after choosing appropriate units for K. The key point to note is that the development of new products reduces the cost of R + D by adding to the stock of general knowledge. Knowledge spillovers thus give rise to dynamic scale economies and sustained technical progress.[52]

When trade occurs the fate of the R + D sector in the poor, less technologically advanced country depends on whether knowledge spillovers are national or global in scope. *Ceteris paribus*, the country with the larger knowledge base has a comparative advantage in conducting R + D. The innovation rate will decline in the poor country, therefore,

---

[51] The R + D sector produces only blueprints. The blueprints are sold to firms that are in the business of producing intermediate inputs.

[52] There is a close parallel here with the literature that analyzes how learning-by-doing affects trade patterns. In Krugman (1987) and Boldrin and Scheinkman (1988), external learning effects produce dynamic scale economies that "lock in" the existing pattern of comparative advantage. The models in these two papers assume continuous learning, but the same conclusion obtains when learning is bounded and there are knowledge spillovers across industries (Young, 1991).

if knowledge does not flow across national boundaries.[53] The growth rate, however, will be higher because trade allows the poor country to purchase the full array of intermediate inputs generated by R + D in the rich country (Feenstra, 1996, pp. 244–245). The domestic R + D sector contracts and may disappear entirely, but n grows more rapidly in (60′). In passing, it should be remarked that this result does not necessarily extend to comparisons less extreme than free trade vs. autarky. Consequently, it does *not* say that all forms of protection are harmful or that productivity growth is likely to be higher in more open economies. The only implication for policy is that the trade regime should be open with respect to imports of intermediate inputs and capital goods. (In other words, trade policy should not reduce n and thereby prevent firms from reaping all economies of specialization.) This is fully compatible with an escalated structure of protection that reduces openness as measured by the ratio of exports (or total imports) to GDP.

There are two ways to escape the conclusion that free trade undermines innovation in LDCs. The first places intermediates in the nontradables sector *and* postulates factor-intensity conditions conducive to expansion of the R + D sector.[54] Consider, for example, the model of a small open economy in Chapter 6 of Grossman and Helpman's *Innovation and Growth in the Global Economy* (1991). In their model, firms use unskilled labor, human capital, and nontradable intermediate inputs to produce an import good and an export good. The supplies of skilled and unskilled labor are perfectly inelastic, and import-competing and export production are equally intermediates-intensive. Production of intermediates requires both labor inputs, but the import and R + D sectors employ only human capital and the export sector hires only unskilled labor.

It is transparent from the assumed factor-intensity conditions that trade results in a reallocation of resources to the R + D sector. Under free trade, the import sector contracts and the export sector expands. Since import and export production are equally intermediates-intensive, there is no direct effect on the demand for intermediates or the price the R + D sector can charge for new product designs. Contraction of the

---

[53] Grossman and Helpman (1991, chapter 8) work with a slightly different model where R + D generates a greater variety of consumer goods. The model produces the conclusion that the country that starts out with more knowledge capital eventually ends up doing all R + D in the world.

[54] If intermediate inputs are nontradable but factor-intensity conditions are not right, then trade is likely to reduce both the innovation rate and the growth rate in the poor country. See Feenstra (1996, pp. 239–241).

import sector, however, is accompanied by a fall in the wage paid to skilled labor. This stimulates expansion in the R + D sector by lowering the cost of producing an innovation.

The other way of helping the R + D sector is to appeal to the possibility that knowledge flows across national borders. If knowledge spillovers are global, then everything discovered by R + D in developed countries is part of the stock of general knowledge capital of firms doing R + D in the Third World. The small knowledge base that slows the pace of innovation in autarky thus ceases to be a handicap when LDCs participate in a globally integrated world economy.[55]

None of this is terribly convincing. Some intermediates may be confined to local markets, but most are highly tradable. Import competition would be expected therefore to cut heavily into the customer base of the domestic R + D sector. Moreover, something is amiss in the notion that higher rates of technological progress can be achieved simply by shifting resources from the rest of the economy to the R + D sector or by tapping into a pool of global knowledge capital. As Romer (1990), Pack (1994), Bardhan (1995), and Rivera-Batiz (1997) emphasize, the innovation business is different in that it requires a set of highly specialized human capital inputs and a complex supporting network of institutions and social and physical infrastructure. This perspective suggests that the mechanisms featured in endogenous growth models operate weakly in LDCs or not at all. Workers laid off in the contracting import sector cannot stroll across the street and start producing innovations; they lack the right type of human capital and/or live in a country that has yet to develop the requisite complementary institutions and infrastructure. Maybe information flows across national boundaries, but when it arrives in Bangladesh, Ecuador, or Kenya the "national innovation system" cannot do much with it.

So where do we stand? Opinions on this are bound to differ. My own view is that the determinants of technological progress remain largely mysterious. We know precious little about how far knowledge spillovers penetrate into the Third World, about the interdependence of trade and information flows, or about why some national innovation systems are dynamic while others are thoroughly moribund. The better part of the action, it seems, is in things that economists do not understand very well.

---

[55] Feenstra (1996, p. 230) stresses that global knowledge spillovers produce this result, not trade per se. It is not necessarily the case, therefore, that more trade is better than less trade. The implications for policy depend on the relationship between trade and information flows.

3.3.4.5   THE EMPIRICAL EVIDENCE

A sizeable body of empirical work has drawn on cross-country data to estimate reduced form equations relating growth to some measure of openness, such as the ratio of exports to GDP, and a list of other potentially relevant variables (investment, the literacy rate, proxies for political instability, etc.).[56,57] The coefficient on the export variable is positive and statistically significant in the great majority of these studies. A host of conceptual and econometric problems, however, make it difficult to assess the importance of this finding:

- **The mechanism through which exports are supposed to raise productivity growth is not modeled explicitly.** Some sort of rationale is usually given for including the export variable, but the connection between theory and empirical specification is quite loose. This is troubling if the goal is to go beyond a first rough pass at the data. There is no clear interpretation of results obtained from reduced form equations that have not been derived from an explicitly specified structural model.
- **Policy instruments are often missing from the set of explanatory variables.** The coefficient on the export variable may not have anything to do with the impact of trade policy on productivity growth. Since the degree of openness depends on factor endowments, technology, and preferences as well as policy, the ratio of exports to GDP (or some other proxy) is not a particularly reliable measure of the orientation of the trade regime.[58] Furthermore, even if it were, comovements of

---

[56] Good reviews of the literature may be found in Yaghmaian (1994), Rodrik (1995, pp. 2938–2941), and Harrison (1996).

[57] Another group of studies investigates the relationship between productivity growth and variables that proxy for the orientation of the trade regime. These studies have not found any clear relationship between total factor productivity growth and import liberalization, the level of protection, or the share of output exported (Pack, 1988, p. 353; Helleiner, 1994, pp. 30–31; Tybout, 1996, pp. 57–59, 63–65). Two studies have also examined the relationship between productivity growth and the factor intensity of production. Dollar and Sokoloff (1990) find that productivity growth is higher in labor-intensive industries, but Nishimizu and Robinson (1984) reach the opposite conclusion.

[58] Pritchett (1996) demonstrates convincingly that quantitative measures of outward orientation are dubious proxies for the policy regime. The share of trade in GDP (adjusted for factor endowments and structural characteristics), the share of imports subject to nontariff barriers, and Leamer's measure of deviation of trade quantities from that predicted by a Heckscher–Ohlin-Vanek model of comparative advantage are almost completely uncorrelated across countries. Rankings of outward orientation thus depend on the chosen criterion.

growth and exports may reflect the influence of other policies, especially macroeconomic policies that increase capacity utilization by enabling restrictions on imported inputs to be relaxed. There is considerable evidence that these qualifications matter. Handoussa, Nishimizu, and Page (1986) find that all productivity growth in Egyptian public-sector firms between 1973 and 1979 owed to greater availability of imported inputs and increased capacity utilization in the import-competing sector, and in Esfahani (1991) the export variable becomes statistically insignificant once the share of imports in GDP is added to the set of regressors. Edwards (1992) estimates a variety of reduced form equations for growth with either a measure of openness or a policy/intervention variable aimed at capturing the effects of export subsidies.[59] There is a positive association between openness and growth, but the coefficient on the policy variable is usually *negative* and statistically significant.

- **The estimates fail tests for robustness.** While many studies find a positive association between indicators of outward-oriented trade policy and growth, the results do not survive small alterations in the conditioning information set (i.e., the set of right-side variables and the sample of countries). Levine and Renelts' (1992) and Levine and Zervos' (1993) comprehensive extreme bounds analysis turn up no evidence of a robust relationship between long-run growth and a variety of fiscal, monetary, and trade policy indicators.[60] Only the investment rate, and possibly certain proxies for financial development, appear to be robustly associated with long-run growth.
- **Do the results reflect a causal relationship?** Since exports are a major component of GDP, it would not be surprising if causality ran from

[59] It is not easy to construct reliable measures of the trade regime. Reinikka (1994) finds, for example, that variations in the tariff rate do not accurately track variations in trade policy in Kenya.

[60] The fragility of the estimates shows up in a number of other studies as well. The statistical significance of the export/openness variable appears to be sensitive to the exclusion of outliers where the average annual growth rate of exports exceeds 20% (Kohli and Singh, 1989; Taylor, 1993, p. 66), to whether the labor input is measured by population or employment growth (Yaghmaian, 1994), and to judgements about what belongs in the complete list of potentially relevant variables. [In De Gregorio (1992) none of the measures of openness or orientation of the trade regime prove significant when the regressors include the initial level of real GDP and variables to control for human capital accumulation and macroeconomic stability.] Case studies and diverse country histories also cast doubt on the notion that there is a robust relationship between openness and growth.

productivity growth to exports rather than the other way around, or if some variable omitted from the model influenced both output and exports. In theory, instrumental variables estimation can handle the problem of correlation between the error term and an explanatory variable; in practice, it is difficult to find suitable instruments for the export variable. Consequently, when estimating reduced form equations for growth there is not much choice but to conduct Granger–Sims causality tests and hope they justify the assumption that the export variable is econometrically exogenous. The findings of Jung and Marshall (1985), Hsiao (1987), Ahmad and Kwon (1991), Bahmani-Oskooee, Mohtadi, and Shabsigh (1991), and Harrison (1996) are not encouraging in this respect. For half of the countries in the Bahmani-Oskooee, Mohtadi, and Shabsigh study and 62% of those in the Jung and Marshall study, causality tests are inconclusive, and in the rest of the sample there is a roughly even split between the cases of export-led growth and export-reducing growth.[61] There is no evidence at all of a causal link running from exports to growth in Ahmad and Kwon's sample of 47 African countries or in Hsiao's test for four Asian NICs.[62] Harrison finds support for the hypothesis that openness Granger-causes growth for two of six openness variables, but one of these (the black market premium) is a variable that measures mainly macroeconomic disequilibrium.

The ambiguous results from causality tests suggest that the built-in correlation between exports and GDP in the national income identity may be a serious problem. This view is reinforced by the failure of some estimates to pass a simple consistency test proposed by Sheehey (1990, 1993). Sheehey's test is based on a comparison of the identity

$$g_y = \omega g_x + (1 - \omega) g_n \tag{61}$$

with the estimates obtained from the regression equations

$$g_y = a_0 + a_1 i + a_2 g_l + a_3 g_x + \varepsilon_t, \tag{62}$$

$$g_y = b_0 + b_1 i + b_2 g_l + b_3 g_n + v_t, \tag{63}$$

---

[61] Bahmani-Oskooee, Mohtadi, and Shabsigh try, strangely, to interpret the cases of export-reducing growth as consistent with the export-led growth hypothesis.
[62] Ahmad and Kwon get the same conclusion when they run the causality tests with manufactured exports instead of total exports. The only evidence of a causal relationship runs in the opposite direction, from growth to total exports for low-income countries and from growth to manufactured exports for middle- and high-income countries.

where g_y, g_x, g_n, and g_l refer to the growth rates of GDP, output in the export sector, output in the nonexport sectors, and the labor force; i is the ratio of investment to GDP; and ω is the share of GDP produced by the export sector. If i and g_l do not accurately measure the growth of capital and labor inputs, or if variations in GDP reflect mostly the impact of omitted variables that influence both g_x and g_n (e.g., technology shocks, cyclical effects, changes in the supply of other inputs), the estimated values of a_3 and b_3 will be suspiciously close to the output shares ω and $1 - \omega$. This is precisely what Sheehey finds when estimating (62) and (63) for Feder's (1983) sample and for a larger sample of 65 countries.

Sheehey's test and the aforementioned studies of causality are not without their own problems.[63] Nevertheless, the results cast doubt on the assumption that in estimates of crude reduced form growth equations a positive and statistically significant coefficient on the export variable reflects something like a production function relationship. Short of estimating more elaborate, structural models, there does not seem much hope of settling the causality issue.

Or maybe there is. If firms benefit from "learning-by-exporting," then current productivity should depend on prior export experience and hence the efficiency gap between exporters and nonexporters should widen over time. But if the productivity gap stems from self-selection alone, it will exist at the time firms enter the export market and exhibit no discernible upward trend thereafter. Using plant-level panel data, Clerides, Lach, and Tybout (1998) test these two competing hypotheses for Colombia, Mexico, and Morocco by estimating cost functions that depend on the firm's exporting history. In all three countries, there is strong support for the self-selection hypothesis but scant evidence of learning-by-exporting. Aw, Chung, and Roberts (1998) carry out similar tests for Taiwan and S. Korea by comparing productivity in different years of firms that recently entered/exited the export market, incumbent exporters, and firms that sell only to the domestic market. While some of the tests are inconclusive, the results again point to self-selection as the source of higher productivity in the export sector. Consistent with self-selection, the productivity gap was significantly positive in nine of ten comparisons between continuous exporters and firms that never ventured out of the domestic market; moreover, in all ten comparisons the gap did not grow progressively larger as called for by learning effects unique to the act of exporting.

---

[63] The tests are applied to crude specifications that include only two or three explanatory variables. In addition, the time series are not very long.

The support for learning-by-exporting is limited to three industries in Taiwan where the productivity gap widened between firms that recently broke into the export market and those that did not. But what looks like learning-by-exporting in these industries could instead reflect self-selection and a finite series of serially correlated productivity shocks (or lagged adjustment of output to a single shock). One merit of this explanation is that it reconciles the results for recent entrants and incumbent exporters: once the technology shocks that induced entry have run their course, the productivity gap plateaus, leaving the trendless gap between established exporters and chronic nonexporters.

- **More recent, widely cited studies suffer from the same set of problems.** The influential studies by Dollar (1992), Ben-David (1993), Sachs and Warner (1995), and Edwards (1998) employ alternative tests and/or more sophisticated methodology to investigate the relationship between trade policy/openness and growth. Rodriguez and Rodrik (1999) have subjected these studies to a lengthy, searching critique only to find that they founder on the same problems as earlier studies. Measurement error is rampant: Dollar's two proxies for the restrictiveness of the trade regime are the variability of the real exchange rate and the ratio of the price level for tradable goods in country i to that in the United States; the former is really a measure of general economic instability, while the latter overlooks the impact of transport costs and is apt to give incorrect rankings when protection is combined with export taxes or subsidies;[64] almost all of the statistical power in the dummy index for openness constructed by Sachs and Warner derives from the black market premium for foreign exchange and the presence of state export monopolies, variables that have little to do with trade policy per se and which effectively assign a value of unity to all non-African countries not experiencing macroeconomic and political difficulties; Edwards' indicators of openness include the Sachs–Warner index, the average black market premium, two subjective indices that contain anomalous rankings suggestive of judgement bias in the classification of countries, a trade tax ratio that is implausibly low for

---

[64] The Lerner symmetry theorem states that an export tax and an import tariff have the same effect on relative prices and the allocation of resources. But since an export tax pushes the domestic price below the world price, a country that levies an export tax as well as a tariff will receive a lower score on Dollar's Distortion index than a country that levies only a tariff. Similarly, countries that use export subsidies to offset protection will be ranked as less outward oriented than countries that impose the same tariffs but do not subsidize exports.

the LDCs in the sample and another source of eccentric country rankings (Chile is no more open than India?), and indices derived from prior regressions that are supposed to isolate the impact of policy on trade flows but almost certainly commingle the influence of policy with measurement error and model specification error. Equally disturbing, almost all of the statistically significant coefficients on openness and the proxies for trade policy disappear when additional variables are introduced to control for macroeconomic instability, political strife and failing institutions, and regional effects (especially location in Sub-Saharan Africa), or when the regressions are reestimated with better data or slightly different sample periods. Rodriguez and Rodrik's conclusion that the results in this group of studies are "largely uninformative" (p. 3) is harsh but altogether fair.

- **The inherent limitations of cross-country data.** It is worthwhile to recall a basic point: regression analysis presumes that observations are drawn from a distinct population. This crucial assumption is obviously not valid when the data come from 40–100 countries whose economies exhibit immense structural diversity.[65] The coefficients obtained from running regressions on such data lack a clear interpretation. They certainly do not tell us anything about behavioral relationships. Cross-country regressions provide, at best, results suggestive of potential empirical regularities.

In light of all these problems, the claim that export-oriented policies are more conducive to growth than protection should be treated with a healthy dose of scepticism. It is not clear whether the ongoing parade of positive, statistically significant coefficients on the openness variable means that empirical studies are rediscovering the same robust stylized fact or the same spurious correlation. Meaningful tests of how trade policy affects productivity growth await the arrival of better theory and better data.

3.4   Concluding Observations

Several major studies have effectively documented the excesses of ISI based on extreme protectionist policies. Unfortunately, however, a large part of the policy spectrum remains uncharted territory. The failure of extreme protectionist policies does not establish that an export-

---

[65] In a study based on time series data for 1960–1982 for 88 LDCs, Ram (1987) finds that there is tremendous diversity in the parameter estimates across countries.

promotion strategy is superior to a moderate, intelligently formulated program of import substitution. And contrary to claims made by advocates of outward-oriented policies, neither theory nor empirical evidence suggests there is likely to be greater exploitation of scale economies, more rapid technological progress, less underemployment, or faster capital accumulation under one strategy than the other.

The immediate prospects for resolving many of the disagreements in the literature do not seem promising. Given the ambiguous predictions of theory, the question of which trade strategy is most conducive to pro-competitive effects will have to be settled mainly by empirical investigation. It is equally doubtful that any decisive breakthroughs are on the horizon that will enable us to better understand how trade policy affects productivity growth; we are clearly a long way from a potentially satisfactory theory of technological progress, let alone a theory that has been validated by the data for LDCs.

Although a great deal of additional work is required if the debate on trade policy is to be better informed, in at least one area it is possible to make quick progress. Intertemporal economics and general equilibrium theory provide the machinery needed to investigate carefully the impact of trade policy on capital accumulation and underemployment. The next two chapters are devoted to this task.

CHAPTER 4

Tools and Tricks of the Trade, Part II: Linear Differential Equations and Dynamic Optimization

This chapter shows how to solve for the perfect foresight path in optimizing, continuous-time dynamic models. The solution procedure involves the use of optimal control theory, the methods for solving linear differential equations, and a working knowledge of how to apply these techniques in general equilibrium models of realistic complexity. I start out in Section 4.1 by developing the techniques for solving linear dynamic systems. Section 4.2 discusses the rudiments of the optimal control solution to dynamic optimization problems. The example in Section 4.3 illustrates how to apply the techniques.

4.1 Linear Differential Equations

A dynamic economic model usually generates a system of nonlinear differential (or difference) equations. Although the nonlinear system often lacks a closed-form solution, a linear approximation of the system can be used to investigate its dynamics in the neighborhood of a stationary equilibrium. For ease of exposition, I demonstrate how this is done in the case of a system of two simultaneous differential equations. The methodology for solving higher order systems is essentially the same and will be discussed later in Section 4.1.3.

Consider the pair of nonlinear differential equations

$$\dot{x}_1 = f(x_1, x_2; \alpha), \tag{1}$$

$$\dot{x}_2 = g(x_1, x_2; \alpha). \tag{2}$$

α is some exogenous variable and $\dot{x}_1$ and $\dot{x}_2$ are derivatives with respect to time ($\dot{x}_1 = dx_1/dt$). The stationary equilibrium, or steady state of the system, (x_1^*, x_2^*), is found by setting $\dot{x}_1 = \dot{x}_2 = 0$ and solving

$$f(x_1, x_2; \alpha) = 0 \tag{3}$$

$$g(x_1, x_2; \alpha) = 0 \tag{4}$$

for x_1 and x_2 as a function of α. Taking a first-order Taylor series expansion of (1)–(2) around a steady state produces

$$\begin{bmatrix} \dot{x}_1 \\ \dot{x}_2 \end{bmatrix} = \begin{bmatrix} f_1 & f_2 \\ g_1 & g_2 \end{bmatrix} \begin{bmatrix} x_1(t) - x_1^* \\ x_2(t) - x_2^* \end{bmatrix}. \tag{5}$$

Since the partial derivatives f_i and g_i are evaluated at (x_1^*, x_2^*), the system in (5) is a linear approximation of the original nonlinear system (1)–(2). Being a linear approximation, it may not accurately describe the paths of x_1 and x_2 at points too far away from the stationary equilibrium.

The general solution to a system of two linear first-order differential equations is

$$x_1(t) - x_1^* = A_1 e^{\lambda_1 t} + A_2 e^{\lambda_2 t}, \tag{6}$$

$$x_2(t) - x_2^* = B_1 e^{\lambda_1 t} + B_2 e^{\lambda_2 t}, \tag{7}$$

where A_i and B_i are constants and λ_i are characteristic roots or eigenvalues. As will be shown later in Section 4.1.2, A_i and B_i depend on the system's parameters and initial conditions. The eigenvalues are the roots of the characteristic equation

$$|J - \lambda I| = 0, \tag{8}$$

where J is the coefficient matrix in (5) and I is the identity matrix (a matrix with 1's on the diagonal and 0's everywhere else). In the present case, the characteristic equation is the quadratic equation

$$\begin{vmatrix} f_1 - \lambda & f_2 \\ g_1 & g_2 - \lambda \end{vmatrix} = \lambda^2 - (f_1 + g_2)\lambda + (f_1 g_2 - f_2 g_1) = 0, \tag{9}$$

whose roots are

$$\lambda_1, \lambda_2 = \frac{f_1 + g_2 \pm \sqrt{(f_1 + g_2)^2 + 4(f_2 g_1 - f_1 g_2)}}{2}. \tag{10}$$

It is easy to verify from (9) and (10) that

$$\operatorname{tr} J = f_1 + g_2 = \lambda_1 + \lambda_2,$$

$$\det J = f_1 g_2 - f_2 g_1 = \lambda_1 \lambda_2.$$

Thus, if $\operatorname{tr} J$, $\det J > 0$, both eigenvalues are positive; if $\operatorname{tr} J < 0$ and $\det J > 0$, both eigenvalues are negative; and if $\det J < 0$, one eigenvalue is positive and the other is negative.

Turning back to (6)–(7), it is evident that the general qualitative properties of the linearized system depend on the characteristics of the eigenvalues. If the term under the square root sign in (10) is negative, the eigenvalues are imaginary and x_1 and x_2 oscillate around the stationary equilibrium. Stability of the system hinges on the signs of the real parts of the eigenvalues. If the real parts of both eigenvalues are negative, the system is locally stable: since the terms $e^{\lambda_1 t}$ and $e^{\lambda_2 t}$ approach zero as $t \to \infty$, x_1 and x_2 converge to their steady-state values x_1^* and x_2^* from any initial position [close to (x_1^*, x_2^*)]. Conversely, if $\lambda_1, \lambda_2 > 0$, the system is unstable. Finally, when one eigenvalue (say λ_1) is positive and the other negative, the stationary equilibrium is a saddle point. All paths for which $A_1, B_1 \neq 0$ veer away from the stationary equilibrium because the term involving the positive eigenvalue dominates the solution as t becomes large. But if the initial conditions are just right, so that $A_1 = B_1 = 0$, λ_1 drops out and x_1 and x_2 follow the stable arm of the solution $(A_2 e^{\lambda_2 t}, B_2 e^{\lambda_2 t})$ that arrives asymptotically at (x_1^*, x_2^*). The stable arm is generally referred to as the saddlepath.

4.1.1   Constructing Phase Diagrams

Phase diagrams are a useful device for analyzing the qualitative nature of the dynamics. Setting $\dot{x}_1 = 0$, we have from the first row of the matrix equation (5) that

$$\left.\frac{x_2 - x_2^*}{x_1 - x_1^*}\right|_{\dot{x}_1 = 0} = -f_1/f_2 \tag{11}$$

is the loci of points for which x_1 is constant. Similarly, x_2 is constant for

$$\left.\frac{x_2 - x_2^*}{x_1 - x_1^*}\right|_{\dot{x}_2 = 0} = -g_1/g_2. \tag{12}$$

Figure 4.1 depicts the phase diagram for the stable system in which $f_1, g_2 < 0$ and $f_2, g_1 > 0$. $X_1 X_1$ and $X_2 X_2$ are the schedules along which $\dot{x}_1 = 0$ and $\dot{x}_2 = 0$. Both schedules slope upward, with $X_1 X_1$ being more steeply sloped than $X_2 X_2$ (det $J > 0$ implies $-f_1/f_2 > -g_1/g_2$). The east/west directional arrow is determined by choosing a point on $X_1 X_1$ and asking whether a horizontal movement to the right (an increase in x_1) causes x_1 to rise or fall over time. Since $\dot{x}_1 = 0$ on $X_1 X_1$ and $f_1 < 0$, x_1 is falling at points to the right of $X_1 X_1$ (where $\dot{x}_1 < 0$) and rising at points to its left (where $\dot{x}_1 > 0$). Similarly, to set the north/south directional arrow, ask how a vertical movement off $X_2 X_2$ affects $\dot{x}_2$. Since $g_2 < 0$,

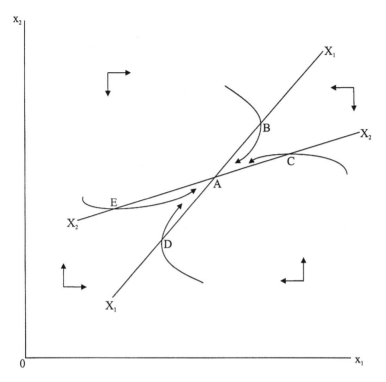

Figure 4.1. The approach to equilibrium in a stable system where the eigenvalues are real.

x_2 is decreasing above X_2X_2 and increasing in the region below the schedule.

In the stable system in Figure 4.1 the eigenvalues are real and the approach to equilibrium involves, at most, a halfcycle.[1] To prove this, consider the nature of the directional pressures at the crossing points B, C, D, and E. The path is horizontal when it crosses X_2X_2 (where $\dot{x}_2 = 0$) and vertical when it crosses X_1X_1 (where $\dot{x}_1 = 0$); consequently, once the path enters the region between the two schedules, it moves on a direct southwesterly or northeasterly line toward point A.

For stable systems having imaginary eigenvalues, the path oscillates around the stationary equilibrium in successively tighter cycles. A case

---

[1] The eigenvalues are real because the discriminant is positive:

$$\text{Discriminant} = f_1^2 + g_2^2 + 4f_2g_1 - 2f_1g_2 = (f_1 - g_2)^2 + 4f_2g_1 > 0.$$

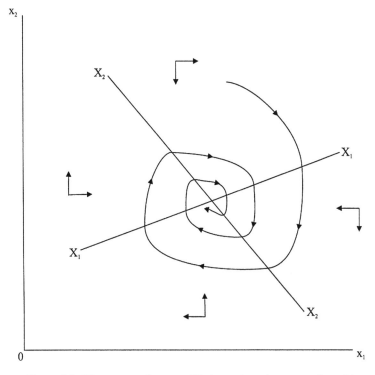

Figure 4.2. The approach to equilibrium when the system is stable and the eigenvalues are imaginary.

of this type is shown in Figure 4.2. Now $g_1 < 0$ and X_2X_2 is negatively sloped. Although the directional arrows pull each variable toward its own schedule, the region between the two schedules no longer traps the path because the cross term g_1 works strongly against a direct approach to equilibrium.[2]

I pass over other configurations consistent with local stability.[3] In this book the equilibria that emerge from solving private agents' intertemporal optimization problems are always saddle points. This is a general characteristic of optimizing dynamic models. Moreover, while a variety of scenarios can produce saddlepoint dynamics, the saddlepoint equilibria of optimizing models are invariably of the type illustrated in

[2] The eigenvalues are imaginary for $g_1 < -(f_1 - g_2)^2/4f_2$. If this inequality does not hold, the roots are real.
[3] See Kamien and Schwarz (1981, pp. 259–263).

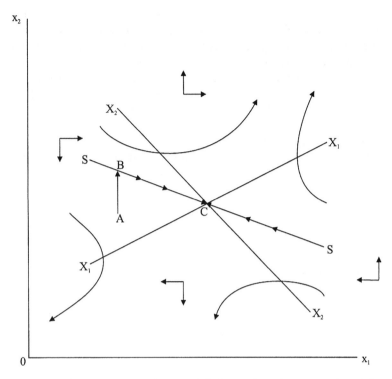

Figure 4.3. The approach to equilibrium when the system is saddle-point stable.

Figure 4.3.[4] One of the variables in the system, x_2, is not tied down by an initial condition; unlike the predetermined variable x_1, it can jump at any point in time. The directional arrow associated with the jump variable usually points away from its own schedule. Thus, in Figure 4.3, where $\partial \dot{x}_2 / \partial x_2 = g_2 > 0$, x_2 is increasing (decreasing) at points above (below) the $X_2 X_2$ schedule. As a result, most adjustment paths end up far away from point C. Most, but not all. Observe that in the northwest/southeast zone between $X_1 X_1$ and $X_2 X_2$ the dynamics pull x_1 and x_2 in the general direction of the stationary equilibrium. There is, in fact, a unique trajectory, the saddlepath SS, that converges to C.

The distinction introduced above between jump variables and predetermined variables is of fundamental importance. While the signs of the

[4] For other saddlepoint configurations, see Seierstad and Sydsaeter (1987, pp. 253–256).

eigenvalues determine whether the stationary equilibrium is a saddle point, in economic models the saddlepoint solution is not meaningful unless the dynamic system has the right number of jump variables. To see this, suppose the economy is at rest at point A and that some shock shifts the stationary equilibrium to point C. If both x_1 and x_2 are predetermined, there is no way to get onto the convergent saddlepath SS. But if x_2 is a jump variable, the equilibrium can shift instantaneously from A to B. The saddlepath is attainable because x_2 can jump to bring about the right initial conditions.

Why focus on the saddlepath when it is but one of an infinite number of paths the economy might follow? In many cases the answer is that other paths can be ruled out as inconsistent with optimizing behavior. This may require some restrictions on preferences and technology, however. A second, more generally applicable rationale appeals to the notion that in a stationary environment it is "sensible" to expect the economy to follow a path that eventually arrives at a stationary equilibrium. This rationale is reinforced by the observation that the saddlepath solution is the only one that guarantees that markets behave in an orderly, stable fashion. If agents do not coordinate on the saddlepath, markets might fall into disarray as nothing ties down the direction or the magnitude of the jump in x_2. The same consideration explains why it is usually *not* desirable for an equilibrium to be locally stable. Since the dynamic systems associated with optimizing models normally have some jump variables, local stability implies a continuum of equilibrium paths and potential market confusion: if the system in Figure 4.3 were locally stable, x_2 could jump *anywhere* (from point A) and the economy would still manage to converge subsequently to the stationary equilibrium C.

4.1.2   Saddlepoint Dynamics: Obtaining Explicit Solutions

In this section I work out the mathematical solutions for the saddlepath and the magnitude of the initial jump AB in Figure 4.3. I am not pursuing formal rigor for its own sake here. Even in simple 2×2 dynamic systems, phase diagrams take one only so far. Explicit mathematical solutions are often required to answer the more interesting questions about the adjustment process. In a macromodel, for example, x_2 might represent investment spending and one might need to know the exact magnitude of the jump in investment AB to determine if some policy is inflationary in the short run.

The first step in the solution procedure is to obtain the eigenvectors associated with the system in (5). Let $\mathbf{Z}_j = (Z_{1j}, Z_{2j})'$ be the eigenvector paired with the jth eigenvalue. An eigenvector is simply a vector that solves $J\mathbf{Z}_j = \lambda_j\mathbf{Z}_j$, that is,

$$\begin{bmatrix} f_1 & f_2 \\ g_1 & g_2 \end{bmatrix}\begin{bmatrix} Z_{1j} \\ Z_{2j} \end{bmatrix} = \begin{bmatrix} \lambda_j Z_{1j} \\ \lambda_j Z_{2j} \end{bmatrix}, \qquad j=1,2. \tag{13}$$

Clearly, any scalar multiple of an eigenvector is also an eigenvector. We are free therefore to set one component in each eigenvector equal to unity. If we set $Z_{1j} = 1$, the second row of the matrix equation in (13) yields[5]

$$Z_{2j} = \frac{g_1}{\lambda_j - g_2}.$$

We can now write the general solution to (5) as

$$\begin{bmatrix} x_1(t) - x_1^* \\ x_2(t) - x_2^* \end{bmatrix} = \begin{bmatrix} 1 & 1 \\ \dfrac{g_1}{\lambda_1 - g_2} & \dfrac{g_1}{\lambda_2 - g_2} \end{bmatrix}\begin{bmatrix} h_1 e^{\lambda_1 t} \\ h_2 e^{\lambda_2 t} \end{bmatrix}. \tag{14}$$

The coefficient matrix on the right side is formed by placing the ith eigenvector in the ith column. h_1 and h_2 are constants determined by initial conditions. The assumption that x_2 jumps so as to bring the economy onto the saddlepath at point B fixes h_1, the constant associated with the positive eigenvalue λ_1. Since $e^{\lambda_1 t}$ grows ever larger over time, x_1 and x_2 will converge to their steady-state values only if $h_1 = 0$. Hence, on the saddlepath $h_1 = 0$ and

$$x_1(t) - x_1^* = h_2 e^{\lambda_2 t}, \tag{15}$$

$$x_2(t) - x_2^* = \frac{g_1}{\lambda_2 - g_2}h_2 e^{\lambda_2 t}. \tag{16}$$

The other constant, h_2, depends on the initial value of the predetermined variable x_1 relative to its new steady-state level x_1^*. At $t = 0$, (15) gives

$$x_1(0) - x_1^* = h_2, \tag{17}$$

and thus

$$x_1(t) - x_1^* = \left[x_1(0) - x_1^*\right]e^{\lambda_2 t}, \tag{18}$$

[5] The same solution emerges when one solves for the eigenvectors using the first row of (13). Since $|J - \lambda I| = 0$, the equations in the two rows of (13) are linearly dependent.

$$x_2(t) - x_2^* = \frac{g_1}{\lambda_2 - g_2}\left[x_1(0) - x_1^*\right]e^{\lambda_2 t}. \tag{19}$$

Equations (18) and (19) tell us where the path is at time t relative to point C in Figure 4.3. To find how far x_1 and x_2 have moved away from their initial values at point A, $x_{1,o}$ and $x_{2,o}$, note that $x_1(0) = x_{1,o}$ (because x_1 is predetermined) and express the solution as

$$x_1(t) - x_{1,o} = \left(x_1^* - x_{1,o}\right)\left(1 - e^{\lambda_2 t}\right), \tag{20}$$

$$x_2(t) - x_{2,o} = x_2^* - x_{2,o} - \frac{g_1}{\lambda_2 - g_2}\left(x_1^* - x_{1,o}\right)e^{\lambda_2 t}. \tag{21}$$

The terms $x_1^* - x_{1,o}$ and $x_2^* - x_{2,o}$ measure the difference between the old and the new steady-state values of x_1 and x_2. From (3) and (4), these are

$$x_1^* - x_{1,o} = dx_1^* = \frac{f_2 g_3 - f_3 g_2}{f_1 g_2 - f_2 g_1}d\alpha \equiv a_1 d\alpha, \tag{22}$$

$$x_2^* - x_{2,o} = dx_2^* = \frac{f_3 g_1 - f_1 g_3}{f_1 g_2 - f_2 g_1}d\alpha \equiv a_2 d\alpha, \tag{23}$$

Substituting the above solutions into (20) and (21) gives

$$x_1(t) - x_{1,o} = a_1(1 - e^{\lambda_2 t})d\alpha, \tag{24}$$

$$x_2(t) - x_{2,o} = \left(a_2 - \frac{g_1}{\lambda_2 - g_2}a_1 e^{\lambda_2 t}\right)d\alpha. \tag{25}$$

Equations (24)–(25) and the expression for λ_2 in (10) define the path CBA. To calculate the initial jump in x_2, evaluate (25) at $t = 0$:

$$\underbrace{x_2(0) - x_{2,o}}_{\substack{\text{Jump in } x_2 \text{ at } t=0 \\ (AB \text{ in Figure 4.3})}} = \left(a_2 - \frac{g_1 a_1}{\lambda_2 - g_2}\right)d\alpha. \tag{26}$$

Although the algebra in dynamic models is often messy, the solution algorithm is simple and always involves the same steps: to find where x_1 and x_2 are at time t, locate the new stationary equilibrium C and move backward along the saddlepath to the appropriate point. This logic is reproduced in (24)–(26). The equation for the saddlepath is [from (15)–(16)][6]

---

[6] Observe that the slope of the saddlepath is the slope of the eigenvector associated with the negative eigenvalue (i.e., the slope of the saddlepath is Z_{22}/Z_{12}).

$$\left.\frac{x_2 - x_2^*}{x_1 - x_1^*}\right|_{saddlepath} = \frac{g_1}{\lambda_2 - g_2}. \tag{27}$$

Thus, in (26) the second term corresponds to $x_2(0) - x_2^*$, the portion of the jump in x_2 associated with the movement up SS from C to B. The first term captures the impact of the shift of the stationary equilibrium from A to C.

4.1.3   Higher Order Systems

The procedure for analyzing a system of two linear differential equations generalizes in a straightforward way to higher order systems. The characteristic equation associated with a system of n linear differential equations is an nth-order polynomial, the solution to which yields n eigenvalues $\lambda_1, \ldots \lambda_n$. As before,

$$tr\, J = \sum_{i=1}^{n} \lambda_i,$$

$$\det J = \lambda_1 \lambda_2 \ldots \lambda_n,$$

and the general solution is of the form

$$\begin{bmatrix} x_1(t) - x_1^* \\ \cdot \\ \cdot \\ \cdot \\ \cdot \\ x_n(t) - x_n^* \end{bmatrix} = \begin{bmatrix} 1 & 1 & \cdot\cdot & 1 \\ Z_{21} & Z_{22} & \cdot\cdot & Z_{2n} \\ \cdot & & & \\ \cdot & & & \\ \cdot & & & \\ Z_{n1} & Z_{n2} & \cdot\cdot & Z_{nn} \end{bmatrix} \begin{bmatrix} h_1 e^{\lambda_1 t} \\ \cdot \\ \cdot \\ \cdot \\ \cdot \\ h_n e^{\lambda_n t} \end{bmatrix}, \tag{28}$$

where $[1, Z_{2j}, \ldots Z_{nj}]'$ is the eigenvector for λ_j. If the real parts of all eigenvalues are negative, the system is locally stable; if they are all positive, it is unstable. The condition for an economically meaningful saddlepoint solution is that the number of jump variables equal the number of positive eigenvalues. With more jump variables than positive eigenvalues, the equilibrium is indeterminate because some of the jump variables are not pinned down by the requirement that the path converge to the stationary equilibrium. When there are too few jump variables, a saddlepath exists but is out of reach: the constant associated with at least one of the positive eigenvalues cannot be set equal to zero. But if the number of jump variables coincides with the number of positive eigenvalues, the number of freely determined jumps is just large enough to ensure that the constant associated with each positive eigenvalue equals zero. The economy is able therefore to lock onto the saddlepath. Suppose, for example, that $n = 9$ and that there are four jump variables, x_1–x_4, and four positive eigenvalues, λ_1–λ_4. Following some shock, appropriate jumps in x_1–x_4 bring the economy onto the saddlepath where $h_1 = h_2 = h_3 = h_4 = 0$ and

$$
\begin{bmatrix}
x_1(t) - x_1^* \\
x_2(t) - x_2^* \\
\cdot \\
\cdot \\
\cdot \\
\cdot \\
\cdot \\
x_9(t) - x_9^*
\end{bmatrix}
=
\begin{bmatrix}
1 & 1 & 1 & 1 & 1 \\
Z_{25} & Z_{26} & Z_{27} & Z_{28} & Z_{29} \\
\cdot & \cdot & \cdot & \cdot & \cdot \\
\cdot & \cdot & \cdot & \cdot & \cdot \\
\cdot & \cdot & \cdot & \cdot & \cdot \\
\cdot & \cdot & \cdot & \cdot & \cdot \\
\cdot & \cdot & \cdot & \cdot & \cdot \\
Z_{95} & \cdot & \cdot & & Z_{99}
\end{bmatrix}
\begin{bmatrix}
h_5 e^{\lambda_5 t} \\
h_6 e^{\lambda_6 t} \\
\cdot \\
\cdot \\
h_9 e^{\lambda_9 t}
\end{bmatrix}.
\tag{29}
$$

The expressions for the remaining constants are obtained by evaluating the solution paths for the predetermined variables x_5–x_9 at $t = 0$. This yields

$$
\begin{bmatrix}
x_{5,0} - x_5^* \\
\cdot \\
\cdot \\
\cdot \\
x_{9,0} - x_9^*
\end{bmatrix}
=
\begin{bmatrix}
Z_{55} & \cdots & Z_{59} \\
\cdot & & \cdot \\
\cdot & & \cdot \\
\cdot & & \cdot \\
Z_{95} & \cdots & Z_{99}
\end{bmatrix}
\begin{bmatrix}
h_5 \\
\cdot \\
\cdot \\
\cdot \\
h_9
\end{bmatrix},
\tag{30}
$$

which can be solved for h_5–h_9 as a function of the changes in the steady-state values of x_5–x_9.

4.1.3.1 PHASE DIAGRAMS IN SYSTEMS WITH TWO STATE VARIABLES

It is possible to draw phase diagrams for higher order systems with two state variables when the solution is a saddle point. The diagrams are genuinely useful, not just pretty pictures. A second state variable is often needed in development models to accomodate a second sector. But the dynamics in higher order systems with two state variables are generally much more complicated than the dynamics in 2×2 systems or higher order systems with one state variable. Any tool that makes it easier to characterize the qualitative properties of the transition path is of value when the system has two state variables.

The Method of Eigenvector Rays

The method of eigenvector rays exploits the presence of zeroes in the coefficient matrix of the linearized system. To illustrate, suppose that in the linearized 4×4 system

$$
\begin{bmatrix} \dot{x}_1 \\ \dot{x}_2 \\ \dot{x}_3 \\ \dot{x}_4 \end{bmatrix} = \begin{bmatrix} f_1^1 & f_2^1 & f_3^1 & f_4^1 \\ f_1^2 & f_2^2 & f_3^2 & f_4^2 \\ f_1^3 & 0 & f_3^3 & 0 \\ 0 & f_2^4 & 0 & f_4^4 \end{bmatrix} \begin{bmatrix} x_1 - x_1^* \\ x_2 - x_2^* \\ x_3 - x_3^* \\ x_4 - x_4^* \end{bmatrix} \tag{31}
$$

x_1 and x_2 are jump variables and the stationary equilibrium is a saddle point. Let λ_3 and λ_4 denote the system's two negative eigenvalues, with $\lambda_3 < \lambda_4$. The eigenvectors associated with λ_3 and λ_4 are obtained from solving

$$
\begin{bmatrix} f_1^1 & f_2^1 & f_3^1 & f_4^1 \\ f_1^2 & f_2^2 & f_3^2 & f_4^2 \\ f_1^3 & 0 & f_3^3 & 0 \\ 0 & f_2^4 & 0 & f_4^4 \end{bmatrix} \begin{bmatrix} Z_{1j} \\ Z_{2j} \\ Z_{3j} \\ Z_{4j} \end{bmatrix} = \lambda_j \begin{bmatrix} Z_{1j} \\ Z_{2j} \\ Z_{3j} \\ Z_{4j} \end{bmatrix}, \qquad j = 3, 4. \tag{32}
$$

Thanks to the zeroes, the third row of this matrix equation yields two *eigenvector rays* in (x_1, x_3) space:

$$
\left. \frac{x_1 - x_1^*}{x_3 - x_3^*} \right|_{\lambda_j = \lambda_3} = \frac{\lambda_3 - f_3^3}{f_1^3} \qquad \text{(nondominant eigenvector ray)} \tag{33}
$$

$$
\left. \frac{x_1 - x_1^*}{x_3 - x_3^*} \right|_{\lambda_j = \lambda_4} = \frac{\lambda_4 - f_3^3}{f_1^3} \qquad \text{(dominant eigenvector ray).} \tag{34}
$$

The ray formed using the largest negative eigenvalue (λ_4) is the dominant eigenvector ray. For want of imagination, I call the other ray the nondominant eigenvector ray. The names are suggested by the solutions

$$
x_1(t) - x_1^* = A_1 e^{\lambda_3 t} + A_2 e^{\lambda_4 t}, \tag{35}
$$

$$
x_3(t) - x_3^* = B_1 e^{\lambda_3 t} + B_2 e^{\lambda_4 t}. \tag{36}
$$

The paths depend on both λ_3 and λ_4, but the term involving the larger eigenvalue dominates the solution as t becomes large.

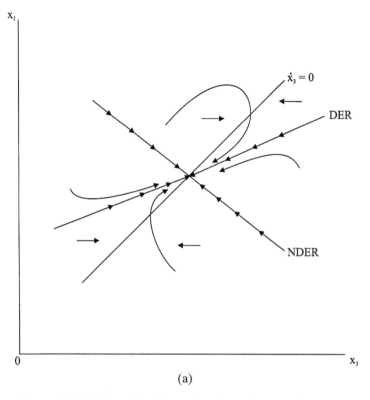

(a)

Figure 4.4. (a) The paths of x_1 and x_3 when the system's two negative eigenvalues are real.

The eigenvector rays and the schedule for $\dot{x}_3 = 0$ supply enough information to track the paths of x_1 and x_3 in Figures 4.4a and b. The paths can be constructed from the east/west directional arrow and the following rules. If the eigenvalues are imaginary, the approach to the steady state is oscillatory. When the eigenvalues are real and the starting point lies on one of the two rays, the path follows that ray to (x_1^*, x_3^*), initial conditions being such that either $A_1 = B_1 = 0$ or $A_2 = B_2 = 0$ in (35)–(36); but if the starting point lies anywhere else, the path never crosses either eigenvector ray and as it approaches the stationary equilibrium it assumes the slope of the dominant eigenvector ray.[7]

The same procedure can be applied to the fourth row in (32) to con-

---

[7] The "starting point" is the position after the jumps in x_1 and x_2 at $t = 0$.

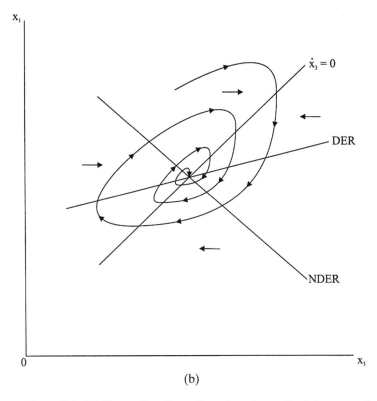

(b)

Figure 4.4. (b) The paths of x_1 and x_3 when the system's two negative eigenvalues are imaginary.

struct a second phase diagram that depicts the paths of x_2 and x_4. In the present example, therefore, the phase space analysis provides a complete picture of the transition path. But this is unusual; it happens only when there are enough equations with the right number of zeroes in the right places.

Dixit's Trick
Dixit's trick (Dixit, 1980) generates a phase diagram for the state variable even when the coefficient matrix lacks zeroes. Go back to (31) and replace the zeroes with the appropriate f_j^i terms. The third and fourth rows then read

$$\dot{x}_3 = f_1^3(x_1 - x_1^*) + f_2^3(x_2 - x_2^*)$$
$$+ f_3^3(x_3 - x_3^*) + f_4^3(x_4 - x_4^*), \tag{37}$$

$$\dot{x}_4 = f_1^4\left(x_1 - x_1^*\right) + f_2^4\left(x_2 - x_2^*\right)$$
$$+ f_3^4\left(x_3 - x_3^*\right) + f_4^4\left(x_4 - x_4^*\right). \tag{38}$$

As yet, there is no phase diagram in sight. But recall that the state variables drive the paths of the jump variables x_1 and x_2. The saddlepoint solution is

$$\begin{bmatrix} x_1(t) - x_1^* \\ x_2(t) - x_2^* \\ x_3(t) - x_3^* \\ x_4(t) - x_4^* \end{bmatrix} = \begin{bmatrix} 1 & 1 \\ Z_{23} & Z_{24} \\ Z_{33} & Z_{34} \\ Z_{43} & Z_{44} \end{bmatrix} \begin{bmatrix} h_3 e^{\lambda_3 t} \\ h_4 e^{\lambda_4 t} \end{bmatrix}, \tag{39}$$

so

$$h_3 e^{\lambda_3 t} = w_1\left[x_3(t) - x_3^*\right] + w_2\left[x_4(t) - x_4^*\right],$$

$$h_4 e^{\lambda_4 t} = w_3\left[x_3(t) - x_3^*\right] + w_4\left[x_4(t) - x_4^*\right],$$

where w_1–w_4 depend on the third and fourth components of the eigenvectors. The solution paths for x_1 and x_2 can thus be written as

$$x_1(t) - x_1^* = (w_1 + w_3)\left[x_3(t) - x_3^*\right] + (w_2 + w_4)\left[x_4(t) - x_4^*\right]$$
$$\equiv k_1\left[x_3(t) - x_3^*\right] + k_2\left[x_4(t) - x_4^*\right],$$

$$x_2(t) - x_2^* = (w_1 Z_{23} + w_3 Z_{24})\left[x_3(t) - x_3^*\right]$$
$$+ (w_2 Z_{23} + w_4 Z_{24})\left[x_4(t) - x_4^*\right]$$
$$\equiv k_3\left[x_3(t) - x_3^*\right] + k_4\left[x_4(t) - x_4^*\right].$$

Substituting these expressions into (37) and (38) gives

$$\left.\frac{x_3 - x_3^*}{x_4 - x_4^*}\right|_{\dot{x}_3 = 0} = -\frac{f_4^3 + f_1^3 k_2 + f_2^3 k_4}{f_3^3 + f_1^3 k_1 + f_2^3 k_3},$$

$$\left.\frac{x_3 - x_3^*}{x_4 - x_4^*}\right|_{\dot{x}_4 = 0} = -\frac{f_4^4 + f_1^4 k_2 + f_2^4 k_4}{f_3^4 + f_1^4 k_1 + f_2^4 k_3}$$

as the loci for which $\dot{x}_3 = 0$ and $\dot{x}_4 = 0$ in state variable space.

4.2   Dynamic Optimization

Optimal control is the most general technique for solving continuous-time dynamic optimization problems. In what follows, I present the optimal control solution for the most basic dynamic optimization problem. For excellent introductions to the use of optimal control in economics, see Arrow and Kurz (1970), Kamien and Schwarz (1981), and Chiang (1992). Seierstad and Sydsaeter (1987) cover much of the same ground, but is more advanced and less user friendly.

In continuous-time macromodels private agents typically solve an intertemporal optimization problem of the type

$$\underset{\{s\}}{\text{Max}} \int_0^\infty f(\mathbf{s}, \mathbf{k}, \alpha) e^{-\rho t} dt, \qquad (40)$$

subject to

$$\dot{k}_i = g^i(\mathbf{s}, \mathbf{k}), \quad i = 1, \dots, n, \qquad (41)$$

where ρ is the discount rate, α is again some exogenous variable, $\mathbf{s} = (s_1, \dots s_m)$ is a vector of control variables, and $\mathbf{k} = (k_1, \dots k_n)$ is a vector of state variables. $\mathbf{s}(t)$ is piecewise continuous and $f(\cdot)$ and $g^i(\cdot)$ are continuous and differentiable.

Static nonlinear programming problems with constraints are solved by setting up the appropriate Lagrangian. A similar approach works for the above dynamic optimization problem. Form the *Hamiltonian*

$$\mathcal{H} = e^{-\rho t} \left[f(\mathbf{s}, \mathbf{k}, \alpha) + \sum_{i=1}^n \phi_i g^i(\mathbf{s}, \mathbf{k}) \right]$$

by attaching time-varying current value multipliers $\phi_i(t)$ to the constraints in (41).[8] (ϕ_i varies over time because the constraints hold period by period.) The *maximum principle* then furnishes the necessary conditions for an optimum:

---

[8] This formulation of the Hamiltonian is a bit unconventional. Usually the Hamiltonian is written as $\mathcal{H} = e^{-\rho t} f(\cdot) + \Sigma_i \tilde{\phi}_i g_i = e^{-\rho t} [f(\cdot) + \Sigma_i \phi_i g_i]$, where $\tilde{\phi}_i$ is the ith present value multiplier and $\phi_i \equiv e^{\rho t} \tilde{\phi}_i$ is the ith current value multiplier. The *current value Hamiltonian* is then defined to be $\mathcal{H}_c \equiv e^{\rho t} \mathcal{H} = f(\cdot) + \Sigma_i \phi_i g_i$. I prefer to work with $\mathcal{H} = e^{-\rho t} [f(\cdot) + \Sigma_i \phi_i g_i]$ because the rule for producing the co-state equation in (42d) is a little easier to remember. When working with the current value Hamiltonian, the co-state equation is generated from $\dot{\phi}_i = \rho \phi_i - \partial \mathcal{H}_c / \partial k_i$.

$$\mathcal{H}_{s_j} = 0 \Rightarrow f_{s_j} + \sum_{i=1}^{n} \phi_i g^i_{s_j} = 0, \qquad j = 1, \ldots, m, \tag{42a}$$

$$\mathcal{H}_{s_j s_j} \leq 0 \Rightarrow f_{s_j s_j} + \sum_{i=1}^{n} \phi_i g^i_{s_j s_j} \leq 0, \qquad j = 1, \ldots, m, \tag{42b}$$

$$\frac{\partial \mathcal{H}}{\partial (e^{-\rho t} \phi_i)} = \dot{k}_i \Rightarrow \dot{k}_i = g^i(\mathbf{s}, \mathbf{k}, \alpha), \qquad i = 1, \ldots, n, \tag{42c}$$

$$\frac{d(e^{-\rho t} \phi_c)}{dt} = -\partial \mathcal{H} / \partial k_c \Rightarrow \dot{\phi}_c = \rho \phi_c - f_{k_c} - \sum_{i=1}^{n} \phi_i g^i_{k_c},$$

$$c = 1, \ldots, n, \tag{42d}$$

$$\lim_{t \to \infty} \phi_i(t) e^{-\rho t} = 0, \qquad i = 1, \ldots, n. \tag{42e}$$

These conditions have natural economic interpretations. As usual, the multipliers can be viewed as shadow prices: $\phi_i(t)$ measures the increment in the value of the objective function of an exogenous increase in k_i at time t, with the path adjusted to be optimal thereafter. Thus $f + \Sigma \ \phi_i g^i = f + \Sigma \ \phi_i \dot{k}_i$ measures the gain in value at time t from current "felicity" and the accumulation of assets that will confer benefits in the future. The control variables are chosen to maximize this gain at each point in time for given values of $\phi_1, \ldots, \phi_n$ and $k_1, \ldots, k_n$. This requires $\mathcal{H}_{s_j} = 0$ and $\mathcal{H}_{s_j s_j} \leq 0$. Equation (42c) simply recovers the constraints in (41), while (42d) says that along an optimal path the return on asset k_c inclusive of capital gains $\dot{\phi}_c / \phi_c$ should equal the discount factor ρ. Finally, the *transversality conditions* in (42e) also belong in the set of necessary conditions. The confusion surrounding this point has recently been resolved by Becker and Boyd (1997). Following their explanation, note that one of the options available to the private agent is to accumulate a little more k_i and hold the asset forever. On an optimal path where all opportunities for intertemporal arbitrage have been fully exploited, this action should not yield a net gain. The most general formulation of the transversality condition is therefore that *unreversed arbitrage* is not profitable in the neighborhood of the optimal path. This *usually* implies that the present value shadow price vanishes in the infinitely long run. There are some special cases, however, in which the optimal solution violates (42e).[9] In these cases, undertaking an unreversed arbitrage on the

---

[9] See Halkin (1974) and Shell (1969). Chiang (1990, pp. 240–251) makes the important point that (42e) does not apply in the Halkin and Shell "counterexamples" because in their examples a fixed terminal state is implicit in the struc-

optimal path results in an infinite loss. The infinite loss cannot be picked up by (42e) because the present value shadow price vanishes only when the private agent is *indifferent* to attempting an unreversed arbitrage. This does not mean that the transversality condition is not one of the necessary conditions for an optimum. The transversality condition is still necessary, but it does not take the usual form stated in (42e).

In the models that appear in later chapters, the transversality condition is (42e) when k_i is freely chosen and $\lim_{t \to \infty} \phi_i(t)e^{-\rho t}k_i = 0$ when the state variable is subject to a nonnegativity constraint. To save space, I will omit the transversality condition from the list of necessary conditions. The condition is satisfied, however, by the saddlepoint solution. Since the saddlepath takes the economy to a stationary equilibrium where all s_j and k_i are constant, the ϕ_i in (42a) also converge to constant values. The present value shadow prices $\phi_i(t)e^{-\rho t}$ thus approach zero asymptotically, as required by the transversality conditions.

The necessary conditions (42a)–(42e) are also sufficient for global optimality provided that f, $\mathbf{g} = [g^1(\mathbf{s}, \mathbf{k}, \alpha), \ldots, g^n(\mathbf{s}, \mathbf{k}, \alpha)]$ and $\boldsymbol{\phi} = [\phi_1(t), \ldots, \phi_n(t)]$ satisfy certain restrictions. If $\mathbf{g}$ is nonlinear in either $\mathbf{k}$ or $\mathbf{s}$, then the Mangasarian sufficiency theorem (Mangasarian, 1965) requires $\phi(t) \geq 0$ for all t and that both f and $\mathbf{g}$ be concave in $(\mathbf{s}, \mathbf{k})$. When $\mathbf{g}$ is linear and f is concave in $(\mathbf{s}, \mathbf{k})$, (42a)–(42e) are necessary and sufficient regardless of the sign of $\phi(t)$; and if f and g are strictly concave, the conditions define the unique global optimum. Most economic models will satisfy these concavity conditions. When they do not, one can appeal to a weaker sufficiency condition derived by Arrow. To evaluate the Arrow condition, let $\bar{\mathbf{s}}(\mathbf{k}, \boldsymbol{\phi})$ refer to the values of $s_1, \ldots s_m$ that satisfy (42a). Plug $\bar{\mathbf{s}}(\mathbf{k}, \boldsymbol{\phi})$ into $\mathcal{H}$ to get the maximized Hamiltonian H

$$\mathsf{H}[t, \bar{\mathbf{s}}(\mathbf{k}, \boldsymbol{\phi}), \mathbf{k}, \boldsymbol{\phi}, \alpha] = e^{-\rho t}\left\{f[\bar{\mathbf{s}}(\mathbf{k}, \boldsymbol{\phi}), \mathbf{k}, \alpha] + \sum_{i=1}^{n} \phi_i g^i[\bar{\mathbf{s}}(\mathbf{k}, \boldsymbol{\phi}), \mathbf{k}]\right\}.$$

The Arrow theorem then states that the necessary conditions in (42a)–(42e) are sufficient for a global optimum if H is concave in $\mathbf{k}$ for given ϕ and for all t.[10]

ture of the optimization problem. (There is no discounting of future felicity $f(\cdot)$ in either example. The optimal path must terminate therefore at the upper bound of f.) The correct transversality condition in such cases is not (42e) but rather the condition that the maximized value of the Hamiltonian equal zero at every point in time.
[10] Arrow's theorem is presented in Arrow and Kurz (1970, p. 45). The Arrow and Mangasarian sufficiency theorems are stated for finite horizon problems. They generalize, however, to the infinite horizon case (Seierstad and Sydsaeter, 1987, pp. 234–236).

4.2.1   Saddlepoint Solutions and Optimal Control

A system of differential equations in $\mathbf{k}$ and ϕ falls out directly from the necessary conditions. It is usually more informative, however, to solve (42a) for $\phi_i = v_i(\mathbf{s}, \mathbf{k}, \alpha), i = 1, \ldots, n$ and work with a system of $n + m$ non-linear differential equations that describe the paths of k_i and the control variables s_i (which are generally of more interest than the unobservable shadow prices ϕ_i). A linear approximation of the system can then be generated by taking a first-order Taylor series expansion around the stationary equilibrium $(\mathbf{s}^*, \mathbf{k}^*)$. Since the freely chosen control variables are *jump* variables, the dynamics will be well defined if the linearized system is a saddle point with m positive eigenvalues.

The lives of economists would be a little more pleasant if this were a complete description of what is involved in solving the private agent's optimization problem in the context of a dynamic general equilibrium model. Sadly, it is not. The set of exogenous variables α typically includes some variables that the private agent views as parametric but which depend indirectly on $\mathbf{s}$ and $\mathbf{k}$ through economywide interactions. Because the paths of $\mathbf{s}$, $\mathbf{k}$, and α are interdependent in general equilibrium, the economy's dynamics and the private agent's intertemporal optimization problem have to be solved jointly in a consistent manner. To see what this entails, suppose α is the vector (P, z), where P is the price of some good that is endogenous in the model and z is exogenous. Terms involving $\dot{P}$ will then appear after differentiating (42a) with respect to time. It is necessary, therefore, to relate the path of P to the paths of s_i and k_i. This is done by solving for P as a function of $s_1, \ldots, s_m$ and $k_1, \ldots, k_n$ in the *pseudostatic variant of the model* where the control and state variables are treated as exogenous. Once the solution for $P = \Lambda(\mathbf{s}, \mathbf{k})$ is in hand, one can replace $\dot{P}$ with $\Lambda_1\dot{s}_1, \ldots, \Lambda_m\dot{s}_m, \Lambda_{m+1}\dot{k}_1, \ldots, \Lambda_{m+n}\dot{k}_n$ and collect terms to form a system of differential equations in $\mathbf{s}$ and $\mathbf{k}$. If P is still present somewhere in level form, then the quasi-reduced form solution $P = \Lambda(\mathbf{s}, \mathbf{k})$ will be used a second time when linearizing the system around a stationary equilibrium.

4.3   An Extended Example

Consider a small LDC that exports an agricultural good and imports a manufactured good that may be used either for consumption or investment. The export good is produced by means of land T and labor L_x and the manufactured good by means of labor L_m and capital K. Technology exhibits constant returns to scale and firms are perfectly competitive. Q_i and C^i denote output and the unit cost function in sector i, while w, v, r, and P_x stand for the wage rate, the land rental, the capital rental, and the price of the export good. The import good is the numeraire ($P_m = 1$) and the total supply of labor is fixed at L.

At a given point in time, the supply side of this economy is defined by the zero-profit conditions

$$P_x = C^x(w, v), \tag{43}$$

$$1 = C^m(w, r); \tag{44}$$

the sectoral labor demands

$$L_m = C^m_w(w, r)Q_m, \tag{45}$$

$$L_x = C^x_w(w, v)Q_x; \tag{46}$$

and the full-employment conditions

$$L_m + L_x = L, \tag{47}$$

$$C^x_v(w, v)Q_x = T, \tag{48}$$

$$C^m_r(w, r)Q_m = K. \tag{49}$$

The equilibrium described by (43)–(49) evolves over time as investment I alters the capital stock. Investment is undertaken by a representative agent who possesses perfect foresight and solves the problem

$$\underset{\{E, I\}}{\text{Max}} \int_0^\infty V(P_x, E)e^{-\rho t}dt \tag{50}$$

subject to

$$E + I = R(P_x, K), \tag{51}$$

$$\dot{K} = I - \delta K, \tag{52}$$

where ρ is the pure time preference rate, E is aggregate consumption, δ is the depreciation rate of capital, and $V(\cdot)$ and $R(\cdot)$ are the indirect utility function and the revenue function.

a. Derive the dynamic system that characterizes the paths of I and K. Demonstrate that the system is saddlepoint stable.
b. Show that the slope of the saddlepath is $dI/dK = \lambda_2 + \delta$, where λ_2 is the negative eigenvalue. Construct the various possible phase diagrams.
c. Suppose the economy is initially at a stationary equilibrium and that P_x increases. Show that on impact investment declines by

$$dI|_{t=0} = \lambda_2 \beta_x (L_x / L_m) K_o \hat{P}_x,$$

where K_o is the initial capital stock and β_x is the wage elasticity of labor demand in sector x. (β_x is defined to be positive.)

d. If investment is undertaken by capitalists instead of a representative agent, then the profit function $\pi(w, K)$ replaces the revenue function in (51). (Note that $\pi_w = -L_m$ and $\pi_K = r$. Also, E now refers to aggregate consumption of just capitalists.) How does this change the solution procedure?

Solution

a. The present value Hamiltonian for the problem in (41)–(43) is

$$\mathcal{H} = e^{-\rho t}\{V[P_x, R(P_x, K) - I] + \phi(I - \delta K)\},$$

where ϕ is the multiplier appended to the constraint (52) and E has been eliminated by substituting the budget constraint into the indirect utility function. The first-order condition associated with the choice variable I is

$$V_E[P_x, R(P_x, K) - I] = \phi. \tag{53}$$

The co-state equation $[d(e^{-\rho t}\phi)/dt = -\partial\mathcal{H}/\partial K]$ reads

$$\dot{\phi} = V_E(\rho + \delta - r), \tag{54}$$

since $V_E = \phi$ and $R_K = r$.

To eliminate the shadow price ϕ, differentiate (53) with respect to time and substitute for $\dot{\phi}$ from (54):

$$r\dot{K} - \dot{I} = (\rho + \delta - r)V_E / V_{EE}. \tag{55}$$

Substituting for $\dot{K}$ from (52), this becomes

$$\dot{I} = r(I - \delta K) + (r - \rho - \delta)V_E / V_{EE}. \tag{56}$$

Before we can linearize (56), we need to know how r depends on K. To obtain the desired solution, we solve the pseudostatic variant of the model where K and I are treated as exogenous variables. From (43)–(44),

$$\hat{v} = \frac{\hat{P}_x - \theta_L^x \hat{w}}{\theta_T^x}, \tag{57}$$

$$\hat{r} = -\frac{\theta_L^m}{\theta_K^m}\hat{w}, \tag{58}$$

where θ_j^i is the cost share of factor j in sector i. The path of the market-clearing wage depends on P_x and the path of K. Substituting for Q_i from (39) and (40), we can write the demands for labor as

$$L_m = KC_w^m(w,r)/C_r^m(w,r), \tag{45'}$$

$$L_x = TC_w^x(w,v)/C_v^x(w,v). \tag{46'}$$

Recall that the Allen–Uzawa partial elasticity of substitution between factors j and s is $\sigma_{js} = C_{js}C/C_jC_s$. After making use of this result and the adding-up restriction $\theta_j\sigma_{jj} = -\theta_s\sigma_{js}$, we have from (45'), (46'), (57), and (58)

$$\hat{L}_m = -\beta_m\hat{w} + \hat{K}, \tag{59}$$

$$\hat{L}_x = -\beta_x(\hat{w} - \hat{P}_x), \tag{60}$$

where $\beta_m \equiv \sigma_{LK}/\theta_K^m$ and $\beta_x \equiv \sigma_{LT}/\theta_T^x$ are the wage elasticities of labor demand. The above solutions and (47) give

$$\hat{w} = b_1 dK + b_2\hat{P}_x, \tag{61}$$

where $b_1 \equiv L_m/(\beta_m L_m + \beta_x L_x)K$ and $b_2 \equiv L_x\beta_x/(\beta_m L_m + \beta_x L_x)$. Hence, the capital rental falls when an increase in K or P_x bids up the market-clearing wage:

$$\hat{r} = -\frac{\theta_L^m}{\theta_K^m}(b_1 dK + b_2\hat{P}_x). \tag{62}$$

Now linearize (52) and (56) around the stationary equilibrium (I^*, K^*), taking into account that $\hat{r} = -(\theta_L^m b_1/\theta_K^m)dK$. Note also that we can ignore how r varies in the first term and how V_E/V_{EE} varies in the second term because at a stationary equilibrium $I = \delta K$ and $r = \rho + \delta$. Linearization thus yields the fairly simple system

$$\begin{bmatrix} \dot{I} \\ \dot{K} \end{bmatrix} = \begin{bmatrix} r & -r\left(\dfrac{\theta_L^m b_1 V_E}{\theta_K^m V_{EE}} + \delta\right) \\ 1 & -\delta \end{bmatrix}\begin{bmatrix} I(t) - I^* \\ K(t) - K^* \end{bmatrix}. \tag{63}$$

The determinant of the coefficient matrix is

$$\Delta = \frac{\theta_L^m b_1 r V_E}{\theta_K^m V_{EE}} < 0.$$

Since $\Delta = \lambda_1 \lambda_2$, one eigenvalue is positive and the other is negative. The stationary equilibrium is therefore a saddle point.

b. Find the system's eigenvectors from

$$\begin{bmatrix} r - r\left(\dfrac{\theta_L^m b_1 V_E}{\theta_K^m V_{EE}} + \delta \right) \\ 1 & -\delta \end{bmatrix} \begin{bmatrix} Z_{1j} \\ Z_{2j} \end{bmatrix} = \begin{bmatrix} \lambda_j Z_{1j} \\ \lambda_j Z_{2j} \end{bmatrix}. \tag{64}$$

Set the first component in each eigenvector equal to unity. The second row of the above matrix equation then produces

$$Z_{2j} = (\lambda_j + \delta)^{-1},$$

and thus the general solution is

$$\begin{bmatrix} I(t) - I^* \\ K(t) - K^* \end{bmatrix} = \begin{bmatrix} 1 & 1 \\ (\lambda_1 + \delta)^{-1} & (\lambda_2 + \delta)^{-1} \end{bmatrix} \begin{bmatrix} h_1 e^{\lambda_1 t} \\ h_2 e^{\lambda_2 t} \end{bmatrix}, \tag{65}$$

where the h_i are determined by initial conditions and $\lambda_1 > 0$ and $\lambda_2 < 0$.

The unique path that converges to the stationary equilibrium is found by setting $h_1 = 0$. This gives

$$I(t) - I^* = h_2 e^{\lambda_2 t}, \tag{66}$$

$$K(t) - K^* = \frac{h_2}{\lambda_2 + \delta} e^{\lambda_2 t}, \tag{67}$$

so the equation for the saddlepath is

$$\left. \frac{I - I^*}{K - K^*} \right|_{\text{saddlepath}} = \lambda_2 + \delta \gtrless 0. \tag{68}$$

To construct the phase diagrams shown in Figures 4.5a and b, derive from (63) the loci for which $\dot{I} = 0$ and $\dot{K} = 0$:

$$\left. \frac{I - I^*}{K - K^*} \right|_{\dot{I}=0} = \frac{\theta_L^m b_1 V_E}{\theta_K^m V_{EE}} + \delta \gtrless 0, \tag{69}$$

$$\left. \frac{I - I^*}{K - K^*} \right|_{\dot{K}=0} = \delta. \tag{70}$$

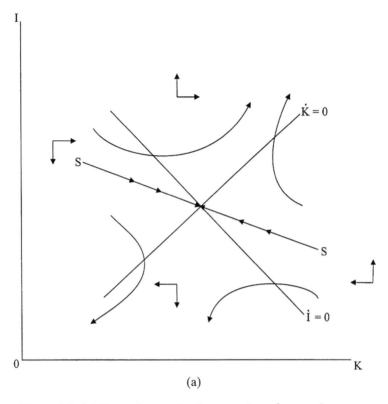

(a)

Figure 4.5. (a) Phase diagram for the case where $\lambda_2 + \sigma < 0$.

The $\dot{K} = 0$ schedule is positively sloped as replacement investment rises
with the size of the capital stock. At points to the left of the schedule,
net investment is positive and the capital stock is increasing; conversely,
K is decreasing in the region to the right of the schedule. The east/west
directional arrow thus points toward the $\dot{K} = 0$ schedule. By contrast, the
north/south directional arrow points *away* from the $\dot{I} = 0$ schedule ($\partial \dot{I}/\partial I$
$= r > 0$). This destabilizing force pulls most paths away from the station-
ary equilibrium, resulting in a saddlepoint solution. Tracing out the paths
in different regions establishes that the convergent saddlepath is flatter
than and slopes in the same direction as the the $\dot{I} = 0$ schedule.
c. At $t = 0$, equations (66)–(67) yield

$$I(0) = I^* + (\lambda_2 + \delta)(K_o - K^*). \tag{71}$$

Subtract the initial level of investment, I_o, from both sides:

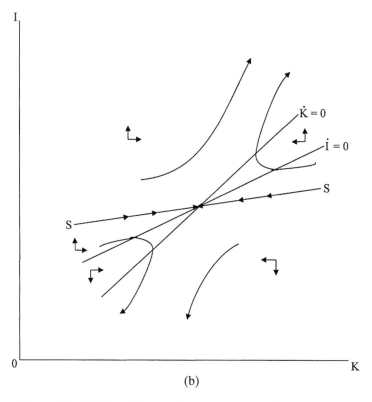

(b)

Figure 4.5. (b) Phase diagram for the case where $\lambda_2 + \sigma > 0$.

$$I(0) - I_o = I^* - I_o + (\lambda_2 + \delta)(K_o - K^*). \tag{72}$$

Since $I^* - I_o = \delta(K^* - K_o)$, this simplifies to

$$\underbrace{I(0) - I_o}_{\text{jump in } I \text{ at } t=0} = \lambda_2 \times \underbrace{(K_o - K^*)}_{\substack{\text{change in the} \\ \text{steady-state} \\ \text{capital stock}}}. \tag{73}$$

Recall that $r = \rho + \delta$ across steady states. Consequently, we can set $\hat{r} = 0$ and solve (62) for K:

$$dK = K^* - K_o = -\beta_x(L_x/L_m)K_o\hat{P}_x < 0. \tag{74}$$

Substituting this into (73) produces

$$I(0) - I_o = dI|_{t=0} = \lambda_2\beta_x(L_x/L_m)K_o\hat{P}_x < 0. \tag{75}$$

d. When $\pi(w, K)$ replaces $R(P_x, K)$, equation (53) becomes

$$V_E[P_x, \pi(w, K) - I] = \phi. \tag{53'}$$

Using (53′) and (54) to eliminate $\dot{\phi}$, we now get

$$r\dot{K} - \dot{w}L_m - \dot{I} = (\rho + \delta - r)V_E/V_{EE}. \tag{55'}$$

To eliminate $\dot{w}$, use the solution in (61) from the pseudostatic variant of the model. Substituting $\dot{w} = wb_1\dot{K}$ into (61) gives

$$(r - wL_m b_1)\dot{K} - \dot{I} = (\rho + \delta - r)V_E/V_{EE}. \tag{55''}$$

The rest of the solution procedure is the same.

CHAPTER 5

Underemployment, Underinvestment, and Optimal Trade Policy

Chapter 3 ended with the discouraging conclusion that we know much more about the consequences of bad trade policy than about the makeup of optimal trade policy. The orthodox critique of protection in LDCs has established to almost everyone's satisfaction that extreme import-substituting policies are detrimental. But what of less extreme policies? Is moderate protection appropriate in some countries? The answer of classical trade theory is a flat no: distortions in goods and factor markets which make protection welfare-improving can be dealt with more effectively by nontrade taxes and subsidies that directly counteract the source of market failure. Most countries are told therefore to move as rapidly and as far toward free trade as political contraints permit. The problem with this uncompromising position is that free trade is not optimal if nontrade taxes and subsidies incur greater administrative costs or present policy makers with a less favorable strategic environment than trade taxes. These qualifications matter. While it is not clear how much adverse strategic effects weaken the case for free trade, there is little doubt that administrative costs are important in practice. Fraud and enforcement problems are likely to undermine even moderately differentiated tax/subsidy systems; consequently, optimal tax policy boils down to finding *simple* systems that minimize demands on administrative capabilities and satisfy a few basic, important objectives (Bird, 1991; Khalizadeh-Shirazi and Shah, 1991; Thirsk, 1991). There is now a broad consensus in the development public finance literature that this means that most countries should rely on a consumption-based VAT (value added tax) to raise revenue and use trade taxes to ameliorate major market failures. Of course, the separation of tasks is not really this clean. Trade taxes are a source of revenue and a VAT of limited scope distorts consumer prices and may also affect the distortions targeted by the trade ministry. The taxes have to be carefully coordinated to achieve the twin objectives of sufficient revenue generation and greater efficiency.

Not much is known about what this implies for policy, except that it will not be optimal to favor the import-competing sector with an effective rate of protection of 150%. Formal theoretical analyses of optimal trade policy in LDCs are generally based on simple static models that allow lump-sum taxes/transfers and ignore both nontradables production and imports of intermediate inputs and capital equipment. Such models cannot say anything about how tariffs should differ across different types of imports or about how trade taxes should be coordinated with other taxes to meet the government's revenue needs. Moreover, in the absence of nontradables production, the tradables sectors compete for a fixed stock of resources. Consequently, protection (an import subsidy) is roughly equivalent to an export tax (subsidy). The overly simplified sectoral structure rules out the possibility that it may be desirable to combine protection with export promotion, a policy mix that seems to have worked well in many countries, including the East Asian success stories.

My objective in this chapter is to examine the connection between trade policy and the problems of underemployment and underinvestment when government spending has to be financed by a combination of trade taxes and a consumption-based VAT. More specifically, I characterize optimal trade policy in a dynamic general equilibrium model that features capital and labor market distortions of the type discussed in Chapter 3. The model incorporates export, import-competing and nontradables production, capital accumulation in all sectors, and imports of intermediate inputs and machinery as well as imports of consumer goods. The extra structural detail enables the model to confront squarely a number of fundamental policy issues: Should the trade regime have a pronounced bias, or is it best to combine protection with export promotion? Is there any rationale for escalation – for having export subsidies and import duties on consumer goods higher than duties on intermediates inputs and capital goods? How sensitive is the design of optimal trade policy to basic structural features of the economy, such as the export share of primary products and the degree of dependence on imported machinery and intermediate inputs?

5.1 The Model

I lay out the model in stages, beginning with the set of goods and factor prices.

5.1.1 Goods and Factor Prices

Firms import intermediate inputs and capital goods and produce a nontraded good, an exportable good, and an importable consumer good. Production of tradable goods is subject to a value added tax v. Nontradables, however, escape taxation as they are produced by small firms who belong to the informal sector. The VAT applies symmetrically to imports, with full rebates for taxes paid on noncompetitive intermediate inputs and capital goods, and exports are zero-rated (i.e., exempt from the tax). These provisions ensure a level playing field for domestic vs. foreign firms. That is, the VAT is structured to be equivalent to an equal-rate tax on consumption of the importable and exportable goods. It is important that the tax applies only to tradable consumer goods. If the VAT covered nontradables as well, it would be a lump-sum tax (under the assumption that labor supply is inelastic). But since the informal sector is beyond the reach of the tax authorities, the VAT is not a cost-less means of raising revenue; it distorts the relative price of tradable consumer goods.

Let P_i denote the price received by firms in sector i ($i = m, n, x$) and P_z the price of imported intermediates. The price of imported capital, the numeraire good, is set at unity. The producer prices of the other traded goods are

$$P_x = 1 + s, \tag{1a}$$

$$P_m = 1 + h, \tag{1b}$$

$$P_z = 1 + g, \tag{1c}$$

where s is the export subsidy and h and g are the respective tariffs on imports of consumer goods and intermediates. The consumer prices for traded goods, P_{mc} and P_{xc}, are marked up by the VAT. To avoid cascading taxes, v enters additively:

$$P_{mc} = 1 + h + v, \tag{1d}$$

$$P_{xc} = 1 + s + v. \tag{1e}$$

Physical capital is produced by combining machinery and a nontraded input (construction). The unit cost function $C^k(1, P_n)$ sets the supply price of capital:

$$P_k = C^k(1, P_n). \tag{1f}$$

Production in the nontradables sector and the import-competing manufacturing sector requires capital, labor, and imported intermediates. Production in the export sector requires these three inputs and also land or some other natural resource. In each sector, firms are perfectly competitive and technology exhibits constant returns to scale. The zero-profit condition thus holds everywhere:

$$P_m = C^m(w_m, P_z, r_m), \tag{2a}$$

$$P_n = C^n(w, P_z, r_n), \tag{2b}$$

$$P_x = C^x(w, P_z, r_x, f), \tag{2c}$$

where $C^i(\cdot)$ is the unit cost function in sector i, w_m is the wage in the manufacturing sector, w is the wage in the nontradables and export sectors; r_i is the capital rental in sector i, and f is the land rental. The capital rentals vary by sector because, once bolted into place, capital is immobile and receives the quasi-rent generated by the prevailing prices for other goods and factors. Prior to installation, capital is equally suitable for production in any sector; after installation, it is a sector-specific input.

The labor market is dualistic. While the wage in the export and nontradables sectors is governed by basic market forces, in the manufacturing sector w_m adjusts so as to preserve workers' real consumption wage, viz.

$$w_m = \varphi b(P_{mc}, P_{xc}, P_n). \tag{3a}$$

The expression on the right side is the expenditure function for homothetic preferences. φ depends on the level of utility, and $b(\cdot)$ corresponds to the exact consumer price index. If the real consumption wage is fixed, φ is constant and w_m varies proportionately with b. Note that for small changes

$$\hat{w}_m = \gamma_n \hat{P}_n + \gamma_m \hat{P}_{mc} + \gamma_x \hat{P}_{xc}, \qquad \gamma_m + \gamma_x + \gamma_n = 1, \tag{3b}$$

where γ_i is the consumption share of good i.

My main reason for adopting the atheoretic rule in (3b) is that the real wage in the formal sector depends partly or wholly on political forces that are not well understood. In some countries w_m is fixed directly by a minimum wage law.[1] In others, unions and firms bargain over the wage, but the outcome of the bargaining process is influenced by which party receives more support from the government.[2] Rather than attempt to bring political elements within the purview of the model, I treat the real wage as an exogenous variable.[3]

---

[1] Examples include Costa Rica, Zimbabwe, Sri Lanka, and Ecuador (where 117 commissions set minimum wages for different sectors).
[2] Tripartite bargaining is very common in LDCs (Svejnar, 1989; Morrison, 1994).
[3] Svejnar (1989) emphasizes that very little is known about the wage determination process in the formal sector.

5.1.2   Technology and Factor Demands

Utilizing Shephard's lemma, the demands for labor L_i, intermediates Z_i, capital K_i, and land T may be stated as

$$L_i = C_w^i Q_i, \qquad (4a\text{–}4c)$$

$$Z_i = C_{p_z}^i Q_i, \qquad (5a\text{–}5c)$$

$$K_i = C_r^i Q_i, \qquad (6a\text{–}6c)$$

$$T = C_f^x Q_x, \qquad (7)$$

where Q_i is gross output.

The nature of technology can be retrieved from the cost functions by using the formulas that link the partial derivatives of C^k, C^m, C^n, and C^x to the Allen–Uzawa partial elasticities of substitution σ_{ji}. The technology for producing capital goods is defined by σ^k, the elasticity of substitution between the nontraded and imported components. If σ^k is small, imports are critical to the investment process – in the limiting case where $\sigma^k = 0$, technology exhibits fixed coefficients and it is impossible to accumulate capital without purchasing additional equipment.

In the import-competing, export, and nontradables sectors I work with two-tiered production functions defined by imposing the restrictions

$$\sigma_{KZ}^i = \sigma_{LZ}^i = \sigma_1^i, \qquad \sigma_{KL}^i = \frac{\sigma_2^i - \theta_Z^i \sigma_1^i}{1 - \theta_Z^i}, \qquad i = m, n$$

$$\sigma_{KZ}^x = \sigma_{LZ}^x = \sigma_{TZ}^x = \sigma_1^x, \qquad \sigma_{KL}^x = \sigma_{KT}^x = \sigma_{TL}^x = \frac{\sigma_2^x - \theta_Z^x \sigma_1^x}{1 - \theta_Z^x}.$$

At the lower tier, domestic primary factors produce a composite input, value added. At the upper tier, value added is combined with imported inputs to produce gross output. σ_1 is the elasticity of substitution between value added and imported inputs, σ_2 is the elasticity of substitution between primary factors, and θ_Z is the cost share of imported inputs. This specification of technology is fairly flexible and allows us to examine the implications for trade policy of two structural rigidities commonly emphasized in the literature: (1) low price responsiveness of supply in the export sector (especially when most exports are primary products), and (2) "dependence" of domestic production on the availability of imports when there is little scope for substitution between primary factors and imported raw materials, parts, and other intermediate inputs (i.e., $\sigma_1^i \ll \sigma_2^i$).

2.1.3 Consumption, Investment, and Capital Accumulation

I_i, K_i, and $D^i(\mathbf{P}_c, u)$ denote investment in sector i, the capital stock in sector i, and the compensated demand for good i. The arguments of the compensated demand function are current utility u and the price vector $\mathbf{P}_c = (P_{mc}, P_n, P_{xc})$. Current utility depends on prices and total consumption spending E as summarized by the indirect utility function $V(\mathbf{P}_c, E)$. The representative agent chooses E and investment in sector i so as to maximize the time separable utility function

$$\int_0^\infty V(\mathbf{P}_c, E)e^{-\rho t}\,dt, \tag{8}$$

subject to the laws of motion for the capital stocks

$$\dot{K}_i = I_i - \delta K_i, \tag{9a–9c}$$

and the budget constraint

$$E + P_k[I + \phi_m(I_m/K_m - \delta)K_m + \phi_x(I_x/K_x - \delta)K_x \\ + \phi_n(I_n/K_n - \delta)K_n] = R(\mathbf{P}, P_z, K_m, K_n, K_x, L_m) + J, \tag{10}$$

where ρ is the pure time preference rate, $\mathbf{P} = (P_m, P_x, P_n)$ is the vector of producer prices, J is lump-sum transfers, $I \equiv I_m + I_n + I_x$ is aggregate investment, and σ is the depreciation rate of capital. The budget constraint requires that spending on consumption and investment not exceed income plus transfers. $R(\cdot)$ measures value added at domestic prices and has the same properties as the revenue function used in earlier chapters: $\partial R/\partial P_i = Q_i$, $\partial R/\partial K_i = r_i$, and $\partial R/\partial L_m = w_m - w$, while $-\partial R/\partial P_z = Z_m + Z_n + Z_x$, the total demand for imported intermediates. In the second term on the left side, $\phi_i(I_i/K_i - \delta)K_i$ captures the costs firms incur when they adjust the capital stock through net investment. Following Lucas (1967), I assume that net investment uses up some capital goods (installed capital differs from purchased capital) and that adjustment costs are non-negative and strictly convex: $\phi_i \geq 0$, $\phi_i(0) = \phi_i'(0) = 0$, $\phi_i' \gtrless 0$ as $I_i \gtrless \delta K_i$ and $\phi_i'' > 0$. Adjustment costs of this type are essential to support the assumption of sector-specific capital. Without adjustment costs, the representative agent sets investment at positive infinity in the sector where the capital rental is highest and lowers investment in the other two sectors to negative infinity. This eliminates the difference in returns before a finite amount of time elapses, effectively reducing the model to one in which capital is intersectorally mobile.

5.1.4   The Government Budget Constraint

Lump-sum transfers are included in the model to create a need for government revenue while side-stepping the issue of how to value government services relative to private consumption. Transfers and export subsidies are paid for by the VAT and tariff collections:

$$J + s[Q_x - D^x(\mathbf{P}_c, u)] = v[D^m(\mathbf{P}_c, u) + D^x(\mathbf{P}_c, u)]$$
$$+ g(Z_m + Z_n + Z_x) + h[D^m(\mathbf{P}_c, u) - Q_m]. \tag{11}$$

If real transfers were fixed, growth would relax the government budget constraint. I assume instead that the need (or social pressure) for government spending increases *pari passu* with the size of the economy. With transfers being a fixed fraction χ of net national product, (11) reads

$$v[D^m(\mathbf{P}_c, u) + D^x(\mathbf{P}_c, u)] = \chi[R(\cdot) - P_k \delta K] + s[Q_x - D^x(\mathbf{P}_c, u)]$$
$$- gZ - h[D^m(\mathbf{P}_c, u) - Q_m], \tag{11'}$$

where $K \equiv K_m + K_n + K_x$ is the aggregate capital stock and $Z \equiv Z_m + Z_n + Z_x$ is total purchases of imported intermediates.

The social planner chooses s, g, h, and v subject to the constraint that (11') be satisfied. In principle, all trade and income taxes could vary continuously. However, not only is it much more difficult to solve the social planner's optimization problem when each policy instrument varies each period,[4] it is also hard to see how the government could effectively commit to a particular trade regime if trade taxes adjust frequently to iron out small swings in the fiscal deficit. Consequently, although it is not a perfect solution, I assume the government sets g, s, and h immediately at their optimal values and adjusts the VAT v to maintain a balanced budget during the adjustment process.[5,6]

---

[4] There is a potential time consistency problem when the government chooses trade taxes period by period.

[5] Since the budget constraint can be written as

$$(v+h)D^m + (v+s)D^x = J + hQ_m + sQ_x - gZ,$$

5.1.5   The Market Clearing Conditions

Prices adjust to equate supply and demand in the markets for labor, land, and the nontraded good. Equation (7) already ensures that the land market clears. The other two markets clear when

$$Q_n = D^n(\mathbf{P}_c, u) + C_n^k(P_n)[I + \phi_m(I_m/K_m - \delta)K_m$$
$$= +\phi_x(I_x/K_x - \delta)K_x + \phi_n(I_n/K_n - \delta)K_n], \tag{12}$$

$$L = L_m + L_n + L_x, \tag{13}$$

where the supply of labor, L, is constant and $C_n^k \equiv \partial C^k/\partial P_n$, the amount of the nontraded input used in the production of one new unit of capital.

5.2   A Sketch of the General Solution Procedure

A model with three sectors, four factors of production, sector-specific capital, and multiple trade taxes does not yield easily digestible results. But neither is it a black box. Despite its size, the model is easy to manipulate; in fact, one can solve by hand for the conditions the optimal trade taxes must satisfy. The main difficulty is that these conditions depend on the eigenvalues and eigenvectors of a high-order dynamic system: the transition path the economy follows from the old to the new steady state

the set of trade and value added taxes is formally equivalent to a system with consumption taxes $v + h$ and $v + s$ and production subsidies h and s. In this system, the common VAT imposes the restriction that the consumption taxes move together when the production subsidies are fixed.

The fact that the set of trade and value added taxes can be viewed as an equivalent set of consumption taxes and production subsidies is not especially meaningful. The equivalence breaks down, with the nod going to trade taxes and the VAT, if unbundling tariffs and export subsidies into separate consumption taxes and production subsidies results in slightly higher administrative costs. I have chosen to ignore collection/disbursement costs in order to focus on the implications of factor market distortions for optimal trade policy. But if they were added to the model, export subsidies would be more costly and tariffs would be useful as a revenue-raising device. Administrative costs strengthen the case for protection and weaken the case for export promotion.

[6] A time-varying VAT gives rise to an intertemporal distortion. As will be shown in Chapter 8, however, the loss from the intertemporal distortion is second-order small. It does not therefore affect the solution for the optimum, which is located by finding small perturbations of the trade taxes that leave welfare unchanged. (In reality, policy changes are discrete; but even then the losses from the intertemporal distortion are very small. See Chapter 8.)

is governed by a 6×6 system of nondecomposable differential equations involving the sectoral capital stocks and investment rates. It is necessary therefore to rely on a mix of numerical and analytical methods. In this section I provide a sketch of the procedure used to derive the optimal policy rules. Section 5.3 describes how the model was calibrated.

5.2.1   The Private Agent's Optimization Problem

It is useful to know that the perfect foresight equilibrium of the large, complicated model described by equations (1)–(13) can be derived by following the procedure outlined in Chapter 4. The mathematics are more involved and much more tedious, but the solution procedure is exactly the same.

To get started, write down the Hamiltonian associated with the private agent's optimization problem. After using the budget constraint (10) to substitute for E in the indirect utility function, we have

$$\mathcal{H} = e^{-\rho t} \{V\{\mathbf{P}_c, R(\mathbf{P}, P_z, K_m, K_n, K_x, L_m) + J$$
$$- P_k[I + \phi_m(I_m/K_m - \delta)K_m + \phi_x(I_x/K_x - \delta)K_x$$
$$+ \phi_n(I_n/K_n - \delta)K_n]\} + \pi_1(I_m - \delta K_m) + \pi_2(I_x - \delta K_x)$$
$$+ \pi_3(I_n - \delta K_n)\},$$

where π_1–π_3 are the multipliers associated with the constraints on capital accumulation. Maximizing $\mathcal{H}$ with respect to the control variables I_i yields the first-order conditions

$$V_E P_k(1 + \phi'_m) = \pi_1, \tag{14a}$$

$$V_E P_k(1 + \phi'_x) = \pi_2, \tag{14b}$$

$$V_E P_k(1 + \phi'_n) = \pi_3, \tag{14c}$$

The corresponding co-state equations are

$$\dot{\pi}_1 = (\rho + \delta)\pi_1 - V_E[r_m + P_k(\phi'_m I_m/K_m - \phi_m)], \tag{15a}$$

$$\dot{\pi}_2 = (\rho + \delta)\pi_2 - V_E[r_x + P_k(\phi'_x I_x/K_x - \phi_x), \tag{15b}$$

$$\dot{\pi}_3 = (\rho + \delta)\pi_3 - V_E[r_n + P_k(\phi'_n I_n/K_n - \phi_n)]. \tag{15c}$$

At this stage in the solution procedure one ignores the dependence of P_n, J, and L_m on K_i and I_i even though the representative agent foresees perfectly the paths of these variables (apart from any jumps caused by unexpected changes in policy). In a competitive environment, the representative agent is small and views P_n and J as independent of his own actions. This is not true, of course, for L_m. (When a plant is built in the manufacturing sector the owners of the firm know whether they have hired more or fewer workers.) The representative agent *qua* investor, however, cares only about the profits obtained from adding to the capital stock, not about the income gained or lost by workers when variations in K_m alter the level of manufacturing sector employment.

5.2.2   The Steady-State Equilibrium

In a steady state K_i and $\pi_1 - \pi_3$ are constant and $\phi = \phi' = 0$. Equations (9a)–(9c) and (15a)–(15c) then state that gross investment offsets depreciation of the capital stock and that in each sector the return on capital $(r_i/P_k - \sigma)$ equals the time preference rate:

$$I_i = \delta K_i, \tag{16a–16c}$$

$$r_i = r = (\rho + \delta)P_k. \tag{17}$$

After replacing E by the expenditure function $E(\mathbf{P}_c, u)$ and substituting for J and I_i from (11) and (16a)–(16c), the private agent's budget constraint and the market clearing condition in the nontradables sector become

$$E(\mathbf{P}_c, u) = R(\mathbf{P}, P_z, K_m, K_n, K_x, L_m) - P_k \delta K + gZ + (h + v)D^m(\mathbf{P}_c, u)$$
$$+ (s + v)D^x(\mathbf{P}_c, u) - hQ_m - sQ_x, \tag{10'}$$

$$Q_n = D^n(\mathbf{P}_c, u) + C_n^k(P_n)\delta K. \tag{12'}$$

The steady-state equilibrium is defined by equations (1a)–(1f), (2a)–(2c), (3a), (4a)–(4c), (5a)–(5c), (6a)–(6c), (7), (10'), (11'), (12'), (13), and (17) – 25 equations that can be solved for the 25 unknowns P_m, P_x, P_n, P_{mc}, P_{xc}, P_z, P_k, r, w_m, w, f, L_i, K_i, Z_i, Q_i, v, and u as a function of L, T, χ, and the three trade taxes g, h, and s.[7] The task can be accomplished in four large steps:

Step 1. Solve (1f), (2a)–(2c), (3a), and (17) for P_k, w_m, w, r, f, and P_n as a function of v, g, h, and s. This is easily done by solving two equations at a time. From (1f) and (17),

$$\hat{r} = \alpha \hat{P}_n, \tag{18}$$

---

[7] Only three of the four policy instruments can be chosen independently. The fourth must take whatever value is required to satisfy the government budget constraint.

where $\alpha \equiv P_n C_n^k / P_k$, the cost share of the nontraded component in the production of capital goods. Equations (2a) and (3a) then yield the solutions for w_m and P_n, following which (2b) and (2c) provide the solutions for w and f.

Step 2. With the expressions for P_n and all factor prices in hand, the factor demands (4)–(7) can be solved for L_i, Z_i, K_x, and Q_i as a function of g, h, s, v, K_m, and K_n.

Step 3. Substitute the semireduced form solutions for L_m, Z_i, and Q_i into (10'), (12'), and (13). This gives three equations relating u, K_n, and K_m to g, h, s, and v.

Step 4. Use the results from Steps 1–3 to solve (11') for v as a function of g, h, and s. To obtain the final solutions for sectoral output and factor demands, plug the solution for v into the semireduced form solutions for K_n and K_m in Step 3 and then substitute these solutions and the solution for v into the solutions for L_i, Z_i, K_x, and Q_i in Step 2.

5.2.3   Pinning Down the Transition Path

One could characterize the transition path in terms of K_i and π_1–π_3. The shadow prices, however, are unobservable. It is more natural and more intuitive to analyze the dynamic system formed by the capital stocks and the investment rates I_i. With this objective in mind, differentiate (14a) with respect to time and equate the resulting expression for $\dot{\pi}_1$ to the one given in (15a). This produces

$$\left(\frac{V_{En}}{V_{EE}} \dot{P}_n + \frac{V_{Em} + V_{Ex}k}{V_{EE}} \dot{v} + \dot{E} \right)(1 + \phi_m') \frac{V_{EE}}{V_E} + \alpha(1 + \phi_m') \frac{\dot{P}_n}{P_n}$$

$$+ \frac{\phi_m''}{K_m} \left(\dot{I}_m - \frac{I_m}{K_m} \dot{K}_m \right) = \rho + \delta + \phi_m + \phi_m'(\rho + \delta - I_m / K_m) - r_m / P_k \qquad (19)$$

where $V_{Ei} \equiv \partial V_E / \partial P_i$ and $k = 0$ or 1, depending on whether the value added tax applies to both tradables sector or just the import sector. To replace the V_{ij} terms in (19) with something more comprehensible and easier to sign, recall that (see Section 2.2.1 of chapter 2)

$$\mu_i \tau - 1 = \frac{V_{Ei}}{V_{EE} D^i},$$

where μ_i is the income elasticity of demand for the good i and $\tau \equiv -V_E / V_{EE} E$, the intertemporal elasticity of substitution. Furthermore, from the expenditure function $E(\mathbf{P}_c, u)$, we have that $\dot{E}/E = \gamma_n \dot{P}_n / P_n +$

$(\gamma_m/P_{mc} + k\gamma_x/P_{xc})\dot{v} + \dot{u}/E$ under the normalization $E_u = 1$. Using these results and assuming homothetic preferences ($\mu_i = 1$), (19) becomes

$$\left[(\alpha - \gamma_n)\frac{\dot{P}_n}{P_n} - \xi\dot{v} - \frac{\dot{u}}{\tau E}\right](1 + \phi'_m) + \frac{\phi''_m}{K_m}\dot{I}_m$$

$$= \frac{\phi''_m I_m}{K_m^2}\dot{K}_m + \rho + \delta + \phi_m$$

$$+ \phi'_m(\rho + \delta - I_m/K_m) - r_m/P_k, \tag{20}$$

where $\xi \equiv \gamma_m/P_{mc} + k\gamma_x/P_{xc}$. Manipulating (14b)–(14c) and (15b)–(15c) in the same manner yields the symmetric solutions

$$\left[(\alpha - \gamma_n)\frac{\dot{P}_n}{P_n} - \xi\dot{v} - \frac{\dot{u}}{\tau E}\right](1 + \phi'_n) + \frac{\phi''_n}{K_n}\dot{I}_n$$

$$= \frac{\phi''_n I_n}{K_n^2}\dot{K}_n + \rho + \delta + \phi_n$$

$$+ \phi'_n(\rho + \delta - I_n/K_n) - r_n/P_k, \tag{21}$$

$$\left[(\alpha - \gamma_n)\frac{\dot{P}_n}{P_n} - \xi\dot{v} - \frac{\dot{u}}{\tau E}\right](1 + \phi'_x) + \frac{\phi''_x}{K_x}\dot{I}_x$$

$$= \frac{\phi''_x I_x}{K_x^2}\dot{K}_x + \rho + \delta + \phi_x$$

$$+ \phi'_x(\rho + \delta - I_x/K_x) - r_x/P_x. \tag{22}$$

We are seeking a set of differential equations where $\dot{I}_x$, $\dot{I}_m$, and $\dot{I}_n$ stand alone on the left side and everything on the right side is a function of either I_i or K_i. This requires that we find solutions which show how P_n, u, r_i, v, and P_k depend on $\mathbf{I} = (I_m, I_n, I_x)$ and $\mathbf{K} = (K_m, K_n, K_x)$. The desired reduced forms

$$P_n = G^1(\mathbf{I}, \mathbf{K}), \quad u = G^2(\mathbf{I}, \mathbf{K}), \quad r_m = G^3(\mathbf{I}, \mathbf{K}),$$

$$r_n = G^4(\mathbf{I}, \mathbf{K}), \quad r_x = G^5(\mathbf{I}, \mathbf{K}), \quad P_k = G^6(\mathbf{I}, \mathbf{K}), \quad v = G^7(\mathbf{I}, \mathbf{K}),$$

are derived by solving the pseudostatic variant of the model in which K_i and I_i are treated as exogenous. The solution procedure is similar to the one employed to pin down the steady-state outcome:

Step 5. Solve equations (1f), (2a)–(2b), and (3a) for P_k, w_m, r_m, and r_n as a function of P_n, h, s, g, v, and w.

Step 6. Solve equations (2c), (6c), and (7) for Q_x, r_x, and f as a function of P_n, h, s, g, v, w, and K_x.

Step 7. The results from Steps 5 and 6 together with the factor demands in (4a)–(4c), (5a)–(5c), (6a), and (6b) yield the solutions for L_i, Z_i, Q_m, and Q_n as a function of h, s, g, v, w, and K_i.

Step 8. Substitute for J from (11) and write the private agent's budget constraint as

$$E(\mathbf{P}_c, u) = R(\mathbf{P}, P_z, K_m, K_n, K_x, L_m) + gZ + (h+v)D^m(\mathbf{P}_c, u)$$
$$+ (s+kv)D^x(\mathbf{P}_c, u) - hQ_m - sQ_x$$
$$- P_k[I + \phi_m(I_m/K_m - \delta)K_m + \phi_n(I_n/K_n - \delta)K_n$$
$$+ \phi_x(I_x/K_x - \delta)K_x]. \tag{10''}$$

After replacing L_m, Q_i, P_k, and Z_i with the semireduced form solutions obtained in Steps 5–7, equation (10'') delivers the semireduced form solution relating u to P_n, h, s, g, v, w, K_i, and I_i.

Step 9. Use the semireduced form solutions for L_i, u, Z_i, and Q_i to solve the government budget constraint (11') and the labor and nontradables market clearing conditions for v, P_n, and w as a function of I_i, K_i and the trade taxes h, s, and g.

Step 10. Return to the semireduced form solutions for u, P_k, and r_i and substitute the reduced form solutions for w, v, and P_n. This gives the final reduced form solutions $G^2(\mathbf{I}, \mathbf{K}) - G^6(\mathbf{I}, \mathbf{K})$. [$G^1(\mathbf{I}, \mathbf{K})$ and $G^7(\mathbf{I}, \mathbf{K})$ are obtained in Step 9.]

Since trade taxes change but once at time $t = 0$, it is not necessary to allow P_m, P_x, and P_z to vary when deriving the reduced form solutions $G^1(\mathbf{I}, \mathbf{K}) - G^7(\mathbf{I}, \mathbf{K})$. The impact effects of the policy changes are required, however, to characterize the welfare outcome and the complete paths of all variables other than I_i and K_i. The solution for L_m, for example, is of the general form $L_m = G^8(\mathbf{I}, \mathbf{K}, h, s, g)$.[8] At $t = 0$, when the economy jumps onto the saddlepath

$$dL_m|_{t=0} = G_1^8 dI_m|_{t=0} + G_2^8 dI_n|_{t=0} + G_3^8 dI_x|_{t=0} + G_7^8 dh + G_8^8 ds + G_9^8 dg.$$

Following the initial jump, the path of L_m is linked to the paths of I_i and K_i:

$$\dot{L}_m = G_1^8 \dot{I}_m + G_2^8 \dot{I}_n + G_3^8 \dot{I}_x + G_4^8 \dot{K}_m + G_5^8 \dot{K}_n + G_6^8 \dot{K}_x.$$

A few mechanical steps now generate equations for $\dot{I}_i$ that are suitable for linearization. Using the reduced form solutions $G^1(\mathbf{I}, \mathbf{K}) - G^7(\mathbf{I}, \mathbf{K})$, we can write (20)–(22) as

---

[8] The effects of induced changes in v and P_n are incorporated into the partial derivatives of $G^8(\cdot)$.

$$(a_{1m} + \phi_m''/K_m)\dot{I}_m + a_{2m}\dot{I}_n + a_{3m}\dot{I}_x$$
$$= \rho + \delta + \phi_m(I_m/K_m - \delta) + \phi_m'(I_m/K_m - \delta)(\rho + \delta - I_m/K_m)$$
$$- G^3(\mathbf{I},\mathbf{K})/G^6(\mathbf{I},\mathbf{K}) - (a_{4m} - I_m\phi_m''/K_m^2)(I_m - \delta K_m)$$
$$- a_{5m}(I_n - \delta K_n) - a_{6m}(I_x - \delta K_x), \tag{23}$$

$$a_{1x}\dot{I}_m + a_{2x}\dot{I}_n + (a_{3x} + \phi_x''/K_x)\dot{I}_x$$
$$= \rho + \delta + \phi_x(I_x/K_x - \delta) + \phi_x'(I_x/K_x - \delta)(\rho + \delta - I_x/K_x)$$
$$- G^4(\mathbf{I},\mathbf{K})/G^6(\mathbf{I},\mathbf{K}) - a_{4x}(I_m - \delta K_m)$$
$$- a_{5x}(I_n - \delta K_n) - (a_{6x} - I_x\phi_x''/K_x^2)(I_x - \delta K_x), \tag{24}$$

$$a_{1n}\dot{I}_m + (a_{2n} + \phi_n''/K_n)\dot{I}_n + a_{3n}\dot{I}_x$$
$$= \rho + \delta + \phi_n(I_n/K_n - \delta) + \phi_n'(I_n/K_n - \delta)(\rho + \delta - I_n/K_n)$$
$$- G^5(\mathbf{I},\mathbf{K})/G^6(\mathbf{I},\mathbf{K}) - a_{4n}(I_m - \delta K_m)$$
$$- (a_{5n} - I_n\phi_n''/K_n^2)(I_n - \delta K_n) - a_{6n}(I_x - \delta K_x), \tag{25}$$

where

$$a_{1i} \equiv (1+\phi_i')\left[(\alpha - \gamma_n)\frac{G_1^1}{P_n} - \frac{G_1^2}{\tau E} - \xi G_1^7\right],$$

$$a_{2i} \equiv (1+\phi_i')\left[(\alpha - \gamma_n)\frac{G_2^1}{P_n} - \frac{G_2^2}{\tau E} - \xi G_2^7\right],$$

$$a_{3i} \equiv (1+\phi_i')\left[(\alpha - \gamma_n)\frac{G_3^1}{P_n} - \frac{G_3^2}{\tau E} - \xi G_3^7\right],$$

$$a_{4i} \equiv (1+\phi_i')\left[(\alpha - \gamma_n)\frac{G_4^1}{P_n} - \frac{G_4^2}{\tau E} - \xi G_4^7\right],$$

$$a_{5i} \equiv (1+\phi_i')\left[(\alpha - \gamma_n)\frac{G_5^1}{P_n} - \frac{G_5^2}{\tau E} - \xi G_5^7\right],$$

$$a_{6i} \equiv (1+\phi_i')\left[(\alpha - \gamma_n)\frac{G_6^1}{P_n} - \frac{G_6^2}{\tau E} - \xi G_6^7\right],$$

and $i = m, n, x$. Equations (23)–(25) yield solutions of the form

$$\dot{I}_m = b_1\{\rho + \delta + \phi_m(I_m/K_m - \delta) + \phi_m'(I_m/K_m - \delta)$$
$$(\rho + \delta - I_m/K_m) - G^3(\mathbf{I},\mathbf{K})/G^6(\mathbf{I},\mathbf{K})\}$$
$$- b_2(I_m - \delta K_m) - b_3(I_n - \delta K_n) - b_4(I_x - \delta K_x), \tag{26}$$

$$\dot{I}_n = b_5 \{ \rho + \delta + \phi_x (I_x/K_x - \delta) + \phi_x'(I_x/K_x - \delta)$$
$$(\rho + \delta - I_x/K_x) - G^4(\mathbf{I},\mathbf{K})/G^6(\mathbf{I},\mathbf{K}) - \delta \}$$
$$- b_6(I_m - \delta K_m) - b_7(I_n - \delta K_n) - b_8(I_x - \delta K_x), \tag{27}$$

$$\dot{I}_x = b_9 \{ \rho + \delta + \phi_n(I_n/K_n - \delta) + \phi_n'(I_n/K_n - \delta)$$
$$(\rho + \delta - I_n/K_n) - G^5(\mathbf{I},\mathbf{K})/G^6(\mathbf{I},\mathbf{K}) \}$$
$$- b_{10}(I_m - \delta K_m) - b_{11}(I_n - \delta K_n) - b_{12}(I_x - \delta K_x), \tag{28}$$

where b_1–b_{12} are functions of a_{1i}–a_{6i}, ϕ_i, ϕ_i', ϕ_i'', and δ. Linearizing (9a)–(9c) and (26)–(28) around the stationary equilibrium $(I_m^*, I_n^*, I_x^*, K_m^*, K_n^*, K_x^*)$ produces

$$
\begin{bmatrix} \dot{I}_m \\ \dot{I}_n \\ \dot{I}_x \\ \dot{K}_m \\ \dot{K}_n \\ \dot{K}_x \end{bmatrix}
=
\begin{bmatrix}
b_1(\rho\phi_m''/K_m - y_{31}) - b_2 & -b_3 - b_1 y_{32} \\
-b_6 - b_5 y_{41} & b_5(\rho\phi_n''/K_n - y_{42}) - b_7 \\
-b_{10} - b_9 y_{51} & -b_{11} - b_5 y_{52} \\
1 & 0 \\
0 & 1 \\
0 & 0
\end{bmatrix}
$$

$$
\begin{matrix}
-b_4 - b_1 y_{33} & b_2\delta - b_1\left(\rho\delta\dfrac{\phi_m''}{K_m} + y_{34}\right) \\
-b_8 - b_5 y_{43} & b_6\delta - b_5 y_{44} \\
b_9(\rho\phi_x''/K_x - y_{53}) - b_{12} & -b_{10} - b_9 y_{54} \\
0 & -\delta \\
0 & 0 \\
1 & 0
\end{matrix}
$$

$$
\begin{matrix}
b_3\delta - b_1 y_{35} & b_4\delta - b_1 y_{36} \\
b_7\delta - b_5\left(\rho\delta\dfrac{\phi_n''}{K_n} + y_{45}\right) & b_8\delta - b_5 y_{46} \\
b_{11} - b_9 y_{55} & b_{12}\delta - b_9\left(\rho\delta\dfrac{\phi_x''}{K_x} + y_{56}\right) \\
0 & 0 \\
-\delta & 0 \\
0 & -\delta
\end{matrix}
\begin{bmatrix} I_m - I_m^* \\ I_n - I_n^* \\ I_x - I_x^* \\ K_m - K_m^* \\ K_n - K_n^* \\ K_x - K_x^* \end{bmatrix},
$$

$$\tag{29}$$

where

$$y_{3j} \equiv \rho G_j^7 + [G_j^3 - (\rho + \delta)G_j^6]/P_k, \quad j = 1,\dots,6$$

$$y_{4j} \equiv \rho G_j^7 + [G_j^4 - (\rho + \delta)G_j^6]/P_k, \quad j = 1,\dots,6$$

$$y_{5j} \equiv \rho G_j^7 + [G_j^5 - (\rho + \delta)G_j^6]/P_k, \quad j = 1,\dots,6$$

Note that there is no need to determine how the coefficients b_1–b_{12} vary with I_i and K_i. These terms drop out since $I_i = \delta K_i$, $\phi = \phi_i' = 0$, and $r_i = (\rho + \delta)P_k$ in a steady state.

All that remains is to pick out the saddlepoint solution and express it in a form that shows where I_i and K_i stand at time t relative to their initial values. Following the procedure outlined in Section 4.1.2 of chapter 4, first solve $|A - \lambda I| = 0$ [where A is the coefficient matrix in (29) and I is the identity matrix] and confirm that three of the system's six eigenvalues are negative. Designate λ_1, λ_2, and λ_3 to be the three negative eigenvalues. The saddlepoint solution is then

$$\begin{bmatrix} I_m(t) - I_m^* \\ I_n(t) - I_n^* \\ I_x(t) - I_x^* \\ K_m(t) - K_m^* \\ K_n(t) - K_n^* \\ K_x(t) - K_x^* \end{bmatrix} = \begin{bmatrix} X_{11} & X_{12} & X_{13} \\ X_{21} & X_{22} & X_{23} \\ X_{31} & X_{32} & X_{33} \\ X_{41} & X_{42} & X_{43} \\ X_{51} & X_{52} & X_{53} \\ X_{61} & X_{62} & X_{63} \end{bmatrix} \begin{bmatrix} h_1 e^{\lambda_1 t} \\ h_2 e^{\lambda_2 t} \\ h_3 e^{\lambda_3 t} \end{bmatrix}, \tag{30}$$

where h_1–h_3 are constants and $X_j = (X_{1j}, X_{2j}, \dots X_{6j})'$, $j = 1, 2, 3$, is the column eigenvector associated with λ_j. The initial values of the predetermined variables K_m, K_n, and K_x fix h_1–h_3. Evaluate (30) at $t = 0$ and let an o subscript refer to the initial steady-state value of a variable. Since $K_i(0) = K_{i,o}$, the last three rows give

$$\begin{bmatrix} X_{41} & X_{42} & X_{43} \\ X_{51} & X_{52} & X_{53} \\ X_{61} & X_{62} & X_{63} \end{bmatrix} \begin{bmatrix} h_1 \\ h_2 \\ h_3 \end{bmatrix} = - \begin{bmatrix} K_m^* - K_{m,o} \\ K_n^* - K_{n,o} \\ K_x^* - K_{x,o} \end{bmatrix}. \tag{31}$$

The solutions for $K_i^* - K_{i,o}$, the changes in the steady-state capital stocks, were derived earlier in Steps 1–4. If we write these solutions as

$$K_m^* - K_{m,o} = c_1(h - h_o) + c_2(s - s_o) + c_3(g - g_o), \tag{32a}$$

$$K_n^* - K_{n,o} = c_4(h - h_o) + c_5(s - s_o) + c_6(g - g_o), \tag{32b}$$

$$K_x^* - K_{x,o} = c_7(h - h_o) + c_8(s - s_o) + c_9(g - g_o), \tag{32c}$$

then

$$
\begin{bmatrix} h_1 \\ h_2 \\ h_3 \end{bmatrix} = - \begin{bmatrix} X_{41} & X_{42} & X_{43} \\ X_{51} & X_{52} & X_{53} \\ X_{61} & X_{62} & X_{63} \end{bmatrix}^{-1} \begin{bmatrix} c_1 & c_2 & c_3 \\ c_4 & c_5 & c_6 \\ c_7 & c_8 & c_9 \end{bmatrix} \begin{bmatrix} h - h_0 \\ s - s_0 \\ g - g_0 \end{bmatrix}.
\tag{33}
$$

Finally, since $I_i^* - I_{i,o} = \delta(K_i^* - K_{i,o})$, we can restate the solution in (30) as

$$
\begin{bmatrix} I_m(t) - I_{m,o} \\ I_n(t) - I_{n,o} \\ I_x(t) - I_{x,o} \\ K_m(t) - K_{m,o} \\ K_n(t) - K_{n,o} \\ K_x(t) - K_{x,o} \end{bmatrix} = \begin{bmatrix} \delta c_1 & \delta c_2 & \delta c_3 \\ \delta c_4 & \delta c_5 & \delta c_6 \\ \delta c_7 & \delta c_8 & \delta c_9 \\ c_1 & c_2 & c_3 \\ c_4 & c_5 & c_6 \\ c_7 & c_8 & c_9 \end{bmatrix} \begin{bmatrix} h - h_o \\ s - s_o \\ g - g_o \end{bmatrix} + \begin{bmatrix} X_{11} & X_{12} & X_{13} \\ X_{21} & X_{22} & X_{23} \\ X_{31} & X_{32} & X_{33} \\ X_{41} & X_{42} & X_{43} \\ X_{51} & X_{52} & X_{53} \\ X_{61} & X_{62} & X_{63} \end{bmatrix} \begin{bmatrix} h_1 e^{\lambda_1 t} \\ h_2 e^{\lambda_2 t} \\ h_3 e^{\lambda_3 t} \end{bmatrix}.
\tag{34}
$$

Equations (33) and (34) describe the paths of I_i and K_i following a change in the policy instruments P_m, P_x, and P_z. For future use, I write the solutions as

$$
\begin{bmatrix} I_m(t) - I_{m,o} \\ I_n(t) - I_{n,o} \\ I_x(t) - I_{x,o} \\ K_m(t) - K_{m,o} \\ K_n(t) - K_{n,o} \\ K_x(t) - K_{x,o} \end{bmatrix} = \begin{bmatrix} \delta c_1 & \delta c_2 & \delta c_3 \\ \delta c_4 & \delta c_5 & \delta c_6 \\ \delta c_7 & \delta c_8 & \delta c_9 \\ c_1 & c_2 & c_3 \\ c_4 & c_5 & c_6 \\ c_7 & c_8 & c_9 \end{bmatrix} \begin{bmatrix} h - h_o \\ s - s_o \\ g - g_o \end{bmatrix}
$$

$$
+ \begin{bmatrix} f_1 & f_2 & \cdots & \cdots & f_9 \\ f_{10} & f_{11} & \cdots & \cdots & f_{18} \\ \cdot & & & & \\ \cdot & & & & \\ \cdot & & & & \\ f_{46} & \cdots & \cdots & & f_{54} \end{bmatrix} \begin{bmatrix} e^{\lambda_1 t} & 0 & 0 \\ e^{\lambda_2 t} & 0 & 0 \\ e^{\lambda_3 t} & 0 & 0 \\ 0 & e^{\lambda_1 t} & 0 \\ 0 & e^{\lambda_2 t} & 0 \\ 0 & e^{\lambda_3 t} & 0 \\ 0 & 0 & e^{\lambda_1 t} \\ 0 & 0 & e^{\lambda_2 t} \\ 0 & 0 & e^{\lambda_3 t} \end{bmatrix} \begin{bmatrix} h - h_o \\ s - s_o \\ g - g_o \end{bmatrix},
\tag{35}
$$

where $f_1 - f_{54}$ can be derived from (33) and (34).

5.2.4 *The Welfare Outcome and Optimal Policy*

The social planner aims to maximize

$$W = \int_0^\infty u(t)e^{-\rho_1 t}dt. \tag{36}$$

The social welfare function coincides with the private agent's objective function when $\rho_1 = \rho$. But if the welfare of future generations is a public good, the private sector saves too little. To correctly represent the community's true preferences, the social planner discounts future utility at the lower rate ρ_1, the time preference rate implicit in the optimal social contract in which everyone agrees to save more.[9]

Mercifully, most of the information needed to determine the welfare outcome is already in our hands since Step 10 provides the solution for u as a function of h, s, g, K_i, and I_i: $u = G^2(\mathbf{I}, \mathbf{K}, h, s, g)$. As in Chapter 3, the optimal values for the policy instruments are derived by perturbing the equilibrium a little and calculating the impact on welfare. Taking a first-order Taylor series expansion of W around the point (h_o, s_o, g_o) gives

$$\begin{aligned}
W - W_o = \int_0^\infty \{ &G_1^2[I_m(t) - I_{m,o}] + G_2^2[I_n(t) - I_{n,o}] + G_3^2[I_x(t) - I_{x,o}] \\
&+ G_4^2[K_m(t) - K_{m,o}] + G_5^2[K_n(t) - K_{n,o}] + G_6^2[K_x(t) - K_{x,o}] \quad (37) \\
&+ G_7^2(h - h_o) + G_8^2(s - s_o) - G_9^2(g - g_o) \} e^{-\rho_1 t} dt.
\end{aligned}$$

Substituting the solutions in (35) into (37) and integrating term by term yields

$$W - W_o = A_1(h - h_o) + A_2(s - s_o) + A_3(g - g_o), \tag{38}$$

where

$$\begin{aligned}
A_1 \equiv &[G_7^2 + c_1(G_4^2 + \delta G_1^2) + c_4(G_5^2 + \delta G_2^2) + c_7(G_6^2 + \delta G_3^2)]/\rho_1 \\
&+ (f_1 G_1^2 + f_{10} G_2^2 + f_{19} G_3^2 + f_{28} G_4^2 + f_{37} G_5^2 + f_{46} G_6^2)/(\rho_1 - \lambda_1) \\
&+ (f_2 + f_{11} + f_{20} + f_{29} + f_{38} + f_{48})/(\rho_1 - \lambda_2) \\
&+ (f_3 + f_{12} + f_{21} + f_{30} + f_{39} + f_{47})/(\rho_1 - \lambda_3),
\end{aligned}$$

---

[9] The market generates too little investment when the marginal value product of capital exceeds the social time preference rate. The simplest way to introduce this distortion is to assume that the social time preference rate is less than the private rate. The implications for commercial policy are similar, however, when the source of the distortion is an income tax or favorable externalities associated with capital accumulation.

$$A_2 \equiv [G_8^2 + c_2(G_4^2 + \delta G_1^2) + c_5(G_5^2 + \delta G_2^2) + c_8(G_6^2 + \delta G_3^2)]/\rho_1$$
$$+ (f_4 G_1^2 + f_{13} G_2^2 + f_{22} G_3^2 + f_{31} G_4^2 + f_{40} G_5^2 + f_{49} G_6^2)/(\rho_1 - \lambda_1)$$
$$+ (f_5 + f_{14} + f_{23} + f_{32} + f_{41} + f_{50})/(\rho_1 - \lambda_2)$$
$$+ (f_6 + f_{15} + f_{24} + f_{33} + f_{42} + f_{51})/(\rho_1 - \lambda_3),$$

$$A_3 \equiv [G_9^2 + c_3(G_4^2 + \delta G_1^2) + c_6(G_5^2 + \delta G_2^2) + c_9(G_6^2 + \delta G_3^2)]/\rho_1$$
$$+ (f_7 G_1^2 + f_{16} G_2^2 + f_{25} G_3^2 + f_{34} G_4^2 + f_{43} G_5^2 + f_{52} G_6^2)/(\rho_1 - \lambda_1)$$
$$+ (f_8 + f_{17} + f_{26} + f_{35} + f_{44} + f_{53})/(\rho_1 - \lambda_2)$$
$$+ (f_9 + f_{18} + f_{27} + f_{36} + f_{45} + f_{54})/(\rho_1 - \lambda_3).$$

The optimal export subsidy and optimal tariffs on intermediates and consumer goods are obtained by solving the three highly nonlinear equations

$$A_1 = 0, \tag{39a}$$

$$A_2 = 0, \tag{39b}$$

$$A_3 = 0, \tag{39c}$$

for s, h, and g. Note that this procedure identifies the *exact* optimum. The solution is *not* distorted by linearization error because the optimum is located by perturbing the initial equilibrium a *small* amount.

5.2.5   Iteration and the Criterion for Convergence to the Optimum

The solution procedure outlined in Sections 5.2.1–5.2.4 evaluates the impact on welfare of small changes in the trade taxes s, h, and g. In a local analysis of this type, variables such as the consumption shares, employment and sectoral output levels, factor cost shares, compensated elasticities of demand, and so on, can be treated as constant because the responses induced by differential changes in the trade taxes are infinitesimally small. But in searching for optimal policies we have to take account of how these variables differ from their free trade values when s, h, and g assume finite values. This presents a technical problem. Since we have eschewed simple functional forms (e.g., Cobb–Douglas), it is not possible to obtain a closed-form solution for the steady-state equilibrium as a function of trade taxes. Furthermore, even if it were, values would have to be assigned to s, h, and g beforehand because the eigenvalues are the roots of a sixth-order polynomial that can be solved only by numerical methods. But if values are preassigned to s, h, and g, all the computer can do is churn out values for A_1, A_2, and A_3; it cannot solve (39a)–(39c) directly for the optimal values of the trade taxes.

The way around this difficulty is to start with initial guesses for the optimal values of s, h, and g; compute the welfare impact for small changes in each trade tax; adjust the initial guesses in the direction indicated by the values of A_1–A_3; and then undertake a new round of welfare calculations. When the updated guesses return $A_1 = A_2 = A_3 = 0$, the trade taxes are at their optimal values.[10] My rule for stopping the iterations is that the elasticity of the welfare gain with respect to each policy instrument be smaller than .0001 when the gain is measured in units of real consumption expenditure. This degree of imprecision would horrify a physicist, but it is plenty good enough for economics: in the final stages of iteration, the computer is trying to ascertain whether the optimal tariff is 12.312% or 12.313%.

5.3   Calibration of the Model

I assume a CES–CRRA utility function, standard CES technology for the production of capital goods, and two-tiered CES production functions in sectors m, n, and x in which value added generated at a lower tier by a CES function of primary factors combines at the upper tier with imported inputs in another CES function. The associated cost and expenditure functions are

$$C^k = \left(k_1^{\sigma^k} + k_2^{\sigma^k} P_n^{1-\sigma^k}\right)^{1/(1-\sigma^k)}, \tag{40}$$

$$P_{van} = \left(k_3^{\sigma_2^n} r_n^{1-\sigma_2^n} + k_4^{\sigma_2^n} w^{1-\sigma_2^n}\right)^{1/(1-\sigma_2^n)}, \tag{41a}$$

$$P_{vam} = \left(k_5^{\sigma_2^m} r_m^{1-\sigma_2^m} + k_6^{\sigma_2^m} w_m^{1-\sigma_2^m}\right)^{1/(1-\sigma_2^m)}, \tag{41b}$$

$$P_{vax} = \left(k_7^{\sigma_2^x} r_x^{1-\sigma_2^x} + k_8^{\sigma_2^x} w^{1-\sigma_2^x} + k_9^{\sigma_2^x} f^{1-\sigma_2^x}\right)^{1/(1-\sigma_2^x)}, \tag{41c}$$

$$C^n = \left(k_{10}^{\sigma_1^n} P_{van}^{1-\sigma_1^n} + k_{11}^{\sigma_1^n} P_z^{1-\sigma_1^n}\right)^{1/(1-\sigma_1^n)}, \tag{42a}$$

[10] As is often the case with optimal taxes based on dynamic models, it is difficult to verify that the second-order conditions are satisfied. One can, however, undertake some simple tests to make sure that the proposed solution is sensible (e.g., that welfare is higher, not lower, and that small changes in each policy instrument from its optimal level reduce welfare).

$$C^m = \left(k_{12}^{\sigma_1^m} P_{vam}^{1-\sigma_1^m} + k_{13}^{\sigma_1^m} P_z^{1-\sigma_1^m}\right)^{1/(1-\sigma_1^m)}, \tag{42b}$$

$$C^x = \left(k_{14}^{\sigma_1^x} P_{vax}^{1-\sigma_1^x} + k_{15}^{\sigma_1^x} P_z^{1-\sigma_1^x}\right)^{1/(1-\sigma_1^x)}, \tag{42c}$$

$$E(\mathbf{P}_c, u) = [u(1-1/\tau)]^{\tau/(\tau-1)} \left(k_{16}^\beta P_n^{1-\beta} + k_{17}^\beta P_{mc}^{1-\beta} + k_{18}^\beta P_{xc}^{1-\beta}\right)^{1/(1-\beta)}, \tag{43}$$

where $k_1 - k_{18}$ are distribution parameters; β is the elasticity of substitution between nontraded, importable, and exportable consumer goods; σ^k is the elasticity of substitution between nontraded and imported capital inputs; P_{vai} is the "price" of value added in sector i; and, to repeat, σ_1^i and σ_2^i are the elasticity of substitution between value added and imported inputs and the elasticity of substitution between primary factors in sector i.

The primitive parameters that describe preferences and technology are the substitution elasticities, the time preference rate ρ, the depreciation rate σ, the second derivatives of the adjustment cost functions ϕ_i'' ($\phi = \phi' = 0$ evaluated at a steady state where $I_i = \delta K_i$), and the distribution parameters $k_1 - k_{18}$. I set β, σ^k, σ_1^i, σ_2^i, ρ, and δ directly and derive $k_1 - k_{18}$ and the endowments of labor L and land T to be consistent with the values assumed for consumption shares, factor cost shares, sectoral value added shares, the value added tax v, and the wage ratio $\psi = w/w_m$ at the initial free trade equilibrium. When units are chosen so that $P_n = P_k = w_m = f = 1$ initially, $r_i = \rho + \delta$ and $\psi = w$. Equations (40)–(43) then yield

$$\theta_L^n = k_{10}^{\sigma_1^n} k_4^{\sigma_2^n} P_{van}^{\sigma_2^n - \sigma_1^n} \psi^{1-\sigma_2^n}, \tag{44a}$$

$$\theta_L^m = k_{12}^{\sigma_1^m} k_6^{\sigma_2^m} P_{vam}^{\sigma_2^m - \sigma_1^m}, \tag{44b}$$

$$\theta_L^x = k_{14}^{\sigma_1^x} k_8^{\sigma_2^x} P_{vax}^{\sigma_2^x - \sigma_1^x} \psi^{1-\sigma_2^x}, \tag{44c}$$

$$\theta_Z^n = k_{11}^{\sigma_1^n}, \tag{45a}$$

$$\theta_Z^m = k_{13}^{\sigma_1^m}, \tag{45b}$$

$$\theta_Z^x = k_{15}^{\sigma_1^x}, \tag{45c}$$

$$\theta_T^x = k_{14}^{\sigma_1^x} k_9^{\sigma_2^x} P_{vax}^{\sigma_2^x - \sigma_1^x}, \tag{46}$$

$$\alpha = k_2^{\sigma^k}, \tag{47}$$

$$\varphi = \frac{1}{\left[k_{16}^{\beta} + k_{17}^{\beta}(1+v)^{1-\beta} + k_{18}^{\beta}(1+kv)^{1-\beta}\right]^{1/(1-\beta)}},$$ (48)

$$\gamma_n = \frac{k_{16}^{\beta}}{\left[k_{16}^{\beta} + k_{17}^{\beta}(1+v)^{1-\beta} + k_{18}^{\beta}(1+kv)^{1-\beta}\right]^{1/(1-\beta)}},$$ (49a)

$$\gamma_m = \frac{k_{17}^{\beta}(1+v)^{1-\beta}}{\left[k_{16}^{\beta} + k_{17}^{\beta}(1+v)^{1-\beta} + k_{18}^{\beta}(1+kv)^{1-\beta}\right]^{1/(1-\beta)}}.$$ (49b)

Since the consumption shares must sum to unity, k_{18} (or one of the other two distribution parameters in the expenditure function) can be fixed arbitrarily at unity. Similarly, $k_{10} = 1 - k_{11}$, $k_{12} = 1 - k_{13}$, and $k_{14} = 1 - k_{15}$ because the cost shares for value added and intermediate inputs sum to unity in each sector. Thus, after assigning values to ρ, δ, ψ, σ_1^i, σ_2^i, β, σ^k, v, α and γ_i, equations (44a)–(49b) and the four zero-profit conditions

$$1 = C^i(\cdot), \qquad i = m, n, x, k \tag{50a–50d}$$

can be solved for ψ, $k_1 - k_9$, k_{11}, k_{13}, and $k_{15} - k_{17}$. (Recall that $r_i = \rho + \delta$ in the expressions for P_{vai}.)

Now turn to the market clearing condition in the nontradables sector. At the free trade steady-state equilibrium

$$D^n + \alpha\delta K = Q_n \tag{51}$$

as $C_n^k = \alpha$ (for $P_k = P_n = 1$) and $I_i = \delta K_i$. The share of value added produced by sector i is $VA_i \equiv (P_i Q_i - P_z Z_i)/R = P_i Q_i(1 - \theta_Z^i)/R$. Hence, after dividing by R, equation (51) can be written as

$$(\gamma_n \bar{E} + \delta\alpha\bar{K})(1 - \theta_Z^n) = VA_n, \tag{51'}$$

where $\bar{E} \equiv E/R$ and $\bar{K} \equiv K/R$. Note also that

$$VA_m + VA_n + VA_x = 1, \tag{52}$$

$$\bar{K} = (\rho + \delta)^{-1}\left(\frac{\theta_K^x}{1 - \theta_Z^x}VA_x + \frac{\theta_K^n}{1 - \theta_Z^n}VA_n + \frac{\theta_K^m}{1 - \theta_Z^m}VA_m\right), \tag{53}$$

and that the budget constraints of the government and the private agent imply

$$\chi = \frac{v\bar{E}}{1 - \delta\bar{K}}\left(\frac{\gamma_m}{1+v} + \frac{k\gamma_x}{1+kv}\right), \tag{54}$$

$$\overline{E} = \frac{1 - \delta\overline{K}}{1 - v[\gamma_m/(1+v) + k\gamma_x/(1+kv)]}.$$ (55)

I assign values to θ_K^i, θ_z^i, v, ρ, δ, and VA_m at the initial free trade equilibrium. The five equations (51′)–(55) thus yield solutions for $\overline{K}$, $\overline{E}$, χ, VA_n, and VA_x.

The sectoral outputs Q_i, the stock of land and the supply of labor have to be consistent with the various normalizations and the initial values assigned to the cost shares at the wage ratio $\psi = w/w_m = w$. The market clearing conditions (7) and (13) provide the restrictions that ensure consistency. For $f = P_x = 1$,

$$\theta_T^x Q_x = T,$$ (7′)

so the values assigned to T and θ_T^x determine Q_x. Furthermore, since

$$VA_j = \frac{Q_j(1 - \theta_z^j)}{\sum_i Q_i(1 - \theta_z^i)},$$

the equations

$$Q_m(1 - \theta_z^m) = VA_m \sum_i Q_i(1 - \theta_z^i),$$

$$Q_n(1 - \theta_z^n) = VA_n \sum_i Q_i(1 - \theta_z^i),$$

can be solved for Q_m and Q_n after substituting for Q_x, VA_m, and VA_n. The aggregate supply of labor then falls out directly after writing (13) as

$$L = \frac{Q_n\theta_L^n + Q_x\theta_L^x}{\psi} + \theta_L^m Q_m.$$ (13′)

There is one last piece of business to take care of. Explicit adjustment cost functions $\phi_i(I_i/K_i - \sigma)K_i$ are not needed to characterize the steady-state equilibrium because $\phi_i = \phi_i' = 0$ at $I_i = \delta K_i$. The second derivatives of the cost functions, however, enter into the solution for the transition path. To tie down these parameters, return to (14a) and observe that π_1/V_E is the shadow price of K_m measured in domestic currency. Thus, $\pi_1/V_E P_k$ is effectively Tobin's q, the ratio of the demand price to the supply price of capital. Adopting this notation, we have from (14a)–(14c) that at a stationary equilibrium

$$\phi_i'' \delta\hat{I}_i/\hat{q}_i = 1, \qquad i = m, n, x.$$

Assume $\phi_i = c_i(I_i/K_i - \delta)^2/2$ and define $\Omega_i \equiv \hat{I}_i/\hat{q}_i$. Under the neutral assumption that $c_i = c$, the q-elasticity of investment spending is the same in each sector and

$$\phi_i'' = c = \frac{1}{\Omega\delta}.$$

The convexity of the adjustment cost functions is determined therefore by the values assigned to the depreciation rate and the q-elasticity of investment spending.

5.3.1 Choice of Parameter Values

Table 5.1 lists the parameter values used to calibrate the model at the initial free trade equilibrium. All of the other variables that enter into the solutions for the optimal trade taxes are determined by these parameter values, the functional forms describing preferences and technology, and restrictions supplied by the market clearing conditions, the budget constraint, and linearization around a stationary equilibrium.

In specifying the parameters of the model I have relied on a mix of real-world data, empirical estimates, and theory. The considerations that went into the choice of each parameter value are described in the following points:

- *Private time preference rate (ρ).* The time preference rate plays two roles in the model: it discounts future utility and determines the steady-state return on capital. This creates something of a dilemma. A value of .05 or less is probably appropriate when using ρ to discount future utility, but a value of .10–.15 is more in keeping with the real return on capital in LDCs. The choice of .08 is an unhappy compromise.
- *Social time preference rate (ρ_1).* The social time preference rate either equals the private time preference rate or is two percentage points lower. In the latter case, the market generates too little investment. The source of market failure could be Sen's isolation paradox; an alternative, closely related explanation is that the welfare of future generations is a public good (Marglin, 1963; Feldstein, 1964).[11]
- *Consumption shares (γ_i).* The consumption shares for the importable and exportable goods are typical of the shares for manufactures and

---

[11] Sen's isolation paradox is compatible with the present model when each agent cares about the welfare of future generations and his own heirs but not the welfare of his contemporaries.

Table 5.1. *Calibration of the model.*

Preferences, Demand-Side Parameters, and the Value Added Tax
$\rho = .08$, $\rho_1 = .06, .08$, $\gamma_m = .30$, $\gamma_n = .45$, $\gamma_x = .25$,
$\beta = .25, .50$, $\tau = .50$, $\upsilon = .10$, $k = 0, 1$

Elasticities of Substitution in Production
$\sigma_1^i = .10, .50$, $\sigma_2^m, \sigma_2^n = .50$, $\sigma_2^x = .10, .50$, $\sigma^k = .25$

Cost Shares
   $\alpha = .35, .55, .65$
   import sector: $\theta_L^m = .225$, $\theta_Z^m = .25$, $\theta_K^m = .525$
   export sector: $\theta_L^x = .31$, $\theta_Z^x = .10$, $\theta_K^x = .15$, $\theta_f^x = .44$
   nontradables sector: $\theta_L^n = .50$, $\theta_Z^n = .05$, $\theta_K^n = .45$

Sectoral Wage Gap, the Depreciation Rate, and the Q-Elasticity of Investment Spending
$\psi = .50, .67$, $\delta = .05$, $\Omega = 2$

Value Added Share of the Import-Competing Manufacturing Sector
$$VA_m = \begin{cases} .07 & \text{when } \alpha = .35 \\ .10 & \text{when } \alpha = .55, .65 \end{cases}$$

The Base Run
   $\rho = .08$, $\gamma_m = .30$, $\gamma_n = .45$, $\gamma_x = .25$, $\beta = .25$, $\tau = .50$, $\upsilon = .10$
   $k = 1$, $\sigma_1^i = .50$, $\sigma_2^i = .50$, $\sigma^k = .25$, $\alpha = .55$, $\psi = .67$, $VA_m = .10$
   $\Omega = 2$, $\delta = .05$, $\theta_L^m = .225$, $\theta_Z^m = .25$, $\theta_K^m = .525$, $\theta_L^x = .31$,
   $\theta_Z^x = .10$, $\theta_K^x = .15$, $\theta_f^x = .44$, $\theta_L^n = .50$, $\theta_Z^n = .05$, $\theta_K^n = .45$

Notation
   α = cost share of domestically produced captial goods
   β = elasticity of substitution in consumption
   ψ = ratio of the wage in the export/nontradables sector to the wage in the import
           sector
   Ω = elasticity of investment spending with respect to q
   γ_i = consumption share of good i
   θ_L^i = cost share of labor in sector i
   θ_K^i = cost share of capital in sector i
   θ_Z^i = cost share of imported intermediates in sector i
   θ_f^x = cost share of land/natural resources in the export sector
   ρ = private time preference rate
   ρ_1 = social time preference rate
   τ = intertemporal elasticity of substitution
   υ = value added tax
   δ = depreciation rate
   k = 0 or 1 depending on the coverage of the value added tax
   VA_m = value added share of the import-competing sector

food in middle-income countries.[12] The consumption share for non-tradables, along with the choices for other parameters, implies a value added share for services around the middle of the range of income-normed values calculated by Chenery and Syrquin (1989).[13]

- *Elasticity of substitution in consumption (β).* Estimates of demand systems with 5–11 goods generally place compensated own-price elasticities of demand in the .15–.60 range.[14] A value of .5 for β yields compensated own-price elasticities ε_i in the lower/middle part of this range: at the initial free trade equilibrium, $\varepsilon_n = .275$, $\varepsilon_m = .35$, and $\varepsilon_x = .375$. But the scope for substitution may be much less when there are 3 goods instead of 5–11. Furthermore, in many countries exportables are dominated by one or two natural resource products that are not consumed at home and food, for which demand is often very price-inelastic.[15] Given this and the high level of aggregation in the model, I set β at .25 in the base run but also examine the outcome for $\beta = .50$.

- *Intertemporal elasticity of substitution (τ).* Most empirical studies find that τ is well below unity. Some of the estimates for developed countries, however, suggest that the intertemporal elasticity is around unity or higher. The assigned value of .5 is consistent with the estimates for different regions obtained by Ostry and Reinhardt (1992) and the simple average of estimates for low- and middle-income countries in Ogaki, Ostry, and Reinhardt (1996).

- *Value added tax (v).* The VAT varies a great deal across LDCs, ranging from a modest 5% in Taiwan and Panama to 35% in Mauritius. The chosen value of 10% is the most common rate for LDCs reported in Cnossen (1991).

The sectoral coverage of the VAT is limited because the large infor-

---

[12] See Chenery and Syrquin (1989, Table 3). The initial consumption share of the exportable in the model, 25%, is approximately equal to the consumption share of food in Colombia in 1980 (de la Cuesta, 1990).

[13] The initial value added share for the nontradables sector ranges from 43 to 47%. This lies between the weighted average figures for low- and middle-income LDCs in 1994 (World Development Report 1996). The share of services (the share of nontradables less the share of domestically produced capital goods) is 38–39%.

[14] See Goldberger and Gamaletsos (1970), Parks and Barten (1973), Lluch et al. (1977, chapter 3), Deaton and Muellbauer (1980, p. 71), Blundell (1988, p. 35), and Blundell, Pashardes, and Weber (1993, Table 3b, p. 581).

[15] The compensated own-price elasticity for food is estimated to be .1 or less for 9 of the 14 countries in Parks and Barten's sample and for 7 of 10 countries in Lluch, Williams, and Powell's sample (when the estimates include those for Caracas and urban households in Mexico).

mal sector is almost always untaxable. Most nontradables/services production therefore eludes the tax net. It is harder to decide how to treat the export sector. Since it is often difficult to tax agriculture for administrative or political reasons (e.g., taboos on taxing food and other necessities), I investigate the case where the tax base is restricted to the import-competing part of the tradables sector. In the base run, the same tax v applies to production in the import and export sectors.

- *Elasticity of substitution between capital and labor (σ_2).* Cross-section and time series estimates of σ_2 give conflicting results. Strangely, for both developed and less developed countries, the estimates in cross-section studies cluster around unity, whereas those based on time series data are typically only half as large (Gaude, 1975; Mansur and Whalley, 1984, pp. 104–105). The same pattern shows up in more recent studies that postulate translog cost or production functions. Berndt and Wood (1975), Behrman (1982), and Corbo and Mellor (1982) find support for a unitary elasticity of substitution, but the estimates for the United States, France, and Germany by Griffin and Gregory (1976) and for India by Laumas and Williams (1981) are on the order of .5 or less.[16] Not surprisingly, after surveying the literature, CGE model builders usually set σ_2 at either unity or a value close to .5.

   I have slightly more faith in the time series estimates. In the base run, therefore, σ_2 takes the value of .5.

- *Elasticity of substitution between primary factors and imported intermediate inputs (σ_1).* There are no reliable estimates of σ_1 for LDCs. Nevertheless, development economists who disagree on many other points seem to agree that σ_1 is not large. Structuralist economists are clearly of this view (Taylor, 1990, pp. 32–33). There is less concensus among neoclassical economists, but most neoclassical CGE models assume fixed input–output coefficients for intermediates (Pereira and Shoven, 1988, pp. 405–406). I set σ_1 at .5 in the base run, but also allow for the possibility that it may be difficult to substitute between imported intermediates and domestic inputs ($\sigma_1 = .1$).[17]

---

[16] The translog function pivots off the Cobb–Douglas function. This raises concerns about the ability of the translog specification to represent technologies with very easy or very limited substitutability [See Pollak, Sickles, and Wales, (1984). The Cobb–Douglas production function, for example, is the only CES form compatible with a translog production function.] Another problem is that the estimates in translog function are sensitive to assumptions made about the dynamics of factor adjustment (Friesen, 1992; Kolstad and Lee, 1993).

[17] This is also the range of values that Bergman (1988) experiments with after surveying the literature on substitutability between energy and value added.

- *Elasticity of substitution between domestic and imported capital inputs* (σ^k). The general view among development economists is that σ^k is probably small in all but the most advanced LDCs. In deference to this view, I fix σ^k at .25.
- *Cost share of domestically produced capital goods* (α). Table 5.2 shows the share of imported machinery and equipment in total gross fixed-capital formation and in gross fixed-capital formation net of residential structures – in the model, capital corresponds to factories, not houses – for different countries for different years. The share exhibits tremendous variation and is very sensitive to the exchange rate. Most of the values lie between .3 and .6, but some are much smaller and others are much larger. Many of the numbers for countries in Sub-Saharan Africa are too low – smuggling is widespread for all types of imports.

  I allow α to take low, middle, and high values of .35, .55, and .65. Moderate levels of protection push the share up by by 3–10 percentage points, so in the numerical solutions α ends up between .38 and .75. When the share of construction in capital formation is 35%, this range is similar to the range that Dervis, de Melo, and Robinson (1982) postulate for their three archetype economies. The middle value of .55 is very close to the stylized value in Taylor's (1990) illustrative SAM and to the value Dervis, de Melo, and Robinson set for the archetype small primary export economy.
- *Cost shares in the import sector* $(\theta_L^m, \theta_Z^m, \theta_K^m)$. Production in the import-substituting manufacturing sector is normally more capital- and intermediates-intensive than production in other sectors. The cost share for labor of 22.5% corresponds to a share of wages in value added of 30%, the average value in the manufacturing sector for low- and middle-income countries in 1990 (WDR, 1993). The share for intermediates (.25) is the same as in Taylor's illustrative SAM.
- *Cost share in the export sector* $(\theta_L^x, \theta_Z^x, \theta_K^x, \theta_T^x)$. The numbers assigned to the cost shares in the export sector reflect the assumption that exportables are predominantly agricultural or primary products. The share for imported intermediates is about equal to the share in agriculture in Nicaragua in the eighties (Gibson, 1990) and S. Korea in 1973 (Dervis, de Melo, and Robinson, 1982). For the primary factors, I chose the cost shares to yield value added shares close to those seen in Colombian agriculture in 1980. The initial value added shares are 34.4% for labor, 16.7% for capital, and 48.9% for land, whereas the corresponding shares in Colombia circa 1980 were 31%, 21%, and 48% (de la Cuesta, 1990). Of course, neither Colombia nor any other country can lay claim to being the "representative" LDC. The cost

Table 5.2. *Share of imported machinery and equipment in GFCF at current prices.*

	Share A[1]	Share B[2]
Bangladesh, 1988	37.3	52.7
India, 1987	15.7	17.9
Pakistan		
1992	40.1	
1989	30.0	33.4
Philippines, 1992	40.2	
Sri Lanka, 1991	31.1	36.9
Thailand, 1989	39.0	51.7
El Salvador, 1992[3]	46.2	54.7
Mexico, 1992	16.9	21.6
Venezuela, 1992	26.8	29.7
Costa Rica, 1993	45.5	
Ecuador, 1992	37.1	40.0
Guatemala, 1994[3]	42.1	
Jamaica[3]		
1993	33.3	
1990	49.8	
Paraguay, 1994[3]	43.1	
Nicaragua[3]		
1993	40.5	
1992	53.6	
Ivory Coast, 1990	36.2	
Mali		
1990	31.2	
1985	63.2	
Nigeria		
1990	47.1	
1988	69.0	
Senegal, 1990	41.7	
Kenya		
1990	54.5	
1985	33.1	
Egypt, 1989	40.6	
Tunisia, 1989	46.3	
Sierra Leone		
1990	55.5	
1985	39.2	
Zaire		
1989	68.2	
1988	35.5	
Congo		
1991	49.2	
1985	33.3	
Malawi, 1990	58.9	
Uganda, 1990	59.9	
Zambia, 1984	50.1	
Zimbabwe		
1991	80.0	
1989	41.2	44.9

[1] Share in total GFCF.
[2] Share in GFCF net of investment in residential structures.
[3] The domestic currency value of imported capital goods is calculated by multiplying the dollar value in Trends in Developing Economies by the period average exchange rate in International Financial Statistics. (The cost share is understated becuase it does not include any duty paid on imported capital goods.)
Sources: Various issues of *United Nations National Accounts Statistics* (Main Aggregates and Detailed Tables), *Trends in Developing Economies*, *Statistical Yearbook for Latin America and the Carribean*, *African Statistical Yearbook*, *Survey of Economic and Social Conditions in Africa*, and *Asian Development Bank: Key Indicators*.

shares are, however, consistent with other empirical evidence bearing on the relative labor intensity of export/agricultural production. The values for θ_L^x, θ_Z^x, and ψ imply that production in the export sector requires 70–130% more labor per unit of value added than production in the import sector. This is in line with the findings of the NBER study of trade and employment in developing countries and the values assigned by Dervis, de Melo, and Robinson to different archetype economies.[18]

- *Cost shares in the nontradables sector (θ_L^n, θ_K^n, θ_Z^n).* There is not much hard empirical information available on the nature of nontradables production. The little there is indicates, however, that nontradables production is much more labor-intensive than tradables production. My choices of .50 for θ_L^n and .05 for θ_Z^n result in the value added share for labor being 50% higher than in agriculture. This agrees with the educated guesses of Dervis, de Melo, and Robinson and the ratios that can be calculated from the data reported for Colombia by de Melo (1977) and for Mexico by Serra-Puche (1984).[19]

- *Sectoral wage gap (ψ).* The wage in manufacturing is initially either 49% or 100% above the wage in the export and nontradables sectors. These two values lie within the range of estimates obtained in empirical studies of the formal sector wage premium (see the earlier discussion in Chapter 3). It should also be noted that ψ is much smaller after trade taxes are chosen optimally. At the steady state associated with an optimal trade policy, the sectoral wage gap is typically 30–70% smaller than at the initial free trade equilibrium.

---

[18] In the NBER data, the ratio for unskilled labor is 1.79 when HOS (Heckscher–Ohlin–Samuelson) export industries are compared with HOS import industries (Krueger, 1981a, Table 5). In the case of NRB (Natural Resource Based) export industries vs. HOS import industries, the ratio for total labor is 2.26 (when the figure for modern sector NRB exports is used for the Ivory Coast in Table 2). The ratio is 1.72–1.73 in Dervis, de Melo, and Robinson's archetypes when marginal laborers are not assigned to any sector; if half are instead allocated to agriculture, the ratio varies from 2.15 to 2.37.

[19] The ratio of the cost share of labor in services to the cost share of labor in agriculture is 1.36 in Serra-Puche, 1.57 in de Melo (using a weighted average of labor's share in services, construction, and transport), and 1.37–1.70 in Dervis, de Melo, and Robinson (depending on how marginal laborers are allocated). The assumption that nontradables production is roughly 50% more labor-intensive than agricultural is also in line with the figures for Brazil in Baer and Fonseca (1987), for South Korea in Kwan and Paik (1995), and for Zambia in Chiwele (1996, Table 11.4).

- *q-elasticity of investment spending (Ω)*. Estimates for developed countries suggest that Ω lies somewhere on the interval .2–1.5.[20] A few estimates have also been undertaken for LDCs, but it is doubtful that the small, thin stock markets in these studies accurately reflect information about the fundamentals that guide private sector investment decisions. The value assigned to Ω, two, equals Shafik's (1990) estimate of the elasticity of investment with respect to the supply price of capital in Egypt. I chose this highish value mainly because the speed of adjustment is very slow at lower values of Ω. In the model of Section 5.2, both internal adjustment costs and diminishing marginal utility of consumption weaken the response of investment to changes in the return on capital. Since the utility function is fairly concave ($\tau = .5$), adjustment of the capital stock is very gradual even when Ω equals two: in most runs, it takes more than 50 years for the aggregate capital stock to cover half of the distance to its new steady-state level.
- *Value added share of the import-competing manufacturing sector (VA_m).* The value added share of the import-competing manufacturing sector is .10 when $\alpha = .55$ or .65 and .07 when $\alpha = .35$. I paired $\alpha = .35$ with a lower value for VA_m because the countries that are most dependent on imported capital goods tend to have smaller manufacturing sectors.

These shares might seem a bit low, but for two reasons I think they are approximately right. First, domestically produced capital inputs other than structures should be counted as output of the manufacturing sector. (In the model, they are classified as part of the nontradables sector.) When the share of construction in capital costs is 35%, the total value added share of the manufacturing sector is 12.8% for $\alpha = .55$ and 14.2% for $\alpha = .65$. While the share in large, semi-industrialized countries is often 20–30%, these values are not atypical of those seen

---

[20] The estimates of Summers (1981), Hayashi (1982), and Alonso-Borrego and Bertolila (1994) imply, respectively, q-elasticities of .30–1.02, .85, and .42–.54 when (as in the model) $I = \delta K$ and $\delta = .05$. Abel and Blanchard (1986) estimate the q-elasticity to lie between .1 and .3. However, the elasticity with respect to the marginal profit component of q exceeds unity. Engel and Foley's (1975) estimates range from .78 to .87 for producer's durable equipment and from 2 to 2.3 for nonresidential construction. Malkiel et al. (1986) estimate the q-elasticity for 12 two-digit SIC industries and obtain values ranging from 0 to 1.85, with half of the estimates equaling or exceeding unity. The estimates for ϕ'' in Galeoti and Schiantarelli (1991) – the "a" parameter in their cost function – yield a q-elasticity of 1.07–1.6 in the present model.

in small low- and middle-income countries. In 1996, the value added
share of manufacturing was below 17% in 15 of 24 countries in Latin
America and the Caribbean (*Statistical Yearbook of Latin America and
the Carribean*, 1997). The weighted average share for low-income
countries (excluding China and India) was 13% in 1994, with shares
of less than 10% being common in Sub-Saharan Africa (World Development Report, 1996).

The second factor to bear in mind is that the initial value
added share is the share at free trade, whereas most observed shares
reflect the impact of protectionist policies. Protection raises the
measured share both by increasing the relative price of manufactured goods and by encouraging resources to move into manufacturing production. These effects can be quite large. The shift to more
liberal trade policies has reduced the share of manufacturing in GDP
by 6–9 percentage points in Colombia, Brazil, Uruguay, and
Argentina.[21]

In the discussion above I put forward the case for particular parameter values one by one. As a final check on the choice of parameter values,
one can also ask whether the structure of production, the degree of openness, the composition of imports, the sectoral distribution of the labor
force, the functional distribution of income, and so on, appear reasonable for LDCs. This information is presented in Table 5.3. The share of
investment in GDP is a little low because net investment is zero at the
initial steady state. All of the other numbers, however, take normal
values. The aggregate capital–output ratio is around 2.8, and the labor
share in national income is close to the stylized value in Taylor's illustrative SAM. Under free trade, the economy is fairly open (exports are
33–38% of GDP), and intermediates and capital goods account for
47–48% of total imports. (This share rises to over 80% at moderate levels
of protection.) Finally, the ratio of employment in services and
construction (i.e., nontradables sector employment) to employment
in agriculture is too high for the poorest countries but realistic for
most other LDCs. The ratio is approximately 1.5 in Latin America; in
the model it lies between 1.34 and 1.70 at the initial free trade
equilibrium.[22]

[21] See the figures in the World Development Report (1996) for the share of manufacturing in GDP in 1980 vs. 1994.
[22] See Table 27 in the *Statistical Yearbook for Latin America and the Caribbean*
(1995). My figure of 1.5 assumes that 6% of the labor force is employed in the
construction sector.

Table 5.3. *Characteristics of the initial equilibrium implied by the choice of parameter values used to calibrate the model.*[1]

Aggregate capital–output ratio
  2.60 when $\alpha = .35$, 2.78 when $\alpha = .55$, 2.81 when $\alpha = .65$

Share of investment in GDP
  13% when $\alpha = .35$, 13.9% when $\alpha = .55$, 14.1% when $\alpha = .65$

Labor's share in national income
  42.0% when $\alpha = .35$, 42.4% when $\alpha = .55$, 42.6% when $\alpha = .65$

Value added share of the nontradables sector
  43.5% when $\alpha = .35$, 46.0% when $\alpha = .55$, 47.4% when $\alpha = .65$

Shares of capital goods and intermediate inputs in total imports
  intermediates: 26.4% when $\alpha = .35$, 31.2% when $\alpha = .55$, 32.3% when $\alpha = .65$
  capital goods: 22.0% when $\alpha = .35$, 18.3% when $\alpha = .55$, 15.1% when $\alpha = .55$

Share of exports in GDP
  38.3% when $\alpha = .35$, 34.1% when $\alpha = .55$, 32.7% when $\alpha = .65$

Ratio of employment in the nontradables sector to employment in the export sector
  1.34 when $\alpha = .35$, 1.60 when $\alpha = .55$, 1.70 when $\alpha = .65$

[1] For the case where $\psi = .50$ and the VAT is levied on both traded goods.

None of this argues that the model is all-encompassing. It is impossible to fit the immense structural diversity of LDC economies under one tent, so choices have to be made. Perhaps the most limiting assumption in the present model is that exports are mainly primary goods produced in the low-wage informal sector. This is the right assumption for Sub-Saharan Africa and for many of the smaller, lesser developed countries in South and Central America.[23] Elsewhere, it is often contrary to the facts: in Brazil, Mexico, Turkey, the East Asian NICs, and other countries,

[23] According to the official data, manufactured goods represented 45% of total merchandise exports in Latin America and the Caribbean in 1996 (World Development Indicators 1998, Table 4.4). This does not belie the claim made in the text. The aggregate figure is deceiving because many lightly processed primary products are classified as manufactured goods and a few large countries supply a disproportionate share of total manufactured exports. (The export share of

manufactures bulk large in the export bundle. The case under examination here is thus common but not generic; it is only one of several important cases that would be investigated in a more general analysis of optimal commercial policy.

5.3.2   The Steady-State Equilibrium in Level Form

In the iterative search for the optimum, it is necessary to recompute the steady-state equilibrium in level form each time the welfare outcome is evaluated for different values of g, s, and h. This is a simple matter once explicit functional forms are in hand for the cost and revenue functions. First derive the expressions for C_w^i, C_r^i, C_f^i, $C_{P_z}^i$, C_n^k, D^i, and $b(P_{mc}, P_{xc}, P_n)$ [which appears in (3a)] from (40)–(43) and (48).[24] After entering these expressions together with those for C^i and E, substituting $\Sigma_i P_i Q_i - P_z Z_i$ for $R(\cdot)$ in (10'), and imposing $I_i = \delta K_i$ and $r_i = r = (\rho + \delta)P_k$, the computer can be instructed to solve for the steady-state equilibrium in the manner outlined in Section 5.2.1. This fixes the values of Q_i, w, P_n, etc., that appear in the expressions for the eigenvectors and eigenvalues of the linearized model.

5.4   The Impact of Small Policy Changes at Free Trade

In this section I examine separately the effects of small (i.e., infinitesimal) changes in each policy instrument at a free trade equilibrium where lump-sum taxes/transfers adjust to keep the government budget in balance. This will prove helpful in understanding the results that follow on optimal trade policy. The exact values for h, s, and g balance numerous, complicated tradeoffs. The general qualitative characteristics of the optimal trade regime, however, depend mainly on how the different policy instruments *directly* affect aggregate capital accumulation and

---

manufactures was 9–36% in 13 of the 16 Latin American countries for which data were available in World Development Indicators, 1998.) Moreover, in some countries foreign firms account for most manufactured exports. These exports should be taken out when calibrating a model that abstracts from direct foreign investment.

[24] The expression for b is

$$b(P_n, P_{mc}, P_{xc}) = \left(k_{16}^\beta P_n^{1-\beta} + k_{17}^\beta P_{mc}^{1-\beta} + k_{18}^\beta P_{xc}^{1-\beta}\right)^{1/(1-\beta)}.$$

employment in the high-wage manufacturing sector. These direct effects are transparent when taxes/transfers are lump sum and the free trade equilibrium is perturbed by small changes in $h, s,$ and g because the losses from the trade distortion are then second-order small and do not interact with the losses due to underemployment, underinvestment, and the distortionary value added tax.

5.4.1   Long-Run Effects on Capital Accumulation, High-Wage Employment, and Real Output

Table 5.4 shows the long-run elasticities of the aggregate capital stock, the sectoral capital stocks, employment in the high-wage manufacturing sector, and net national product (NNP) with respect to P_m, P_x, and P_z. The share of domestically produced capital goods varies from .35 to .65, and firms operate nonnested CES production functions ($\sigma_1^i = \sigma_2^i$). All parameters other than those specified in the table take their base run values. In the upper half of each panel, the supply response in the export sector is highly inelastic ($\sigma^x = .1$); in the lower half, technology is equally flexible in the three sectors ($\sigma^m = \sigma^x = \sigma^n = .5$).

At a broad qualitative level, there is nothing in the results that disagrees with intuition. Protection promotes capital accumulation and employment growth in the manufacturing sector but lowers the equilibrium capital stock in the export sector. Export promotion, naturally, has the opposite effects. The one result that might not have been guessed beforehand is the positive relationship between the price of imported intermediates and capital accumulation in the export sector. An increase in P_z causes contraction in the import-competing manufacturing sector, where the cost share of intermediates is large. Capital decumulation and layoffs in the import sector depress, in turn, the wage in the export and nontradables sectors and the demand for domestically produced capital inputs. The overall effect on the supply of nontradables is ambiguous, but the reduction in demand ensures that P_n falls. The fall in the wage and decrease in the cost of capital goods ($\hat{P}_k = \alpha\hat{P}_n < 0$) more than offset the impact of a higher price for intermediates in the export sector. Consequently, K_x increases after the general equilibrium interactions have had their full say.

While the signs of the numbers in Table 5.4 generally conform to expectations, the magnitudes do not. What stands out in this respect are the strikingly large elasticities for capital accumulation and employment in the manufacturing sector. As just noted, in the case where P_z increases, this reflects the much greater cost share of imported intermediates in the

Table 5.4. *Long-run elasticities of the aggregate capital stock (K), the sectoral capital stocks (K_i), high-wage employment (L_m), and Net National Product (NNP) with respect to P_m, P_x, and P_z.*

σ_1^x, σ_2^x	K	K_m	K_n	K_x	L_m	NNP	α
			Elasticity with respect to P_m				
.1	3.52	17.18	1.89	−.542	16.87	.958	.35
	1.81	6.60	1.02	−.430	6.57	.533	.55
	1.34	5.01	.736	−.394	5.07	.401	.65
.5	7.71	43.31	3.38	−2.71	43.00	2.14	.35
	3.98	16.81	1.93	−2.15	16.78	1.20	.55
	3.03	13.10	1.48	−1.97	13.16	.929	.65
			Elasticity with respect to P_x				
.1	−.487	−3.12	−.155	.260	−3.24	−.140	.35
	−.324	−1.62	−.099	.253	−1.76	−.102	.55
	−.282	−1.46	−.082	.251	−1.60	−.091	.65
.5	−1.64	−11.08	−.572	1.30	−11.19	−.473	.35
	−1.16	−5.93	−.454	1.27	−6.07	−.364	.55
	−1.05	−5.41	−.421	1.26	−5.54	−.332	.65
			Elasticity with respect to P_z				
.1	−1.03	−5.09	−.519	.130	−5.05	−.280	.35
	−.560	−2.09	−.289	.100	−2.12	−.166	.55
	−.432	−1.66	−.214	.090	−1.71	−.131	.65
.5	−2.13	−11.91	−.913	.648	−11.86	−.593	.35
	−1.13	−4.71	−.528	.498	−4.75	−.341	.55
	−.876	−3.72	−.409	.449	−3.77	−.268	.65

manufacturing sector and the way in which the conflicting general equilibrium effects play out in the nontradables and export sectors. It is not so easy, however, to explain the other numbers. The own-price elasticity $\hat{K}_m/\hat{P}_m$ is 13–32 times larger than $\hat{K}_x/\hat{P}_m$ when $\sigma^x = .1$ and 7–16 times larger when $\sigma^x = .50$. Moreover, although the elasticities are smaller for an increase in P_x, their relative magnitudes are similar. The cross-price elasticity $\hat{K}_m/\hat{P}_x$ is 4–15 times the size of the own-price elasticity $\hat{K}_x/\hat{P}_x$.

Several factors contribute to the huge elasticities for K_m. The small size of the manufacturing sector matters but is not the whole story: when VA_m is .20 instead of .10 or .07, the own- and cross-price elasticities for K_m decrease substantially but are still much greater than those for K_x and K_n. The far more important sectoral asymmetries stem from differences in the relative factor intensities of production. Manufacturing production is relatively most intensive in the variable input that is in perfectly elastic supply, imported intermediates, and relatively least intensive in the two inputs that are in fixed supply, labor and land. General equilibrium interactions therefore do not restrain expansion or contraction in the manufacturing sector to nearly the same extent as in the nontradables and export sectors.

In the long run, the very strong elastic response of capital accumulation in the manufacturing sector overwhelms everything else that affects the aggregate capital stock, high-wage employment and real output. Export subsidies and tariffs on intermediates thus reduce K, L_m, and NNP. Tariffs on consumer imports, by contrast, exert a powerful positive effect on each of these variables. The elasticities for L_m are almost identical to the large elasticities for K_m; and though the manufacturing sector is small, the elasticities for K exceed three and those for NNP lie between .93 and 2.14 when $\sigma^x = .5$. In short, the picture painted by these results agrees with the themes emphasized by early labor surplus models: manufacturing is the most dynamic sector in the economy and rapid capital accumulation is the key to reducing underemployment $(\hat{L}_m \approx \hat{K}_m)$.

In runs that specify different values for σ_2^i, σ_1^i, σ^k, θ_L^i, θ_Z^i, θ_T^x, α, ψ, and β, the elasticities retain the same signs as in Table 5.4. The magnitudes, however, are sensitive to some primitive parameters. The two most important parameters are the ones shown in the table – α, the share of domestically produced capital goods, and σ^x, the elasticity of substitution in the export sector. A small value for σ^x lowers the elasticity of supply in the export sector directly; in general equilibrium, the elasticities in the import and nontradables sectors also decrease because when σ^x is small there is less reallocation of labor between these two sectors and the export sector. The value of α is critical in determining the slope of the supply curve in the industry that builds factories by combining imported and domestic components. An investment boom bids up the prices of domestically produced equipment and structures but not the price of imported capital inputs. Aggregate capital accumulation can proceed further therefore without strongly increasing the total cost of building a factory when the cost share of imported machinery is large (i.e., α is small).

5.4.2   The Speed of Adjustment

After P_m changes, the new steady state is very far away.[25] Furthermore, both diminishing marginal utility of consumption and internal adjustment costs favor gradual capital accumulation. The transition to the new steady state is therefore quite slow. The panel for $\Omega = 1,000,000$ in Table 5.5 shows how long it takes for K, K_m, and NNP to cover half the distance from the old to the new steady state when internal adjustment costs are negligible. In the case where $\alpha = .55$ and $\sigma^i = .5$ in all sectors, K and NNP traverse this ground in 17 years. But with even modest adjustment costs, the transition is much slower.[26] For $\Omega = 2$, the halfway point is not reached until 65 years out. A value of ten for Ω implies very small adjustment costs, but still adds nearly 20 years to the length of the transition path. Trade policy has small but enduring effects on capital accumulation and growth.

5.4.3   Real Wages and Underemployment

In Chapter 3 I argued that there is no presumption labor will fare better under an export-oriented strategy than under ISI. I am now in a position to spell out in detail why I dissent from the majority view on this issue.

According to conventional wisdom, an escalated structure of protection weakens labor demand by drawing resources into the capitalintensive import-competing sector at the expense of labor-intensive exportables production and by spurring firms to utilize more capital-intensive technology. Both of these mechanisms operate in the model. Nevertheless, the real wage in the informal sector (i.e., sectors n and x) always increases in the long run under an escalated structure of protection. Across steady states, equations (1f) and (17) yield

$$\hat{r} = \alpha \hat{P}_n.$$

It then follows from (1a)–(1e), (2a), (2b), and (3b) that

---

[25] Far away in the sense that the elasticities associated with P_m are very large. The analysis is confined to small changes.
[26] The medium-/long-term response is sensitive to adjustment costs when (as in the model and most LDCs) the cost share of capital is high (Wilcoxen, 1993).

Table 5.5. *Time it takes for the aggregate capital stock (K), the capital stock in the import sector (K_m), and Net National Product (NNP) to complete half of the transition path when P_m increases.*

		$\Omega = 2$		
σ_1^x, σ_2^x	K	K_m	NNP	α
.10	49.16	47.03	48.53	.35
	29.19	27.54	28.49	.55
	25.01	23.67	24.29	.65
.50	120.12	118.27	119.41	.35
	65.42	63.47	64.57	.55
	56.71	54.79	55.80	.65

		$\Omega = 10$		
σ_1^x, σ_2^x	K	K_m	NNP	α
.10	20.69	18.28	20.24	.35
	13.78	12.09	13.37	.55
	11.97	10.60	11.57	.65
.50	49.06	46.64	48.53	.35
	28.20	25.89	27.63	.55
	24.04	21.81	23.46	.65

		$\Omega = 1,000,000$		
σ_1^x, σ_2^x	K	K_m	NNP	α
.10	12.16	9.42	11.75	.35
	9.66	7.66	9.30	.55
	8.77	6.97	8.41	.65
.50	25.87	22.86	25.33	.35
	17.20	14.37	16.66	.55
	14.88	12.01	14.32	.65

$$\hat{P}_n = \frac{1 - \theta_L^m \gamma_m P_m / P_{mc}}{F} \hat{P}_m - \frac{\theta_Z^m}{F} \hat{P}_z - \frac{\theta_L^m \gamma_x P_x}{P_{xc} F} \hat{P}_x - \frac{\theta_L^m}{F} \left(\frac{\gamma_m}{P_{mc}} + \frac{\gamma_x k}{P_{xc}} \right) dv \quad (56)$$

$$\hat{w} = \frac{(1 - \theta_L^m \gamma_m P_m / P_{mc})(1 - \theta_K^n \alpha)}{\theta_L^n F} \hat{P}_m - \frac{\theta_Z^n F + \theta_Z^m (1 - \theta_K^n \alpha)}{\theta_L^n F} \hat{P}_z$$

$$- \frac{\theta_L^m \gamma_x (1 - \theta_K^n \alpha) P_x}{P_{xc} \theta_L^n F} \hat{P}_x - \frac{\theta_L^m}{\theta_L^n F} \left(\frac{\gamma_m}{P_{mc}} + \frac{k \gamma_x}{P_{xc}} \right) (1 - \theta_K^n \alpha) dv, \quad (57)$$

where $F \equiv \theta_L^m \gamma_n + \theta_K^m \alpha$. In this section only, $v = dv = 0$ (taxes are lump sum). In the *actual* model, however, the solutions are more complicated because changes in tariffs and the export subsidy are paired with compensating changes in the value added tax v. The required adjustment in v depends, moreover, not only on whether revenues from trade taxes rise or fall, but also on how changes in real income affect consumption of tradables, the base for the value added tax. The information in Table 5.4 fills in this part of the equation: a tariff on consumer imports raises real income while export subsidies and tariffs on intermediates have the opposite effect. Export subsidies require, therefore, an increase in v while tariffs on consumer goods allow v to be reduced. Knowing this, it is easy to confirm from (56)–(57) that, after including the induced adjustment in the VAT, $\hat{w}/\hat{P}_m > \hat{P}_n/\hat{P}_m > 1$ and $\hat{w}/\hat{P}_x < \hat{P}_n/\hat{P}_x < 0$. Thus, the real wage of workers in the nontradables and export sectors increases unambiguously in the case of a tariff on consumer imports but decreases unambiguously when the government subsidizes exports.

These results stem from the tight link between goods and factor prices under perfect competition. A tariff on consumer goods lowers the real prices of intermediate inputs and capital in the nontradables and import sectors. Hence, the zero-profit conditions in the two sectors cannot be satisfied unless both product wages, w_m/P_m and w/P_n, increase. This requires, in turn, that a higher product wage in the nontradables sector be accompanied by a sufficiently large increase in the relative price of the nontraded good (so that $\hat{P}_n > \hat{w}_m > \hat{P}_m$). Conversely, since an export subsidy pushes up wage costs in the import sector (w_m rises with P_x if $\gamma_x > 0$), the product wage w/P_n and the relative price of the nontraded good must fall, implying $\hat{w} < \hat{P}_n < 0$. The same conclusion holds for a tariff on intermediates provided an increase in g is not associated with too large a reduction in v (or that v increases).

The claim that protection is harmful to labor might still be valid if the shift to more capital- and intermediates-intensive technology lowered employment in the high-wage manufacturing sector. But, as we saw earlier, L_m and K_m move closely together. Also, for each trade tax, the sign of the impact on the real wage ω, the aggregate capital stock K, and total purchases of intermediates Z is of the same sign as the impact on L_m. Thus, there seems to be a strong positive relationship in the long run between aggregate capital accumulation, imports of intermediates, and overall labor demand.

The fact that L_m, K, Z, and ω always move in the same direction is definitely not a fluke. It reflects instead a basic assumption about the nature of technology. Almost all of the functional forms that economists use to describe technology have the feature that factors of production

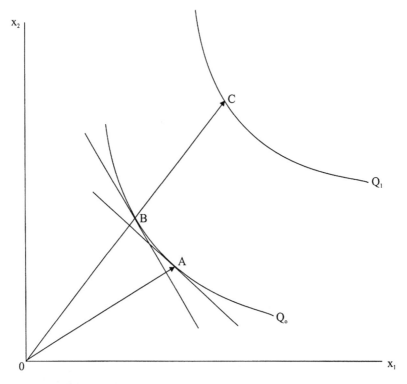

Figure 5.1. The output effect vs. the substitution effect when inputs are gross complements.

are gross complements, that is, that the demand for input i rises when the price of input j falls. This is illustrated in Figure 5.1. When the price of x_2 falls, firms substitute away from x_1 but also produce a higher level of output. Normally point C lies northeast of point A; the output effect dominates the substitution effect so that the demand for x_1 increases even though technology OC is more x_2-intensive than technology OA.

Gross complementarity is the key to understanding why the favorable treatment accorded to imported intermediates and capital goods under an escalated structure of protection strengthens rather than depresses labor demand. The greater utilization of intermediates immediately increases labor productivity in the import-competing and nontradables sectors. In addition, when the import-competing sector is relatively capital-intensive, protection stimulates investment spending by driving up the capital rental, r, relative to the cost of building capital, P_k.

Over time, therefore, the supply of complementary capital inputs also increases. The growth in the capital stock together with larger purchases of intermediates ensures that eventually labor demand in the import sector (and possibly the nontradables sector) increases strongly enough to bid up the real wage in the informal sector.

5.4.3.1   THE TRANSITIONAL DYNAMICS

A comparison of steady-state outcomes tells us only what happens in the very long run. To make a compelling case for the view that protection is favorable to labor, we need to demonstrate that workers are better off during the early phases of the adjustment process that brings the economy from the old to the new steady state. Do the real wage in the informal sector and total real labor income increase immediately? If not, are any decreases short-lived?

In the short run the sectoral capital stocks are fixed and the outcome hinges on how the tariff affects employment and the market clearing price in the nontradables sector. Focus first on the implications of lower employment in the nontradables sector. If L_n declines, then the wage increases in terms of both the nontraded good and the export good, which together comprise 70% of the consumption basket. A great deal depends therefore on the flexibility of technology in the export sector. If σ^x is small, wage increases do not induce the export sector to release much labor; as a result, higher employment in the import-competing sector comes mainly at the expense of employment in the nontradables sector. *Ceteris paribus*, this favors an immediate increase in the real wage.

The other important factor is the size of the induced increase in the price of the nontraded good. When employment contracts in the non-tradables sector, a small decrease in P_n/P_m implies that the wage either increases in terms of the importable or falls by a modest amount ($\hat{P}_m > \hat{w} > \hat{P}_n$, but $\hat{P}_n$ is "close" to $\hat{P}_m$). To see when the increase in P_n is large, consider the state of excess demand for nontradables at $t = 0$. A little reflection (and some algebra) establishes that, for $\sigma^k = 0$, demand exceeds supply at $\hat{P}_n = \hat{P}_m$ iff

$$I(\alpha - \gamma_n)\frac{\hat{I}}{\hat{P}_m}\bigg|_{t=0} - \gamma_n(w_m - w)L_m(\Lambda_x + \Lambda_z) > D^n \varepsilon_x^n - Q_n(\eta_x + \eta_z),$$

where η_i and Λ_i are the general equilibrium elasticities of Q_n and L_m with respect to P_i ($\eta_x, \eta_z, \Lambda_x, \Lambda_z < 0$).[27] The increase in P_n relative to P_x and P_z

---

[27] The adding-up restrictions $\eta_n + \eta_m = -(\eta_x + \eta_z)$ and $\Lambda_m + \Lambda_n = -(\Lambda_x + \Lambda_z)$ have been used to state the solution in terms of η_x, η_z, Λ_x, and Λ_z.

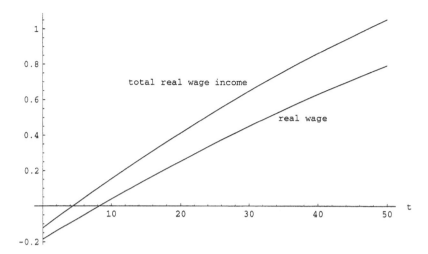

Figure 5.2. Time-dated elasticities of the real wage in the informal sector and of total real wage income with respect to the tariff on imported consumer goods when $\alpha = .55$ and $\sigma^x = .50$.

raises supply and induces consumers to substitute away from nontradables toward exportables. These effects are picked up by the terms on the right side of the inequality sign. The two terms on the left side capture the impact on demand of the upward jumps in investment spending and manufacturing sector employment at $t = 0$. The increase in manufacturing sector employment is associated with a real income gain of $(w_m - w)dL_m$ and higher demand for nontraded consumer goods. Higher investment spending is financed by higher saving, so the net impact on demand depends on whether the share of nontraded inputs used in producing capital goods is larger or smaller than the share of nontradables in aggregate consumption. An immediate increase in the real wage ω is most likely therefore when the labor market is highly distorted, the share of domestically produced capital goods is relatively large, and nontradables and exportables are weak general equilibrium substitutes (i.e., ε_x^n and η_x are small).

This pattern is evident in Table 5.6 and Figure 5.2. The real wage increases immediately when supply is inelastic in the export sector ($\sigma^x = .1$) and $\alpha = .55, .65$. More importantly, when labor suffers losses at the beginning of the adjustment process, they are small and short-lived. The real wage recovers to its previous level within 2.5–12 years and total real labor income recovers in less than 5 years (with one exception). Observe also that the long-run gains are *very* large and *inversely* corre-

Table 5.6. *Short- and long-run elasticities for the real wage in the informal sector and total real labor income and the time* t* *at which the variable equals its initial value.*

	Impact of an increase in P_m						
	Real wage in informal sector			Total real labor income			
σ_1^x, σ_2^x	Impact	t^*	Long run	Impact	t^*	Long run	α
.1	−.120	2.52	3.74	−.085	1.68	3.93	.35
	.016	—	2.22	.043	—	2.21	.55
	.056	—	1.73	.076	—	1.72	.65
.50	−.238	11.87	3.74	−.189	7.20	4.84	.35
	−.185	8.25	2.22	−.122	4.37	2.75	.55
	−.168	8.27	1.73	−.108	4.32	2.16	.65

	Impact of an increase in P_x						
σ_1^x, σ_2^x	Impact	t^*	Long run	Impact	t^*	Long run	α
.1	.072	21.33	−.494	.053	15.66	−.554	.35
	.048	8.08	−.402	.024	4.29	−.430	.55
	.041	5.64	−.373	.017	2.48	−.398	.65
.50	.293	122.48	−.494	.248	72.83	−.831	.25
	.270	67.42	−.402	.206	37.32	−.655	.55
	.263	57.83	−.373	.199	31.22	−.608	.65

	Impact of an increase in P_z						
σ_1^x, σ_2^x	Impact	t^*	Long run	Impact	t^*	Long run	α
.1	−.031	—	−1.18	−.037	—	−1.23	.35
	−.068	—	−.776	−.070	—	−.764	.55
	−.080	—	−.645	−.079	—	−.632	.65
.50	−.076	—	−1.18	−.077	—	−1.47	.35
	−.086	—	−.776	−.085	—	−.901	.55
	−.089	—	−.645	−.087	—	−.742	.65

lated with the short-run losses. Thus, the charge in the orthodox critique that protection depresses labor demand is simply wrong. Workers in the informal sector might have to put up with slightly lower real wages for 5–10 years, but the payback on this investment is sizeable. Overall, protection is good for labor.

The orthodox critique is closer to the mark in its evaluation of how export promotion affects the labor market. In the long run, aggregate capital decumulation pulls down the real wage in the informal sector and

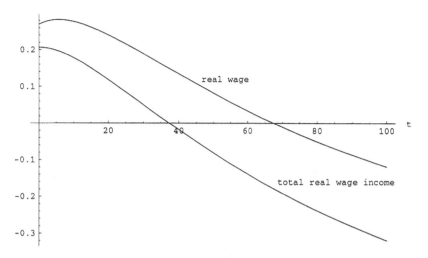

Figure 5.3. Time-dated elasticities of the real wage in the informal sector and of total real wage income with respect to the export subsidy when $\alpha = .55$ and $\sigma^x = .50$.

reduces the number of high-wage manufacturing jobs. But the long run is very far away when technology is moderately flexible in the export sector. In the cases where $\sigma^x = .5$, expansion of the labor-intensive export sector keeps ω higher for more than 50 years. Furthermore, the wage-depressing effects of capital decumulation in the import-competing and nontradables sectors may not become apparent for a decade or longer. In Figures 5.3 and 5.4, the real wage increases steadily for 8–15 years before starting on its long downward trek.

5.4.4   *Protection Plus Export Promotion*

It is not hard to deduce from the results in Table 5.4 that the optimal trade regime will be biased toward import substitution. The bias, however, is not nearly as pronouced as one might expect. Export subsidies can be helpful in offsetting the byproduct distortions tariffs incur in consumption and production patterns. Consider in particular the effects of equal effective rates of protection in the import and export sectors brought about by proportionate increases in P_m, P_z, and P_x. Since the real equilibrium is homogeneous of degree zero in the export price and *all* import prices, this set of policies is equivalent to a subsidy on imported machinery. As can be seen from Tables 5.7 and 5.8, the implicit subsidy promotes aggregate capital accumulation and increases employment in

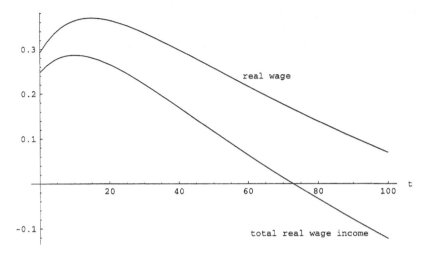

Figure 5.4. Time-dated elasticities of the real wage in the informal sector and of total real wage income with respect to the export subsidy when $\alpha = .35$ and $\sigma^x = .50$.

Table 5.7. *Long-run elasticities of the aggregate capital stock (K), the sectoral capital stocks (K$_i$), high-wage employment (L$_m$), and Net National Product (NNP) in the case of protection plus export promotion.*[1]

				Elasticity with respect to P_m			
σ_1^x, σ_2^x	K	K_m	K_n	K_x	L_m	NNP	α
.1	3.036	14.059	1.737	−.282	13.63	.818	.35
	1.484	4.976	.923	−.177	4.813	.431	.55
	1.054	3.550	.655	−.143	3.473	.310	.65
.5	6.069	32.234	2.813	−1.410	31.806	1.672	.35
	2.821	10.874	1.480	−.883	10.711	.837	.55
	1.987	7.693	1.063	−.714	7.617	.597	.65

[1] Protection plus export promotion is defined to be the case where P_m, P_x, and P_z increase proportionately.

the high-wage manufacturing sector. In addition, it drives up the real wage in the informal sector more quickly than does protection alone, which matters for policy when the short- and medium-run impact on the distribution of income is an issue of concern. These benefits have to be balanced against two costs. First, the subsidy distorts the choice between

Table 5.8. *Short- and long-run effects of protection plus export promotion on the real wage in the informal sector and total real labor income.*

σ_1^x, σ_2^x	Real wage in informal sector			Total real labor income			
	Impact	t^*	Long run	Impact	t^*	Long run	α
.1	−.048	.806	3.247	−.031	.527	3.379	.35
	.064	—	1.820	.067	—	1.784	.55
	.097	—	1.361	.093	—	1.326	.65
.50	.055	—	3.247	.059	—	4.011	.35
	.085	—	1.820	.084	—	2.091	.55
	.095	—	1.361	.092	—	1.547	.65

imported and domestically produced capital goods. Second, in the more realistic model of Section 5.2, the subsidy has to be paid for by increasing the distortionary value added tax. These two costs increase slowly with the subsidy because both the elasticity of substitution in consumption and the elasticity of substitution between capital inputs are small ($\beta = \sigma^k = .25$). This suggests that optimal trade policy will often call for relatively flat structures of protection and export promotion (vis-à-vis intermediates) and only a slight bias toward import substitution.

5.5   The Optimal Structure of Protection

I start by examining the solutions for the optimal tariffs on consumer goods and intermediate inputs when the export subsidy is fixed at zero. This is mainly an exercise in positive analysis: the objective is not so much to determine what tariffs should be when export subsidies/taxes are infeasible as to develop a framework for judging how badly protectionist policies went astray in the pre-1980 period. Despite all that has been written about the evils of import-substituting industrialization, some aspects of this issue are still unsettled. To be sure, people of sound mind now agree that tariffs are preferable to quotas and that effective rates of protection of 200–400% are far too high. But what are we to make of the success that Mexico, Colombia, Kenya, Pakistan, Malaysia, Brazil, Thailand, the Ivory Coast, and other countries achieved under moderate import-substituting programs?[28] Was moderate protection

[28] Devarajan (1991) asks the same question: how did the Ivory Coast achieve 8% growth (until the government undertook a massive and ill-advised expansion in public investment in the late seventies) when prices were not "right"?

actually harmful, or did it just fall short of the first-best? Did policy makers in these and most other countries grant preferential treatment to imported intermediates and capital goods because they suffered from "priority illusion" (Bhagwati, 1978, p. 21), or was an escalated structure of protection a sensible reponse to the problems of underemployment and underinvestment? Answers can be found here and there in the literature, but they are not the product of any formal theoretical analysis. Little, Scitovsky, and Scott (1970) conjecture, on the basis of some back-of-the-envelope calcuations (pp. 147–148), that high wages in the industrial sector might justify a tariff of 20%. Rodrik (1992a) allows that it might be as high as 50%. Mitra (1991) argues for a uniform tariff no higher than 10–15%, but also cautions that theory needs to investigate the conditions under which such rules-of-thumb are highly inappropriate.

The present model is flexible enough to support an investigation of the type Mitra recommends. The solutions for the optimal tariffs in Table 5.9 cover 36 different cases where the wage in manufacturing is initially 50–100% higher than in the nontradables and export sectors and the social time preference rate either equals or is two percentage points below the private time preference rate. The first panel is the base run and those that follow show how sensitive optimal policy is to the share of imported capital goods $(1 - \alpha)$, the breadth of the tax base, the elasticity of supply in the export sector, the scope for substitution between consumer goods, the flexibility of technology, and the speed of adjustment to the steady state. In each panel, only one parameter takes a value different from that specified in the base run.

A quick scan of Table 5.9 reveals that the numbers change little going from one panel to the next. Three rules-of-thumb are quite robust:

1. **A sharply escalated structure of protection is the right way to combat underemployment and underinvestment.** g equals or exceeds h only in the two cases where $\rho_1 = .08$ and it is difficult to substitute between intermediates and primary factors $(\sigma_1^i = .1)$. In the other 34 cases, the tariff on intermediates is 10–80% of the tariff on consumer imports. Since the ratio of producer prices for imported equipment and manufactured goods is $1/(1 + h)$, 8.5 of the 9 panels support the same conclusion that the optimal tariff structure is highly escalated. This is the natural corollary of the high elasticities for the aggregate capital stock and manufacturing sector employment in Table 5.4; a tariff structure that lowers the relative prices of imported equipment and intermediates promotes aggregate capital accumulation and encourages greater utilization of inputs complementary to labor.

Table 5.9. *The optimal structure of protection when the export subsidy equals zero.*

	Base run[1]					
	$\rho_1 = .08$			$\rho_1 = .06$		
ψ	h	g	ERP	h	g	ERP
.50	13.158	8.730	14.65	22.852	13.732	25.97
.67	7.767	4.988	8.70	15.466	7.811	18.08

	$\alpha = .35$					
	$\rho_1 = .08$			$\rho_1 = .06$		
ψ	h	g	ERP	h	g	ERP
.50	11.470	8.298	12.54	20.213	13.430	22.52
.67	6.475	4.440	7.16	13.114	7.093	15.16

	$\alpha = .65$					
	$\rho_1 = .08$			$\rho_1 = .06$		
ψ	h	g	ERP	h	g	ERP
.50	13.804	8.660	15.55	23.578	13.231	27.13
.67	8.276	5.050	9.36	16.145	7.632	19.05

	VAT on the importable good only					
	$\rho_1 = .08$			$\rho_1 = .06$		
ψ	h	g	ERP	h	g	ERP
.50	12.821	11.024	13.42	21.338	16.423	23.00
.67	7.655	6.627	8.00	14.916	10.286	16.48

	$\sigma_1^x = \sigma_2^x = .10$					
	$\rho_1 = .08$			$\rho_1 = .06$		
ψ	h	g	ERP	h	g	ERP
.50	14.415	10.859	15.61	23.550	14.328	26.70
.67	9.028	7.262	9.62	16.747	9.326	19.27

Table 5.9. *(cont.)*

| | $\beta = .50$ | | | | | |
| | $\rho_1 = .08$ | | | $\rho_1 = .06$ | | |
ψ	h	g	ERP	h	g	ERP
.50	12.702	9.017	13.94	21.687	13.345	24.53
.67	7.747	5.550	8.48	14.958	7.785	17.40

| | $\sigma_1^i = .10$ | | | | | |
| | $\rho_1 = .08$ | | | $\rho_1 = .06$ | | |
ψ	h	g	ERP	h	g	ERP
.50	14.703	14.703	14.703	22.637	9.546	27.03
.67	8.779	9.090	8.68	14.630	1.497	19.04

| | $\sigma_1^i = \sigma_2^i = 1$ | | | | | |
| | $\rho_1 = .08$ | | | $\rho_1 = .06$ | | |
ψ	h	g	ERP	h	g	ERP
.50	14.262	10.335	15.60	24.792	17.799	27.21
.67	8.384	5.662	9.31	16.721	10.786	18.78

| | $\Omega = 10$ | | | | | |
| | $\rho_1 = .08$ | | | $\rho_1 = .06$ | | |
ψ	h	g	ERP	h	g	ERP
.50	12.784	8.471	14.24	23.145	13.586	26.42
.67	7.611	4.889	8.53	15.841	7.696	18.62

[1] Parameter values for the Base Run are stated in Table 5.1.

2. **If factor markets are distorted by underemployment but not under-investment, then the optimal tariff on consumer imports is on the order of 5–15%.** For $\rho_1 = \rho = .08$, the optimal tariff on consumer imports is only 11–15% and the associated effective rate of protection (ERP) never exceeds 16%, even when the wage in manufacturing at the free trade equilibrium is double the wage paid in other sectors. In the cases where the sectoral wage gap is 49% at free trade ($\psi = .67$), h drops to 6–9% and the ERP to 7–10%.

3. **Severe underemployment and underinvestment justify, at most, tariffs on consumer imports of 20–25% and an ERP of 30%.** The numbers are higher but still quite low when $\rho_1 = .06$. The optimal tariff on consumer imports never exceeds 25%, and the ERP lies between 15% and 28%. Sadly, the highest values for h (24.8%) and the ERP (27.2%) are produced by the profession's favorite Cobb–Douglas production function. The various structural/institutional rigidities invoked in support of import-substituting policies do not make much difference and in some cases favor lower instead of higher protection.

Why are the optimal tariffs invariably small when the distortions they help to alleviate are so large? The explanation is rooted in basic principles familiar from the theory of optimal taxation. In dynamic models, supply is very elastic over the medium and long run in sectors that produce under conditions of constant returns to scale. The large elasticities for capital accumulation and employment in the manufacturing sector imply that import demand is also extremely elastic and hence that the costs of the trade distortion rise rapidly with the tariff h. As a result, the optimal tariff on consumer imports is small even though protection is highly effective in reducing underemployment and underinvestment.

In connection with this last remark, it should be emphasized that the "small" tariffs matter in the long run. Table 5.10 shows how the aggregate capital stock, the share of high-wage employment, the distribution of income, and imports of manufactured consumer goods differ at free trade and the new stationary equilibrium. The structural changes are fairly minor for the small ERPs of 7–10% that are optimal when $\rho_1 = .08$ and $\psi = .67$. But in the other cases (excepting Cobb–Douglas technology) the aggregate capital stock grows 25–100%, the employment share of manufacturing rises from 3–5% to 10–16%, the sectoral wage gap decreases 35–80%, and the real wage in the informal sector increases 20–45%. Note also that, more often than not, the economy ends up as a net exporter of manufactured consumer goods after the adjustment process is complete. When this happens, h becomes an export subsidy supported by a matching tariff on the final stretch of the transition path.

The significance of the steady-state results depends on the case under consideration and one's prior beliefs about the importance of convex adjustment costs and what constitutes a reasonable speed of adjustment to the steady state. *If* Table 5.5 is a reliable guide for large policy changes, then the adjustment process is half complete after 25–30 years when supply in the export sector is highly inelastic. This applies, however, to only one panel in Table 5.9. In all of the other cases, $\sigma_1^x = \sigma_2^x = .5$ and the

Table 5.10. *Long-run effects of the optimal structure of protection when the export subsidy equals zero.*

				Free trade				
	$K_n + K_m + K_x$	VA_m	$D^m/Q_m - 1$	w_m/w	L_m/L	ω	Total RWI	v
Base run, $\psi = .50$	1292	.10	.854	2	.037	.072	28.2	.10
Base run, $\psi = .67$	1292	.10	.854	1.49	.049	.096	28.2	.10
$\alpha = .35, \psi = .50$	1072	.07	1.68	2	.026	.072	24.9	.10
$\alpha = .35, \psi = .67$	1072	.07	1.68	1.49	.034	.096	24.9	.10
$\alpha = .65, \psi = .50$	1348	.10	.851	2	.036	.072	29.3	.10
$\alpha = .65, \psi = .67$	1348	.10	.851	1.49	.049	.096	29.3	.10
VAT on import good only								
$\psi = .50$	1256	.10	.813	2	.037	.079	30.3	.10
$\psi = .67$	1256	.10	.813	1.49	.049	.106	30.3	.10

				Optimal policy				
	$K_n + K_m + K_x$	VA_m	$D^m/Q_m - 1$	w_m/w	L_m/L	ω	Total RWI	v
Base run								
$\psi = .50, \rho_1 = .08$	1800	.228	−.219	1.66	.097	.086	34.9	.106
$\psi = .50, \rho_1 = .06$	2094	.287	−.402	1.53	.131	.094	38.1	.159
$\psi = .67, \rho_1 = .08$	1583	.181	.003	1.31	.096	.109	32.2	.093
$\psi = .67, \rho_1 = .06$	1832	.241	−.268	1.20	.135	.119	35.2	.122
$\alpha = .35$								
$\psi = .50, \rho_1 = .08$	1767	.252	−.310	1.54	.115	.093	33.4	.115
$\psi = .50, \rho_1 = .06$	2171	.324	−.494	1.37	.163	.104	37.4	.183
$\psi = .67, \rho_1 = .06$	1790	.263	−.350	1.11	.159	.129	33.6	.132

				Optimal policy				
	$K_n + K_m + K_x$	VA_m	$D^m/Q_m - 1$	w_m/w	L_m/L	ω	Total RWI	v
$\alpha = .65, \rho_1 = .06$								
$\psi = .50$	2021	.265	−.339	1.59	.115	.090	37.8	.144
$\psi = .67$	1804	.224	−.200	1.24	.121	.115	35.4	.114
VAT on import good only								
$\psi = .50, \rho_1 = .06$	1986	.279	−.393	1.55	.126	.101	40.2	.156
$\psi = .67, \rho_1 = .06$	1756	.236	−.265	1.21	.132	.130	37.4	.109
$\sigma_{1,2}^x = .10$								
$\psi = .50, \rho_1 = .08$	1562	.165	.109	1.61	.065	.089	35.1	.075
$\psi = .50, \rho_1 = .06$	1735	.204	−.123	1.46	.084	.098	38.6	.098
$\psi = .67, \rho_1 = .06$	1588	.173	.048	1.16	.091	.123	36.0	.086
$\sigma_1^i = .10$								
$\psi = .50, \rho_1 = .08$	1800	.229	−.215	1.66	.097	.086	35.0	.090
$\psi = .50, \rho_1 = .06$	2106	.287	.398	1.52	.131	.094	38.3	.174
$\psi = .67, \rho_1 = .06$	1845	.241	−.265	1.19	.136	.120	35.4	.142
$\sigma_1^i = \sigma_2^i = 1$								
$\psi = .50, \rho_1 = .08$	2211	.292	−.412	1.66	.137	.086	35.7	.132
$\psi = .50, \rho_1 = .06$	2668	.350	−.534	1.54	.177	.093	38.7	.208
$\psi = .67, \rho_1 = .06$	2242	.304	−.443	1.21	.186	.119	35.3	.150

$K_n + K_m + K_x$ is the aggregate capital stock; VA_m is the share of value added produced by the import-competing sector; $D^m/Q_m - 1$ is the ratio of imports to domestic production in sector m; w_m/w is the ratio of the wage in the import sector to the wage in the export and nontradables sectors; L_m/L is the share of the labor force employed in sector m; ω is the real consumption wage in the export and non-tradables sectors; Total RWI is total real wage income; and v is the value added tax.

halfway point is not reached until 60–70 years have elapsed (more in the case of $\alpha = .35$). If this seems unreasonable, the parameter Ω can be assigned the much larger value of ten, as would be appropriate if internal adjustment costs were nearly linear. The solutions for the optimal tariffs are then virtually the same (compare the panels for the Base Run and $\Omega = 10$ in Table 5.9), but most of the journey to the new steady state is accomplished within 25–50 years. This provides, in many ways, a better fit with the stylized facts of the development process under protection. Suppose, for example, that in the base run case where $\psi = .50$ and $\rho_1 = .06$ adjustment is 99% complete after 50 years. Moderate protection then raises the average growth rate of the aggregate capital stock by a percentage point, while the average growth rates of employment and value added in manufacturing increase more strongly, by 2.1 and 2.7 percentage points, respectively. The direction of trade in manufactured consumer goods turns around after 30–40 years. For higher tariffs that push import substitution too hard and too fast, the process runs out of steam in 15–25 years.

5.6   The Full Optimal Solution

Table 5.9 represents a victory of sorts for conventional wisdom. Although some protection is desirable, the optimal level of protection is very low compared to the levels seen during the pre-1980 period and the levels that prevail today in much of the Third World. Indeed, the tariffs are so small that in many cases the trade regime would be classified as "export-oriented" according to the mildly eccentric criteria employed by much of the literature (viz., light protection and no explicit taxation of exports).

In the full optimal solution that allows policy makers to subsidize or tax exports, the results diverge radically depending on whether underinvestment is or is not a problem. Not much changes in Tables 5.11 and 5.12 when $\rho_1 = .08$. An export tax of 5–15% is introduced to facilitate a 3–10 point cut in the tariff on consumer goods and payment (in 15 of 18 cases) of a small subsidy on intermediates. The full optimal solution involves just a bit of tinkering to reduce the costs of the trade distortion; the aggregate capital stock, the real wage in the informal sector, and the share of high-wage employment do not change appreciably.

This conclusion, that the constrained and unconstrained solutions amount to pretty much the same thing, is sensitive to the assumption that the social time preference rate equals the private time preference rate. The freedom to manipulate the export subsidy makes a great difference to the nature of optimal policy when decentralized markets fail to deliver

Table 5.11. *The optimal structure of protection and export promotion.*

| | Base run[1] | | | | | |
| | $\rho_1 = .08$ | | | $\rho_1 = .06$ | | |
ψ	h	s	g	h	s	g
.50	4.939	−9.969	−1.345	38.681	18.500	32.059
.67	2.868	−6.235	−1.266	35.339	24.662	31.662

| | $\alpha = .35$ | | | | | |
| | $\rho_1 = .08$ | | | $\rho_1 = .06$ | | |
ψ	h	s	g	h	s	g
.50	5.642	−8.689	.114	30.358	15.116	26.671
.67	3.086	−5.176	−.596	26.288	20.440	25.177

| | $\alpha = .65$ | | | | | |
| | $\rho_1 = .08$ | | | $\rho_1 = .06$ | | |
ψ	h	s	g	h	s	g
.50	4.267	−10.550	−2.322	43.960	21.503	35.513
.67	2.488	−6.747	−1.854	41.075	28.020	35.751

| | VAT on the importable good only | | | | | |
| | $\rho_1 = .08$ | | | $\rho_1 = .06$ | | |
ψ	h	s	g	h	s	g
.50	3.408	−11.796	−.624	36.224	17.840	33.850
.67	2.050	−7.373	−.611	33.805	24.046	33.175

| | $\sigma_1^x = \sigma_2^x = .10$ | | | | | |
| | $\rho_1 = .08$ | | | $\rho_1 = .06$ | | |
ψ	h	s	g	h	s	g
.50	6.252	−9.768	.572	39.441	18.000	33.143
.67	3.540	−7.006	.097	34.954	22.298	31.646

Table 5.11. *(cont.)*

		$\rho_1 = .08$			$\rho_1 = .06$	
			$\beta = .50$			
ψ	h	s	g	h	s	g
.50	4.206	−9.968	−1.599	36.689	17.102	31.086
.67	2.165	−6.840	−1.681	33.652	22.492	30.603

		$\rho_1 = .08$			$\rho_1 = .06$	
			$\sigma_1^i = .10$			
ψ	h	s	g	h	s	g
.50	4.633	−11.164	−1.424	38.204	17.025	31.976
.67	2.922	−6.800	−.595	35.164	23.893	31.818

		$\rho_1 = .08$			$\rho_1 = .06$	
			$\sigma_1^i = \sigma_2^i = 1$			
ψ	h	s	g	h	s	g
.50	2.010	−15.437	−3.972	38.216	17.134	32.838
.67	1.752	−8.634	−2.383	37.590	27.598	34.897

		$\rho_1 = .08$			$\rho_1 = .06$	
			$\Omega = 10$			
ψ	h	s	g	h	s	g
.50	5.677	−8.755	−.402	41.594	21.737	35.120
.67	3.306	−5.550	−.710	37.754	27.341	34.199

[1] Parameter values for the Base run are stated in Table 5.1.

the socially desirable level of aggregate investment. In the right half of Table 5.11, where $\rho_1 = .06$, employment in manufacturing and the capital stock in each sector are too low at the initial free trade equilibrium. Consequently, optimal policy calls for a substantial, economywide reduction in the relative price of imported equipment. This is engineered by much higher tariffs on consumer imports and large export subsidies. h lies between 30 and 44% in every case save one, while s ranges from 15 to

Table 5.12. *Long-run effects of the optimal structure of protection and export promotion.*

	$K_n + K_m + K_x$	VA_m	$D^m/Q_m - 1$	w_m/w	L_m/L	ω	Total RWI	v
Free trade								
Base run, $\psi = .50$	1292	.10	.854	2	.037	.072	28.2	.10
Base run, $\psi = .67$	1292	.10	.854	1.49	.049	.096	28.2	.10
$\alpha = .35$, $\psi = .50$	1072	.07	1.68	2	.026	.072	24.9	.10
$\alpha = .35$, $\psi = .67$	1072	.07	1.68	1.49	.034	.096	24.9	.10
$\alpha = .65$, $\psi = .50$	1348	.10	.851	2	.036	.072	29.3	.10
$\alpha = .65$, $\psi = .67$	1348	.10	.851	1.49	.049	.096	29.3	.10
VAT on import good only								
$\psi = .50$	1256	.10	.813	2	.037	.079	30.3	.10
$\psi = .67$	1256	.10	.813	1.49	.049	.106	30.3	.10

	$K_n + K_m + K_x$	VA_m	$D^m/Q_m - 1$	w_m/w	L_m/L	ω	Total RWI	v
Optimal policy								
Base run								
$\psi = .50$, $\rho_1 = .08$	1732	.228	−.202	1.70	.095	.084	34.1	.080
$\psi = .50$, $\rho_1 = .06$	2187	.281	−.407	1.48	.132	.097	39.2	.212
$\psi = .67$, $\rho_1 = .08$	1543	.180	.023	1.34	.094	.107	31.7	.076
$\psi = .67$, $\rho_1 = .06$	1950	.236	−.284	1.15	.138	.125	35.6	.192
$\alpha = .35$								
$\psi = .50$, $\rho_1 = .08$	1693	.253	−.296	1.59	.113	.090	32.6	.087
$\psi = .50$, $\rho_1 = .06$	2272	.315	−.496	1.32	.164	.108	38.6	.229
$\psi = .67$, $\rho_1 = .06$	1919	.255	−.362	1.05	.161	.136	35.0	.200

	$K_n + K_m + K_x$	VA_m	$D^m/Q_m - 1$	w_m/w	L_m/L	ω	Total RWI	v
Optimal policy								
$\alpha = .65$, $\rho_1 = .06$								
$\psi = .50$	2106	.261	−.347	1.54	.117	.093	38.9	.200
$\psi = .67$	1910	.220	−.218	1.19	.124	.120	36.7	.184
VAT on import good only								
$\psi = .50$, $\rho_1 = .06$	2074	.274	−.402	1.50	.127	.105	41.4	.233
$\psi = .67$, $\rho_1 = .06$	1864	.230	−.282	1.16	.134	.135	38.8	.213
$\sigma^x_{1,2} = .10$								
$\psi = .50$, $\rho_1 = .08$	1513	.165	.136	1.65	.064	.087	34.4	.049
$\psi = .50$, $\rho_1 = .06$	1807	.201	−.140	1.42	.086	.101	39.6	.150
$\psi = .67$, $\rho_1 = .06$	1670	.171	.018	1.12	.093	.128	37.0	.152
$\sigma^i_1 = .10$								
$\psi = .50$, $\rho_1 = .08$	1735	.230	−.200	1.70	.095	.084	34.2	.075
$\psi = .50$, $\rho_1 = .06$	2182	.281	−.402	1.48	.131	.097	39.2	.206
$\psi = .67$, $\rho_1 = .06$	1946	.235	−.277	1.15	.137	.125	36.6	.188
$\sigma^i_1 = \sigma^i_2 = 1$								
$\psi = .50$, $\rho_1 = .08$	1979	.291	−.389	1.74	.131	.082	34.3	.090
$\psi = .50$, $\rho_1 = .06$	2877	.344	−.539	1.49	.179	.096	39.8	.257
$\psi = .67$, $\rho_1 = .06$	2557	.299	−.461	1.14	.191	.125	37.0	.231

$K_n + K_m + K_x$ is the aggregate capital stock; VA_m is the share of value added produced by the import-competing sector; $D^m/Q_m - 1$ is the ratio of imports to domestic production in sector m; w_m/w is the ratio of the wage in the import sector to the wage in the export and nontradables sectors; L_m/L is the share of the labor force employed in sector m; ω is the real consumption wage in the export and non-tradables sectors; Total RWI is total real wage income; and v is the value added tax.

28%. Large increases in the VAT and the tariff on intermediates are required to pay for the large export subsidies. Escalation in the structure of protection/promotion is confined therefore mainly to imported capital goods: the real producer price of intermediates rises 4–14% in the export sector and decreases a slight 1–6% in the import sector.

The principal advantage of having the export subsidy as another policy instrument is that the domestic relative prices P_m/P_x, P_m/P_z, and P_x/P_z can be brought closer to world relative prices. This substantially reduces the costs of the trade distortion because, to repeat, the general equilibrium supply elasticities are very large, especially in the import-competing sector. The full optimal solution also pushes the three sectoral capital stocks closer to their socially optimal levels, but the gains from this are not dramatic. The values for the aggregate capital stock in Table 5.12 are 4–14% higher (for $\rho_1 = .06$) than their counterparts in Table 5.10. (The *increase* in the aggregate capital stock, however, is 10–33% greater than the increase in Table 5.10.) Greater accumulation of capital comes with the nice side benefit of a more equitable distribution of income, but, again, the numbers are small. Across steady states, the real wage in the export and nontradables sectors increases an additional 3–5%.

5.7   Incorporating Distributional/Poverty-Reduction Objectives into the Social Welfare Function

Suppose the social planner values a peso in the hands of a worker in the low-wage informal sector more than a peso in the hands of the representative agent. Distributional considerations then have a voice in the determination of optimal policy. The social welfare function in (36) is amended to

$$W = \int_0^\infty \left\{ u(t) + \Theta \left[\frac{w_m(L_m - L_{m,o}) + w(L_x + L_n)}{b(P_{mc}, P_{xc}, P_n)} \right] \right\} e^{-\rho_1 t} dt , \qquad (36')$$

where $\Theta' > 0$ and $b(\cdot)$ is the exact consumer price index. The term $w_m(L_m - L_{m,o})/b$ is included in the argument of Θ because the distributional objective is to raise the real income of the poor who work in the informal sector at the initial free trade equilibrium. Thus distributional gains can be achieved either by increasing the real wage in the informal sector or by creating more jobs in the formal industrial sector. At constant prices

$$dW = \int_0^\infty \left\{ du + \frac{\Theta'}{b} [(w_m - w) dL_m + (L_x + L_n) dw] \right\} e^{-\rho_1 t} dt .$$

Since $u = V(P_{mo}, P_{xo}, P_n, E)$, we can substitute $V_E dE$ for du and express the welfare gain in pesos as

$$\frac{dW}{V_E} = \int_0^\infty \{dE + \underbrace{\frac{\Theta'}{V_E b}}_{\Lambda}[(w_m - w)dL_m + (L_x + L_n)dw]\}e^{-\rho_1 t} dt.$$

The weight on the distributional/poverty-reduction objective, $\Lambda = \Theta'/V_E b$, is simply the marginal rate of substitution between national consumption and real income of the poor in the social welfare function. Its value can be fixed once policy makers reveal (off the record) how many pesos of national consumption they would be willing to sacrifice in order to purchase one extra peso of real income for workers in the informal sector. Obviously, this involves a rough interpersonal utility comparison. Capitalists, landowners, and workers in the formal sector pay for both the cut in national consumption and for the extra peso transferred to workers in the informal sector. Implicitly, therefore, one peso given to the poor is judged to produce the same increase in social welfare as $1 + \Lambda$ pesos given to the "average" nonpoor individual.

The weight on the distributional/poverty-reduction objective presumably changes with the fortunes of workers in the informal sector. Exactly how it changes is a matter to be determined by social policy. I assign Λ a value of unity at the free trade equilibrium and assume that the weight declines point for point as the percentage gap between the formal and informal sector wage decreases relative to its initial level. In other words,

$$\Lambda = \Lambda|_{\text{free trade}} \times \frac{(w_m - w)/w}{(w_{m,o} - w_o)/w_o} = \frac{(w_m - w)/w}{(w_{m,o} - w_o)/w_o},$$

so $\Lambda = 0$ and the battle against poverty is won only when the low-wage informal sector disappears.

Table 5.13 collects the solutions for optimal policy in the base run. In the first panel, where $s = 0$, the optimal ERP increases from 9–26% to 16–33%. (For comparison, the solutions that ignore distributional concerns are shown in parentheses below.) This is qualitatively and quantitatively consistent with earlier results. An escalated structure of protection helps the poor; the benefits of protection are greater therefore when the social welfare function includes a distributional objective. But since the costs of the trade distortion rise rapidly when export subsidies are disallowed, the increase in the ERP is limited to 6–8 percentage points. More protection is desirable, but not much more.

Optimal policy changes dramatically, however, when the export subsidy is a policy instrument. For $\rho_1 = .08$, the distributional objective

Table 5.13. *Optimal commercial policy in the base run when there is a distributional objective.*[1]

Optimal structure of protection ($s = 0$)

ψ	$\rho_1 = .08$			$\rho_1 = .06$		
	h	g	ERP	h	g	ERP
.50	19.987 (13.158)	11.623 (8.730)	22.84 (14.65)	28.358 (22.852)	15.874 (13.732)	32.66 (25.97)
.67	14.421 (7.767)	8.447 (4.988)	16.45 (8.70)	20.299 (15.466)	10.554 (7.811)	23.64 (18.08)

Full optimal solution

ψ	$\rho_1 = .08$						$\rho_1 = .06$					
	h	s	g	ERP_m	ERP_x	Bias	h	s	g	ERP_m	ERP_x	Bias
.50	35.264 (4.939)	18.290 (-9.969)	29.878 (-1.345)	37.06 (7.08)	17.04 (-10.90)	1.17 (1.21)	70.054 (36.681)	48.256 (18.500)	63.663 (32.059)	72.21 (40.92)	46.59 (17.04)	1.18 (1.20)
.67	25.186 (2.868)	13.910 (-6.235)	22.055 (-1.266)	26.24 (4.27)	13.02 (-6.78)	1.12 (1.12)	50.990 (35.339)	38.987 (24.662)	47.719 (31.662)	52.09 (36.58)	38.03 (23.90)	1.10 (1.10)

[1] The numbers in parentheses refer to the outcome when there is no distributional objective. Bias is measured as $(1 + ERP_m)/(1 + ERP_x)$.

makes it optimal to raise the ERP in the import-competing sector from 4% to 26–38% and to replace an export tax of 6–10% with a subsidy of 13–18%. When underinvestment is added to the list of distortions at the laissez faire equilibrium, the optimal tariff on consumer imports doubles and the optimal export subsidy increases nearly threefold. The import-competing sector enjoys an ERP of 52–72%, but this is paired with an ERP of 38–47% for the export sector and a slight reduction in the bias of the trade regime.

The large values of s in the full optimal solution reflect not only the role the export subsidy plays in reducing the costs of the trade distortion, but also its own separate contribution to the distributional/poverty-reduction objective. It may seem paradoxical that the contribution to the distributional objective is positive given that export subsidies reduce the real wage in the informal sector across steady states. But the long run is preceded by a medium run of 30–40 years in which the real wage is substantially higher (see Figure 5.3). Moreover, the protectionist component of the optimal policy package is large enough to ensure that the real wage continues to rise after the stimulus from the export subsidy dies out. The adverse long-run effects are limited therefore to *smaller increases* in the real wage far out on the transition path where the weight on the distributional objective Λ has fallen from unity to a number below .5. The lengthy medium run of positive benefits combined with the steadily declining value of Λ makes for a favorable intertemporal tradeoff when the discount rate is 6–8%. This result is almost certainly not unique to the base run in the current model; it should extend to other parameter settings and other models provided labor demand is moderately elastic and production relatively labor-intensive in the export sector. I conjecture that in most cases distributional considerations call for more protection, more export promotion, and little change in the overall bias of the trade regime.

5.8   Further Remarks on the Nature of Optimal Trade Policy

Two points should be kept in mind when using the results in Tables 5.11–5.13 to argue that optimal trade policy combines moderate protection with export promotion. First, a large export subsidy is not always the same thing as export promotion. Despite the large subsidies, the producer price of the primary good falls relative to the producer prices for both importables and nontradables in the long run. The export subsidy does raise the producer price relative to the price of capital (P_x/P_k always increases), but this does not prevent output Q_x or the capital stock K_x from decreasing across steady states. The export sector may expand for a few years before growth accelerates in the import and nontradables sectors. But that is all. There is no surge in export production until the adjustment process has been underway for several decades (at least) and the direction of trade changes in manufactured consumer goods.

The second point concerns the size of the VAT after import substitution is complete and the economy enters the phase where it exports both manufactures and primary products. In some cases the tax ends up at a high level that probably violates political and/or administrative constraints (i.e., the ability to control evasion). Values around 25% are particularly suspect (Agha and Houghton, 1996). The solutions in several of the cases where $\rho_1 = .06$ are therefore problematic.[29] The pursuit of optimal export promotion may require the government to expand the tax base or find new sources of revenue.

5.9   Concluding Observations

Protection should be moderate but highly escalated with respect to both intermediate inputs and capital goods if underemployment is the only distortion in factor markets or if political/administrative constraints rule out export subsidies in the primary sector. Moderate means, specifically, that the optimal ERP is unlikely to exceed 30% and will often be less than 20%. Much higher rates of effective protection of 40–70% can be justified for the import-competing sector when export subsidies are feasible and policy makers wage battle against both underemployment and underinvestment. High levels of protection, however, go together with high export subsidies in the primary sector: in the right half of Tables 5.11 and 5.13, the ERP in the primary export sector ranges from 14 to 47% and is tightly correlated with the ERP in the import sector.

These guidelines do not support the extreme anti-protectionism in vogue today, but they are, I believe, consistent with much that we have learned in the past 50 years about trade policy in LDCs. Successful trade regimes in East Asia and elsewhere have generally been distinguished by moderate levels of protection, low duties on imported capital goods, and substantial export incentives.[30] Case studies suggest that this combi-

[29] This is especially relevant to the full optimal solutions in the case where the social welfare function incorporates a distributional objective. In the lower right panel of Table 5.13 (full optimal solution, $\rho_1 = .06$), the VAT is 25.1% for $\psi = .67$ and 34.7% for $\psi = .50$.

[30] In 1978, tariffs on consumer goods were twice as high as tariffs on capital goods in S. Korea and Thailand but only 1–1.3 times as high in India, Brazil, and Argentina (Langhammer, 1987). Hong (1981, 1991) emphasizes that export

nation of policies promoted rapid capital accumulation and the switch
from domestic to export markets that was critical to maintaining high
growth in the manufacturing sector after import substitution had run its
course.[31] This is also what happens in the model. After domestic firms
corner the whole market in manufactured consumer goods, the tariff h
doubles as an export subsidy and the growth momentum achieved under
import substitution spills over into exports.[32] Nor is the export phase a
minor event at the tail end of the transition path. In the cases where
$\rho_1 = .06$ in Table 5.11, exports of manufactured goods rise to 4–25% of
GDP. The path the economy follows has the look of what Taylor (1993)
calls the import-substitute-then-export (ISTE) strategy.

The other important feature of the model, discussed at length in
Section 5.4.3, is that an escalated structure of protection strengthens
labor demand and reduces underemployment. It is difficult to judge how
well this prediction accords with the empirical record. Econometric estimates of the impact of trade policy on employment are few in number,
do not properly control for the influence of other factors, and neglect
indirect effects stemming from induced capital accumulation and greater
utilization of imported intermediates. The same criticisms apply to case
studies and other informal methods of empirical investigation. None of
this would matter if the data pointed again and again to the conclusion
that an escalated structure of protection weakens labor demand. But
they do not. Many countries have achieved satisfactory or high rates of
employment growth and real wage growth under protection.[33] To confuse

incentives and extreme preferential treatment of imported intermediates and
capital goods were part of a conscious strategy in S. Korea to promote capital
accumulation.

[31] Virtually all successful exporters of manufactured goods (with the exception
of Hong Kong) experienced a prior period of strong import-substitution–based
growth. It is also interesting to note that the leading industrial sectors changed
little in S. Korea, Turkey, and Taiwan when the shift from import substitution to
export expansion took place (Helleiner, 1990).

[32] Note that the tariff and export subsidy cannot differ. If the export subsidy is
lower, firms will shift sales to the domestic market until they receive the same
price at home and abroad. The effective tariff is then equal to the export subsidy.

[33] Manufacturing output grew at 10+ percent and manufacturing sector employment at 4+ percent in the sixties and seventies in Thailand, Malaysia, and Tunisia.
Protection was moderate in Malaysia and Thailand and quite high in Tunisia
(Akrasanee, 1981; Nabli, 1981; Lewis, 1989; Akrasanee and Wiboonchutikula,
1994). In Colombia, manufacturing employment growth averaged only 1% from
1957 to 1966, but the real wage grew at an annual rate of 5.5%. After 1966, real
wage growth moderated and employment growth rose to 3% (Thoumi, 1981).

the issue further, the literature often ascribes an export-oriented strategy to these countries. In the Ivory Coast, for example, manufacturing sector employment grew at 10.8% per annum between 1960 and 1974. The average ERP in 1972 was 105% for the "priority" firms that produced 79% of value added in HOS (Heckscher–Ohlin–Samuelson) import industries and 62% for "common law" firms that produced the rest. The ERPs for priority and common law firms in HOS export industries were 58% and 9%,[34] yet the Ivory Coast is classified in the NBER study as a country that followed an export promotion strategy.

Pakistan fared well under import substitution for most of the 1960–1987 period. Labor demand increased strongly enough to absorb a growing labor force at rising real wages (McCleary, 1991).

[34] These and the other figures cited for the Ivory Coast are from Monson (1981, pp. 248, 270).

CHAPTER 6

Liberalization and the Transition Problem, Part I: Transitory Unemployment

The results in Chapter 5 argue that most LDCs pursued excessively protectionist policies in the recent past. This conclusion agrees with conventional wisdom, but it does not, on its own, justify aggressive trade liberalization. Attempts to reduce protection to more moderate, sensible levels have been neither easy to sustain nor clearly welfare-improving. While some liberalization programs have worked well, many others have confirmed policy makers' worst fears that lower trade barriers will increase unemployment and worsen the balance of payments deficit. Prior to the nineties, one or both of these problems often provoked a reversal of the trade reform after a fairly short period of time. The NBER project organized by Bhagwati and Krueger examined 22 liberalization episodes in the pre-1980 period; in 16 of the 22 episodes, the attempt at reform was abandoned within five years.[1] A more recent World Bank study (Michaely, Papageorgiou, and Choksi, 1991) reports similarly discouraging figures. The study was confined to liberalization attempts outside of Sub-Saharan Africa that lasted at least two years, which undoubtedly skewed the sample toward successful outcomes. Nevertheless, the failure rate was 64% overall and 83% for first attempts to liberalize severely distorted trade regimes.[2]

There are two important aspects to the liberalization problem. The first is the problem of making the transition – the problem of how to get from here to there. The second concerns the extent to which adjustment costs matter for the welfare arithmetic. Is it worthwhile to liberalize if the reform may not last longer than five years? For reforms that are viable, how much do costs during the transition reduce the desirable amount of liberalization?

This chapter focuses primarily on the problem of transitory high

[1] See Krueger (1978, pp. 219–220) for a breakdown of the 22 liberalization episodes into failures and successes. Krueger counts three programs that were sustained for three to four years as "intermediate successes."
[2] Michaely, Papageorgiou, and Choksi (1991, pp. 35, 40). My figures exclude episodes in Israel and New Zealand and count "partially sustained" episodes as failed attempts.

187

unemployment. In Chapter 8, I analyze the reasons why liberalization may give rise to unexpectedly large payments deficits and the welfare costs of speculative import sprees.

6.1   The Problem of Transitory High Unemployment

The orthodox critique of import-substituting industrialization contends that protection weakens the demand for labor and depresses the real wage paid to workers outside the industrial sector. A fine balancing act is required to reconcile this tenet with the fact that liberalization often leads to higher unemployment in the short and medium run. Thus, when summarizing the findings of the NBER project, Krueger (1978) first acknowledges that adjustment problems may arise when imports contract:

> the process of transition will be easier, and therefore more likely to result in sustained liberalization, if import flows increase following devaluation; if devaluation must be accompanied by a cut in real imports, it will be much more difficult. Many of the Latin American Phase III "failures" started at a time when imports were high and had to be reduced. (p. 224)

then asserts

> In most of the cases of recession encountered in the country studies, in fact, the real villain of the piece appears to have been the sharp cutback in the rate of increase of the money supply. In most instances it was the attempt to control domestic inflation, and not liberalization, that resulted in slowdowns in the rate of economic growth. (p. 238)

and in the end settles for the cautious, heavily qualified position

> The appropriate conclusion is probably that a healthy skepticism should be maintained about any sizable impact of the Phase III package on the level of economic activity, except when a sharp cutback in imports accompanies devaluation. There are enough offsetting factors working in both directions that it would very likely require large changes in import flows, in the exchange rate, or in other variables before it could be assumed that the devaluation package would be a major factor in determining changes in the level of economic activity or prices. (p. 243)

Michaely, Papageorgiou, and Choksi (1991) take a much stronger position. They emphasize that the country studies in the World Bank project did not uncover any evidence that liberalization adversely affects employment or growth in the short run:

The clear conclusion indicated by the data and analyses of the country studies is that, by and large, liberalization attempts have not incurred significant transition costs by way of unemployment. A suspicion of some slight negative impact of liberalization on employment is detected only in Argentina 1 and 2, Philippines 1, and Spain 1 and 2.... In sum, it appears warranted to infer that liberalization attempts that fall within the range of the large number of observed post–World War II experiences are unlikely to do much harm to employment.... This evidence appears to dispel the notion that trade liberalization policies incur short-term economic costs in the guise of a general loss of production. On the contrary, a clear inference emerges from the evidence that trade liberalization is positively associated with a general economic expansion. (pp. 80, 81, 90)

This view strikes me as overly sanguine. The empirical regularities cited in the World Bank study are based on simple cross-tabulations of the data and comparisons of the economy before, during, and after liberalization. This methodology is too crude to isolate the impact of trade reform from that of other policies and shocks.[3] Moreover, there are serious problems with the way the country studies identify liberalization episodes and measure their intensity and duration. In some cases, liberalization has not even occurred – the so-called liberalization program comprises only a devaluation and other stabilization measures (Greenaway, 1993). The study's vague, undifferentiated concept of liberalization also adds to the difficulty of interpretation. It embraces lower duties and less restrictive quotas on consumer goods, intermediate inputs and capital goods, export-promotion policies, substitution of tariffs for quotas, and tidying-up operations that reduce the variance of protection but have only a modest impact on its overall level. As will become clear in subsequent sections, it does not make sense to toss everything into the same pot because different types of trade reform would be expected to have quite different effects on employment.[4] Given this, the absence of an explicit counterfactual model, and the fact that the project examined mostly *mild* liberalization episodes,[5] it is dubious to assert that "the evidence appears to dispel the notion that trade liberalization policies incur short-term economic costs in the guise of a general loss of

---

[3] See Collier (1993), Greenaway (1993), and Greenaway and Morrissey (1993) on this and other criticisms that follow.
[4] As Helleiner remarks (1991, p. 534), "One is left yearning for more analysis of such issues as the effects of different kinds of import liberalization. ..."
[5] See Helleiner (1990) and Thomas (1991). Decreases in protection of the import-competing sector were quite modest up to the late eighties.

production."[6] On the contrary, though the empirical record is messy, it seems hard to deny that a temporary increase in unemployment is a potential danger in liberalization programs. Some studies that focus more narrowly on the labor market conclude that liberalization reduces employment growth significantly in the short run.[7] A number of the country studies in the NBER project also reach this conclusion, and there is certainly nothing in the outcome of Latin American liberalization programs in the early nineties that contradicts it.[8] The most disturbing evidence, however, comes from post-1980 liberalization episodes in Sub-Saharan Africa:

- Senegal experienced large job losses following a two-stage liberalization program that reduced the average effective rate of protection from 165% in 1985 to 90% in 1988. By the early nineties, employment

[6] Policy makers do not appear to share this view. Israel, for example, chose to liberalize very gradually over a period of 25 years because of concerns about the adverse effects of tariff cuts on employment (Bruno, 1988). The same fear lies behind the slow pace of liberalization in India (Joshi and Little, 1995).

[7] Rama (1994) estimates that each one percentage point reduction in the tariff-inclusive import price leads to a .4–.5 percentage point drop in manufacturing sector employment in Uruguay. This implies that the removal of all trade barriers would eliminate jobs for 5% of the workforce. Ravenga (1994) comes up with a smaller employment elasticity of .2–.3 for the Mexican liberalization of 1985–1988. And while the recent World Bank study supervised by Michaely et al. concludes that Chile's bold liberalization program in the late seventies did not cost the economy any jobs, most experts on the Chilean economy believe otherwise. Meller (1994) estimates the overall reduction in industrial sector employment at approximately 10% (p. 127) – a figure that should be compared with average annual employment growth in the sixties of 2.9%. Foxley (1983) estimates the job losses from trade liberalization to be as large or larger.

[8] See the accounts in Baldwin (1975) and Behrman (1976) of the 1960–62 liberalization episode in the Philippines and the 1957–58 and 1965–66 episodes in Chile. It should also be noted that there is evidence in the World Bank project of strong contractionary effects in some episodes for Israel, Spain, and Yugoslavia.

Liberalization in the early nineties seems to have resulted in large job losses in the formal sector and a substantial worsening in underemployment in Peru (Sheahan, 1994), Nicaragua (Aravena, 1996; Geske Dijkstra, 1996), Ecuador (Larrea, 1998), and Brazil. Nor is the evidence from other parts of Latin America particularly encouraging: "the regional record as it now stands suggests that the 'normal' outcome is a sharp deterioration in income distribution, with no clear evidence that this shift is temporary in character" (Berry, 1999a, p. 4). "No example of an outward-oriented Latin American country achieving an improvement in distribution through the combination of market outcomes and its own redistributive efforts has yet been identified" (Berry, 1999b, p. 27).

cuts had eliminated one-third of all manufacturing jobs (Weissman, 1991; African Development Bank, 1995, p. 84).

- The chemical, textile, shoe, and automobile assembly industries virtually collapsed in Cote d'Ivoire after tariffs were abruptly lowered by 40% in 1986 (Stein, 1992). Similar problems have plagued liberalization attempts in Nigeria. The capacity utilization rate fell to 20–30%, and harsh adverse effects on employment and real wages provoked partial policy reversals in 1990, 1992, and 1994.
- In Sierre Leone, Zambia, Zaire, Uganda, Tanzania, and the Sudan, liberalization in the eighties brought a tremendous surge in consumer imports and sharp cutbacks in foreign exchange available for purchases of intermediate inputs and capital goods.[9] The effects on industrial output and employment were devastating. In Uganda, for example, the capacity utilization rate in the industrial sector languished at 22% while consumer imports claimed 40–60% of total foreign exchange (Loxley, 1989).
- The beverages, tobacco, textiles, sugar, leather, cement, and glass products sectors have all struggled to survive competition from imports since Kenya initiated a major trade liberalization program in 1993 (African Development Bank, 1998; Ministry of Planning and National Development, 1998). Contraction in these sectors has not been offset by expansion elsewhere in manufacturing. The period 1993–1997 saw the growth rates of output and employment in manufacturing fall to 2.6% and 2.2%, respectively (Ministry of Planning and National Development, 1998, p. 164).
- Manufacturing output and employment grew rapidly in Ghana after liberalization in 1983 and generous aid from the World Bank greatly increased access to imported inputs. But when liberalization spread to consumer imports, employment plunged from 78,700 in 1987 to 28,000 in 1993 (African Development Bank, 1995, p. 397). The employment losses owed mainly to the fact that "large swathes of the manufacturing sector had been devastated by import competition" (African Development Bank, 1998, p. 45).
- Following trade liberalization in 1990, formal sector job growth slowed to a trickle in Zimbabwe and the unemployment rate jumped from 10 to 20%.[10] Adjustment in the nineties has also been difficult for much

---

[9] See Cornia, van der Hoeven, and Mkandawire (1992); Stein (1992); Wagao (1992); Zack-Williams (1992); Sepehri (1993); Stewert (1994); and Mommen (1996). Nicaragua suffered from the same problem when it liberalized imports in 1990 (Aravena, 1996; Geske Dijkstra, 1996).

[10] The country was hit by a severe drought in 1991–92, but employment was still depressed three years later despite a 25% cut in the real wage. See Marquette (1997).

of the manufacturing sector in Mozambique, Cameroon, Tanzania, Malawi, and Zambia. Import competition precipitated sharp contractions in output and employment in the short run, with many firms closing down operations entirely (African Development Bank, 1998, pp. 45, 51).

It is easy to see why unemployment might increase if tariffs were lowered but other policy instruments were left unchanged: since employment would fall in industry at the same time as consumers switched expenditures away from nontraded goods toward imports, a reduction in the nominal wage would probably be required to clear the labor market.[11] But it is surely asking a lot of any labor market, even the "flexprice" informal market, that the nominal wage fall instantaneously to whatever level is needed to maintain full employment.[12,13] Many liberalization programs therefore combine lower tariffs with devaluation and an upfront real wage cut in the industrial sector. The aim of this policy package is to lessen the need for difficult adjustments in the labor market. The accompanying real wage cut, if large enough, allows liberalization to be compatible with higher employment in industry. A sufficiently large devaluation prevents the price of imported consumer goods from falling and reduces the product wage in export industries, which would seem to increase the chance for workers laid off in the import-competing sector to find jobs in other sectors at a constant or rising nominal wage.

Surprisingly, broader adjustment programs of this type have not been highly successful even when workers accede to large real wage cuts. The country studies in the NBER project and the outcome of post-1980 liberalization attempts in Sub-Saharan Africa point to cuts in imported inputs as the likely source of difficulties. I examine this hypothesis in the next section by developing a macroeconomic model that incorporates a

[11] If the efficiency gains are large enough, the demand for nontraded goods might increase despite layoffs in the industrial sector and a fall in the price of imports. It is then possible that overall labor demand will increase.
[12] Advocates of World Bank liberalization programs do not dispute this. See, for example, Little et al. (1993, p. 101).
[13] The difficulties the CFA countries experienced in trying to engineer a depreciation of the real exchange rate without adjustment of the nominal rate attest to the downward inflexibility of wages and prices. After suffering through a ten-year recession that lowered real output per capita by 30% but failed to restore external balance, the countries admitted defeat and devalued the currency vis à vis the franc by 50% in January 1994 [see Devarajan and Rodrik (1991) and O'Connell (1997)].

general specification of technology but does not assume perfect downward flexibility of the wage in the informal sector.

6.2   Compensated Devaluation, Wage Rigidity, and Unemployment

To bring nominal variables into the picture with a minimum of complications, I keep the macroeconomic framework simple. The capital account is closed and high-powered money M is the only financial asset in the economy. There is no government consumption, and net tariff revenues (i.e., revenues less the cost of any export subsidies) are rebated to the public in a lump-sum fashion. The sole function of the central bank is to swap domestic currency for foreign currency at the fixed exchange rate v.

The general equilibrium structure of the model is also very simple. Competitive firms hire capital K_i, labor L_i, and imported inputs Z_i to produce an importable consumer good and an export good according to a pair of linearly homogeneous production functions. Intermediate inputs enter duty-free, but consumer imports are subject to a tariff h that is much larger than the export subsidy s. ($s < 0$ signifies an export tax.) The trade regime is thus characterized by an escalated structure of protection and a bias toward import substitution.

Since the focus is now on short- and medium-run adjustment problems, I ignore investment spending and treat the sectoral capital stocks as fixed. As usual, world prices equal unity. Domestic prices are therefore

$$P_m = v(1+h), \tag{1}$$

$$P_x = v(1+s), \tag{2}$$

$$P_z = v, \tag{3}$$

while

$$P_i = C^i(w_i, r_i, v), \tag{4}$$

$$L_i = C^i_w Q_i, \tag{5}$$

$$Z_i = C^i_v Q_i, \tag{6}$$

$$K_i = C^i_r Q_i, \tag{7}$$

define the zero-profit conditions and sectoral factor demands.

In normal times the wage in the protected industrial sector is fully indexed to the price level. At the start of the adjustment program, however, indexation provisions may be adjusted or temporarily suspended so as to engineer a real wage cut:

$$\hat{w}_m = \alpha\hat{P} = \alpha(\gamma_m \hat{P}_m + \gamma_x \hat{P}_x), \qquad \gamma_m + \gamma_x = 1, \tag{8}$$

where γ_i is the consumption share of good i, $P \equiv P_m^{\gamma m} P_x^{\gamma x}$ is the price level, and $\alpha \leq 1$ measures the real wage cut.

Wage adjustment in the export sector is asymmetric. Nothing prevents the price of labor from rising quickly to eliminate excess demand, but adjustment in the downward direction is difficult as workers will not agree to nominal wage cuts unless they feel threatened by persistent, open unemployment. I model this by assuming that w_x decreases gradually when labor demand falls below labor supply:

$$\frac{\dot{w}_x}{w_x} = -b(1 - L_m - L_x) \quad \text{for} \quad L_m + L_x < 1. \tag{9}$$

The supply of labor is fixed at unity, so the parameter b determines the responsiveness of the wage to the unemployment rate $1 - L_m - L_x$.

Finally, the private agent solves the problem

$$\max_{\{E,S\}} \int_0^\infty [V(P_m, P_x, E) + \phi(M/P)]e^{-\rho t} dt, \tag{10}$$

subject to

$$E = R(\cdot) + vh[D^m(P_m, P_x, E) - Q_m] - vs[Q_x - D^x(P_m, P_x, E)] - S, \tag{11}$$

$$\dot{M} = S, \tag{12}$$

where S is saving; D^i is the *uncompensated* demand function for good i; and $\phi(M/P)$ is an increasing, strictly concave function that measures the nonpecuniary services generated by real money balances.[14] The revenue function differs depending on the state of the labor market. When there is open unemployment,

$$R(\cdot) = R(P_m, P_x, P_z, L_m, L_x), \qquad R_4 = w_m, R_5 = w_x, \tag{13}$$

---

[14] There is nothing wrong with putting money in the utility function when the transactions technology is stable. Feenstra (1986) has shown that there is an equivalence between models where liquidity costs appear in the budget constraint and those that put money in the utility function. The shopping-time model of McCallum can also be represented as a model with money in the utility function (McCallum, 1983).

whereas in periods of full employment

$$R(\cdot) = R(P_m, P_x, P_z, L_m), \qquad R_4 = w_m - w_x. \tag{13'}$$

The adjustment program involves reductions in h and s, a devaluation of the currency, and an administratively imposed real wage cut in the import-competing sector. The *compensated* or *net devaluation* in sector i is defined as $\hat{P}_i/\hat{v}$, the ratio of the percentage increase in P_i to the percentage devaluation of the currency. Clearly, the larger the liberalization component of the program, the smaller the net devaluation; if the devaluation is fully offset by cuts in the tariff and export subsidy (or an increase in the export tax), the net devaluation is zero in both sectors.[15]

6.2.1 The Short-Run Effect on Sectoral Employment[16]

The short-run effect on unemployment depends on whether total labor demand, $L_m + L_x$, rises or falls at the initial wage that firms pay in the export sector. To make this calculation, use (7) to eliminate Q_i in (5):

$$L_i = C_w^i(w_i, r_i, v) K_i / C_r^i(w_i, r_i, v). \tag{14}$$

As K_i is fixed,

$$\hat{L}_i = \theta_K^i (\sigma_{LK}^i - \sigma_{KK}^i)\hat{r}_i + \theta_Z^i(\sigma_{LZ}^i - \sigma_{KZ}^i)\hat{v} + \theta_L^i(\sigma_{LL}^i - \sigma_{LK}^i)\hat{w}_i, \tag{15}$$

where θ_j^i is the cost share of factor j and σ_{jf} is the partial elasticity of substitution between factors j and f. The earnings of the fixed factors are determined residually by the zero-profit conditions (4):

$$\hat{r}_i = \left(\hat{P}_i - \theta_Z^i\hat{v} - \theta_L^i\hat{w}_i\right)/\theta_K^i . \tag{16}$$

Substituting this into (15) produces

$$\hat{L}_i = a_1^i\hat{P}_i - a_2^i\hat{v} - a_3^i\hat{w}_i, \tag{17}$$

where

$$a_1^i \equiv \sigma_{LK}^i - \sigma_{KK}^i > 0,$$

---

[15] In many of the episodes studied by the NBER project, the net devaluation for exports was smaller than that for imports (Krueger, 1978, p. 73). Michaely et al. (1991) also note that it is fairly common to combine lower export incentives with devaluation.

[16] The analysis in this section is based on Buffie (1984).

$$a_2^i \equiv \theta_Z^i(\sigma_{LK}^i + \sigma_{KZ}^i - \sigma_{KK}^i - \sigma_{LZ}^i) \gtrless 0,$$

$$a_3^i \equiv \theta_L^i(2\sigma_{LK}^i - \sigma_{KK}^i - \sigma_{LL}^i) > 0.$$

From (8) and (17),

$$\hat{L}_m = (a_1^m - \alpha\gamma_m a_3^m)\hat{P}_m - a_2^m\hat{v} - a_3^m\alpha\gamma_x\hat{P}_x, \tag{18}$$

while in the export sector

$$\hat{L}_x\big|_{\text{constant } w} = a_1^x\hat{P}_x - a_2^x\hat{v}. \tag{19}$$

a_3 must be positive given strict concavity of the production function in L and Z alone. a_1 is also positive under the weak assumption that labor is not an inferior factor. The sign of the cross-price term is ambiguous due to possibly countervaling output and substitution effects, but in the normal case where labor and intermediates are gross complements a_2 is positive. Reflecting the homogeneity property of factor demands, $a_1^i - a_2^i - a_3^i = 0$.

Equations (18) and (19) return different results for different types of adjustment programs and for different types of technology. But while the details of technology and policy matter, the general implication of the solutions is that adjustment in the labor market is likely to be difficult in programs where the weight of the liberalization component is large. Consider the outcome when the nominal wage is held fixed in the import sector. For $\alpha = 0$,

$$\frac{\hat{L}_i}{\hat{v}} = \left(\frac{\hat{P}_i}{\hat{v}} - \theta_Z^i\right)(\sigma_{LK}^i - \sigma_{KK}^i) - \theta_Z^i(\sigma_{KZ}^i - \sigma_{LZ}^i). \tag{20}$$

The first term is of the same sign as $\hat{r}_i$, while the sign of the second depends on which primary factor substitutes more easily with imported intermediates. Employment always falls when $\sigma_{KZ} \geq \sigma_{LZ}$ and the liberalization component of the adjustment program lowers nominal profits. More striking still, employment may decline in both sectors even though nominal profits increase and product wages fall by the full amount of the net devaluations. Nor is there any assurance that large real wage cuts will at least stave off large reductions in employment. For $\hat{P}_i/\hat{v} = \theta_Z^i = .25$, $\sigma_{KZ}^i = .75$, $\sigma_{LZ}^i = .25$, and $\hat{v} = .50$, employment contracts 6.25% despite a 12.5% cut in the real wage.

These results are consistent with our finding in Chapter 5 that an escalated structure of protection is helpful in reducing underemployment. The flip side of this finding is the depressing conclusion that liberalization programs will encounter problems on the employment front if real wages are not sufficiently flexible. A compensated devaluation raises the real price of imported intermediates by $\hat{v}/\hat{P}_i - 1$. When firms react by purchasing fewer intermediates, labor productivity falls (assuming L_i and Z_i are gross complements). The product wage w_i/P_i must decrease therefore to prevent employment from declining in sector i. What is disconcerting is that the requisite cuts in product wages may not be feasible unless nominal wages are downwardly flexible.

In what follows, I assume $s = 0$ initially and that unemployment increases in the short run. The first assumption serves mainly to simplify the analysis. When examining the employment effects of a compensated devaluation in the export sector, it does not matter whether $\hat{P}_x/\hat{v} < 1$ reflects a reduction in an existing export subsidy or an increase in an export tax that initially equals zero. In the latter case, however, the comparison of short-run costs and long-run gains involves less algebra because the (small) export tax does not create a trade distortion [i.e., the term $vs(Q_x - D^x)$ drops out of (11)]. This makes it easier to calculate how excessive protection is at the initial equilibrium and how much liberalization increases welfare in the long run.

The reason for concentrating on the case where unemployment increases temporarily is that the alternative case is not very interesting from an analytical standpoint. If full employment prevails from the outset and h exceeds its *ex ante* optimal level, then liberalization is welfare-improving and the balance of payments registers a surplus at all points on the transition path to the new steady state.[17] The interesting issues have to do with how the welfare calculations and the dynamics differ when a bout of unemployment is required to beat the wage in the export sector down to its equilibrium level. How much liberalization is desirable after taking account of the welfare losses associated with transitory unemployment? Might severe contraction in one or more branches of the tradables sector cause a temporary worsening in the balance of payments?

6.2.2   The Transition Path

The private agent chooses saving so that

$$V_E(P_m, P_x, E) = \pi, \tag{21}$$

$$\dot{\pi} = \rho V_E - \phi'/P, \tag{22}$$

---

[17] These results will be transparent after the transition path is derived in the next two sections.

where π is the multiplier paired with the constraint in (12). These two conditions can be collapsed into one by differentiating (21) with respect to time and substituting for $\dot{\pi}$ from (22):

$$V_{EE}\dot{E} = \rho V_E - \phi'/P. \tag{23}$$

The economy's dynamics are governed by (9), (12), and the differential equation for saving implicit in (23) and the private agent's budget constraint (11). Starting from an initial equilibrium where the external accounts balance (i.e., $Q_x - D^x = Z_x + Z_m + D^m - Q_m$ initially),

$$\hat{E} = \gamma_m \hat{P}_m + \gamma_x \hat{P}_x + \theta_L^m \frac{P_m Q_m}{EF} \hat{L}_m + \theta_L^x \frac{P_x Q_x}{EF} \hat{L}_x$$
$$- \frac{\gamma_m \varepsilon h}{F(1+h)}(\hat{P}_m - \hat{P}_x) - \frac{h}{1+h}\frac{P_m Q_m}{EF}\hat{Q}_m - \frac{dS}{FE}, \tag{24}$$

where $F \equiv 1 - \gamma_m h/(1 + h)$, $\varepsilon > 0$ is the compensated own-price elasticity of demand for the imported good, and we have made use of the Slutsky decompositions $\hat{D}^m/P_m = -\varepsilon - \gamma_m$ and $\hat{D}^m/P_x = \varepsilon - \gamma_x$. (Note that the compensated own- and cross-price elasticities are equal when there are just two goods.) On the transition path, L_m, P_m, P_x, and Q_m are all constant and the ordinary derivatives in (24) become time derivatives. Thus,

$$F\dot{E} = P_x Q_x \theta_L^x a_3^x b(1 - L_x - L_m) - \dot{S},$$

and

$$\dot{S} = \frac{F}{V_{EE}}\left[\frac{\phi'(M/P)}{P} - \rho V_E(P_m, P_x, E)\right] + P_x Q_x \theta_L^x a_3^x b(1 - L_x - L_m). \tag{25}$$

Linearizing (25) around the stationary equilibrium $(M^*, w_x^*, 0)$ gives

$$\dot{S} = \rho S + c(w_x - w_x^*) + \frac{FE\rho}{M}\left(\frac{\phi''M}{V_{EE}E\rho P^2}\right)(M - M^*), \tag{26}$$

where $c \equiv L_x a_3^x(\rho + bL_x a_3^x) > 0$. It is readily shown from (22) that $\phi''M/V_{EE}E\rho P^2$ is the expenditure or income elasticity of money demand. Set this elasticity equal to unity and define μ to be the ratio of money balances to national income ($\mu \equiv M/E$). The system formed by (26) and the linearized versions of (9) and (12) is then

$$\begin{bmatrix} \dot{S} \\ \dot{w}_x \\ \dot{M} \end{bmatrix} = \begin{bmatrix} \rho & c & F\rho/\mu \\ 0 & -bL_x a_3^x & 0 \\ 1 & 0 & 0 \end{bmatrix} \begin{bmatrix} S \\ w_x - w_x^* \\ M - M^* \end{bmatrix}. \tag{27}$$

The general solution to (27) is

$$S(t) = \lambda_2 k_2 e^{\lambda_2 t} + \lambda_3 k_3 \Omega e^{\lambda_3 t}, \tag{28}$$

$$w_x(t) - w_x^* = k_3 e^{\lambda_3 t}, \tag{29}$$

$$M(t) - M^* = k_2 e^{\lambda_2 t} + k_3 \Omega e^{\lambda_3 t}, \tag{30}$$

where

$$\Omega \equiv -\frac{c}{F\rho/\mu + \lambda_3(\rho - \lambda_3)},$$

$$\lambda_1, \lambda_2 = \frac{\rho \pm \sqrt{\rho^2 + 4F\rho/\mu}}{2},$$

$$\lambda_3 = -bL_x a_3^x.$$

Since the system possesses two negative eigenvalues and two predetermined variables (w_x and M), the stationary equilibrium is saddlepoint stable.

The long-run impact of liberalization on the market clearing wage (w_x^*) and desired wealth (M^*) picks out a particular solution. At t = 0, equations (29) and (30) give

$$k_2 = M_o - M^* - k_3 \Omega,$$

$$k_3 = w_{x,o} - w_x^*.$$

From (17), (18), and the full-employment condition $L_m + L_x = 1$, we get

$$\frac{w_x^* - w_{x,o}}{w_{x,o}} = \delta \hat{v}, \tag{31}$$

where

$$\delta \equiv \left[\frac{L_m}{L_x}(a_1^m - \alpha\gamma_m a_3^m)\frac{\hat{P}_m}{\hat{v}} + \left(a_1^x - \frac{L_m}{L_x}a_3^m \alpha\gamma_x \right)\frac{\hat{P}_x}{\hat{v}} - \frac{L_m}{L_x}a_2^m - a_2^x \right] \bigg/ a_3^x$$

is negative by assumption. To derive the solution for the change in money balances, set $\dot{\pi} = 0$ in (22) and define $V_{Ei} \equiv \partial V_E/\partial P_i$. Differentiation with respect to P_i, M, and E then produces

$$\frac{V_{Em}}{V_{EE} D^m} \gamma_m \hat{P}_m + \frac{V_{Ex}}{V_{EE} D^x} \gamma_x \hat{P}_x + \hat{E} = \hat{M} + (\tau - 1)(\gamma_m \hat{P}_m + \gamma_x \hat{P}_x).$$

$V_{Ei}/V_{EE} D^i = \tau - 1$ under homothetic preferences, so this simplifies drastically to

$$\frac{M^* - M_o}{M_o} = \frac{E^* - E_o}{E_o}. \tag{32}$$

Equations (4), (7), and (8) provide

$$\hat{Q}_m = a_4 \hat{P}_m - a_5 \hat{v} - a_6 \hat{P}_x, \tag{33}$$

where

$$a_4 = -\sigma_{KK}^m - \theta_L^m \alpha \gamma_m (\sigma_{KL}^m - \sigma_{KK}^m),$$

$$a_5 = \theta_Z^m (\sigma_{KZ}^m - \sigma_{KK}^m),$$

$$a_6 = \alpha \gamma_x \theta_L^m (\sigma_{KL}^m - \sigma_{KK}^m).$$

Substitute for $\hat{Q}_m$ and set $dS = 0$ and $dL_x = -dL_m$ in (24). After consolidating a few terms, there emerges

$$\frac{E^* - E_o}{E_o} = f\hat{v}, \tag{34}$$

where

$$f \equiv \gamma_m \frac{\hat{P}_m}{\hat{v}} + \gamma_x \frac{\hat{P}_x}{\hat{v}} + \theta_L^m \frac{P_m Q_m}{EF} (1 - \psi) \left[(a_1^m - \alpha \gamma_m a_3^m) \frac{\hat{P}_m}{\hat{v}} - a_3^m \alpha \gamma_x \frac{\hat{P}_x}{\hat{v}} - a_2^m \right]$$

$$- \frac{\gamma_m \varepsilon h}{F(1 + h)} \left(\frac{\hat{P}_m}{\hat{v}} - \frac{\hat{P}_x}{\hat{v}} \right) - \frac{h}{1 + h} \frac{P_m Q_m}{EF} \left(a_4 \frac{\hat{P}_m}{\hat{v}} - a_6 \frac{\hat{P}_x}{\hat{v}} - a_5 \right)$$

and $\psi \equiv w_x / w_m$. The complete solutions for the paths of S, w_x, and M are therefore

$$S(t) = [\lambda_2 (\delta w_{x,o} \Omega - M_o f) e^{\lambda_2 t} - \lambda_3 \Omega \delta w_{x,o} e^{\lambda_3 t}] \hat{v}, \tag{28'}$$

$$w_x(t) - w_{x,o} = \delta w_{x,o} (1 - e^{\lambda_3 t}) \hat{v}, \tag{29'}$$

$$M(t) - M_o = [M_o f(1 - e^{\lambda_2 t}) + \delta w_{x,o} \Omega(e^{\lambda_2 t} - e^{\lambda_3 t})] \hat{v}. \tag{30'}$$

Before proceeding further with the analysis of the adjustment process, it is worth drawing attention to the implications of (32) and (34) for the

long-run effects on welfare and the payments balance. Note in particular that, since the solution for the change in real money balances is the
same as that for real expenditure, the long-run impact on welfare
depends only on how the adjustment program affects allocative efficiency. Formally, let

$$U = V(P_m, P_x, E) + \phi(M/P).$$

Then

$$\frac{dU}{V_E E} = (1 + \rho\mu) \underbrace{\left(\frac{E^* - E_o}{E_o} - \gamma_m \hat{P}_m - \gamma_x \hat{P}_x \right)}_{\text{change in real expenditure}},$$

$$\Rightarrow \frac{F}{P_m Q_m (1 + \rho\mu) V_E} \frac{dU}{\hat{v}} = \frac{D^m}{Q_m} \varepsilon \frac{h}{1+h} \left(\frac{\hat{P}_x}{\hat{v}} - \frac{\hat{P}_m}{\hat{v}} \right)$$

$$+ \theta_L^m (1 - \psi) \left[(a_1^m - \alpha\gamma_m a_3^m) \frac{\hat{P}_m}{\hat{v}} - a_3^m \alpha\gamma_x \frac{\hat{P}_x}{\hat{v}} - a_2^m \right]$$

$$- \frac{h}{1+h} \left(a_4 \frac{\hat{P}_m}{\hat{v}} - a_6 \frac{\hat{P}_x}{\hat{v}} - a_5 \right), \tag{35}$$

as $V_{P_i}/V_E = -D^i$ by Roy's Identity and $\phi'/P = \rho V_E$ for $\dot{\pi} = 0$. The first term
captures the gain from reducing the consumption distortion ($\hat{P}_x/\hat{v} >
\hat{P}_m/\hat{v}$) while the second and third terms pick up the gain/loss from the
changes in employment and output in the import-competing sector. I
assume the sum of the last two terms is positive so that in the long run
liberalization improves allocative efficiency both in production and consumption. Nominal and real expenditure thus increase across steady
states. Since the nominal money supply grows only when the private
sector sells more foreign exchange to the central bank than it buys,
this implies as well that the adjustment program generates a cumulative
payments surplus.

6.2.3   Short-Run vs. Long-Run Effects on the Balance of Payments

The paths for the payments surplus B and private saving are one and
the same as the paths of the money supply and the stock of foreign
exchange reserves. To track the path of M, note from (27) and (28)–(30)
that

$$B = \dot{M} = S(t) = \lambda_2 [M(t) - M^*] - \Omega(\lambda_2 - \lambda_3) [w_x(t) - w_x^*]. \tag{28''}$$

The positive term $\lambda_2(M - M^*)$ reflects the pull of the long-run fundamentals: since $\phi(M/P)$ is concave, the private agent faces an incentive to increase saving immediately so that the path from M_o to M^* will be direct. On the other hand, given that real income rises in the long run, it is also tempting to smooth the path of consumption by saving less during the short run when real income is temporarily low.[18] This opposing effect shows up in the second term. Observe that

$$\lambda_2 - \lambda_3 \gtreqless 0 \quad \text{as} \quad \rho - 2\lambda_3 \gtreqless \sqrt{\rho^2 + 4F\rho/\mu},$$

or, equivalently,

$$\lambda_2 - \lambda_3 \gtreqless 0 \quad \text{as} \quad F\rho/\mu + \lambda_3(\rho - \lambda_3) \lesseqgtr 0.$$

But $-[F\rho/\mu + \lambda_3(\rho - \lambda_3)]$ also sets the sign of Ω The $\dot{M} = 0$ schedule in Figure 6.1 is thus negatively sloped.

If w_x could adjust to keep the economy operating at full employment, liberalization would immediately shift the equilibrium from A to B and hence foreign exchange reserves would rise monotonically toward their higher steady-state level through a series of payments surpluses.[19] But when nominal wage cuts are slow to materialize, policy makers may have to contend with both higher unemployment and payments deficits in the short run. This is the case shown in Figure 6.2. The central bank loses foreign exchange reserves over the period $(0, t_1)$ while the economy moves from A to D, but thereafter the external accounts are in the black, and from t_2 onward (i.e., the JC stretch of the path) the stock of reserves exceeds its prereform level.

To determine whether short-run payment deficits are a nagging worry or a serious problem, I calculated the initial impact on B, the values of t_1 and t_2, and the cumulative reserve loss at t_1 for an economy where

$$\gamma_m = .30, \sigma_{KL}^i = .5, \psi = .667, h = .50, \mu = .10,$$
$$\theta_Z^x = .10, \lambda_3 = -.2, -1, \beta = .25;$$

$$\sigma_{KZ}^i = .75, \text{ and } \sigma_{LZ}^i = .25 \text{ or } \sigma_{KZ}^i = \sigma_{LZ}^i = .5;$$

---

[18] This suggests that the intertemporal elasticity of substitution τ should appear in (28″). It does not, however, because when the income elasticity of money demand equals unity and the utility function is separable, τ sets the concavity of both $\phi(M/P)$ and of the indirect utility function $V(\cdot)$. The two effects are perfectly offsetting because, *ceteris paribus*, the private agent desires equally smooth paths for consumption and money balances.

[19] The solution in the case of continuous full employment is obtained by deleting (29′) and setting Ω equal to zero in (28′) and (30′). ($\Omega \to 0$ as $b \to \infty$.) This yields $S(t) = -\lambda_2 M_o f e^{\lambda_2 t} > 0$.

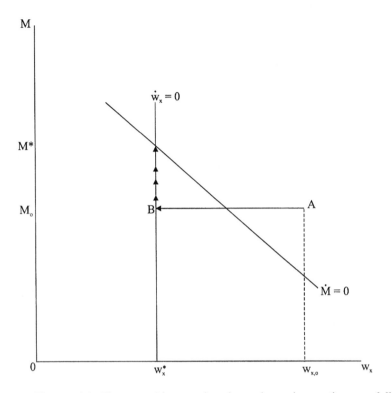

Figure 6.1. The transition path when there is continuous full employment.

$\theta_Z^m = .25$, $\theta_L^m = .225$, and $\theta_L^x = .36$ (base run)

or $\theta_Z^m = .40$, $\theta_L^m = .30$, and $\theta_L^x = .45$;

$\hat{P}_m/\hat{v} = 0$ and either $\hat{P}_x/\hat{v} = 0$ or $\hat{P}_x/\hat{v} = a_2^x/a_1^x$;

reserves are initially one-half of the monetary base (roughly equivalent to 3–4 months of imports); and the share of sector m in total value added is 20% when $\theta_Z^m = .25$ and 17% when $\theta_Z^m = .40$. This set of parameter values encompasses diverse structural characteristics and different types of adjustment patterns.[20] Substitution patterns are either neutral or biased against labor. Cost shares may take normal values, as in the base

---

[20] The results are highly insensitive to β and h. The numbers that follow in Tables 6.2–6.5 change very little when $h = .25$ and $\beta = .50$.

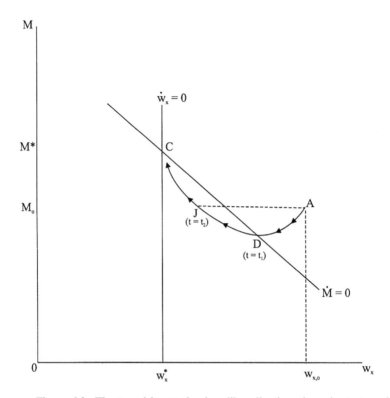

Figure 6.2. The transition path when liberalization gives rise to transitory unemployment and an initial series of payments deficits.

run, or production may be highly intermediates and labor-intensive.[21] The degree of wage flexibility also varies a fair bit. Each value of λ_3 is associated with a different value of b and a different path of unemployment. The speed of adjustment depends on $1 - e^{\lambda_3 t}$, which measures how far w_x has progressed at time t toward its market clearing level w_x^* (see Table 6.1). For $\lambda_3 = -.2$, adjustment is very slow and the wage is still 37% above its equilibrium level after five years. $\lambda_3 = -1$ implies, by contrast, that adjustment in the labor market is nearly complete after two years.

---

[21] The cost shares in the base run reflect the average values for low- and middle-income countries (see the discussion in Chapter 5). In some LDCs, however, labor's share in value added is as high as 50%. The cost share of imported intermediates in manufacturing was 35–40% in Nicaragua and Sri Lanka and 50% in Tanzania in the eighties (Gibson, 1990; Maasland, 1990; Krumm, 1993).

Table 6.1. *Value of* $[w_x(t) - w_{x,o}]/(w_x^* - w_{x,o})$ *at time* t.

λ_3				t			
	1	2	3	4	5	8	10
−.2	.18	.33	.45	.55	.63	.80	.86
−.4	.33	.55	.70	.80	.86	.96	.98
−.6	.45	.70	.83	.91	.95	.99	.998
−.8	.55	.80	.91	.96	.98	.998	≈1
−1	.63	.86	.95	.98	.99	≈1	≈1

The final element in calibration of the model is the mix of trade liberalization and devaluation. The values for $\hat{P}_i/\hat{v}$ indicate that liberalization involves either a pair of fully compensated devaluations – a policy advocated by Little, Scitovsky, and Scott (1970, p. 26) – or a fully compensated devaluation in the import sector and a positive net devaluation in the export sector equal to a_2^x/a_1^x. In the first case, employment contracts sharply in both sectors and exports traverse a J curve, decreasing in the short run before increasing in the medium/long run.[22] In the second case, employment falls in the import sector but does not change initially in the export sector. This latter case can also be interpreted as one where wages are flexible but labor is not instantaneously mobile and firms adopt a "wait and see" strategy before deciding that liberalization will survive long enough to justify an increase in hiring. Production in the export sector is then fixed at $t = 0$ and λ_3 determines how strong the supply response is in the medium run compared to the long run.

Tables 6.2 and 6.3 contain mostly good news. In the lower panels, where L_x does not change in the short run, the balance of payments either improves immediately or worsens by a small amount for a year or less. The numbers are less favorable when liberalization is implemented through fully compensated devaluations in both sectors, but not so bad as to endanger the reform. Although the values for t_2 are large, the period of payments deficits never lasts longer than 2.4 years and the cumulative reserve loss at t_1 is small. This reflects the strong stabilizing influence of the long-run fundamentals: the desire of the private sector to accumulate wealth in line with its long-run increase in real income holds the payments deficit to a tolerable level even when liberalization is severely

---

[22] See Bhagwati (1978, p. 183) for examples and a discussion of the J-curve phenomenon.

Table 6.2. *The impact effect on the payments deficit and the values of* t_1, t_2 *and the cumulative reserve loss at* t_1 *in the base run.**

	Fully compensated devaluations in both sectors							
	$\sigma_{KZ} = .75, \sigma_{LZ} = .25$				All $\sigma_{ij} = .50$			
λ_3	$B(0)$	t_1	t_2	$RL(t_1)$	$B(0)$	t_1	t_2	$RL(t_1)$
−.2	−1.57	2.48	13.65	−.276	−.96	2.44	12.70	−.167
−.4	−2.38	1.85	9.00	−.326	−1.46	1.83	8.49	−.199
−.6	−2.95	1.52	7.23	−.335	−1.82	1.51	6.84	−.205
−1	−3.68	1.17	5.63	−.319	−2.27	1.16	5.32	−.195

	Positive net devaluation in the export sector leaves L_x unchanged at $t = 0$							
	$\sigma_{KZ} = .75, \sigma_{LZ} = .25$				All $\sigma_{ij} = .50$			
λ_3	$B(0)$	t_1	t_2	$RL(t_1)$	$B(0)$	t_1	t_2	$RL(t_1)$
−.2	.42	—	—	—	.31	—	—	—
−.4	.18	—	—	—	.16	—	—	—
−.6	.01	—	—	—	.05	—	—	—
−1	−.21	.188	.397	−.004	−.08	.117	.242	−.001

* In the import sector, the cost share of intermediates is 25% and the value-added share of labor is 30%. The corresponding values in the export sector are 10% and 40%. $B(0)$ is the semielasticity of the payments deficit at $t = 0$ with respect to v, expressed as a percentage of initial total expenditure [i.e., $B(0) = v(dB/dv)/E$]. RL refers to the elasticity of the cumulative reserve loss at t_1 with respect to v. A dash indicates that reserves increase continuously.

contractionary in the short run. Temporary contraction in the traded goods sectors is thus, at most, a contributing factor in balance of payments problems.[23] The main cause of the problem lies elsewhere.

6.2.3.1   SOCIAL SAFETY NETS AND THE TRADE BALANCE

A liberalization program that increases unemployment will not be terribly popular with the general public. Due to this and policy makers' genuine concern about the short-run distributional effects of adjustment, social safety nets are more common now than in earlier periods. But

---

[23] A modest payments deficit may, however, incite speculation that the reform is not sustainable (O'Connell, 1997, p. 107). As will be shown in Chapter 8, this can lead to very large payments deficits that force a quick policy reversal.

Table 6.3. *The impact effect on the payments deficit and the values of* t_1, t_2 *and the cumulative reserve loss at* t_1 *when production is highly intermediate and labor-intensive.**

	Fully compensated devaluations in both sectors							
	$\sigma_{KZ} = .75, \sigma_{LZ} = .25$				All $\sigma_{ij} = .50$			
λ_3	$B(0)$	t_1	t_2	$RL(t_1)$	$B(0)$	t_1	t_2	$RL(t_1)$
-.2	-3.05	2.42	12.15	-.528	-1.99	2.39	11.43	-.341
-.4	-4.69	1.81	8.19	-.633	-3.08	1.79	7.80	-.412
-.6	-5.83	1.50	6.61	-.654	-3.84	1.48	6.32	-.427
-1	-7.30	1.15	5.14	-.624	-4.82	1.13	4.91	-.409

	Positive net devaluation in the export sector leaves L_x unchanged at $t = 0$							
	$\sigma_{KZ} = .75, \sigma_{LZ} = .25$				All $\sigma_{ij} = .50$			
λ_3	$B(0)$	t_1	t_2	$RL(t_1)$	$B(0)$	t_1	t_2	$RL(t_1)$
-.2	-.50	1.12	2.77	-.048	-.29	.98	2.34	-.024
-.4	-1.32	1.12	3.00	-.123	-.83	1.07	2.79	-.074
-.6	-1.88	.99	2.69	-.153	-1.21	.95	2.54	-.095
-1	-2.61	.78	2.17	-.166	-1.70	.75	2.06	-.105

* The value-added share of labor is 50% in both sectors, while the cost share of intermediates is 40% in the import sector and 10% in the export sector. $B(0)$ is the semielasticity of the payments deficit at $t = 0$ with respect to v, expressed as a percentage of initial total expenditure [i.e., $B(0) = v(dB/dv)/E$]. RL refers to the elasticity of the cumulative reserve loss at t_1 with respect to v.

while a social safety net can reduce the losses suffered by the newly unemployed and make it easier to sell liberalization, it also worsens the trade balance if higher spending on unemployment compensation or public sector employment schemes drives up the fiscal deficit. It is correct but not particularly helpful to object that the safety net should be financed by reducing other expenditures or by raising taxes. The government will probably have its hands full trying to neutralize the fiscal consequences of the tariff cut (i.e., a loss of revenues, assuming the initial tariff is below its revenue-maximizing level).[24] So the question remains:

[24] In the ensuing analysis, I maintain the assumption that lump-sum transfers equal tariff revenues. The fiscal deficit is therefore exactly equal to spending on the safety net.

Table 6.4. *The impact effect on the payments deficit and the values of* t_1, t_2 *and the cumulative reserve loss at* t_l *in the base run when there is a social safety net.**

| | Fully compensated devaluations in both sectors | | | | | | | |
| | $\sigma_{KZ} = .75$, $\sigma_{LZ} = .25$ | | | | All $\sigma_{ij} = .50$ | | | |
λ_3	$B(0)$	t_1	t_2	RL(long run)	$B(0)$	t_1	t_2	RL(long run)
−.2	−3.81	—	—	−3.05	−2.35	—	—	−1.90
−.4	−4.21	—	—	−1.50	−2.61	—	—	−.93
−.6	−4.50	5.05	—	−.73	−2.78	5.01	—	−.61
−1	−4.86	2.38	—	−.57	−3.01	2.36	—	−.35

| | Positive net devaluation in the export sector leaves L_x unchanged at $t = 0$ | | | | | | | |
| | $\sigma_{KZ} = .75$, $\sigma_{LZ} = .25$ | | | | All $\sigma_{ij} = .50$ | | | |
λ_3	$B(0)$	t_1	t_2	RL(long run)	$B(0)$	t_1	t_2	RL(long run)
−.2	−.24	—	—	−.63	−.10	—	—	−.38
−.4	−.37	—	—	−.17	−.18	—	—	−.09
−.6	−.45	1.84	—	−.02	−.23	1.54	7.57	.003
−1	−.56	.70	1.87	.10	−.30	.60	1.49	.08

* In the import sector, the cost share of intermediates is 25% and the value-added share of labor is 30%. The corresponding values in the export sector are 10% and 40%. $B(0)$ is the semielasticity of the payments deficit at $t = 0$ with respect to v, expressed as a percentage of initial total expenditure [i.e., $B(0) = v(dB/dv)/E$]. RL refers to the elasticity of the reserve loss across steady states with respect to v. Dashes in the columns for t_1 and t_2 indicate that the balance of payments is continuously in deficit and that the stock of foreign exchange reserves never regains its preform level.

can the balance of payments withstand the temporarily higher fiscal deficits that accompany the introduction of a moderately protective safety net?

Tables 6.4 and 6.5 show the outcome when unemployment compensation is one-half of the initial wage in the export sector and the safety net is paid for entirely by printing money. Despite the increase in the fiscal deficit, there is still some good news. In the case where factor intensities are normal and labor demand contracts only in the import sector, the reserve losses are manageable even when adjustment in the labor market is difficult and slow. Elsewhere, however, the desire to minimize the social costs of adjustment conflicts with the objective of external balance: the payments deficit increases very sharply in the short run and the cumulative deficit often wipes out a large part or all of the central

Table 6.5. *The impact effect on the payments deficit and the values of* t_1, t_2 *and the cumulative reserve loss at* t_1 *when production is highly intermediate and labor-intensive and there is a social safety net.**

	Fully compensated devaluations in both sectors							
	$\sigma_{KZ} = .75, \sigma_{LZ} = .25$				All $\sigma_{ij} = .50$			
λ_3	$B(0)$	t_1	t_2	RL(long run)	$B(0)$	t_1	t_2	RL(long run)
-.2	-7.56	—	—	-6.12	-4.99	—	—	-4.06
-.4	-8.38	—	—	-2.99	-5.54	—	—	-1.98
-.6	-8.95	4.99	—	-1.95	-5.92	4.96	—	-1.28
-1	-9.68	2.34	—	-1.11	-6.41	2.31	—	-.73

	Positive net devaluation in the export sector leaves L_x unchanged at $t = 0$							
	$\sigma_{KZ} = .75, \sigma_{LZ} = .25$				All $\sigma_{ij} = .50$			
λ_3	$B(0)$	t_1	t_2	RL(long run)	$B(0)$	t_1	t_2	RL(long run)
-.2	-2.74	—	—	-2.72	-1.78	—	—	-1.81
-.4	-3.15	—	—	-1.17	-2.05	—	—	-.77
-.6	-3.43	3.96	—	-.65	-2.24	3.88	—	-.42
-1	-3.79	1.66	—	-.24	-2.49	1.62	—	-.15

* The value added share of labor is 50% in both sectors, while the cost share of intermediates is 40% in the import sector and 10% in the export sector. $B(0)$ is the semielasticity of the payments deficit at $t = 0$ with respect to v, expressed as a percentage of initial total expenditure [i.e., $B(0) = v(dB/dv)/E$]. RL refers to the elasticity of the reserve loss across steady states with respect to v. Dashes in the columns for t_1 and t_2 indicate that the balance of payments is continuously in deficit and that the stock of foreign exchange reserves never regains its preform level.

bank's foreign exchange reserves.[25] In some cases, therefore, a social safety net is not viable without external financial support. Fortunately, the World Bank and the IMF are often willing to put up the necessary funds.

One other point is worth mentioning. Observe that faster adjustment

---

[25] If the elasticities are approximately correct for large changes, then the percentage reserve loss is the figure in the column for RL mutliplied by the percentage gross devaluation. The large elasticities for $\lambda_3 = -.2, -.4$ thus imply very large reserve losses. It should also be noted here that unemployment compensation itself may be the cause of slow adjustment in the labor market. This argues that λ_3 is more likely to be small in Tables 6.4 and 6.5 than in Tables 6.2 and 6.3.

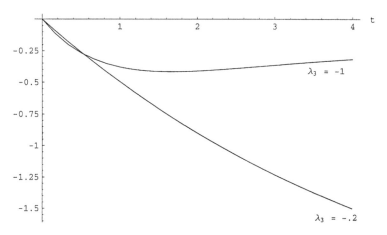

Figure 6.3. Time-dated elasticity of foreign exchange reserves with respect to v when production is highly intermediate and labor-intensive, $\sigma_{KZ} = .75$ and $\sigma_{LZ} = .25$.

always goes together with larger deficits in the short run but smaller reserve losses in the long run. The reason is that the incentive to dissave in the short run is greater when unemployment is short-lived and liberalization is more akin to a temporary, adverse income shock. But a short recession also reduces outlays on the social safety net; since the increase in the nominal money supply depends only on the increase in nominal expenditure across steady states, the lower path for the fiscal deficit ensures that the loss in reserves will be smaller in the long run.[26] The message for policy makers is thus: do not pay excessive attention to the immediate impact on the balance of payments; liberalization programs that produce similar deficits in the short run may have quite different effects in the long run. Figure 6.3 illustrates the point nicely. In the short run, the deficit increases more and the loss of reserves is slightly greater when $\lambda_3 = -1$ instead of $-.2$. But for $\lambda_3 = -1$, the payments deficit disappears midway through the second year and the total loss in foreign exchange reserves is trivial (12% for a gross devaluation of 50%). By contrast, when $\lambda_3 = -.2$, the payments deficits are persistent and the eventual loss in reserves is very large.

---

[26] The change in foreign exchange reserves at time t equals $M(t) - M_o - .5w_{xo}\int_0^t(1 - L_x - L_m)dt$.

6.2.4   Credibility and Transitory Unemployment

The assumption that the nominal wage in the export sector is inflexible downward in the short run is realistic but also ad hoc. A better model would explain why wages are slow to adjust in the downward direction and how (if at all) the forces that delay adjustment in the labor market depend on the announced policy reform. (There might be a relationship between b, the parameter that determines the speed of wage adjustment, and the mix of policies that comprise the reform program.) Our model does not do this, and consequently it is incomplete and perhaps even inconsistent: employment increases when w_x falls because firms offer jobs that pay more than workers' reservation price; but if workers released by the import sector find it advantageous to take these jobs, what prevents them from immediately bidding the wage down to its equilibrium level? Many new classical macroeconomists would answer emphatically: "Nothing, absolutely nothing," invoking the general principle that the market will always find a way to realize mutually beneficial trades.

There is another way of interpreting the model that overcomes this objection and reconciles transitory unemployment with perfect bidirectional wage flexibility in the export (informal) sector. Without stating so explicitly, I assumed that the adjustment program was perfectly credible. But when credibility has been damaged by numerous past failures, continuous full employment requires both that w_x be downwardly flexible and that labor immediately relocate to the export sector even though job losses in industry might be temporary. This ignores the possibility that workers laid off in the import sector may find it preferable to endure a spell of unemployment rather than incur relocation costs twice or risk permanent loss of a privileged, high-wage job. Hence, if the reform is initially expected to be short-lived, a certain amount of time would have to elapse before any of the unemployed would seek jobs in the export sector. The short-run losses on the production side would then be the same as in the cases where employment in the export sector does not change at $t = 0$, with the pace of adjustment afterward depending on the distribution of beliefs – on how many workers revise their beliefs as time passes and the expected policy reversal does not materialize. The fallout of weak credibility is thus persistent unemployment, low labor mobility, and slowly declining wages in the informal sector.

While a model with slowly adjusting wages is adequate to capture the production losses stemming from weak credibility, it misses other potentially important welfare costs. If workers fear a reversal of the trade reform, then so also do consumers. Imperfect credibility creates an incentive therefore to purchase imports today before their price increases in the future. This distorts saving behavior and may result in payments deficits many times larger than would occur if liberalization were widely believed to be permanent. These problems will be taken up subsequently in Chapter 8.

6.2.5   The Welfare Costs of Transitory Unemployment

Asymmetric wage flexibility complicates the analysis of optimal policy reform as there may be adjustment costs to dismantling protection which have no counterpart when the economy moves from free trade to the equilibrium associated with the optimal trade regime. Suppose, for example, that the government manipulates only the tariff on consumer imports (the case the model is set up to handle). There is no need to worry about unemployment for increases in h because w_x rises when the industrial sector draws labor away from the export sector. The optimal tariff h^* is calculated therefore by balancing at the margin the benefits of higher employment in industry against the costs of the byproduct distortions caused by protection. The tariff that is optimal *ex ante*, however, is not the tariff that policy makers should aim for if the price of liberalization is a spell of transitory unemployment. Since the gains from moving *closer* to the *ex ante* optimal tariff have to compensate for the costs of adjusting, it is optimal to stop short of h^*. (The benefits of reducing protection shrink to zero as h approaches h^*, but the costs of transitory unemployment remain.) For policy purposes, it is obviously important to know how far the stopping point is from the *ex ante* optimal tariff. If $h^* = .20$ and the labor market can be expected to clear within five years, does liberalization cease to be desirable at $h = .23$ or at $h = .40$? In the former case, one should make amends for past sins; in the latter, it is best to let bygones be bygones and live with a moderate amount of excess protection.

Two problems arise when attempting to confront this issue in the current model. First, the welfare gains that accrue from the administered real wage cut in the industrial sector should not be attributed to liberalization. Second, the increase in the general price level acts like a wealth levy by reducing real money balances. The saving the private sector undertakes merely to rebuild real money balances is associated with a welfare loss, but this might be offset by the value of the extra foreign exchange reserves the government acquires.

To sidestep these problems, I set $\alpha = 1$ (the adjustment program does not include a real wage cut in the import sector) and remove money from the model. I also assume that weak credibility is the source of adjustment problems in the labor market. The structure of beliefs is such that labor is completely immobile for a period of T years: anticipating a policy reversal, all of the workers laid off in the import sector at first judge it worthwhile to remain unemployed; at time T, however, the reform passes some critical test for credibility (e.g., tariffs are not increased after the agreement with the IMF expires) and the unemployed relocate en masse to the export sector where the wage adjusts immediately to give everyone a job.[27,28]

When money is absent from the model, saving is zero and expenditure equals income each period. During the period the liberalization program lacks credibility, $\hat{L}_x = 0$ in (24) and[29]

$$E(t) - E_o - D^m dP_m = \frac{Q_m}{F} \left[\theta_L^m (a_1^m - \gamma_m a_3^m) \right.$$

$$\left. - \frac{h}{1+h} \left(a_4 + \frac{D^m}{Q_m} \varepsilon \right) \right] dP_m, \qquad 0 \leq t \leq T.$$

After the tariff cut becomes credible at T, the unemployed go to work in the export sector and the first term inside the brackets gets scaled down by $(1 - \psi)$:

$$E(t) - E_o - D^m dP_m = \frac{Q_m}{F} \left[\theta_L^m (1 - \psi)(a_1^m - \gamma_m a_3^m) \right.$$

$$\left. - \frac{h}{1+h} \left(a_4 + \frac{D^m}{Q_m} \varepsilon \right) \right] dP_m, \qquad t \geq T.$$

Define $\overline{U} \equiv \int_0^\infty V(P_m, P_x, E)e^{-\rho t} dt$. Then the sum of the welfare gains over the two periods is

[27] There is no loss of generality in this specification. With a smooth distribution of beliefs, employment in the export sector would increase continuously at the rate $\dot{L}_x = k$. But for any k, one can find a value of T that produces the same present value losses from transitory unemployment.
[28] As mentioned earlier, weak credibility also lowers welfare by distorting saving behavior. This welfare loss, however, is a second-order effect. It does not affect the solutions here because the optimum is located by finding the point at which a small change in the tariff leaves welfare unchanged.
[29] Multiply through by $\hat{v}$ and set $\hat{v} = \hat{P}_x = 0$. I assume for simplicity that the government manipulates only the tariff on consumer imports; the objective of the analysis is only to determine how far away the optimal stopping point is from the *ex ante* optimum, not the exact nature of optimal commercial policy.

$$\frac{F}{Q_m V_E}\frac{d\overline{U}}{dP_m}=\int_0^T \theta_L^m(a_1^m-\gamma_m a_3^m)e^{-\rho t}dt+\int_T^\infty \theta_L^m(1-\psi)(a_1^m-\gamma_m a_3^m)e^{-\rho t}dt$$

$$-\int_0^\infty \frac{h}{1+h}\left(a_4+\frac{D^m}{Q_m}\varepsilon\right)e^{-\rho t}dt.$$

To find the optimal stopping point, set $d\overline{U}/dP_m$ equal to zero and solve for h. This gives[30]

$$h_1=\frac{\theta_L^m(a_1^m-\gamma_m a_3^m)(1-\psi e^{-\rho T})}{a_4+\varepsilon D^m/Q_m-\theta_L^m(a_1^m-\gamma_m a_3^m)(1-\psi e^{-\rho T})}.$$

The *ex ante* optimal tariff emerges, trivially, when $T=0$. Thus

$$h^*=\frac{\theta_L^m(a_1^m-\gamma_m a_3^m)(1-\psi)}{a_4+\varepsilon D^m/Q_m-\theta_L^m(a_1^m-\gamma_m a_3^m)(1-\psi)}.$$

6.2.5.1 THE OPTIMAL *EX ANTE* TARIFF VS. THE OPTIMAL STOPPING POINT

Figure 6.4 depicts the solution for the optimal tariff cut. The initial tariff h_o exceeds the *ex ante* optimal tariff h^* at which the marginal benefit of reducing underemployment equals the marginal cost of the trade distortion. A tariff cut thus increases allocative efficiency. This gain is reflected in the first quadrant by the movement down the MBTL (marginal benefit of trade liberalization) schedule from point A toward h^*. The MCTU schedule keeps track of the marginal costs of transitory unemployment. (MCTU is horizontal in the diagram, but it could be positively or negatively sloped.) At the optimal stopping point h_1 the long-run efficiency gains from further trade liberalization just compensate for the costs of additional transitory unemployment. If MCTU lies above point A, the cure is worse than the disease – the tariff should be kept at h_o. The opposite extreme outcome is also possible: $\lim_{\rho\to 0} h_1\to h^*$ because for $\rho=0$ the optimal policy is to ignore losses on the transition path and choose h to maximize welfare in the postadjustment period (T,∞).

Closed-form solutions for h_1 and h^* do not exist except in special, very simple cases. Numerical methods are required therefore to determine

[30] The nature of technology in the export sector does not directly affect the solution for the optimal stopping point because employment in the export sector is constant up to time T and then jumps upward by the amount of layoffs in the import sector. (All unemployment is eliminated at time T when labor moves to the export sector and w_x falls to its market clearing level.)

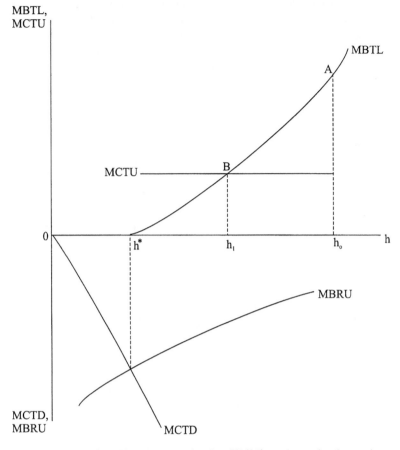

Figure 6.4. The *ex ante* optimal tariff (h^*) vs. the optimal stopping point when liberalization causes transitory unemployment.

how far the government should cut the tariff toward its *ex ante* optimal level. To calibrate the model, I assume the same functional forms as in Chapter 5. The private agent has CES preferences and firms operate two-tiered CES production functions. As before, β, σ_1, and σ_2 are the elasticities of substitution between importables and exportables in consumption, between value added and imported inputs, and between capital and labor. At the initial equilibrium,

$$h_o = .40, \qquad \psi = .67, \qquad \gamma_m = .30, \qquad VA_m = .20$$
$$\theta_Z^m = .25, \qquad \theta_Z^x = .10, \qquad \theta_L^m = .225, \qquad \theta_L^x = .36.$$

The initial tariff of 40% generates an effective rate of protection of
61.5%. The values for the sectoral wage gap, the consumption share, and
the cost shares are the same as in Section 6.1.3.

The parameters σ_1^i, σ_2^i, β, T, and ρ determine how much the tariff cut
improves allocative efficiency after the economy returns to full employ-
ment, how much labor demand contracts in the short run, how long
unemployment persists, and how short-run losses are weighted relative
to long-run gains. Each of these crucial parameters is allowed to take
multiple values:

$$\beta = .15, .25, .50; \qquad T = 1, 3, 5; \qquad \rho = .02, .05, .075, .10;$$
$$\sigma_1^i = .10, .50; \qquad \sigma_2^i = .5, 1.$$

This range of values covers a variety of scenarios: slow vs. rapid adjustment in the labor market; heavy vs. light discounting of future gains; and
easy vs. difficult substitution between domestic factors of production and
imported inputs.

The different panels in Tables 6.6 and 6.7 show how h_1 varies with σ_1,
ρ, and T for given values of σ_2 and β. The number in parentheses in the
upper northwest cell is the *ex ante* optimal tariff h^*. Since labor reallo-
cates immediately in response to an increase in the tariff, h^* is independent of T and ρ. Note also that h^* is very small – the initial level of
protection is way too high.

There is something for everyone in these two tables. Those who
support liberalization will no doubt draw attention to the fact that in 43
of the 48 cases where $\rho \leq .05$ and $T \leq 3$ the optimal stopping point lies
within 5 percentage points of the *ex ante* optimal tariff. Critics can
respond to this, however, by pointing out that for higher discount rates
and/or longer spells of unemployment the gap between h_1 and h^* is often
sizeable. For example, when $\sigma_2 = 1$, $\sigma_1 = .1$, $\beta = .15$, $\rho = .075$, and $T = 5$,
it is optimal to maintain the existing tariff of 40% . If credibility can
be established more quickly and unemployment lasts three years
instead of five, h_1 decreases 6 points but is still appreciably higher than
h^* (33.8% vs. 19.1%).

These results may seem surprising given that the initial tariff is so
much higher than the *ex ante* optimal tariff and that the economy attains
higher utility in the long run. But while these factors matter, they are
often not enough to overcome liberalization's basic handicap: the long-
run efficiency gains are little triangles whereas the losses from unemployment are beefy rectangles. Consequently, high discounting and a few
years of high unemployment may sharply limit the desirable amount of
liberalization.

Table 6.6. *The optimal* ex ante *tariff vs. the optimal stopping point when the elasticity of substitution between capital and labor equals .5.**

		$\beta = .15$			
σ_1	$\rho = .02$	$\rho = .05$	$\rho = .075$	$\rho = .10$	T
.1	16.4 (15.5)	17.7	18.8	19.9	1
	18.2	22.0	25.1	28.1	3
	19.9	26.1	31.0	35.6	5
.5	11.9 (11.3)	12.8	13.5	14.2	1
	13.1	15.6	17.6	19.5	3
	14.2	18.3	21.3	24.1	5

		$\beta = .25$			
σ_1	$\rho = .02$	$\rho = .05$	$\rho = .075$	$\rho = .10$	T
.1	13.2 (12.5)	14.2	15.0	15.8	1
	14.5	17.4	19.7	22.0	3
	15.8	20.5	24.1	27.4	5
.5	10.1 (9.6)	10.8	11.4	12.0	1
	11.1	13.2	14.8	16.4	3
	12.0	15.4	17.9	20.2	5

		$\beta = .50$			
σ_1	$\rho = .02$	$\rho = .05$	$\rho = .075$	$\rho = .10$	T
.1	8.8 (8.3)	9.4	9.9	10.4	1
	9.6	11.4	12.9	14.2	3
	10.4	13.3	15.5	17.5	5
.5	7.2 (6.8)	7.7	8.1	8.5	1
	7.9	9.3	10.5	11.6	3
	8.5	10.8	12.6	14.1	5

* The optimal *ex ante* tariff is stated in parentheses in the cell for $\rho = .02$ and $T = 1$.

6.3 Liberalization via Increased Quotas

Liberalization programs come in all shapes and sizes. The program we examined in Section 6.1.1 is often implemented in the later stages of the liberalization process.[31] In the early stages, it is more com-

[31] See Michaely et al. (1991, pp. 55, 134). Thomas (1991, p. 48) observes that liberalization of imported inputs used in export production is the policy most consistently adopted in World Bank trade adjustment programs.

Table 6.7. *The optimal* ex ante *tariff vs. the optimal stopping point when the elasticity of substitution between capital and labor equals unity.**

		$\beta = .15$			
σ_1	$\rho = .02$	$\rho = .05$	$\rho = .075$	$\rho = .10$	T
.1	20.4 (19.1)	22.3	23.9	25.5	1
	22.9	28.8	33.8	39.1	3
	25.5	35.5	40.0	40.0	5
.5	15.7 (14.8)	17.0	18.1	19.2	1
	17.5	21.4	24.7	28.0	3
	19.2	25.8	31.3	36.6	5

		$\beta = .25$			
σ_1	$\rho = .02$	$\rho = .05$	$\rho = .075$	$\rho = .10$	T
.1	16.9 (15.9)	18.4	19.6	20.9	1
	18.9	23.4	27.3	31.2	3
	20.9	28.6	35.2	40.0	5
.5	13.5 (12.7)	14.6	15.5	16.4	1
	15.0	18.3	21.0	23.7	3
	16.4	21.9	26.4	30.7	5

		$\beta = .50$			
σ_1	$\rho = .02$	$\rho = .05$	$\rho = .075$	$\rho = .10$	T
.1	11.6 (10.9)	12.5	13.3	14.1	1
	12.8	15.7	18.1	20.4	3
	14.1	18.8	22.7	26.5	5
.5	9.7 (9.2)	10.5	11.2	11.8	1
	10.8	13.1	14.9	16.8	3
	11.8	15.6	18.6	21.4	5

* The optimal *ex ante* tariff is stated in parentheses in the cell for $\rho = .02$ and $T = 1$.

mon to see a loosening of quotas on imports of noncompetitive intermediate inputs and capital goods.[32] Restrictions on consumer imports are usually not relaxed until sometime later and are frequently
combined with higher tariffs to maintain the existing level of

[32] There are many exceptions, however. The foreign exchange auctions adopted
in Uganda, Sierre Leone, Zambia, and Somalia eliminated quotas in intermediates and consumer goods simultaneously.

protection. (The tariffs may be lowered later on through a compensated devaluation.)

In this section I investigate the consequences of early-stage liberalization programs in an economy where quotas apply to all types of imports. The model laid out in equations (1)–(12) is easily adapted for this purpose. Interpret Z_i as the quota on imports of intermediates in sector i and assume that consumer imports are subject to a quota G (which will not vary), that exports are neither taxed nor subsidized ($s = 0$), and that production functions are separable between imported intermediates and primary factors. The difference between domestic and world prices define *implicit* tariffs of h, g_m, and g_x on the three types of imports. The price equations (1)–(3) are replaced therefore by

$$h = P_m - v, \tag{1'}$$

$$P_x = v, \tag{2'}$$

$$g_i = P_{zi} - v, \qquad i = m, x, \tag{3'}$$

where P_{zi} is the price of intermediates in sector i.[33]

The zero-profit conditions and sectoral factor demands (4)–(7) apply as before, except P_{zi} appears in place of v. The rest of the model consists of (8), (9), the market clearing condition for the industrial good

$$D^m(P_m, P_x, E) = Q_m + G, \tag{36}$$

and the maximization problem defined by (10), (12), and the budget constraint

$$E = R(\cdot) + hG + g_m Z_m + g_x Z_x - S, \tag{11'}$$

where the middle three terms measure rents conferred by import licenses and the revenue function is now either $R(P_m, P_x, P_{zm}, P_{zx}, L_m, L_x)$ or $R(P_m, P_x, P_{zm}, P_{zx}, L_m)$.

In the model with tariffs, prices were exogenous and imports were endogenous. With quotas, the assignment of exogenous vs. endogenous variables is reversed. The only modification in the solution procedure therefore is that import quantities shift from the left to the right side in various equations. For $\alpha = 1$ (the real wage is fixed in sector m) and

---

[33] Equation (3') assumes that import licenses cannot be resold. If the resale of licenses cannot be prevented, then $g_m = g_x$ and Z_m and Z_x are endogenously determined.

$\sigma_{KZ}^m = \sigma_{LZ}^m = \sigma_1$ (the m superscript will not be needed for either σ_1 or σ_{KL}),[34] we have from (4)–(6) and (8)

$$\hat{P}_{zm} = c_1\hat{P}_m - c_2\hat{P}_x - c_3\hat{Z}_m, \tag{37}$$

where

$$c_1 \equiv \frac{c_3}{\theta_K^m}\{\sigma_1[\theta_K^m + \theta_Z^m(1 - \gamma_m\theta_L^m)] + \sigma_{KL}\theta_L^m[1 - \gamma_m(1 - \theta_Z^m)]\},$$

$$c_2 \equiv c_1 - 1,$$

$$c_3 \equiv \frac{\theta_K^m}{\sigma_1[\theta_K^m + \theta_Z^m(1 - \theta_L^m)] + \sigma_{KL}\theta_L^m\theta_Z^m}.$$

Equations (18), (33), and (37) can be solved for $\hat{P}_{zm}$, $\hat{L}_m$, and $\hat{Q}_m$ [replace $\hat{v}$ in (18) and (33) with $\hat{P}_{zm}$]. The solutions for $\hat{L}_m$ and $\hat{Q}_m$ are

$$\hat{Q}_m = \eta_m(\hat{P}_m - \hat{v}) + \eta_z\hat{Z}_m, \tag{38}$$

$$\hat{L}_m = \delta_m(\hat{P}_m - \hat{v}) + \delta_z\hat{Z}_m, \tag{39}$$

where

$$\eta_m \equiv \sigma_1\theta_L^m\gamma_x c_3[\sigma_{KL}(1 - \theta_Z^m) + \sigma_1\theta_Z^m]/\theta_K^m,$$

$$\eta_z \equiv c_3\theta_Z^m[\sigma_1(1 - \theta_L^m) + \sigma_{KL}\theta_L^m]/\theta_K^m,$$

$$\delta_m \equiv \sigma_1\gamma_x c_3[\sigma_{KL}(1 - \theta_Z^m) + \sigma_1\theta_Z^m]/\theta_K^m,$$

$$\delta_z \equiv \theta_Z^m c_3[\sigma_{KL}(1 - \theta_Z^m) + \sigma_1\theta_Z^m]/\theta_K^m.$$

These solutions, along with the private agent's budget constraint and the market clearing condition in the industrial sector, tie down the steady-state outcome. Across steady states,

$$\hat{E} = \gamma_m\hat{P}_m + \gamma_x\hat{v} + (1 - \psi)\frac{w_mL_m}{E}\hat{L}_m + \frac{g_mZ_m}{E}\hat{Z}_m + \frac{g_xZ_x}{E}\hat{Z}_x, \tag{40}$$

---

[34] Recall that σ_{KL} is not a substitution parameter of the production function. If σ_2 denotes the elasticity of substitution between capital and labor in the production of value added, then $\sigma_{KL} = (\sigma_2 - \theta_Z^m\sigma_1)/(1 - \theta_Z^m)$. See example #2 in Chapter 2.

$$\hat{Q}_m = \frac{D^m}{Q_m}[(\varepsilon - \gamma_x)\hat{v} - (\varepsilon + \gamma_m)\hat{P}_m + \hat{E}]. \tag{41}$$

The long-run effects on P_m, M, and welfare U are thus

$$\hat{P}_m = n_1\hat{Z}_x - n_2\hat{Z}_m + \hat{v}, \tag{42}$$

$$\frac{dU}{V_E E} = \frac{P_m Q_m}{E}(1 + \rho\mu)\left\{\frac{g_x Z_x}{P_m Q_m}[1 + (1 - \psi)\gamma_m \theta_L^m \delta_m / F]\hat{Z}_x \right.$$
$$\left. + \left[(1 - \psi)\theta_L^m(\delta_z - \delta_m n_2) + \frac{g_m}{1 + g_m}\theta_Z^m\right]\hat{Z}_m\right\}, \tag{43}$$

$$\hat{M} = \left\{\frac{g_x Z_x}{E}[1 + (1 - \psi)\gamma_m \theta_L^m \delta_m / H] + \gamma_m n_1\right\}\hat{Z}_x$$
$$+ \left\{\left[(1 - \psi)\theta_L^m(\delta_z - \delta_m n_2) + \frac{g_m}{1 + g_m}\theta_Z^m\right]\frac{P_m Q_m}{E} - \gamma_m n_2\right\}\hat{Z}_m + \hat{v},$$
$$\tag{44}$$

where

$$n_1 \equiv \gamma_m g_x Z_x / HP_m Q_m,$$

$$n_2 \equiv H^{-1}\left\{\eta_z - \gamma_m\left[(1 - \psi)\theta_L^m \delta_z + \frac{g_m}{1 + g_m}\theta_Z^m\right]\right\}$$

$$H \equiv \eta_m + \varepsilon D^m / Q_m - \gamma_m(1 - \psi)\theta_L^m \delta_m.$$

The procedure for deriving the transition path is slightly more involved than before because P_m varies over time. From (21)–(22), (38), and (41),

$$V_{EE} E[(\tau - 1)\gamma_m \dot{P}_m / P_m + \dot{E}/E] = \rho V_E - \phi'/P, \tag{45}$$

$$[\eta_m + (\varepsilon + \gamma_m)D^m / Q_m]\frac{\dot{P}_m}{P_m} = \frac{D^m}{Q_m}\frac{\dot{E}}{E}, \tag{46}$$

where

$$\frac{\dot{E}}{E} = \gamma_m\frac{\dot{P}_m}{P_m} + (1 - \psi)\frac{w_m L_m}{E}\frac{\dot{L}_m}{L_m} - \frac{\dot{S}}{E} \tag{47}$$

when the labor market clears and

$$\frac{\dot{E}}{E} = \gamma_m \frac{\dot{P}_m}{P_m} + \frac{w_m L_m}{E} \frac{\dot{L}_m}{L_m} + \frac{w_x L_x}{E} \frac{\dot{L}_x}{L_x} - \frac{\dot{S}}{E} \tag{47'}$$

if unemployment exists. (Note that P_x, Z_m, and Z_x change only once, at $t = 0$.) In the simpler case where liberalization is consistent with continuous full employment, (39), (45), (46), and (47′) give

$$V_{EE} N\dot{S} = \phi'(M/P) - \rho V_E (P_m, P_x, E), \tag{48}$$

where

$$N \equiv 1 + \frac{\gamma_m}{H} [(1-\psi)\theta_L^m \delta_m + \tau D^m/Q_m].$$

Linearizing (12) and (48) around the stationary equilibrium $(0, M^*)$ produces the saddlepoint solution

$$S(t) = -\lambda_2 (M^* - M_o) e^{\lambda_2 t}, \tag{49}$$

$$M(t) - M_o = (M^* - M_o)(1 - e^{\lambda_2 t}), \tag{50}$$

where

$$\lambda_2 = \frac{\rho[1 + (1-\tau)\gamma_m D^m/Q_m HN] - \sqrt{\rho^2 [1 + (1-\tau)\gamma_m D^m/Q_m HN]^2 + 4\rho/\mu N}}{2}$$

is the system's negative eigenvalue and (44) provides the appropriate expression for $M^* - M_o$.

6.3.1   Larger Quotas for Imports of Intermediates in the Export Sector

Consider first the long-run effects of allowing firms in the export sector more access to imported intermediates ($\hat{Z}_x > 0$, $\hat{Z}_m = \hat{v} = 0$). Since imports of consumer goods and of intermediates in the industrial sector are fixed by their respective quotas, an increase in Z_x raises real income directly by the amount $g_x dZ_x = g_x Z_x \hat{Z}_x$. (The gain from lessening a trade distortion is the product of the trade tax and the change in the import or export volume.) Part of the income gain is spent on consumption of industrial goods, so P_m and L_m increase. Thus, greater usage of intermediates in the export sector indirectly promotes employment in the high-wage industrial sector. This additional gain – the gain from lower underemployment – shows up in the term involving $1 - \psi$ in (43).

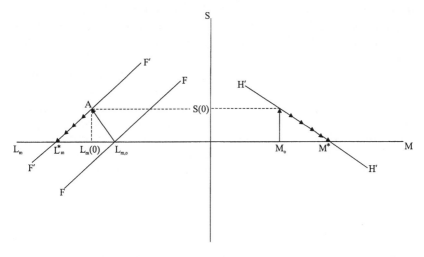

Figure 6.5. The paths of high-wage employment, private saving, and the trade surplus when quotas are loosened for imported intermediates in the export sector.

The impact on the external accounts is equally pleasant. The increase in real income and the increase in the price level ensure an increase in money demand and a cumulative payments surplus. After the adjustment process is complete, the central bank's holdings of foreign exchange reserves are higher by the amount

$$M^* - M_o = g_x Z_x \mu \left[1 + \frac{(1 - \psi)\gamma_m \theta_L^m \delta_m + D^m / Q_m}{H} \right] \hat{Z}_x. \qquad (51)$$

On the transition path the price of the industrial good and employment in the industrial sector are below their steady-state levels because the private agent saves to accumulate more money balances. A little reflection establishes, however, that P_m and L_m always exceed their pre-reform values. Suppose the labor market clears continuously so that equations (49)–(50) describe the dynamics of saving (or the payments surplus) and money balances. Figure 6.5 then applies. HH in the first quadrant is the saddle path. In the second quadrant, the downward sloping FF schedule shows how L_m varies with S for given values of the exchange rate and the three quotas.

When Z_x increases, the stationary equilibrium shifts from $(M, L_{m,o})$ to (M^*, L_m^*) and saving jumps upward to $S(0)$. If the assumption of continuous full employment is to be correct, point A must lie to the left of $L_{m,o}$.

To confirm that this is the case, note that at $t = 0$ the private agent saves only part of the gain $g_x dZ_x$; the rest is spent, so the demand curve in the industrial sector shifts to the right, pushing up P_m and increasing the demand for labor.[35] Following the upward jumps in P_m, L_m, and S, the equilibrium path moves smoothly down $H'H'$ and $F'F'$. This is the sort of adjustment process that policy makers pray for: on the way to the long-run equilibrium (M^*, L_m^*) the balance of payments is in surplus, real income is higher and rising, and underemployment is lower and falling. Furthermore, since both the trade distortion and underemployment are lower at all points on the transition path, the reform is unambiguously welfare-improving.[36]

6.3.2   Larger Quotas for Imports of Intermediates in the Industrial Sector

Quota liberalization in the industrial sector also has the potential to reduce underemployment, raise welfare, and improve the balance of payments. None of these benefits is guaranteed, however, for an increase in Z_m leads to greater production and a fall in the price of industrial goods. After substituting for $\hat{P}_m$ in (39) and cancelling terms, we have that in the long run

---

[35] Observe from (11'), (36), (49), and (51) that

$$\hat{P}_m\big|_{t=0} = \frac{\gamma_m g_x Z_x}{P_m Q_m H}\left\{1 + \lambda_2 \mu\left[\frac{\gamma_m}{H}\frac{D^m}{Q_m} + 1 + (1-\psi)\theta_L^m \gamma_m \frac{\delta_m}{H}\right]\right\}\hat{Z}_x.$$

The term enclosed by braces is positive for

$$\frac{2}{\mu} + \rho[1 + (1-\tau)\gamma_m D^m/Q_m HN]\left\{1 + \frac{\gamma_m}{H}[(1-\psi)\theta_L^m \gamma_m \delta_m + D^m/Q_m]\right\}$$

$$> \sqrt{\rho^2[1 + (1-\tau)\gamma_m D^m/Q_m HN]^2 + 4\rho/\mu N}$$

$$\times\left\{1 + \frac{\gamma_m}{H}[(1-\psi)\theta_L^m \gamma_m \delta_m + D^m/Q_m]\right\},$$

which reduces to $1/\mu > 0$ after squaring both sides and canceling terms. Hence, $L_m(0) > L_{m,o}$.

[36] The increase in P_m tends to lower welfare by reducing real money balances in the short run. If this loss is not offset by the value of the extra foreign exchange reserves that the government obtains, then the central bank should order a helicopter drop of money that prevents real money balances from decreasing initially. Welfare is then sure to increase and the balance of payments still improves (though to a lesser extent).

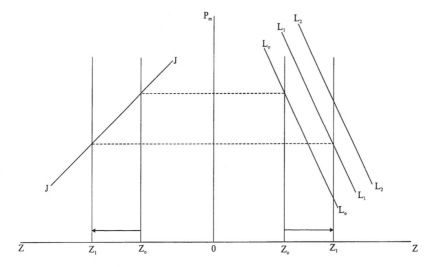

Figure 6.6. The impact on industrial sector employment when the conditions in (53) and (53′) hold.

$$\hat{L}_m > 0 \qquad \text{iff } \varepsilon \frac{D^m}{Q_m} > \sigma_1 \gamma_x \left(1 - \gamma_m \frac{g_m}{1 + g_m} \right). \tag{52}$$

With only two consumption goods, $\varepsilon = \beta \gamma_x$, where the elasticity of substitution β is evaluated at the initial equilibrium. (For small changes, it does not matter whether β is constant or a function of prices.) So the above simplifies further to

$$\hat{L}_m > 0 \qquad \text{iff } \beta > \sigma_1 \frac{Q_m}{D^m} \left(1 - \gamma_m \frac{g_m}{1 + g_m} \right). \tag{53}$$

And when there is a proportionate across-the-board increase in quotas for intermediates ($\hat{Z}_m = \hat{Z}_x$),

$$\hat{L}_m > 0 \qquad \text{iff } \beta > \sigma_1 \frac{Q_m}{D^m} \left[1 - \gamma_m \frac{g_m}{1 + g_m} \left(1 + \frac{g_x Z_x}{g_m Z_m} \right) \right]. \tag{53'}$$

These conditions are easily understood with the aid of Figure 6.6. The JJ schedule in the second quadrant shows how the market clearing price of the industrial good varies with Z. In the first quadrant, the contour curves $L_o L_o$, $L_1 L_1$, and $L_2 L_2$ depict combinations of P_m and Z consistent with progressively higher levels of employment. The curves are negatively sloped because an increase in Z shifts the labor demand schedule

Table 6.8. *Elasticities of industrial sector employment and the real wage in the export sector with respect to the quotas Z_i when $\sigma_1 = \beta$.*

β	Only Z_m changes		Z_m and Z_x change		
	L_m	$\tilde{w}_x$	L_m	$\tilde{w}_x$	g_i
.25	.086	.380	.115	.765	.25
	.108	.368	.155	.742	.50
	.123	.360	.183	.727	.75
.50	.054	.187	.072	.378	.25
	.068	.180	.097	.365	.50
	.077	.175	.115	.357	.75

out by raising the marginal product of labor. (Recall that labor and intermediates are gross complements.) Thus, if employment is to remain at its initial level, P_m must fall to raise the product wage by a matching amount. The smaller is σ_1, the larger the required drop in P_m and the more steeply sloped is LL. (For Leontief technology, the contour curves are vertical.)

Import liberalization increases the supply of intermediates from Z_o to Z_1. If substitution is easier in consumption than between value added and imported inputs, then JJ is flatter in slope than LL and employment increases. More generally, (53) and (53′) require only that σ_1 not be too much larger than β. On the right side, both Q_m/D^m and [·] are less than unity. These terms adjust for the difference in the scales of domestic production and consumption ($Q_m/D^m = 1 - G/D^m$) and for the favorable impact the gains from trade exert on the demand for industrial goods. Since the strength of the demand effect depends on the implicit tariffs g_m and g_x, liberalization is most likely to reduce underemployment when quotas are highly restrictive, especially in programs that increase quotas proportionately in the industrial and export sectors.[37] [The borderline value of σ_1 implied by (53′) is often nearly double or more that of β for plausible cases where $g_m, g_x \geq .50$.]

When (53) and (53′) hold workers benefit not only from the creation of more high-wage jobs but also from higher real wages in the export sector ($\hat{w}_x > 0 > \hat{P}_m$). Furthermore, these effects can be quantitatively weighty.

---

[37] This is consistent with the finding in Michaely et al. (1991, p. 88) that "strong" liberalization of severely restricted regimes often triggered an immediate, strong surge in growth and employment.

Table 6.9. *Elasticities of industrial sector employment and the real wage in the export sector with respect to the quotas* Z_i *when* $\sigma_1 = .5\beta$.

β	Only Z_m changes		Z_m and Z_x change		
	L_m	$\tilde{w}_x$	L_m	$\tilde{w}_x$	g_i
.25	.449	.558	.474	1.341	.25
	.471	.543	.512	1.316	.50
	.486	.533	.538	1.298	.75
.50	.295	.264	.312	.654	.25
	.309	.256	.336	.641	.50
	.318	.251	.352	.632	.75

Tables 6.8 and 6.9 show the elasticities of industrial sector employment and the real wage in the export sector ($\tilde{w}_x \equiv w_x/P_x^{\gamma x} P_m^{\gamma m}$) with respect to Z_i when the model is calibrated in the same way as in Section 6.1.4. In the least favorable cases where $\beta = \sigma_1$ and $g_m = g_x = .25$ initially, the gains in industrial sector employment are modest – 1.3–4.2% for a 25% increase in the quota – but the elasticity for $\tilde{w}_x$ ranges from .175 to .761. When the foreign exchange bottleneck is more severe ($\sigma_1 = .5\beta$), the entries for L_m are three to five times larger and most of the elasticities for $\tilde{w}_x$ lie between .5 and 1.3.

The preceding results were derived under the assumption that it is not necessary to supplement liberalization with a devaluation of the currency to keep the payments deficit in check. This may not be correct, however. As in the case of quota liberalization in the export sector, higher real income pulls in the direction of a payments surplus by raising the demand for real money balances. But the price level definitely falls when only Z_m increases and is likely to fall when Z_m and Z_x increase proportionately. If the decrease in the price level supplies the private agent with more real money balances than he desires, liberalization will be followed by a series of payments deficits.

It can be demonstrated with some effort that liberalization usually *does* worsen the payments deficit.[38] But this does not alter the prospects for reducing underemployment in the short or long run. Conditions (53) and (53′) still apply when quota liberalization is accompanied by

[38] Liberalization produces a payments deficit in all 24 cases covered by Tables 6.8 and 6.9.

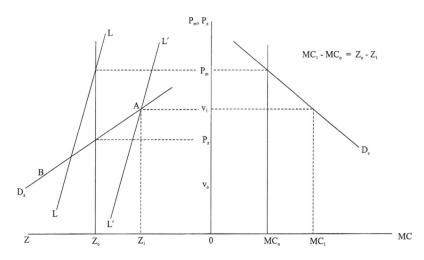

Figure 6.7. The impact of a foreign exchange auction when exports are fixed in the short-run.

a devaluation large enough to prevent a payments deficit.[39] To see this, note that the real steady-state equilibrium is independent of v and that the distinction between short- and long-run effects disappears when the exchange rate is set to ensure that $M^* = M_o$. In terms of Figure 6.5, if HH coincides with $H'H'$ and FF shifts to the left, then L_m jumps immediately to L_m^*. All of the results presented earlier are valid therefore when the government adjusts the exchange rate to maintain external balance.

6.3.3   Foreign Exchange Auctions and Liberalization

Certain types of trade reform hit the industrial sector very hard by simultaneously decreasing the price of imported consumer goods and increasing the price of imported inputs. This seems to have happened in liberalization programs in some parts of Sub-Saharan Africa. In these programs a system of comprehensive foreign exchange rationing that discriminated heavily against consumer imports was replaced by a foreign exchange auction. This case is depicted in Figure 6.7. All foreign exchange is initially rationed, but preferential treatment is accorded to imports of intermediates. For holders of foreign exchange licenses, the

[39] Collier (1991) refers to this combination of policies as a "trade-liberalizing devaluation."

prices of both imported consumer goods and imported intermediates is given by the official exchange rate v_o. The government reserves the lion's share of foreign exchange for intermediates, so the implicit tariff on intermediates, $P_z - v_o$, is much lower than that on consumer products, $P_m - v_o$. As earlier in Figure 6.6, the LL schedule in the second quadrant is an isoemployment contour slowing the combinations of P_m and Z consistent with constant employment in the industrial sector.

When a foreign exchange auction is introduced, firms and consumers compete on equal terms for the available supply of foreign exchange. If export production is inelastic in the short run, the total supply of foreign exchange is fixed and hence consumer imports increase at the expense of intermediates as the exchange rate rises from v_o to its market clearing level v_1.[40] Since the greater availability of consumer imports depresses P_m at the same time as lower purchases of intermediates reduce the marginal product of labor, the level of employment $L'L'$ may be far below that of LL. This certainly fits with the experiences of Uganda, Zambia, and Sierre Leone, where foreign exchange auctions allowed consumer imports to claim a large share of foreign exchange and the industrial sector suffered tremendous job losses.

In the above story, export production was inelastic, and consequently consumers and firms had to compete for a fixed supply of foreign exchange. The foreign exchange auction works much better, however, if exports respond strongly to the increase in the exchange rate (more likely in the medium and long run than in the short run). Higher exports cause the currency to appreciate by increasing the supply of foreign exchange. If the increase in supply is great enough, the equilibrium may shift from A to a point like B, at which higher imports of intermediates support higher employment in industry.[41] The condition for this to occur, however, is much stricter than the condition in (53) because P_m falls more when imports of consumer goods increase as well as imports of intermediates. For employment to increase, the supply response in the export sector must be large and the elasticity of substitution between labor and imported intermediates must be very small.[42]

---

[40] Changes in Z shift the D_c schedule and changes in MC shift the D_z schedule. These shifts are omitted to avoid cluttering the diagram.

[41] In Ghana, the introduction of a foreign exchange auction in 1986 was instrumental in reviving growth by increasing firms' access to imported intermediates and capital equipment. This fits with the explanation in the text. Aid from the World Bank and the IMF greatly increased the supply of foreign exchange, enabling the economy to move to a point like B.

[42] An increase in employment is possible only when the isoemployment contour is more steeply sloped than the D_z schedule.

6.4   Concluding Observations

There are no neat and tidy results that describe how liberalization affects unemployment and economic welfare. The outcome depends on whether imports of intermediates increase or decrease, the nature of technology, the credibility of liberalization, the speed of adjustment in the labor market, and the other policies that round out the reform program. Liberalization programs that reduce tariffs or loosen quotas on consumer goods also raise the real price of imported intermediates, encouraging firms to cut back on their purchases. For most types of technology, this causes labor demand to contract. Unemployment need not increase if the real wage is cut simultaneously; unfortunately, however, the employment-preserving real wage cut may be quite large, especially when technology does not permit much substitution away from intermediates or when capital substitutes more easily with intermediates than labor.

When total labor demand falls, the path to higher steady-state welfare entails a period of transitory unemployment. If it is difficult to substitute between imported intermediates and domestic inputs, and if adjustment in the labor market is slow either because liberalization lacks credibility or because wages in the export sector are inflexible in the downward direction, the losses from high unemployment during the adjustment process are substantial. Even moderate cuts in tariffs that far exceed their *ex ante* optimal level may then be welfare-worsening. This conclusion is not likely to sit well with many people, but it is just common sense. When technology is inflexible and nominal or real wage rigidities impede reallocation of the labor force, liberalization hits the economy with an adverse supply shock that it is ill-equipped to handle. The only way out of this dilemma is to delay liberalization until it can be coordinated with real wage cuts that lower the costs of adjustment enough to ensure an overall welfare gain.[43] It is important to recall here that our results for the optimal stopping point held the real wage fixed in the import sector to isolate the effects of trade liberalization per se. But if workers will agree to real wage cuts only when liberalization threatens to inflict large job losses, it may be more appropriate to view the two policies as com-

---

[43] If weak credibility is the problem, larger real wage cuts in the export sector will be ineffective and possibly harmful. (The lower the real wage in the export sector, the more the cost-benefit calculation favors sitting out a period of temporary unemployment.) The only way to avoid adjustment problems in this case is to coordinate liberalization with a sufficiently large real wage cut in the import sector.

ponent parts of an indivisible reform program. The catch is that the threat to destroy jobs must be credible. If there is a time consistency problem, the real wage concessions needed to make liberalization welfare-improving will not be forthcoming because workers realize that the government will reverse the reform when faced with persistent high unemployment.

Difficulties with transitory, high unemployment are much less likely in liberalization programs that increase the availability of imported inputs. More generous quotas for imports of intermediates reduce underemployment (i.e., the share of high-wage jobs increases) and raise the real wage in the informal sector provided the elasticity of substitution between intermediates and domestic factors of production is not too much larger than the elasticity of substitution in consumption. Moreover, if the two elasticities are of the same order of magnitude or the elasticity of substitution in production is relatively small, the favorable effects on underemployment and real wages are quantitatively large. The same conclusions presumably apply to larger quotas for imports of capital equipment, although a careful theoretical analysis of this case has yet to appear.

The contrasting results for different types of liberalization programs bear importantly on how one reads the empirical evidence. The results in Sections 6.1 and 6.2 are capable not only of explaining the sharply contractionary effects of some liberalization programs in Sub-Saharan Africa, but also of reconciling these episodes with the generally optimistic findings of the World Bank study led by Michaely, Papageorghiou, and Choksi. As noted earlier, trade reform in Sub-Saharan Africa has often involved sharp cuts in tariff/quotas on consumer imports and a considerable reduction in the share of foreign exchange allocated to imports of intermediates and capital goods. By contrast, the most common type of liberalization in the episodes studied by the World Bank project was the removal of quotas on imports of noncompetitive intermediate inputs and capital equipment; liberalization of competitive inputs and consumer goods came later, if at all. The mixed findings for employment and growth could reflect therefore the offsetting effects of other policies (especially coordinated real wage cuts) or the mixed effects of pro- and anti-employment liberalization programs.[44] At present, there is no basis for general pronouncements about the likely impact of liberalization on labor demand

---

[44] This point is acknowledged in the World Bank study. Michaely et al. recognize (1991, p. 76) that it is dubious to correlate import ratios and employment when imports of intermediates increase.

and unemployment in the short run. Empirical investigation needs to be better informed by theory so as to distinguish how different types of trade reform affect unemployment in economies possessing different structural characteristics.

CHAPTER 7

Tools and Tricks of the Trade, Part III:
The Dynamics of Temporary Shocks

In Chapter 4 we analyzed the behavior of the system

$$\dot{x}_1 = f(x_1, x_2; \alpha), \tag{1}$$

$$\dot{x}_2 = g(x_1, x_2; \alpha), \tag{2}$$

following an unanticipated, permanent shock that shifted the stationary equilbrium from $(x_{1,o}, x_{2,o})$ to (x_1^*, x_2^*). The phase diagram for this system is reproduced in Figure 7.1. x_2 is a jump variable and x_1 is predetermined. Immediately after the shock, x_2 jumps by AB so as to bring the equilibrium onto the saddlepath $S'S'$. As x_1 increases, the path moves along $S'S'$ until it arrives at the stationary equilibrium C.

The transitional dynamics are more complicated when the shock is temporary rather than permanent. Suppose the public knows that the shock that hits the economy at $t = 0$ will last only up to time t_1. While the shock persists, the transition path is governed by the dynamic system associated with (x_1^*, x_2^*). Because the shock is temporary, however, point A remains the long-run stationary equilibrium. Convergence to the steady state at A requires that the equilibrium lie somewhere along the saddlepath at time t_1. The path that fulfills this requirement usually involves one jump in x_2 at $t = 0$, and possibly a second jump at t_1. Furthermore, the equilibrium path is almost always a *nonconvergent* path of the system associated with point C. It is rarely optimal to simply traverse $S'S'$ prior to time t_1 and then jump to SS when the shock is reversed. Nor is there any general presumption that the equilibrium path will "shadow" the saddlepath $S'S'$ up to time t_1. In many cases, the transitional dynamics for temporary and permanent shocks are qualitatively different; the path for the temporary shock may well look like $ADEF$.

Our main motivation for studying permanent vs. temporary shocks is that the same distinction applies to credible vs. noncredible policy reforms. The economic landscape in the Third World is littered with failed attempts at reform. Knowing the history of failure, the public is likely to be sceptical of government pronouncements of a change in the policy regime – more likely than not, the newest attempt at reform will be

233

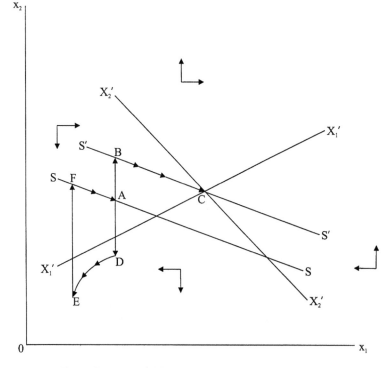

Figure 7.1. A case where the path for a temporary shock is qualitatively different from the path for a permanent shock.

reversed at some later date. Noncredible reforms are thus analagous to temporary shocks.

7.1   The General Methodology

Let the exogenous variable α increase at $t = 0$ and then fall back to its original value at time t_1. The stationary equilibria associated with the original value and the higher value of α are $(x_{1,o}, x_{2,o})$ and (x_1^*, x_2^*), respectively. During the period $(0, t_1)$, x_1 and x_2 evolve according to [see equation (14) in Chapter 4]

$$x_1(t) - x_1^* = h_1 e^{\lambda_1 t} + h_2 e^{\lambda_2 t}, \qquad 0 \leq t \leq t_1, \tag{3}$$

$$x_2(t) - x_2^* = \frac{g_1}{\lambda_1 - g_2} h_1 e^{\lambda_1 t} + \frac{g_1}{\lambda_2 - g_2} h_2 e^{\lambda_2 t}, \qquad 0 \leq t \leq t_1. \tag{4}$$

From t_1 onwards, the path coincides with the saddlepath that converges to the original steady state

$$x_1(t) - x_{1,o} = h_3 e^{\lambda_2 t}, \qquad t \geq t_1, \tag{5}$$

$$x_2(t) - x_{2,o} = \frac{g_1}{\lambda_2 - g_2} h_3 e^{\lambda_2 t}, \qquad t \geq t_1. \tag{6}$$

Note that h_1 is not set equal to zero in (3) and (4) because nothing constrains the economy to follow the saddlepath $S'S'$ during the phase $(0, t_1)$.

The mathematical task we face is to find solutions for the three constants h_1, h_2, and h_3. This requires three boundary conditions that tell us something about where x_1 and x_2 are at the crucial transition points $t = 0$ and $t = t_1$. The fixed values for the predetermined variable provide two boundary conditions. Evaluating (3) at $t = 0$ yields the restriction

$$h_1 + h_2 = x_{1,o} - x_1^*. \tag{7}$$

Moreover, at $t = t_1$, equations (3) and (5) must give the same value for x_1. Thus,

$$h_1 e^{\lambda_1 t_1} + (h_2 - h_3) e^{\lambda_2 t_1} = x_{1,o} - x_1^*. \tag{8}$$

The third boundary condition fixes the position of the jump variable x_2 just before the shock is reversed at t_1. How this is done depends on the nature of the model. If x_2 is the price of some asset, it will usually be possible to rule out a jump by appealing to an arbitrage argument: since the public knows the shock is temporary, a jump in x_2 would be foreseen; but this is clearly incompatible with a perfect foresight equilibrium as it implies that market participants passively accept an infinite capital loss when the price falls and pass up the opportunity to make infinite, risk-free profits when the price rises.

In optimizing models where x_2 is a control variable, a similar but less direct arbitrage argument can be exploited. Consider the optimization problem

$$\underset{\{x_2\}}{\text{Max}} \int_0^\infty \psi(x_1, x_2, \alpha) e^{-\rho t} dt, \tag{9}$$

subject to

$$\dot{x}_1 = f(x_1, x_2, \alpha). \tag{10}$$

The optimal path satisfies the first-order condition

$$\psi_2(x_1, x_2, \alpha) = -\phi f_2(x_1, x_2, \alpha) \tag{11}$$

and the co-state equation

$$\dot{\phi} = [\rho - f_1(x_1, x_2, \alpha)]\phi - \psi_1(x_1, x_2, \alpha), \tag{12}$$

where ϕ is the multiplier attached to the constraint (10). To continue working with the same model, suppose (11) and (12) have been manipulated to obtain $\dot{x}_2 = g(x_1, x_2, \alpha)$.

The arbitragelike aspect to the solution arises from restrictions that optimizing behavior places on the path of ϕ. $\phi(t)$ is a shadow price that measures the welfare gain from a small increase in x_1 at time t. The crucial implication of this is that ϕ jumps only when the private agent adjusts in response to the arrival of new information. If ϕ jumped at any other time, the existing path would not be optimal: the private agent could secure a higher level of welfare by selecting a different path for x_2 that delivered a little bit more or a little bit less of x_1 just before the *foreseen* jump in ϕ.[1]

In the case under examination, new information arrives only at time $t = 0$ because the public is assumed to know from the outset that the increase in α is temporary. ϕ jumps therefore at $t = 0$ but not at $t = t_1$. This and the fact that x_1 is predetermined enable us to tie down the third boundary condition. Since neither ϕ nor x_1 changes when α falls at time t_1, x_2 has to jump by

$$dx_2|_{t_1} = -\frac{\phi f_{23} + \psi_{23}}{\psi_{22} + \phi f_{22}} d\alpha|_{t_1} \equiv J \tag{13}$$

to preserve the equality in (11). This jump connects the solution paths in (4) and (6):

$$J = \underset{\substack{\text{value of } x_2 \text{ as } t \\ \text{approaches } t_1 \text{ from} \\ \text{above in (6)}}}{x_2(t_1^+)} - \underset{\substack{\text{value of } x_2 \text{ as } t \\ \text{approaches } t_1 \text{ from} \\ \text{above in (4)}}}{x_2(t_1^-)}$$

$$\Rightarrow J = x_{2,0} - x_2^* + \frac{g_1}{\lambda_2 - g_2}(h_3 - h_2)e^{\lambda_2 t_1} - \frac{g_1}{\lambda_1 - g_2}h_1 e^{\lambda_1 t_1}. \tag{14}$$

Equations (7), (8), and (14) yield explicit solutions for h_1, h_2, and h_3 after calculating the eigenvalues and the impact of an increase in α on the steady-state values of x_1 and x_2.

---

[1] The rule that ϕ does not jump at t_1 assumes that in general equilibrium x_2 is not an exogenous variable; if it is, then the foreseen jump in ϕ implies that some price adjusts at time t_1 to eliminate opportunities for profitable intertemporal arbitrage. This case does not arise in the models that appear in Chapter 8.

The solution procedure is the same in the general case where there are n predetermined variables $x_1, \ldots, x_n$ and m control variables $x_{n+1}, \ldots, x_{n+m}$. A total of $2n + m$ constants appear in the $2(n + m)$ equations that describe the paths of the x_i during the phases $(0, t_1)$ and (t_1, ∞). $2n$ boundary conditions are obtained directly by evaluating the solution paths for $x_1, \ldots, x_n$ at $t = 0$ and $t = t_1$. To derive the other m boundary conditions, one solves the m first-order conditions for the jumps $J_1, \ldots, J_m$ in $x_{n+1}, \ldots, x_{n+m}$. The jumps can then be used to link the end of the solution path for phase $(0, t_1)$ to the beginning of the solution path for phase (t_1, ∞) – i.e., setting $J_1 = x_{n+1}(t_1^+) - x_{n+1}(t_1^-)$, $J_2 = x_{n+2}(t_1^+) - x_{n+2}(t_1^-)$, $\ldots, J_m = x_{n+m}(t_1^+) - x_{n+m}(t_1^-)$ produces an additional m restrictions on the constants $h_1, h_2, \ldots, h_{2n+m}$.

7.2   An Example

Assume in the example in Chapter 4 that the increase in the world market price of the export good is temporary. When P_x increases at $t = 0$, the public anticipates, correctly, that the price will drop back to its previous level at time t_1.

a. Show that when $\delta = 0$ the path of investment is

$$I(t) = \begin{cases} \beta_x K_o(L_x/L_m)\lambda_1 e^{\lambda_1 t} + [e^{\lambda_1(t-t_1)}\lambda_1 - \lambda_2 e^{\lambda_2 t - \lambda_1 t_1}](\lambda_1 - \lambda_2)^{-1} \\ \{P_x D^x \tau + P_x X + \beta_x K_o(L_x/L_m)[\lambda_2(e^{\lambda_1 t_1} - 1) \\ -\lambda_1 e^{\lambda_1 t_1}]\}\hat{P}_x, \qquad 0 \le t \le t_1, \\[2ex] \dfrac{\lambda_2}{\lambda_1 - \lambda_2} e^{\lambda_2 t}\{(P_x D^x \tau + P_x X)(e^{-\lambda_2 t_1} - e^{-\lambda_1 t_1}) \\ + \beta_x K_o(L_x/L_m)[\lambda_1(1 - e^{-\lambda_2 t_1}) \\ -\lambda_2(1 - e^{-\lambda_1 t_1})]\}\hat{P}_x, \qquad t \ge t_1. \end{cases}$$

   where $X \equiv Q_x - D^x$, the volume of exports.
b. Explain why investment spending might increase in the short run and sketch the phase diagrams that cover the various possible paths of I and K.

Solution

We can start from equation (65) in Chapter 4. Setting $\delta = 0$, we have that over the period $(0, t_1)$

$$I(t) = h_1 e^{\lambda_1 t} + h_2 e^{\lambda_2 t}, \qquad 0 \le t \le t_1, \tag{15}$$

$$K(t) - K^* = \frac{h_1}{\lambda_1} e^{\lambda_1 t} + \frac{h_2}{\lambda_2} e^{\lambda_2 t}, \qquad 0 \le t \le t_1. \tag{16}$$

After t_1, the economy traverses the saddlepath that leads back to the original steady state $(0, K_o)$:

$$I(t) = h_3 e^{\lambda_2 t}, \qquad t \ge t_1, \tag{17}$$

$$K(t) - K_o = \frac{h_3}{\lambda_2} e^{\lambda_2 t}, \qquad t \ge t_1. \tag{18}$$

Evaluating (16) at $t = 0$ gives

$$\frac{h_1}{\lambda_1} = K_o - K^* - \frac{h_2}{\lambda_2}. \tag{19}$$

Also, since (16) and (18) have to return the same value for $K(t)$ at t_1,

$$\frac{h_1}{\lambda_1} e^{\lambda_1 t_1} + \frac{e^{\lambda_2 t_1}}{\lambda_2} (h_2 - h_3) = K_o - K^*,$$

or

$$\frac{h_2}{\lambda_2} (e^{\lambda_2 t_1} - e^{\lambda_1 t_1}) - \frac{h_3}{\lambda_2} e^{\lambda_2 t_1} = (K_o - K^*)(1 - e^{\lambda_1 t_1}). \tag{20}$$

The solution for the change in the steady-state capital stock is [see equation (74) in Chapter 4]

$$K_o - K^* = K_o \beta_x (L_x / L_m) \hat{P}_x. \tag{21}$$

Thus,

$$h_1 / \lambda_1 = K_o \beta_x (L_x / L_m) \hat{P}_x - h_2 / \lambda_2, \tag{22}$$

$$h_2 (e^{\lambda_2 t_1} - e^{\lambda_1 t_1}) - h_3 e^{\lambda_2 t_1} = \lambda_2 (1 - e^{\lambda_1 t_1}) K_o \beta_x (L_x / L_m) \hat{P}_x. \tag{23}$$

At t_1, I jumps so as to place the equilibrium on the original saddlepath. The jump in I can be determined from the first-order condition

$$V_E[P_x, R(P_x, K) - I] = \phi. \tag{24}$$

Since optimizing behavior rules out foreseen jumps in ϕ and K is predetermined, I must adjust to keep the marginal utility of consumption constant when P_x falls. This requires

$$dI|_{t_1} = \left(\frac{V_{Ex}}{V_{EE}} + Q_x \right) dP_x|_{t_1}, \tag{25}$$

where $V_{Ex} \equiv \partial V_E / \partial P_x$. Define $X \equiv Q_x - D^x$, the export volume, and make use of the result that $V_{Ex} / V_{EE} D^x = \tau - 1$ when preferences are homothetic. The jump in I can then be stated as

$$dI|_{t_1} = (D^x \tau + X)dP_x|_{t_1} = -(D^x \tau + X)dP_x. \tag{25'}$$

The jump in (25') must be consistent with the jump that connects the paths for I in (15) and (17). Letting t approach t_1 from below in (15) and from above in (17) gives

$$I(t_1^-) = h_2\left(e^{\lambda_2 t_1} - \frac{\lambda_1}{\lambda_2}e^{\lambda_1 t_1}\right) + \beta_x K_o(L_x/L_m)\lambda_1 e^{\lambda_1 t_1}\hat{P}_x, \tag{26}$$

$$I(t_1^+) = h_3 e^{\lambda_2 t_1}. \tag{27}$$

Thus,

$$h_3 e^{\lambda_2 t_1} + h_2\left(\frac{\lambda_1}{\lambda_2}e^{\lambda_1 t_1} - e^{\lambda_2 t_1}\right) = [\beta_x K_o(L_x/L_m)\lambda_1 e^{\lambda_1 t_1}$$
$$- P_x D^x \tau - P_x X]\hat{P}_x. \tag{28}$$

Solving (22), (23), and (28) for h_1, h_2, and h_3 produces

$$h_1 = \left\{\lambda_1 \beta_x K_o L_x/L_m + \frac{e^{-\lambda_1 t_1}}{\lambda_1 - \lambda_2}\{P_x D^x \tau + P_x X\right.$$
$$\left. + \beta_x K_o(L_x/L_m)[\lambda_2(e^{\lambda_1 t_1} - 1) - \lambda_1 e^{\lambda_1 t_1})]\}\right\}\hat{P}_x, \tag{29}$$

$$h_2 = -\frac{\lambda_2}{\lambda_1 - \lambda_2}e^{-\lambda_1 t_1}\{P_x D^x \tau + P_x X + \beta_x K_o(L_x/L_m)$$
$$[\lambda_2(e^{\lambda_1 t_1} - 1) - \lambda_1 e^{\lambda_1 t_1})]\}\hat{P}_x, \tag{30}$$

$$h_3 = \frac{\lambda_2}{\lambda_1 - \lambda_2}\{(P_x D^x \tau + P_x X)(e^{-\lambda_2 t_1} - e^{-\lambda_1 t_1}) + \beta_x K_o(L_x/L_m)$$
$$[\lambda_1(1 - e^{\lambda_2 t_1}) - \lambda_2(1 - e^{-\lambda_1 t_1})]\}. \tag{31}$$

Substituting for h_1–h_3 in (15) and (17) gives

$$I(t) = \begin{cases} \beta_x K_o(L_x/L_m)\lambda_1 e^{\lambda_1 t} + [e^{\lambda_1(t-t_1)}\lambda_1 - \lambda_2 e^{\lambda_2 t - \lambda_1 t_1}] \\ (\lambda_1 - \lambda_2)^{-1}\{P_x D^x \tau + P_x X + \beta_x K_o(L_x/L_m) \\ [\lambda_2(e^{\lambda_1 t_1} - 1) - \lambda_1 e^{\lambda_1 t_1}]\}\hat{P}_x, \qquad 0 \le t \le t_1, \\[2ex] \frac{\lambda_2}{\lambda_1 - \lambda_2}e^{\lambda_2 t}\{(P_x D^x \tau + P_x X)(e^{-\lambda_2 t_1} - e^{-\lambda_1 t_1}) \\ + \beta_x K_o(L_x/L_m)[\lambda_1(1 - e^{-\lambda_2 t_1}) \\ - \lambda_2(1 - e^{-\lambda_1 t_1})]\}\hat{P}_x, \qquad t \ge t_1. \end{cases} \tag{32}$$

b. At $t = 0$,

$$\underbrace{I(0)}_{\substack{\text{initial jump} \\ \text{in } I}} = [e^{-\lambda_1 t_1}(P_x D^x \tau + P_x X) + \underbrace{\lambda_2 \beta_x K_o (L_x/L_m)(1 - e^{-\lambda_1 t_1})}_{\substack{\text{impact on } I \text{ when} \\ \text{the increase in } P_x \text{ is} \\ \text{permanent}}}]\hat{P}_x. \tag{33}$$

The first term is positive and the second is negative, so I may fall or rise on impact. The negative term reflects the tendency for investment to decline when higher labor demand in the export sector bids up the wage (thereby lowering profits in the import sector). This is the mechanism that induces capital decumulation when the increase in P_x is permanent. Consequently, I falls initially if t_1 is sufficiently large. The solution that we obtained earlier in Chapter 4 now emerges as a limiting case:

$$\lim_{t_1 \to \infty} I(0) = \lambda_2 \beta_x K_o (L_x/L_m)\hat{P}_x < 0.$$

Two positive effects oppose the contractionary pull exerted by a higher wage. First, the private agent wishes to set aside some of the temporary income gain to support higher consumption in the future. The pursuit of a smooth consumption path thus calls for higher investment over the period $(0, t_1)$. This effect shows up simply as $P_x X e^{-\lambda_1 t_1}$ because the windfall gain conferred by the price increase is proportional to the export volume.

The second positive effect operates through the relative price of current consumption. A *temporary* increase in P_x makes current consumption expensive relative to future consumption (i.e., consumption after t_1). The private agent has an incentive therefore to save and invest during the period $(0, t_1)$ while the price of consuming the export good is high. The strength of this effect depends on the size of the intertemporal elasticity of substitution scaled by domestic consumption of the exportable good.

It is apparent from (33) that the intertemporal substitution and consumption smoothing effects will produce an upward jump in investment when the price increase is relatively short-lived. To find the borderline value of t_1, set $I(0) = 0$ in (33). This yields

$$I(0) > 0 \quad \text{iff} \quad t_1 < -\frac{\ln\left(\dfrac{\lambda_2 \beta_x K_o L_x/L_m}{\lambda_2 \beta_x K_o L_x/L_m - P_x D^x \tau - P_x X}\right)}{\lambda_1}. \tag{34}$$

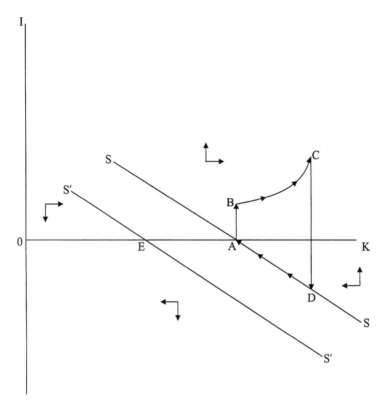

Figure 7.2. The transition path when investment increases on impact.

The paths for I and K are depicted in the phase diagrams in Figures 7.2 and 7.3. When capital does not depreciate, the $\dot{K}=0$ schedule coincides with the horizontal axis and the saddlepath is negatively sloped. The increase in P_x shifts the stationary equilibrium from point A to point E.

Figure 7.2 applies when the condition on t_1 in (34) holds. In this case, I jumps upward by AB on impact and then increases smoothly throughout the period where the higher export price prevails. When the price falls at t_1, a large downward jump in investment shifts the equilibrium from point C to point D on the saddlepath SS. From D, the path moves gradually back to the preshock steady state A.

When $I(0) < 0$, the intertemporal substitution and consumption-smoothing effects ensure that the initial downward jump is smaller than

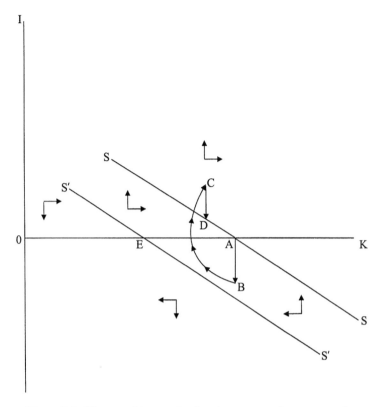

Figure 7.3. The transition path when investment decreases on impact.

in the case where the price increase is permanent. Hence, point B in Figure 7.3 is above $S'S'$. Furthermore, since I jumps downward at time t_1, the path must cross the horizontal axis prior to t_1 so as to reach point C above SS. We also know that point C lies to the left of point A: $I(t_1^+) > 0$ only if $h_3 > 0$; but when $h_3 > 0$, equation (18) says that $K(t_1) < K_o$.

CHAPTER 8

Liberalization and the Transition Problem, Part II: Credibility and the Balance of Payments

A certain amount of trade reform can be accomplished by enhancing the incentives for export production, reducing dispersion in effective rates of protection, and loosening quotas on imports of intermediate inputs and capital goods. But after these opportunities have been exploited, it is necessary to get on with the more difficult business of dismantling the high tariffs and restrictive quotas that protect firms in the import-competing industrial sector. At this stage in the liberalization process, lack of credibility can do serious damage. As we saw in Chapter 6, expectations of a policy reversal weaken the incentive for workers laid off in the import sector to seek jobs in the export sector. The same point applies to physical capital and other inputs that cannot shift costlessly from one sector to another. Thus, even if other policies prevent unemployment from increasing, there is a cost to weak credibility in that the gains from trade on the production side will be slower to materialize.

This chapter focuses on the connection between lack of credibility and another aspect of the transition problem: sudden, large increases in spending on consumer imports. *Some* increase in consumer imports is expected and desired in liberalization programs that aim for a significant reduction in the level of protection. The problem is that the objective is often greatly overfulfilled. In Chile (1978), Mexico (1987), Turkey (1989), Kenya (1976, 1980, 1988), Tanzania (1984), Zaire (1983–86), Zambia (1986), the Sudan (1979), Uganda (1985), Senegal (1986), Sierre Leone (1988), Cote d'Ivoire (1984), Guinea (1983–86), Vietnam (1989), Ecuador (1990–94), and elsewhere, liberalization was followed by a surge in consumer imports inconsistent with plausible values for price and income elasticities of demand.[1] This suggests the private sector did not believe the reform would last – that it viewed liberalization as a one-time opportunity to purchase imports at exceptionally favorable prices.

---

[1] See the accounts in Loxley (1989), Stein (1992), Zack-Williams (1992), Sepehri (1993), Celasun (1994), Ros (1994), Arulpragasam and del Ninno (1996), Mommen (1996), Reinikka (1996), Truong and Gates (1996), and Larrea (1998).

243

At least two questions come to mind when consumers bet heavily against the viability of trade reform. First, are there real, tangible welfare costs to consumption binges induced by expectations of a policy reversal? The answer to this question is – yes, very much so. Calvo has demonstrated in a series of elegant papers that imperfect credibility distorts intertemporal choice. This, the possibility of additional losses from transitory unemployment, and the low success rate in liberalization attempts should give policy makers pause before they endorse a program of deep tariff cuts. A failed attempt at reform may be positively harmful, not just a missed opportunity.

The second issue concerns the impact on the balance of payments. I take up this issue in Section 8.2 by comparing the effects of credible and noncredible reforms. The comparison reveals that noncredible reforms often produce much larger deficits. Consequently, a level of foreign exchange reserves that would comfortably support a permanent, credible reform may be depleted in a year or less when liberalization lacks credibility. In these circumstances, policy makers face a coordination problem: expectation of success is a self-fulfilling equilibrium, but so also is expectation of failure – what happens is what the private sector expects.

Since the aforementioned costs of weak credibility stem from its impact on saving behavior, I put production problems to the side in this chapter by working with models in which everyone is employed and all imports are consumer goods.

8.1   Temporary Liberalization and the Saving Distortion

Imperfect credibility is itself a distortion. This is easy to demonstrate in a two-period version of the infinite horizon model in Calvo (1986). Assume all output is exported, all consumer goods are imported, that production in the export sector is fixed at Q, and that the representative agent can borrow or lend as much as he likes in a perfect world capital market where the interest rate r equals his time preference rate ρ. As will become apparent momentarily, the point of these special assumptions is to have a setup where the solutions to the maximization problems of the private agent and the social planner coincide whenever the current level of protection is credible. The private agent maximizes

$$U(C_1) + \frac{U(C_2)}{1+r}, \tag{1}$$

subject to the lifetime budget constraint

$$C_1(1+h_1)+\frac{C_2(1+h_2)}{1+r}=Q+h_1C_1+\frac{Q+h_2C_2}{1+r}, \qquad (2)$$

where C_i is consumption in period i; h_i is the tariff in period i; and, on the right side, h_iC_i is the lump-sum rebate of tariff revenues in period i. The first-order conditions yield the textbook rule that C_1 and C_2 will be chosen so that the marginal rate of substitution equals the relative price of current consumption:

$$\frac{U'(C_2)}{U'(C_1)}=\frac{1+h_2}{1+h_1}. \qquad (3)$$

This and the consolidated budget constraint

$$C_1+\frac{C_2}{1+r}=Q\frac{2+r}{1+r} \qquad (2')$$

can be solved for C_1 and C_2.

The social planner ignores the tariffs by maximizing $U(C_1) + U(C_2)/(1 + r)$ subject to (2'). The socially optimal values of C_1 and C_2 thus satisfy

$$\frac{U'(C_1)}{U'(C_2)}=1. \qquad (4)$$

The social planner's solution is point A in Figure 8.1. This is also the competitive equilibrium when the tariff is the same in the two periods. [For $h_1 = h_2$, equations (3) and (4) are identical.] Protection is harmless because there are no relative prices in an economy that specializes in both production and consumption.

Now suppose the tariff is lowered in period one. If the private sector believes the reduction in the tariff is permanent, then $h_1 = h_2$ and the competitive equilibrium remains at A, the social optimum. But a *finite* tariff cut expected to be reversed in period two shifts the equilibrium to B. Welfare falls because the private agent decides to consume more in period one even though, for the economy as a whole, the price of current vs. future consumption has not changed; temporary liberalization thus distorts intertemporal choice by making current consumption look cheaper than it really is.

Two subtle aspects of Calvo's analysis merit comment. First, the saving distortion associated with temporary liberalization is a *second-order* effect. The envelope theorem states here that in the neighborhood of the social optimum small induced changes in C_1 and C_2 leave welfare unchanged. Consequently, an infinitesimal decrease in h_1 alone does

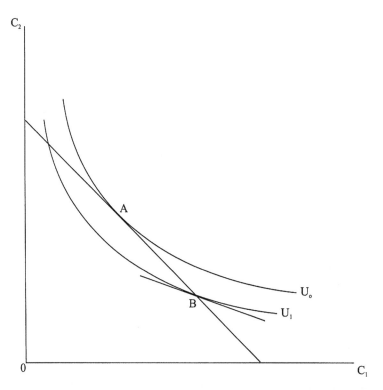

Figure 8.1. The welfare loss from lack of credibility in a simple Calvo-type model.

not produce a first-order welfare loss when $h_1 = h_2$ at the initial equilibrium.

The second point to note is that the welfare loss from imperfect credibility does not depend on whether private sector fears of a policy reversal prove correct. The reason, of course, is that time runs in one direction; it is not possible to go back and undo previous dissaving when, contrary to expectations, the government does not revert to its old protectionist policies. The private agent may experience regret upon learning that the lower tariff will be maintained, but this is inconsequential – point B remains the competitive equilibrium. In short, what distorts the saving decision of the private agent is the *expectation* of a policy reversal; it is not necessary for the policy reversal to actually occur (Calvo, 1987, 1988).

8.2   A More General Analysis of Temporary Liberalization[2]

The central message of Calvo's papers is that temporary liberalization programs which lack credibility may be welfare-worsening. To draw sharper conclusions, one needs to know how the length of the liberalization period, the size of the tariff cut, and the values of certain critical primitive parameters influence the costs of the saving distortion relative to the gains from trade. A more general welfare analysis of this type promises, in particular, to say something about the extent to which weak credibility limits the case for trade reform. I tackle this issue head-on by deriving the solution for the optimal tariff cut under the assumption that the public anticipates the subsequent policy reversal.

Employing our usual notation, let $V(P_m, E)$, $R(P_m)$, and $D(P_m, E)$ denote, respectively, the indirect utility function, the revenue function, and the Marshallian demand function for the import good, where $P_m = 1 + h$ is the price of the import good ($P_x = 1$) and E is total consumption expenditure. As before, foreign bonds b are the only store of wealth. The private agent thus maximizes

$$U = \int_0^\infty V(P_m, E)e^{-\rho t} dt, \tag{5}$$

subject to

$$\dot{b} = R(P_m) + h[D(P_m, E) - R'(P_m)] + rb - E. \tag{6}$$

The government decides at time $t = 0$ to reduce the tariff from its current level h_2 to h_1. If the tariff cut were fully credible, it would be optimal to set h_1 equal to zero – to go all the way to free trade. Owing to past failures, however, the public is highly sceptical of the government's announcement that liberalization is permanent. To keep things very simple, assume, following Calvo, that both the policy maker and the public know the tariff cut will will be reversed at time T. The optimal value of h_1 is then determined by weighing the benefits of greater allocative efficiency against the costs of the saving distortion in the manner shown in Figure 8.2. Some liberalization is desirable because, starting from the initial equilibrium where $h_1 = h_2$, the gain in allocative efficiency

---

[2] Much of this section is reprinted from *Journal of International Economics*, 47, E. Buffie, "Optimal Trade Liberalization and the Welfare Costs of Imperfect Credibility," pages 371–378, Copyright (1999), with permission from Elsevier Science. The analysis that follows, however, is based on a two-sector version of the three-sector model developed in that paper.

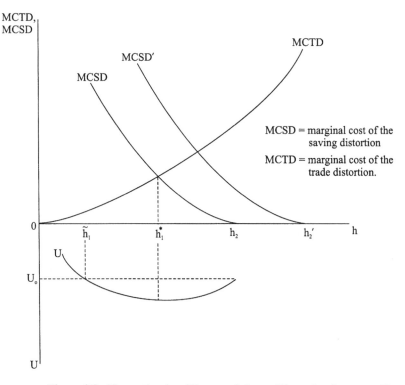

Figure 8.2. The optimal tariff cut and the tariff cut that leaves welfare unchanged.

from an infinitesimal decrease in h_1 is a first-order effect whereas the loss from the saving distortion is second-order small. But as a wedge opens up between h_1 and h_2, further tariff cuts yield smaller efficiency gains and the second-order costs of the saving distortion cease to be negligible. At the optimal tariff, h_1^*, the costs of further worsening the saving distortion counterbalance the benefits of reducing the trade distortion.

The assumption of a mass point in expectations at time T simplifies the analysis but is not critical to the results. Calvo motivates the assumption by arguing that policy reversals are purely exogenous events that occur at a well-defined time (e.g., elections). An alternative rationale is supplied by Rodrik (1989b): even protectionist governments may agree to tariff cuts as a way of obtaining aid from the World Bank and the International Monetary Fund; recognizing this, the public may expect protectionist policies to reappear shortly after the structural adjustment program comes to an end.[3]

If the watershed event at T passes without a policy reversal, the tariff h_1 becomes credible and the economy enjoys greater gains from trade forever. In what follows, I assume the government in power at $t = 0$ is so risk averse that it ignores the possibility of gains beyond time T. The solutions correspond therefore to the conservative maximin rule: the tariff cut is chosen to maximize welfare in the worst-case scenario where the reform cannot be sustained. This, and the assumption the public is certain the reform is temporary, bias the results strongly against the conclusion that large tariff cuts will be optimal.[4]

8.2.1 The Optimal Policy Rule

The path of expenditure is the only input needed to derive the optimal value of h_1. Accordingly, start by examining the necessary conditions that characterize the solution to the private agent's optimization problem. These are

$$V_E(P_m, E) = \pi, \tag{7}$$

$$\dot{\pi} = \pi(\rho - r), \tag{8}$$

where π is the multiplier associated with the constraint (6). Observe that π rises or falls continuously if $\rho \neq r$. In models of this type it is necessary therefore to assume $\rho = r$. Given this assumption, the economy eventually settles into a stationary equilibrium where the current account is in balance. Furthermore, the dynamics simplify greatly. For $\rho = r$, the shadow price π jumps at $t = 0$ but is constant thereafter. Consequently, the path of E is flat over the intervals $[0, T)$ and $[T, \infty)$, with jumps occuring at $t = 0$ and $t = T$. Let E_1 and E_2 refer to the constant levels of expenditure during these two intervals. Because π does not jump at T, equation (7) implies

$$V_E(1 + h_1, E_1) = V_E(1 + h_2, E_2). \tag{9}$$

---

[3] A third possibility is that the public anticipates the return of protection when the most recent commodity boom comes to an end (Bevan, Collier, and Gunning, 1990). Reinikka (1996) provides direct empirical support for the Calvo hypothesis: the private sector in Kenya appears to have correctly anticipated several policy reversals.

[4] Calvo and Mendoza (1994) show that the welfare losses from weak credibility are smaller the lower the subjective probability of a policy reversal.

A second relationship between E_1 and E_2 is embedded in the budget constraint (6). Since the paths of consumption and income are flat from T onwards, the current account balance will equal zero only if

$$E_2 = R(1+h_2) + h_2[D(1+h_2, E_2) - R'(1+h_2)] + rb_T. \tag{10}$$

To determine b_T, the stock of bonds at the end of the liberalization period, define $y \equiv R(1+h_1) + h_1[D(1+h_1, E_1) - R'(1+h_1)] - E_1$ and write (6) as

$$\dot{b} = y + rb, \qquad 0 \le t \le T. \tag{11}$$

y is constant, so this differential equation can be solved directly to get

$$b_T = b_o e^{rT} + \frac{y}{r}(e^{rT} - 1), \tag{12}$$

where b_o is initial bond holdings. Substituting for b_T in (10) gives

$$E_1 + \frac{E_2}{e^{rT} - 1} = R(1+h_1) + h_1[D(1+h_1, E_1) - R'(1+h_1)]$$
$$+ \frac{R(1+h_2) + h_2[D(1+h_2, E_2) - R'(1+h_2)] + rb_o e^{rT}}{e^{rT} - 1}. \tag{13}$$

Before solving (9) and (13) for E_1 and E_2, it will be helpful to introduce a bit of new notation and to place a mild restriction on preferences. Let $D^1 \equiv D(1+h_1, E_1)$ and $Q^1 \equiv R'(1+h_1)$ denote consumption of the import good and domestic production in the import-competing sector during the liberalization phase, let γ_i be the consumption share of the import good when the import price is $1 + h_i$, and let ε and η be the compensated elasticity of demand and the elasticity of supply for the import good evaluated at $P_m = 1 + h_1$. Also, assume that preferences are homothetic and that the instantaneous utility function is of the form $u = J^{1-1/\tau}/(1 - 1/\tau)$, where aggregate consumption is a CES index of the import and export goods and $\tau \equiv -V_E/V_{EE}E$ is the intertemporal elasticity of substitution. Equations (9) and (13) then yield

$$dE_1 - \frac{E_1}{E_2} dE_2 = D^1(1-\tau)dh_1, \tag{14}$$

$$\left(1 - \frac{h_1}{1+h_1}\gamma_1\right)dE_1 + \left(1 - \frac{h_2}{1+h_2}\gamma_2\right)\frac{dE_2}{e^{rT} - 1}$$
$$= \left[\left(1 - \frac{h_1}{1+h_1}\gamma_1\right)D^1 - \frac{h_1}{1+h_1}(D^1\varepsilon + Q^1\eta)\right]dh_1, \tag{15}$$

after noting that under homothetic preferences γ equals the marginal propensity to consume the import good and $V_{EPm}/V_{EE}D^1 = \tau - 1$. The solutions for E_1 and E_2 are

$$\frac{dE_1}{dh_1} = D^1 - \Delta^{-1}\left[\frac{D^1\tau}{e^{rT}-1}\left(1-\frac{h_2}{1+h_2}\gamma_2\right)\right.$$

$$\left. +\frac{h_1}{1+h_1}\frac{E_1}{E_2}(D^1\varepsilon+Q^1\eta)\right], \tag{16}$$

$$\frac{dE_2}{dh_1} = \Delta^{-1}\left[D^1\tau\left(1-\frac{h_1}{1+h_1}\gamma_1\right)-\frac{h_1}{1+h_1}(D^1\varepsilon+Q^1\eta)\right], \tag{17}$$

where

$$\Delta \equiv \left(1-\frac{h_1}{1+h_1}\gamma_1\right)\frac{E_1}{E_2}+(e^{rT}-1)^{-1}\left(1-\frac{h_2}{1+h_2}\gamma_2\right).$$

The impact on welfare can now be derived from (5), (16), and (17). First split the utility integral into the two components:

$$U = \int_0^T V(1+h_1, E_1)e^{-rt}dt + \int_T^\infty V(1+h_2, E_2)e^{-rt}dt.$$

Since E_1 and E_2 are constant, so also are $V(1 + h_1, E_1)$ and $V(1 + h_2, E_2)$. Thus,

$$U = \frac{1-e^{-rT}}{r}V(1+h_1, E_1)+\frac{e^{-rT}}{r}V(1+h_2, E_2),$$

from which we obtain

$$\frac{re^{rT}}{e^{rT}-1}\frac{dU}{dh_1} = V_E\left[\frac{dE_1}{dh_1}-D^1+(e^{rT}-1)^{-1}\frac{dE_2}{dh_1}\right], \tag{18}$$

as $-V_P(1 + h_1, E_1)/V_E(1 + h_1, E_1) = D^1$ by Roy's Identity and $V_E(1 + h_1, E_1) = V_E(1 + h_2, E_2)$ by (9). To locate the optimal tariff, substitute for dE_i/dh_1, set $dU/dh_1 = 0$, and solve for h_1. This leads to

$$\frac{h_1^*}{1+h_1^*} = \frac{h_2}{1+h_2}\frac{\tau\gamma_2}{\tau\gamma_1+(\varepsilon+\eta Q^1/D^1)[1+(e^{rT}-1)E_1/E_2]}. \tag{19}$$

As expected, the crucial variables are T, the length of the liberalization period; τ, which determines how much a temporary decrease in the import price distorts intertemporal choice by tilting real consumption toward the present; and $\varepsilon + \eta Q^1/D^1$, which determines the price-responsiveness of import demand and hence how large the gains from trade are during the liberalization phase. In polar cases where these variables assume extreme values, it is optimal to follow free trade or to forsake liberalization altogether. For $\tau = 0$, $h_1^* = 0$ as the fall in the relative price of current consumption does not distort saving. Free trade is also approximately optimal when T is very large: $\lim_{T \to \infty} h_1^* = 0$ since an infinitely lived liberalization program is effectively a permanent, credible reform. At the opposite extreme, $h_1^* = h_2$ when $\varepsilon = \eta = 0$. This is Calvo's result that liberalization is harmful if there are no gains from trade.

It is not generally possible to infer from (19) the optimal amount of liberalization because E_1, E_2, ε, η, γ_1, γ_2, and Q^1/D^1 are functions of h_1 or h_2. A closed-form solution exists, however, in the special case where $\eta = 0$ and the utility function is logarithmic in a Cobb–Douglas index of aggregate consumption. Logarithmic, Cobb–Douglas preferences imply $\tau = 1$, $E_1 = E_2$, $\gamma_1 = \gamma_2 = \gamma$, and $\varepsilon = 1 - \gamma$.[5] After imposing these conditions and $\eta = 0$, equation (19) yields

$$h_1^* = \frac{h_2 \gamma}{\gamma + (1 + h_2)(1 - \gamma)e^{rT}}. \tag{20}$$

A couple of interesting, suggestive conclusions follow from this solution. Note that, since h_1^* is increasing in h_2, two structurally identical economies should *not* levy the same tariff during the liberalization phase; rather, the tariff should be higher in the economy where it was initially and will subsequently be higher. The postcollapse tariff matters because the marginal gains from trade depend on the level of h_1 (free trade being optimal *ex ante*) while the loss from the saving distortion depends on the gap between h_1 and h_2. Thus, in the economy that is initially more protectionist, the marginal cost of exacerbating the saving distortion equals the marginal benefits of superior allocative efficiency at a point further away from free trade (see Figure 8.2). But apologists for protection should not get too excited about this result, for the optimal percentage tariff cut, $(h_2 - h_1^*)/h_2$, is also increasing in h_2; the general rule implicit in (20) is that, *ceteris paribus*, more protectionist economies should liberalize more but stop further away from free trade than less protectionist economies.[6]

---

[5] To see that $E_1 = E_2$, note from (14) that $\hat{E}_1 = \hat{E}_2$ for $\tau = 1$.

[6] The optimal tariff during the liberalization period depends only on the postcollapse tariff. The more general case where the postcollapse tariff h_2 is less than the initial tariff h_o is analytically equivalent, however, to a two-stage reform in which the government first institutes a permanent, fully credible tariff cut of $h_o - h_2$ and then attempts a further noncredible tariff cut. When focusing on temporary tariff cuts, it is appropriate therefore to assume that the initial and postcollapse tariffs coincide.

This rule is sensible and agrees with intuition, but, unfortunately, it is based on a particular closed-form solution of the model. More generally applicable rules can be derived directly from (19); however, if something is known either about the degree of intertemporal vs. intratemporal substitution or about the relative magnitudes of the elasticities that determine the costs of the saving distortion vis à vis the gains from trade. Since we have assumed a CES–CRRA utility function, $\varepsilon = \beta(1 - \gamma_1)$, where β is the elasticity of substitution between importable and exportable consumer goods. In the benchmark case where $\tau = \beta$,

$$\frac{h_1^*}{1+h_1^*} = \frac{h_2}{1+h_2}\frac{\gamma_2}{\gamma_1 + (1-\gamma_1 + \eta Q^1/\tau D^1)[1 + (e^{rT}-1)E_1/E_2]}. \quad (21)$$

Set $\eta = 0$ and ignore the term $(e^{rT} - 1)E_1/E_2$ so that the solution overstates the true value of h_1^*. Some trivial algebra then produces

Proposition 1　*If $\beta \geq \tau$, then*

$$\frac{h_2 - h_1^*}{h_2} > 1 - \frac{\gamma_2}{1 + h_2(1-\gamma_2)}. \quad (22)$$

In words: no matter how short the liberalization period, it is optimal to reduce the tariff by more than $(1 - \gamma_2)\%$ when the intratemporal elasticity of substitution equals or exceeds the intertemporal elasticity of substitution.

Consider next the outcome when the elasticities that govern the saving and trade distortions are of equal magnitude. In this case, $\tau = \varepsilon + \eta Q^1/D^1$ and

$$h_1^* < \frac{h_2 \gamma_2}{1+\gamma_1 + h_2(1+\gamma_1 - \gamma_2)},$$

which implies

Proposition 2　*If $\tau \leq \varepsilon + \eta Q^1/D^1$, then*

$$\frac{h_2 - h_1^*}{h_2} > 1 - \frac{\gamma_2}{1+\gamma_1 + h_2(1+\gamma_1 - \gamma_2)}. \quad (23)$$

Corollary 2.1　*If $\tau \leq \varepsilon + \eta Q^1/D^1$ and $h_2 > 1 - \gamma_2/(1 + \gamma_1)$, then the optimal tariff cut is at least $(1 - .5\gamma_2)\%$.*

Although reliable estimates of τ, ε, and η are wanting, the overall tenor of these results is that a substantial amount of liberalization is desirable, credibility problems nothwithstanding. The consumption share of importable manufactured goods is well below .5 in most LDCs. (The share of output produced by the protected manufacturing sector generally lies between 10 and 25%, while imports of consumption goods rarely amount to more than 10% of GDP.) Furthermore, Propositions 1 and 2 have a strong conservative bias in that they are based on the maximin criterion and presume the reversal of the reform is nearly instantaneous. Since the propositions also rely on neutral assumptions about the relative magnitudes of the key elasticities τ, β, and η, one can argue that a tariff cut of at least 50% is optimal when choosing from behind the veil of ignorance. [The validity of the policy rules in (22) and (23) requires only that τ not be too much larger than β or $\varepsilon + \eta Q^1/D^1$.] This may be cold comfort should it turn out, *ex post*, that a much smaller tariff cut is optimal. But even then, a tariff cut of 50% is unlikely to overshoot the optimal tariff to the point of being harmful; in fact, the results presented in the next section suggest the stronger conclusion that a move to free trade is often welfare-improving.

8.2.2   *Model Calibration*

Let o and 2 subscripts/superscripts refer to the preliberalization equilibrium and to the equilibrium after the policy reversal. To calibrate the model, I assume that output is produced by labor L_i and a fixed factor K_i according to CES production functions in which the elasticity of substitution equals σ. At the initial equilbrium,

$$r = .05, \qquad b_o = 0, \qquad K_m = 100, \qquad \theta_{L,o}^m = .30,$$
$$\theta_{L,o}^x = .45, \qquad VA_{m,o} = .20, \qquad \gamma_o = .30,$$

where θ_L^i is the cost share of labor in sector i and VA_m is the share of GDP produced by the import-competing sector (measured at domestic prices).[7]

The length of the liberalization period T, the initial tariff h_2, and the substitution elasticities σ, β, and τ determine how the gains from trade weigh up against the losses from the intertemporal distortion. Searching for robust policy rules, I allow these crucial variables to assume multiple values:

$$T = 1, 5, \qquad h_2 = .3, .5, 1, \qquad \beta = .15, .25, .50,$$
$$\tau = .25, .5, 1, 2, \qquad \sigma = 0, .50.$$

---

[7] The values for b_o and K_m do not affect the welfare outcome. (K_m affects only the size of the economy and b_o determines whether total consumption expenditure is initially above or below real output.)

The liberalization episode may be short or fairly long-lived ($T = 5$); the initial tariff may be low, moderately high, or very high;[8] and the intertemporal elasticity of substitution may vary from .25 to 2. As regards the intratemporal elasticity of substitution, the values .25 and .50 are consistent with the middle- and lower-end estimates in systemwide demand functions for 5–11 goods. But since the scope for substitution may be much less at higher levels of aggregation, I also carry out runs for $\beta = .15$. Finally, there may be modest efficiency gains in production or none at all ($\sigma = 0$). The case of zero gains deserves serious attention because in the presence of adjustment costs it may not be optimal for labor to move from the import sector to the export sector and then back again at time T. As Rodrik (1989a, 1992) has observed, weak credibility acts like a tax of factor mobility.

Our assumptions about technology and preferences imply

$$\eta = \sigma \theta_L^m \frac{L_x}{L_m \theta_K^x + L_x \theta_K^m},$$

$$D^i = \frac{k_2^\beta (1 + h_i)^{-\beta} E_i}{1 + k_2^\beta (1 + h_i)^{1-\beta}},$$

$$\theta_L^m = g_2 [w/(1 + h_1)]^{1-\sigma},$$

$$\theta_L^x = g_4^\sigma w^{1-\sigma},$$

$$\varepsilon = \beta(1 - \gamma_1),$$

$$\gamma_1 = \frac{k_2^\beta (1 + h_1)^{1-\beta}}{1 + k_2^\beta (1 + h_1)^{1-\beta}},$$

$$C^m = (g_1^\sigma v_m^{1-\sigma} + g_2^\sigma w^{1-\sigma})^{1/(1-\sigma)},$$

$$C^x = (g_3^\sigma v_x^{1-\sigma} + g_4^\sigma w^{1-\sigma})^{1/(1-\sigma)},$$

$$C_v^m = (g_1^\sigma v_m^{1-\sigma} + g_2^\sigma w^{1-\sigma})^{\sigma/(1-\sigma)} (g_1/v_m)^\sigma,$$

$$C_v^x = (g_3^\sigma v_x^{1-\sigma} + g_4^\sigma w^{1-\sigma})^{\sigma/(1-\sigma)} (g_3/v_x)^\sigma,$$

$$C_w^m = (g_1^\sigma v_m^{1-\sigma} + g_2^\sigma w^{1-\sigma})^{\sigma/(1-\sigma)} (g_2/w)^\sigma,$$

$$C_w^x = (g_3^\sigma v_x^{1-\sigma} + g_4^\sigma w^{1-\sigma})^{\sigma/(1-\sigma)} (g_4/w)^\sigma,$$

[8] Nowadays tariffs are seldom above 100%, but quotas often generate very large implicit tariffs. Note also from the Lerner symmetry theorem that a 100% tariff has the same effect on relative prices and the allocation of resources as a 50% tariff and a 25% export tax.

where k_2 and g_1–g_4 are distribution parameters ($k_1 = 1$), v_i is the rental of the fixed factor in sector i, and C^i is the unit cost function in sector i. The values assigned to $VA_{m,o}$, $\theta^i_{L,o}$, γ_o, σ, τ, β, K_m, and h_2 suffice to determine k_2, g_1–g_4, the total supply of labor (L), the supply of the fixed factor in the export sector (K_x), and the sectoral outputs $Q_{m,o}$, and $Q_{x,o}$. Moreover, $\gamma_2 = \gamma_o$, $Q_{m,2} = Q_{m,o}$, and $Q_{x,2} = Q_{x,o}$ since the consumption shares and all supply variables return to their preliberalization values at time T. Thus, after being armed with the above formulae, the computer can solve (19),

$$E_1 + \frac{E_2}{e^{rT} - 1} = Q_x + Q_m + h_1 D^1 + \frac{Q_{x,2} + Q_{m,2} + h_2 D^2}{e^{rT} - 1}, \tag{24}$$

$$\frac{E_1}{E_2} = \left[\frac{1 + k_2^\beta (1+h_1)^{1-\beta}}{1 + k_2^\beta (1+h_2)^{1-\beta}} \right]^{(\tau-1)/(\beta-1)}; \tag{25}$$

the zero-profit conditions

$$1 + h_1 = C^m, \tag{26}$$

$$1 = C^x; \tag{27}$$

the sectoral labor demands

$$L_i = C^i_w Q_i; \tag{28a–28b}$$

and the full employment conditions

$$K_i = C^i_v Q_i, \tag{29a–29b}$$

$$L_m + L_x = L, \tag{30}$$

jointly for E_1, E_2, w, v_m, v_x, L_m, L_x, Q_m, Q_x, and h_1^*. The solution for $\tilde{h}_1$, the tariff cut that leaves welfare unchanged, is found by replacing (19) with

$$V^o = (1 - e^{-rT})V^1 + e^{-rT}V^2, \tag{31}$$

where

$$V^i = \frac{E_i^{1-1/\tau} \left[1 + k_2^\beta (1+h_i)^{1-\beta} \right]^{(\tau-1)/\tau(\beta-1)}}{1 - 1/\tau},$$

$$V^o = \frac{E_o^{1-1/\tau} \left[1 + k_2^\beta (1+h_2)^{1-\beta} \right]^{(\tau-1)/\tau(\beta-1)}}{1 - 1/\tau},$$

and E_o is preliberalization consumption expenditure.

Table 8.1. *The values of* h⃰ *and* h̃₁ *when the initial tariff is 30%.*

τ	β = .15		β = .25		β = .50		σ
	T = 1	T = 5	T = 1	T = 5	T = 1	T = 5	
.25	.105	.091	.072	.061	.040	.034	0
	(—)	(—)	(—)	(—)	(—)	(—)	
	.057	.048	.046	.039	.031	.026	.50
	(—)	(—)	(—)	(—)	(—)	(—)	
.50	.158	.143	.118	.104	.072	.061	0
	(.027)	(—)	(—)	(—)	(—)	(—)	
	.099	.085	.081	.070	.056	.048	.50
	(—)	(—)	(—)	(—)	(—)	(—)	
1	.210	.196	.172	.156	.117	.103	0
	(.123)	(.097)	(.054)	(.025)	(—)	(—)	
	.152	.136	.131	.115	.097	.083	.50
	(.017)	(—)	(—)	(—)	(—)	(—)	
2	.248	.238	.220	.207	.170	.154	0
	(.197)	(.178)	(.145)	(.120)	(.055)	(.026)	
	.205	.190	.185	.169	.148	.132	.50
	(.116)	(.088)	(.080)	(.050)	(.016)	(—)	

8.2.3   Numerical Solutions

Tables 8.1–8.3 present the solutions for the 144 cases defined by the alternative values of β, h_2, σ, τ, and T. There are two numbers in each cell; the first refers to h_1^* and the second (in parentheses below) to $\tilde{h}_1$. A negative sign for $\tilde{h}_1$ indicates that free trade is welfare-improving.

The numerical solutions tell the same story as Propositions 1 and 2, but in sharper, more quantitatively precise terms. Five results are worth emphasizing:

1. The optimal percentage tariff cut always increases with the size of the initial tariff. The rule that more protectionist economies should liberalize more thus appears to be generally valid.
2. For $\tau \simeq \beta$, the optimal tariff cut is very large, ranging from 76 to 91%. In small, very poor LDCs where τ is likely to be on the order of .25 or less (Ogaki, Ostry, and Reinhart, 1996), it is often optimal to drop the tariff below 10%.
3. Even when there are no gains from trade in production ($\sigma = 0$) and τ is three to four times larger than β, the optimal tariff cut is close to or greater than 50%.

Table 8.2. *The values of* h_1^* *and* $\tilde{h}_1$ *when the initial tariff is 50%.*

τ	$\beta = .15$		$\beta = .25$		$\beta = .50$		σ
	$T = 1$	$T = 5$	$T = 1$	$T = 5$	$T = 1$	$T = 5$	
.25	.160	.139	.107	.091	.059	.049	0
	(—)	(—)	(—)	(—)	(—)	(—)	
	.084	.071	.067	.056	.045	.038	.50
	(—)	(—)	(—)	(—)	(—)	(—)	
.50	.251	.224	.182	.158	.107	.091	0
	(.030)	(—)	(—)	(—)	(—)	(—)	
	.151	.129	.123	.104	.084	.071	.50
	(—)	(—)	(—)	(—)	(—)	(—)	
1	.340	.316	.274	.247	.180	.156	0
	(.192)	(.147)	(.075)	(.028)	(—)	(—)	
	.242	.214	.205	.179	.147	.126	.50
	(.017)	(—)	(—)	(—)	(—)	(—)	
2	.408	.391	.359	.335	.269	.241	0
	(.321)	(.288)	(.229)	(.186)	(.078)	(.030)	
	.334	.308	.299	.271	.233	.205	.50
	(.183)	(.134)	(.121)	(.071)	(.018)	(—)	

4. A 50% tariff cut is always welfare-improving when $\tau \leq 1$.
5. Going all the way to free trade is welfare-improving if either $\tau \leq .50$ or $\tau \leq 2\beta$.[9]

These results constitute additional, powerful support for the position that potential credibility problems should not deter policy makers from undertaking ambitious trade reforms. The third result is especially notable in this connection. Uncertainty about the longevity of the reform and about the magnitudes of key parameters may make it hard to calculate the precise value of h_1^*, but the rule that the optimal tariff cut is at least 50% is highly robust. It shold be clear by now that the robustness of the rule derives from certain advantages that liberalization has in the battle of warring triangles. The welfare arithmetic is inherently favorable to liberalization because the intertemporal distortion applies to only a small fraction of total consumption (20–30%) and because in the neighborhood of the initial equilibrium the gains from

---

[9] I ignore here the three cases where $\tilde{h}_1$ is between .01 and .03 and the welfare loss from elimination of the tariff is negligible.

Table 8.3. *The values of* h*$_1$ *and* h̃$_1$ *when the initial tariff is 100%.*

τ	$\beta = .15$		$\beta = .25$		$\beta = .50$		σ
	$T = 1$	$T = 5$	$T = 1$	$T = 5$	$T = 1$	$T = 5$	
.25	.267 (—)	.228 (—)	.169 (—)	.143 (—)	.089 (—)	.075 (—)	0
	.130 (—)	.109 (—)	.102 (—)	.086 (—)	.068 (—)	.057 (—)	.50
.50	.450 (.01)	.395 (—)	.308 (—)	.264 (—)	.169 (—)	.143 (—)	0
	.250 (—)	.210 (—)	.198 (—)	.166 (—)	.132 (—)	.111 (—)	.50
1	.646 (.334)	.592 (.240)	.497 (.097)	.439 (.01)	.302 (—)	.257 (—)	0
	.435 (—)	.377 (—)	.357 (—)	.305 (—)	.244 (—)	.206 (—)	.50
2	.798 (.611)	.759 (.537)	.684 (.411)	.631 (.317)	.480 (.107)	.421 (.02)	0
	.639 (.329)	.579 (.224)	.557 (.202)	.495 (.098)	.412 (.01)	.354 (—)	.50

trade are first-order in magnitude whereas the losses from lack of credibility are second-order small. Consequently, the optimal tariff cut is at least 50% if the intertemporal elasticity of substitution is not extremely large relative to the elasticities that govern the gains from trade.

Lest these remarks be misunderstood, I hasten to add that they are largely model-specific. The 50% rule breaks down if workers laid off in the import-competing sector experience an extended spell of unemployment. There is more to this than just the fact that the losses from several years of high unemployment are often sizeable compared to the gains from trade. Dissaving in response to transitory unemployment also exacerbates the distortion of intertemporal choice (too much consumption today relative to consumption in the future) caused by weak credibility. The two distortions interact, so the loss when both exist exceeds the sum of the independent losses.

There is another reason to err on the side of caution. The costs of weak credibility *may* be substantially greater when consumers accelerate purchases of durables (Calvo, 1989) or when uncertainty about future policies provokes a collapse of investment by increasing the option value of

waiting (Rodrik, 1991).[10,11] The current model, however, ignores investment spending and assumes that all consumer imports are nondurable
goods. Strictly speaking, therefore, it captures only the losses from one
particular type of intertemporal distortion. The conclusion that, in the
absence of other adjustment problems, tariff cuts of 50–80% are optimal
is thus tentative. Further work is needed to develop a complete theoretical and quantitative analysis of the costs of the different intertemporal
distortions associated with weak credibility.

8.2.4   Temporary Quota Liberalization

In the present context, the distinction between quotas and tariffs is
potentially important. A temporary tariff cut affects the trade distortion
in future periods via its impact on saving, future income, and future
import demand. Under a quota, by contrast, the import volume is fixed
exogenously and hence there is no automatic link between today's and
tomorrow's trade distortion. This consideration has led Calvo (1988) and
Falvey and Kim (1992) to conjecture that temporary quota liberalization
does not distort intertemporal choice. A lot rides on this conjecture; if it
is correct, then full liberalization is optimal in countries where quotas
are the principal instrument of protection.

   The model is easily adapted to handle protection by quotas instead of
tariffs. The private agent's budget constraint now reads

$$\dot{b} = R(1 + h) + hZ + rb - E, \tag{32}$$

where Z is the import quota and the *implicit* tariff h is determined by
the market clearing condition

$$D(1 + h, E) = R'(1 + h) + Z. \tag{33}$$

The same first-order conditions apply, so

$$V_E(1 + h, E) = \pi, \tag{34}$$

and π is constant after its initial jump at $t = 0$. Equations (33) and (34)
imply that, as in the tariff case, the paths of E and h are flat over the

---

[10] When the private agent consumes durables k wealth is $A = b + k$. The agent
can thus instantaneously swap b for k without reducing saving. This suggests that
a temporary tariff cut may greatly accelerate purchases of durables and badly
distort intertemporal choice even when the intertemporal elasticity of substitution is low.
[11] The data and rough estimates in Reinikka (1996) indicate that the costs from
stockpiling durables were generally small in Kenya (.3% of GDP or less, except
possibly in the 1980 liberalization episode).

intervals $[0, T)$ and $[T, \infty)$. The only change in (13), therefore, is that the import volumes are replaced by quotas:

$$E_1 + \frac{E_2}{e^{rT} - 1} = R(1 + h_1) + h_1 Z_1 + \frac{R(1 + h_2) + h_2 Z_2 + rb_o e^{rT}}{e^{rT} - 1}. \qquad (35)$$

The critical issue is whether there is some indirect link between Z_1, the quota during the liberalization period, and Z_2, the quota imposed at the time of the policy reversal. It is easy to confirm that free trade is optimal for the period $[0, T)$ if Z_2 is independent of Z_1 (as when $Z_2 = Z_o$). In this case, temporary liberalization does not affect the severity of the trade distortion in the future. Consequently, there is no reason not to reap all the gains from trade for as long as is possible.

The problem with this nice result is that it ignores the motive for protection. It is probably more sensible to assume that at T the quota will be set so as to restore the previous implicit level of protection. But under this policy rule, Z_2 varies inversely with E_2 to prevent h_2 from falling. Since saving connects Z_1 and E_2, there comes a point at which the gains from more liberalization in the short run have to be traded off against the costs of a more restrictive quota in the long run (i.e., a smaller Z_2). Not surprisingly, the solution for the optimal quota is to choose Z_1 so that the implicit tariff satisfies (19), the solution in the case where a tariff is the instrument of protection. To establish this formally, note that

$$D^1(1 + h_1, E_1) = R'(1 + h_1) + Z_1, \qquad (36)$$

$$D^2(1 + h_2, E_2) = R'(1 + h_2) + Z_2, \qquad (37)$$

(9) and (35) can be solved for E_1, E_2, Z_2, and h_1 as a function of Z_1. Choosing Z_1 is thus equivalent to choosing h_1 in the model of Section 8.2. If the public fears that future policy makers will grant firms the same level of protection as before, then the credibility problem is exactly the same for quota and tariff liberalization.

8.3   Payments Deficits, Multiple Equilibria, and Self-Fulfilling Failures[12]

The government quickly reversed its position and instituted modified quantitative restrictions. . . . It is obvious that, the Bank's protestations

---

[12] Much of this section is reprinted from *Journal of International Economics*, 38, E. Buffie, "Trade Liberalization, Credibility and Self-Fulfilling Failures," pages 51–73, with permission from Elsevier Science.

aside, import restrictions and exchange controls will always be employed whenever foreign exchange reserves fall rapidly (Cheru, 1989, pp. 95–96).

[There is] overwhelming evidence attesting to the inference that the fate of a liberalization policy is determined, first and foremost, by developments in the balance of payments position. A significant deficit, involving a substantial loss of foreign exchange reserves, is most likely to abort a liberalization attempt.... The authors of ten country studies.... explicitly reach this conclusion (Michaely et al., 1986, pp. 14–15).

[T]he new policy which was introduced in 1985 in Zambia was sprung on the government by President Kaunda with very little internal debate or preparation. It was in fact only supported by the President himself, and by two other ministers. It was opposed publicly and consistently by the remainder of the Cabinet and the Central Committee of the ruling party in almost daily speeches up and down the country. In those circumstances, producers would have been extremely foolish to invest significant resources in increased production in the expectation that the policy would be sustained. Moreover, it became rational to buy not only current needs for foreign exchange but future needs as well, in the expectation that the availability of foreign exchange would be restricted when the policy was reversed. This became a self-fulfilling prophecy (Harvey, 1996, p. 131).

However, in the African context, ... typically reserve levels are so low that almost any reduction in the level will be interpreted as a threat to sustainability (Collier, Greenaway, and Gunning, 1997, p. 329).

Import restrictions [in Zimbabwe] were lifted on the first items shifted to the OGIL in October 1990. There followed a surge of imports, most of it apparently speculative.... The increase in imports was roughly double that anticipated. Since there were no disbursements to support the OGIL the government was forced into borrowing US$155m. on a commercial short-term basis in mid-1991 and attempting to depress import demand by introducing a 20 percent tariff surcharge on all OGIL items and new limitations on forex allocations for those items not so far included (Gibbons, 1996, p. 353).

We do not as yet have a satisfactory explanation for the stylized fact that liberalization attempts are often undermined by unexpectedly large payments deficits. While sharp contraction in the tradables sector may cause a temporary deficit, the cumulative reserve loss will be tolerably small if the liberalization program is welfare-improving in the long run and the unemployed are told to fend for themselves (i.e., there is no social safety net – see the analysis in Section 6.2.3 of Chapter 6). Calvo's models of temporary liberalization can explain why saving falls and the current account worsens, but not why large deficits appear in the overall balance of payments: when foreign bonds are the only vehicle for dissaving, current account deficits are financed entirely by capital inflows; the central bank never experiences a loss in reserves because it never hands over hard currency for domestic money.

The objective of this section is to determine whether there may be a self-fulfilling aspect to the failure of liberalization attempts when it is widely known that the government will abandon the reform if the central bank suffers an unacceptably large loss in reserves. I pose the issue in the context of a simple perfect foresight model where the government has the financial resources to cover any payments deficits that result when it succeeds in convincing the public that the shift in policy is permanent. The liberalization program is thus fundamentally sound and a successful, lasting reform is an equilibrium outcome. The announced reform may, nevertheless, not be perfectly credible if there exists a second equilibrium in which expectations of a policy reversal prove self-fulfilling. When this second, bad equilibrium competes with the good equilibrium the government is trying to promote, liberalization is inherently risky: whether the reform succeeds or fails depends entirely on private sector expectations.

The analysis is organized into six sections. The first two sections lay out the model and characterize the impact of a sustained liberalization. After these preliminaries are out of the way, Sections 8.3.3–8.3.6 develop the dynamics for a temporary liberalization and investigate the conditions under which there exist multiple self-fulfilling equilibria. The central theme to emerge from the results is that self-fulfilling failures remain a serious threat even when the government's stockpile of reserves is several times larger than needed to underwrite a sustained, credible liberalization.

8.3.1   The Model

For the most part I shall work with a competitive, two-sector general equilibrium model in which the capital account is closed and money is the only asset. This very simple model has enough structure to capture what is critical to the issue at hand: when analyzing the likelihood of a self-fulfilling failure, what is needed from the real side of the economy is the size of the efficiency gain produced by liberalization; in a competitive general equilibrium model the gains are confined to reductions in triangles (which are not so little in LDCs), but this is not restrictive because the gains can be made as large or small as desired by setting the trade elasticities appropriately.

The most important consequence of making domestic money the sole asset is that balance of payments problems are automatically equated with current account deficits. When the capital account is open, however, a current account deficit may be accompanied by large capital inflows and an overall payments surplus. The implications of this will be discussed in Section 8.3.5.

Turning to specifics, the model is the same as in Section 8.2, except domestic money replaces foreign bonds. The representative private agent chooses the path of saving so as to maximize

$$\int_0^\infty [V(P_m, E) + \phi(M/P)]e^{-\rho t}\, dt, \tag{38}$$

subject to

$$E + S = R(P_m) + h[D(P_m, E) - R'(P_m)], \tag{39}$$

$$\dot{M} = S, \tag{40}$$

where $P \equiv P_m^\gamma$ is the consumer price index and γ is the consumption share of the import good.

Let π be the multiplier associated with (40). The solution to the private agent's optimization problem then generates the familiar first-order conditions

$$V_E(P_m, E) = \pi, \tag{41}$$

$$\dot{\pi} = \rho\pi - \phi'/P. \tag{42}$$

On the transition path, the tariff is constant (h is reduced once at $t = 0$, not in stages) and (39), (41), and (42) yield

$$-V_{EE}g^{-1}\dot{S} = \rho V_E(P_m, E) - \frac{\phi'(M/P)}{P}, \tag{43}$$

where $g \equiv (1 + h\gamma_x)/(1 + h)$ and $\gamma_x = 1 - \gamma$ is the consumption share of the export good.

Equations (40) and (43) determine the paths of private saving and nominal money balances. Linearizing this pair of equations around a stationary equilibrium produces

$$\begin{bmatrix} \dot{S} \\ \dot{M} \end{bmatrix} = \begin{bmatrix} \rho & \dfrac{\phi'' g}{V_{EE}P^2} \\ 1 & 0 \end{bmatrix} \begin{bmatrix} S \\ M - M^* \end{bmatrix}. \tag{44}$$

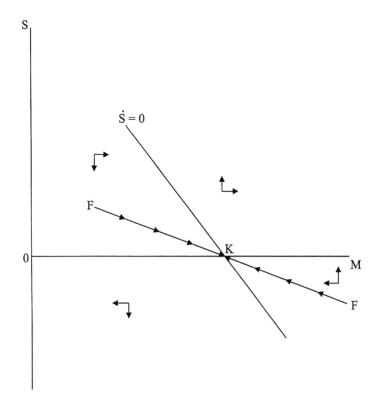

Figure 8.3. The dynamics for saving and money balances.

Figure 8.3 depicts the same specie-flow adjustment process encountered earlier in Chapter 6. The steady state K is a saddle point with a unique convergent path FF to equilibrium. To the left of K, saving is positive, the trade balance shows a surplus, and money balances are increasing. Conversely, when M is above its steady-state level, private dissaving gives rise to payments deficits and decreases in the money supply.

8.3.2   Sustained Liberalization

The new long-run equilibrium values of E and M can be obtained from (39) and (43) by deleting the terms involving S. Under the assumption that the income elasticity of money demand equals unity, M and E increase proportionately:

$$\hat{E}/\hat{P}_m = \gamma(1-k),$$ (45)

$$f \equiv \hat{M}/\hat{P}_m = \gamma(1-k),$$ (46)

where

$$k \equiv [\varepsilon + \eta(1 - Z/D)]\frac{h}{1+h\gamma_x},$$

Z is imports, and ε and η are, as before, the compensated elasticity of demand and the elasticity of domestic supply for the importable good.

Since the change in the money supply measures the cumulative payments surplus, reserves fall (or rise) by $fM_o\hat{P}_m$. To economize on notation, assume the money supply equals the stock of reserves (i.e., in the past, money has been created only through reserve accumulation). f then represents the long-run elasticity of reserves with respect to P_m.

The impact on the cumulative payments surplus turns on the relative weight of two conflicting effects. The reduction in the tariff tends to lower nominal money demand by lowering the price level. Opposing this effect is the increase in real income brought about by liberalization. The magnitude of the real income effect depends on the initial level of protection (h), the income elasticity of demand (assumed to equal unity), the marginal propensity to consume the importable, and the elasticity of import demand as determined by ε, η, and Z/D. If the tariff is initially small ($h \le .30$), it is improbable that liberalization will generate a strong enough income effect to produce a cumulative payments surplus. But for the very high levels of protection seen in many LDCs, this possibility cannot be dismissed out-of-hand.

I assume the government has a large enough reserve cushion to absorb any cumulative payments deficit caused by a credible liberalization. A permanent and successful liberalization is therefore an equilibrium outcome. The next section investigates whether it is the only equilibrium when the private sector knows that some reserve loss larger than f will induce the government to revert to protectionist policies.[13]

---

[13] Multiple equilibria would not be a potential problem if the public were convinced that the government would respond to payments deficits by devaluing the currency. But many policy makers fear that devaluation will worsen inflationary pressures and drive up real interest rates. Krugman concludes, therefore, that "as a practical matter the balance of payments problem cannot be easily dismissed" (1993, p. 46).

8.3.3   Temporary Liberalization and Self-Fulfilling Failures

If a policy reversal is possible at some later date, there is no guarantee the economy will jump onto the saddlepath that converges to the long-run equilibrium characterized by a lower tariff. The private sector may instead coordinate on a path consistent with the expectation that liberalization will be temporary. To establish that such a path is an equilibrium path, it must be shown that the payments deficit eventually becomes so large that the government does, in fact, abandon the trade reform.

When the policy experiment is expected to end at some time t_1, the adjustment process is governed by a nonconvergent path during the phase in which the tariff is lower. Over the period $(0, t_1)$,

$$S(t) = \lambda_1 b_1 e^{\lambda_1 t} + \lambda_2 b_2 e^{\lambda_2 t}, \qquad t \leq t_1, \tag{47}$$

$$M(t) - M^* = b_1 e^{\lambda_1 t} + b_2 e^{\lambda_2 t}, \qquad t \leq t_1, \tag{48}$$

where $\lambda_1 > 0$ and $\lambda_2 < 0$ are eigenvalues and the b_i are constants determined by initial conditions.

From t_1 onward the tariff is at its original level and the economy traverses the saddlepath that leads back to the preliberalization equilibrium. Along this path, S and M evolve according to

$$S(t) = \lambda_2 b_3 e^{\lambda_2 t}, \qquad t \geq t_1, \tag{49}$$

$$M(t) - M_o = b_3 e^{\lambda_2 t}, \qquad t \geq t_1, \tag{50}$$

where b_3 is another constant and M_o is the preliberalization value of nominal money balances.

To find the particular nonconvergent path that links up with the original saddlepath at t_1, first exploit two pieces of information provided by initial conditions on the stock of nominal money balances. As M is predetermined, at $t = 0$ equation (48) gives

$$b_2 = -\left(b_1 + f M_o \hat{P}_m\right).$$

So the path of money balances during the liberalization phase is

$$\frac{M(t) - M_o}{M_o} = f(1 - e^{\lambda_2 t})\hat{P}_m + (e^{\lambda_1 t} - e^{\lambda_2 t})b_1 / M_o, \qquad t \leq t_1. \tag{51}$$

Furthermore, this nonconvergent path must yield precisely the same value for M at time t_1 as the convergent path (50). This implies

$$b_3 e^{\lambda_2 t_1} + b_1(e^{\lambda_2 t_1} - e^{\lambda_1 t_1}) = (1 - e^{\lambda_2 t_1})f M_o \hat{P}_m. \tag{52}$$

The third piece of information needed to tie down b_1–b_3 is obtained from the first-order condition (41): $V_E(P, E) = \pi$. Foreseen jumps in π and the marginal utility of expenditure are inconsistent with optimizing behavior since the private agent could increase welfare by selecting a smoother consumption path. Hence, in a perfect foresight equilibrium, private saving S must jump so as to keep V_E constant when the tariff is restored to its original level at t_1. Making use of the formula $\tau = 1 + V_{PmE}/V_{EE}D$, the required jump in S is found to be

$$S(t_1^+) - S(t_1^-) = J\hat{P}_m(t_1), \tag{53}$$

where

$$J \equiv D(1 + h\gamma_x)\left[\tau - h\frac{\varepsilon + \eta(1 - Z/D)}{1 + h\gamma_x}\right].$$

Equating this solution for the jump in S to the one obtained from (47) and (49) yields

$$b_3\lambda_2 e^{\lambda_2 t_1} + b_1(\lambda_2 e^{\lambda_2 t_1} - \lambda_1 e^{\lambda_1 t_1}) = J\hat{P}_m(t_1) - \lambda_2 e^{\lambda_2 t_1} fM_o\hat{P}_m. \tag{54}$$

Equations (52) and (54) can be solved for b_1 and b_3. The solution for b_1 is

$$b_1 = \frac{J + fM_o\lambda_2}{(\lambda_1 - \lambda_2)e^{\lambda_1 t_1}}\hat{P}_m.$$

Plugging this into (51) produces

$$\frac{[M(t) - M_o]/M_o}{\hat{P}_m} = f(1 - e^{\lambda_2 t}) + \frac{f\lambda_2 + J/M_o}{\lambda_1 - \lambda_2}$$
$$\times [e^{\lambda_1(t - t_1)} - e^{\lambda_2 t - \lambda_1 t_1}], \qquad t \leq t_1. \tag{55}$$

Define $\psi \equiv [(M - M_o)/M_o]/\hat{P}_m$ to be the cumulative percentage reserve loss that provokes the government to scrap the reform and assume $\psi > f$ [the solution in (46)] to ensure that a sustained liberalization is potentially credible. Now, when the liberalization program is *actually* reversed, the reserve loss in (55) equals ψ by definition. The existence of multiple equilibria thus hinges on whether the equality

$$\psi - f = f\left\{\frac{\lambda_2}{\lambda_1 - \lambda_2}[1 - e^{(\lambda_2 - \lambda_1)t_1}] - e^{\lambda_2 t_1}\right\}$$
$$+ \frac{J}{M_o(\lambda_1 - \lambda_2)}[1 - e^{(\lambda_2 - \lambda_1)t_1}] \tag{56}$$

holds for some positive value of t_1. If so, a self-fulfilling failure (SFF hereafter) is an equilbrium.

Several fairly general results can be pried loose from (56). Starting with a check on the correctness of the solution, SFFs should not occur when the government has unlimited access to foreign exchange. This trivial result is confirmed by (56). Observe that $\psi - f$ represents the extra reserve loss the government is prepared to tolerate in order to strengthen the credibility of the trade reform. Since the expression on the right side of the equality sign is finite, sustained liberalization is the only equilibrium path if the government's reserve cushion is large enough.

It is not surprising that the government can make liberalization perfectly credible by building up a sufficiently large stock of reserves in advance. What is less obvious and more interesting is that the reform may be perfectly credible even if it is undertaken without any reserve cushion (i.e., $\psi - f = 0$ or $\psi = 0$ when $f < 0$). As shown in Figures 8.4a and b, this is the case whenever saving jumps downward at t_1 (i.e., $J < 0$). When sustained liberalization produces a cumulative payments surplus, temporary liberalization does likewise and hence the government never experiences a drain on its foreign exchange reserves. In the case where sustained liberalization causes a payments deficit, temporary liberalization is associated with smaller deficits (or surpluses) that keep the economy's path from crossing the vertical line running through M^*. Thus, regardless of the size of the reserve cushion, expectations of a policy reversal cannot be self-fulfilling. More precisely, from (53) and (56), we have

Proposition 3 *A sufficient condition for sustained liberalization to be the only equilibrium outcome is*

$$\tau < \frac{h}{1+h\gamma_x}[\varepsilon + \eta(1 - Z/D)]. \tag{57}$$

Proof: *The equality in (56) is never satisfied when $J < 0$. If $f > 0$, (56) fails to hold as both terms on the right side are negative. On the other hand, when f is negative the equality is violated because*

$$G(t_1) \equiv 1 - e^{\lambda_2 t_1} + \frac{\lambda_2}{\lambda_1 - \lambda_2}[1 - e^{(\lambda_2 - \lambda_1)t_1}]$$

is nonnegative for $t_1 \geq 0$. [$G(0) = 0$ and $G' > 0$ for $t_1 > 0$.]

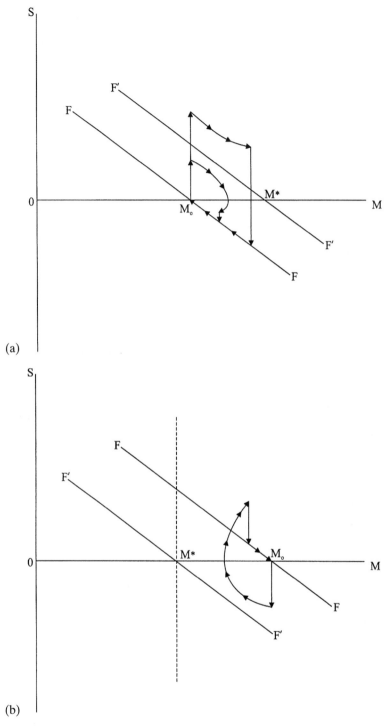

Figure 8.4. (a) The adjustment process when sustained liberalization produces a payments surplus and saving jumps downward at time t_1. (b) The adjustment process when sustained liberalization produces a payments deficit and saving jumps downward at time t_1.

Proposition 3 implies, *inter alia*, that liberalization is easier to sustain when the level of protection is initially high. The rationale for this important policy result lies in the nature of the income shocks associated with a temporary reform. A temporary tariff reduction produces a temporary real income gain. This creates an incentive to save more in the short-run, which counterbalances the opposite incentive arising from the anticipation of higher future import prices. The positive income effect is stronger the larger the temporary real income gain and the more averse the private agent is to a nonsmooth consumption path. The chances for success are best, therefore, in economies where the import sector is highly protected and the intertemporal elasticity of substitution is small.

When Proposition 3 does not apply, there is no guarantee that the equilibrium is unique and a reserve cushion may be needed to rule out the possibility of an SFF. In the normal case where sustained liberalization worsens the payments balance, it is easy to solve explicitly for the size of the required reserve cushion. Turning back to (56), call the term on the right side $K(t_1)$. For $f \geq 0$ and $J > 0$ (no reserve cushion is needed if $J < 0$), K is increasing in t_1 and approaches its maximum asymptotically. An SFF exists therefore only if $\lim_{t_1 \to \infty} K(t_1) > \psi - f$, or if

$$\psi - f < \frac{f\lambda_2 + J/M_o}{\lambda_1 - \lambda_2}.$$

After slight manipulation, this yields

Proposition 4 *When sustained liberalization causes a cumulative payments deficit, it is the unique equilibrium if and only if*

$$\psi - f > \frac{f}{2}(\rho/X - 1) + \frac{\gamma(1 + h\gamma_x)}{\mu(1 + h)X}\left\{\tau - \frac{h}{1 + h\gamma_x}[\varepsilon + \eta(1 - Z/D)]\right\}, \qquad (58)$$

where

$$X \equiv \sqrt{\rho^2 + 4\rho(1 + h\gamma_x)/\mu(1 + h)}$$

and $\mu \equiv M/E$, *the ratio of money balances to national income (which equals E at a steady state).*

Consider next the less plausible case where sustained liberalization generates a payments surplus. For $f < 0$ and $J > 0$, the right-side term in (56) attains its maximum in finite time when $e^{\lambda_1 t_1} = 1 + J/M_o f\lambda_2$, which implies

Proposition 5 *When sustained liberalization produces a payments surplus and $\tau > k$, sustained reform is the unique equilibrium only if*

$$\psi > \gamma(k-1)\left\{ e^{[(\rho-X)/2]t_1} + \frac{X-\rho}{2X}(e^{[(\rho+X)/2]t_1} - e^{[(\rho-X)/2]t_1}) - 1\right\}, \quad (59)$$

evaluated at

$$t_1 = \frac{2}{\rho+X}\ln\left[1 + \frac{2(1+h\gamma_x)(\tau-k)}{\mu(1+h)(k-1)(X-\rho)}\right].$$

The import of Propositions 4 and 5 is that the government usually has to hold at least a modest reserve cushion to ensure that the private sector coordinates on the desired equilibrium. Even when sustained liberalization generates a payments surplus, a small reserve cushion may not suffice to prevent SFFs. To illustrate, suppose $\rho = .05$, $\gamma_x = \varepsilon = \gamma = .5$, $h = \eta = 1.25$, $\mu = .10$, $Z/D = .20$, and $\tau = 1.5$. Although $f = -.077$, the condition in (59) then requires $\psi > 1.001$.

An interesting aspect of the dynamics in this case is that the actual course of events is likely to validate the wrong set of beliefs. Figure 8.5 shows what happens when the reserve cushion is too small and the private sector, steeped in pessimism, coordinates on SFF as the economy's equilibrium path. The liberalization program lasts until the path arrives at point C and is associated with a steadily worsening payments deficit.[14] At point C, the reform is abandoned and the payments surplus instantly shifts from a deficit to a surplus. All of the evidence conspires to support the mistaken belief that protection is good for the balance of payments.

Most of what can be said at a general theoretical level is collected in Propositions 3–5. For policy purposes, however, one would like to know this and much more, for example: Just how large must the reserve cushion be to rule out SFFs for reasonable values of ρ, τ, h, etc.? When multiple equilibria exist, do SFFs occur within a believable period of time? With view to answering questions of this type, I calibrate the model and present numerical solutions for a wide range of cases.

8.3.4   Some Numerical Solutions

While many parameters enter into (56), the preceding analysis argues that the most important, by far, are the intertemporal elasticity of sub-

---

[14] Saving may increase initially. In this case, there would be payments surpluses in the first phase of the temporary reform.

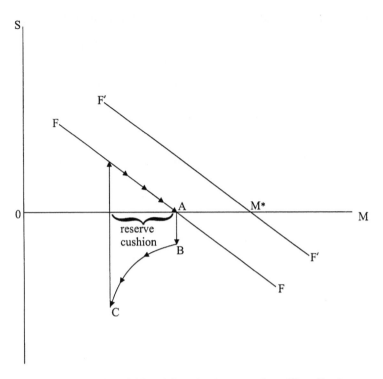

Figure 8.5. A self-fulfilling failure in the case where liberalization produces a payments surplus.

stitution τ; the initial tariff h; the reserve cushion $\psi - f$; and the elasticities of substitution β, σ^m, and σ^x that enter into the demand elasticity ε and the supply elasticity η.[15] These parameters play pivotal roles in determining the efficiency gains from liberalization, the relative strengths of the conflicting income and substitution effects operating on private saving, and the reserve loss that the government is willing to absorb in an attempt to sustain its reform program. Accordingly, in calibrating the model, I again set

$$\rho = .05, \quad \mu = .10, \quad \gamma = .30, \quad VA_m = .20, \quad \theta_L^m = .30 \quad \text{and} \quad \theta_L^x = .45,$$

[15] $\varepsilon = \beta(1 - \gamma)$. With respect to the supply elasticity η, I assume that labor is the only mobile factor of production in the short run and that $\sigma^m = \sigma^x$. The expression for η therefore is the same as that stated in Section 8.2.2.

but let τ, h, σ^i, β, and ψ take on a variety of low and high values:

$$h = .3, .5, 1; \qquad \sigma^m = \sigma^x = 0, 1; \qquad \psi = f, 1.5f, .5, 1, 1.5, 2;$$
$$\beta = .25, .50; \qquad \tau = .25, .5, .75, 1, 2.$$

As before, I allow for the possibility that firms will not respond to relative price changes that are expected to be short-lived.[16,17] (t_1 turns out to be smaller than .6 in 172 of the 235 cases where SFFs occur.) The efficiency gains from liberalization may be limited therefore to a smaller byproduct distortion of consumption patterns (the case when $\sigma = 0$). Note also that liberalization may be attempted with no reserve cushion, a very ample cushion, or something inbetween. When $\psi = f$, the government abandons the liberalization program as soon as the cumulative payments deficit exceeds the deficit associated with a successful, sustained reform. $\psi = 2$, on the other hand, implies that the government is willing to tolerate a huge reserve loss – a loss five to ten times larger than that produced by a perfectly credible liberalization – to see the reform through. It is probably more realistic to think of this as the case of a small country that has financial backing from friends with deep pockets (i.e., the World Bank and the IMF).

8.3.4.1   RESERVE CUSHIONS AND UNIQUENESS: THE PRICE OF PURCHASING CREDIBILITY

Tables 8.4–8.6 show the results of evaluating equation (56) for the different values assigned to σ, β, τ, ψ, and h. U indicates that sustained liberalization is the unique equilibrium. When there are two equilibria, the entry shows the time at which the reform would be reversed on the path associated with an SFF. The payments deficit produced by a sustained liberalization is given by the value for f in the far right column.[18] (For

---

[16] There is a fair bit of ground between $\sigma = 0$ and $\sigma = 1$. The results when $\sigma = .5$, however, differ little from those for $\sigma = 0$.

[17] When lack of credibility is itself to blame for the muted supply response, different values of σ have to be used in characterizing the transitional dynamics and the efficiency gains from a sustained reform. This refinement does not alter the results substantively. (The answer as to whether the equilibrium is unique is almost always the same and the values for t_1 are very close.)

[18] f tends to be small because I have assumed that foreign exchange reserves initially equal the money supply. If reserves are instead one-half of the initial money supply (roughly six months' worth of imports), then the solutions are unchanged

Table 8.4. *Time at which the policy reversal occurs when the initial tariff is 30%.*

			$\beta = .25$			
σ	$\tau = .25$	$\tau = .50$	$\tau = .75$	$\tau = 1$	$\tau = 2$	ψ
0	.72	.26	.16	.12	.05	f (.287)
	1.52	.44	.26	.18	.08	1.5f
	2.37	.54	.31	.21	.10	.5
	U	2.49	.82	.51	.21	1
	U	U	2.55	1.01	.34	1.5
	U	U	U	2.59	.50	2
1	1.10	.29	.17	.12	.05	f (.269)
	3.24	.49	.26	.18	.08	1.5f
	U	.66	.34	.23	.10	.5
	U	U	.97	.57	.22	1
	U	U	U	1.17	.36	1.5
	U	U	U	U	.53	2

			$\beta = .50$			
σ	$\tau = .25$	$\tau = .50$	$\tau = .75$	$\tau = 1$	$\tau = 2$	ψ
0	.95	.28	.16	.12	.05	f (.274)
	2.38	.47	.26	.18	.08	1.5f
	U	.62	.33	.23	.10	.5
	U	U	.92	.55	.22	1
	U	U	U	1.12	.35	1.5
	U	U	U	5.29	.52	2
1	1.80	.31	.17	.12	.05	f (.256)
	U	.53	.27	.18	.08	1.5f
	U	.80	.38	.25	.10	.5
	U	U	1.17	.61	.22	1
	U	U	U	1.32	.37	1.5
	U	U	U	U	.54	2

the chosen parameter values, the efficiency gains from liberalization are never large enough to produce a payments surplus.)

The general message conveyed by the three tables is that SFFs will frequently be a problem even if the government takes the precaution of

but all of the numbers in the column for ψ double in value. For example, when $\sigma = 0$ and $\beta = .25$ in Table 8.4, the numbers in the column for ψ change to $f = .574$, $1.5f = .861$, 1, 2, 3, 4. As is evident from the solution in (56), all that matters is the ratio ψ/f.

Table 8.5. *Time at which the policy reversal occurs when the initial tariff is 50%.*

	$\beta = .25$					
σ	$\tau = .25$	$\tau = .50$	$\tau = .75$	$\tau = 1$	$\tau = 2$	ψ
0	.85	.28	.17	.12	.06	$f(.281)$
	1.95	.47	.27	.19	.09	1.5 f
	4.32	.60	.33	.23	.10	.5
	U	4.23	.91	.55	.22	1
	U	U	4.18	1.12	.36	1.5
	U	U	U	4.13	.53	2
1	2.11	.33	.18	.12	.05	$f(.253)$
	U	.56	.28	.19	.08	1.5 f
	U	.86	.40	.26	.11	.5
	U	U	1.21	.64	.23	1
	U	U	U	1.43	.38	1.5
	U	U	U	U	.57	2

	$\beta = .50$					
σ	$\tau = .25$	$\tau = .50$	$\tau = .75$	$\tau = 1$	$\tau = 2$	ψ
0	1.48	.31	.17	.12	.05	$f(.261)$
	U	.53	.28	.19	.08	1.5 f
	U	.77	.38	.25	.11	.5
	U	U	1.10	.62	.23	1
	U	U	U	1.32	.38	1.5
	U	U	U	U	.56	2
1	U	.39	.18	.12	.05	$f(.234)$
	U	.67	.29	.19	.08	1.5 f
	U	1.27	.46	.28	.11	.5
	U	U	1.63	.73	.24	1
	U	U	U	1.86	.40	1.5
	U	U	U	U	.60	2

accumulating a substantial reserve cushion. In between the regions characterized by very large efficiency gains *and* a very small intertemporal elasticity is a sizeable zone where the equilibrium is seldom unique. For $\sigma = 0$, $\tau = \beta = .25$, and $h = .30$, .50, multiple equilibria exist until $\psi = 1$. And when the intertemporal elasticity lies between one-half and unity, success cannot be guaranteed unless the government puts up a big stake – financial resources sufficient to ride out a cumulative payments deficit

Table 8.6. *Time at which the policy reversal occurs when the initial tariff is 100%.*

			$\beta = .25$			
σ	$\tau = .25$	$\tau = .50$	$\tau = .75$	$\tau = 1$	$\tau = 2$	ψ
0	1.21	.32	.18	.13	.06	$f(.269)$
	3.95	.54	.29	.20	.09	1.5f
	U	.74	.38	.26	.11	.5
	U	U	1.10	.63	.24	1
	U	U	U	1.35	.39	1.5
	U	U	U	U	.59	2
1	U	.44	.20	.13	.05	$f(.227)$
	U	.79	.32	.20	.08	1.5f
	U	1.71	.52	.31	.12	.5
	U	U	2.19	.83	.26	1
	U	U	U	2.53	.44	1.5
	U	U	U	U	.66	2

			$\beta = .50$			
σ	$\tau = .25$	$\tau = .50$	$\tau = .75$	$\tau = 1$	$\tau = 2$	ψ
0	U	.40	.19	.13	.05	$f(.238)$
	U	.69	.31	.20	.08	1.5f
	U	1.25	.48	.30	.12	.5
	U	U	1.69	.77	.26	1
	U	U	U	1.99	.43	1.5
	U	U	U	U	.64	2
1	U	.72	.22	.13	.05	$f(.196)$
	U	1.47	.35	.20	.07	1.5f
	U	U	.73	.38	.13	.5
	U	U	U	1.10	.28	1
	U	U	U	U	.48	1.5
	U	U	U	U	.73	2

six to eight times larger than that produced by a perfectly credible liberalization.[19]

While SFFs occur in 65% of the cases covered by Tables 8.4–8.6, the results also suggest one somewhat encouraging conclusion. Observe that for $\tau \le .75$ and $\psi = 2$ the equilibrium is always unique. Thus, if it is taken

[19] In the cases where $\sigma = 0$, $\tau = 1$, and $h \le .50$, SFFs are possible even when $\psi = 2$. The equilibrium is unique, however, for values of ψ slightly above 2.

on faith that the intertemporal elasticity is smaller than .75 in LDCs, SFFs can probably be ruled out when external donors are willing to back sound liberalization programs with generous balance of payments support.

8.3.5   The Outcome under an Open Capital Account

The treatment of the capital account is crucial because it determines the nature of the relationship between private saving and the balance of payments. Under a closed capital account, dissaving is associated with a larger payments deficit and a lower path for money balances. If the capital account is open, however, dissaving leads to *higher* money demand, capital inflows, and a smaller payments deficit (or possibly a payments surplus). As a result, the condition sufficient to ensure uniqueness of equilibrium when the capital account is closed may give rise to multiple equilibria when the capital account is open, and vice versa. This powerful duality proposition suggests the need to qualify the view prevalent in the existing literature that capital controls should be kept in place until liberalization of the current account is complete (e.g., McKinnon, 1982; Edwards, 1984; Calvo, 1988); under certain circumstances, prior liberalization of the capital account enhances the prospects for a successful, credible trade reform.

To incorporate capital account transactions in the simplest possible manner, assume the time preference rate ρ equals the world market interest rate r and that all interest earned on government reserves is rebated to the public in a lump-sum fashion.[20] Given these two assumptions, the solution for expenditure is

$$\hat{E} = \gamma(1-k)\hat{P}_m + \frac{1+h}{1+h\gamma_x}\left(r\frac{dA}{E} - \frac{dS}{E}\right), \tag{60}$$

where A is the stock of nominal wealth (money + foreign bonds). Equation (41) still holds, but now the multiplier π remains constant over time (after a possible jump at $t = 0$) and (42) is replaced by

---

[20] The assumption that government reserves now earn interest serves to eliminate an artificial income effect. When the government invests its reserves in foreign bonds, instantaneous portfolio swaps by the private sector do not change real income. (The changes in private and government bond holdings are perfectly offsetting.) Furthermore, since the outcome of the liberalization attempt is determined at $t = 0$ (see the ensuing analysis in the text), there is no time for the current account to alter the total stock of foreign assets. As in the case of a closed capital account, the only income effects that matter are those arising from the reduction in the trade distortion.

$$\frac{\phi'(M/P)}{PV_E(P_m, E)} = r. \tag{61}$$

Both (42) and (61) state that the marginal rate of substitution between money and consumption equals the interest rate. In (61), however, the interest rate is fixed. This radically changes the general equilibrium relationship between saving (or expenditure) and money demand. When capital controls are in place, the only way to dissave is to run down money balances; the interest rate then rises in step with the marginal rate of substitution to reconcile lower money holdings with higher expenditure. But with perfect capital mobility, the interest rate is constant and hence money demand and expenditure tend to move in the same direction. Consequently, a larger current account deficit will be accompanied by a smaller overall payments deficit and smaller reserve losses. Unlike when the capital account is closed, expectations of a policy reversal will be self-defeating rather than self-fulfilling if they weaken the incentive to save.

The dynamics are easy to characterize when the reform is perfectly credible: all variables jump immediately to their new steady-state levels and equation (46) again determines whether the central bank gains or loses reserves. The instantaneous change in the money supply is brought about by either a capital inflow or a capital outflow; as in most optimizing intertemporal models, a permanent income shock that leaves rates of return unchanged does not alter saving or the current account balance.

When the reform is expected to be temporary, the term $\tau - k$ again determines whether the stimulus to saving from the temporary real income gain is stronger or weaker than the opposite pull exerted by the anticipation of higher future import prices. Saving jumps back to zero at time t_1 and follows the path

$$\frac{S(t)}{E} = \gamma \frac{1 + h\gamma_x}{1 + h}(\tau - k)e^{r(t-t_1)}\hat{P}_m, \qquad t \le t_1, \tag{62}$$

during the liberalization phase $(0, t_1)$. All other variables, including the money supply, jump at $t = 0$ and then follow perfectly flat paths until they jump to their steady-state levels at time t_1. Since the path of M is flat over the interval $(0, t_1)$, the outcome of the liberalization attempt is decided immediately at $t = 0$. SFFs correspond to what Calvo has called "one-instant" liberalizations.

The condition for an SFF to exist can now be derived in three short steps. From (60) and (62),

$$\hat{E}\big|_{t=0} = \gamma(1-\tau)\hat{P}_m.$$ (63)

Differentiating (61) and substituting for E produces

$$\hat{M}\big|_{t=0} = \gamma(1-\tau)\hat{P}_m.$$ (64)

Setting this against the solution in (46) (which still determines the impact on the payments balance of a credible reform) gives

Proposition 6 *When the capital account is open,*

$$\psi - f > \gamma(k - \tau)$$ (65)

is necessary and sufficient for sustained liberalization to be the unique equilibrium.

In striking contrast to the results obtained earlier, SFFs are now least (most) likely when the efficiency gains from liberalization are small (large) and the intertemporal elasticity of substitution is large (small). This reflects the fact that, under an open capital account, lower saving is associated with higher expenditure, greater money demand, and a smaller overall payments deficit. Since saving is unchanged in the case of a permanent liberalization, expectations of a policy reversal cannot be self-fulfilling if they provoke a decrease in saving. Thus, $\tau > k$ rules out SFFs as it implies that a temporary reform would result in a smaller reserve loss than a permanent reform (see Figure 8.6). The inequality in Proposition 3 gets turned around because, in essence, money and saving switch from being "substitutes" when the capital account is closed to "complements" when the capital account is open.

From a policy standpoint, the value of the contrasting results is that they spell out clearly when capital controls are desirable. Calvo (1988) has argued in favor of capital controls on the grounds that they prevent the private sector from dissaving, thereby eliminating the intertemporal distortion created by an anticipated policy reversal (see also Falvey and Kim, 1992, p. 912). This result falls out of Calvo's model because the foreign asset is the only available vehicle for dissaving (there are no other assets) and credibility of the reform is determined by exogenous factors (the intentions of future policy makers). We reach the different conclusion that capital controls are harmful when $\tau < k$ because our model differs on both of these points. Since money is an alternative store of wealth, capital controls do not prevent dissaving or current account deficits. More importantly, capital account transactions strengthen credibility whenever they lessen the reserve loss that would occur under a

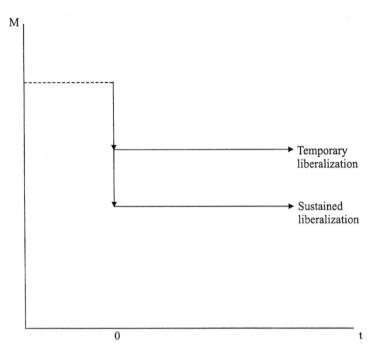

Figure 8.6. Paths of money balances for temporary and sustained liberalizations when $\tau > k$ and the capital account is open.

temporary reform.[21] For $\tau > k$, an open capital account eliminates the potential intertemporal distortion by making the announced reform perfectly credible.

8.4 Fiscal Deficits, Payments Deficits, and Credibility

African trade liberalization attempts suffer from problems of credibility and sustainability, which are typically reflected by reversals of trade liberalization initiatives – as amply demonstrated by the varying experiences of the ten case study countries. Mauritius and Uganda are the only two countries in this sample that did not reverse policy.... Most policy reversals revealed in the case studies were triggered by balance-of-payments and *fiscal incompatibility* (Oyejide, 1996, p. 29; emphasis is mine).

---

[21] Mellor (1994) makes the same point.

In the preceding analysis I assumed that lump-sum transfers were continuously equal to tariff revenues in order to abstract from *potential* fiscal problems. Potential with emphasis because there is no general presumption that liberalization worsens the fiscal deficit. The empirical evidence in Greenaway and Milner's (1993) sample of eleven liberalizing countries is distinctly mixed. Moreover, some types of trade reform would be expected to increase revenues. This is obviously true of tariffs that replace quotas and of cuts in export taxes and import duties that initially exceed their revenue-maximizing level. Simplification and consolidation of trade taxes may also yield a fiscal gain by lowering administrative costs and making evasion more difficult (Greenaway and Milner, 1993).

While liberalization does not always reduce revenues, there are plenty of examples where it has done just that and the losses have run to several percentage points of GDP.[22] In such cases, the fiscal dimension of liberalization occupies center stage in the reform process. If the government fails to increase other taxes or cut expenditures sufficiently, the loss in tariff revenues leads to larger fiscal deficits and persistent current account deficits that eventually force a reversal of the reform. The connection between the two deficits and the inevitability of failure are particularly transparent in the simple optimizing models of Sections 8.2 and 8.3. The current account surplus in the models is the sum of private saving and the fiscal surplus; but since private saving is zero in the long run, the economy cannot reach a steady state where the external accounts balance if the government runs a fiscal deficit. Liberalization is not sustainable therefore when it is not supported by adequate fiscal adjustment.

The point that credibility requires proper coordination of trade reform and fiscal policy is well understood and beyond dispute. Certain

---

[22] Revenue shortfalls provoked partial or full policy reversals in the Philippines (1991), Kenya (1983), Morocco (a special import tax was imposed in 1987, after liberalization in 1984 reduced trade revenues by 4% of GDP), Guinea (1990, 1992), Bangladesh (late 1980s), Malawi (tariffs raised multiple times in the eighties), Senegal (revenue needs have forced a steady retreat from trade liberalization since 1989), Costa Rica (higher tariffs imposed in 1995 to offset large revenue losses from liberalization in the preceding four years), Mexico (1995), Brazil (1995), and Colombia (1996). [See the World Trade Organization's *Trade Policy Review*, Mulaga and Weiss (1996), *Economic Survey of Latin America and the Caribbean* for 1995–96 and 1996–97, Chibber and Khalizadeh-Shirazi (1991), Faini (1994), and Arulpragasam and del Ninno (1996).] Liberalization over the period 1980–91 was associated with a fall in the share of trade taxes in total tax revenue from 42.8% to 27.8% in Cote d'Ivoire and from 39.1% to 13.4% in Botswana (Jebuni, 1997).

subtle aspects of the relationship between *ex ante* fiscal adjustment, the *ex post* fiscal deficit, and credibility, however, are not so well appreciated. For one thing, weak credibility may cause large fiscal deficits instead of the other way around. But if it is wrong to automatically blame higher fiscal deficits for the failure of liberalization, one also has to be careful not to commit the opposite error. Even when lack of fiscal adjustment is clearly the root cause of failure, speculative import sprees may prop up tariff revenues enough to conceal the underlying fiscal problem. Paradoxically, the fiscal surplus may be positive and increasing throughout the liberalization phase precisely because inadequate fiscal adjustment renders the attempted reform noncredible.

8.4.1   Weak Credibility May Itself Be the Cause of Fiscal Deficits

Liberalization cannot be credible unless the government keeps fiscal deficits at bay when tariff revenues decline. The implications of this observation are not entirely straightforward. If fiscal policy is not compatible with permanent liberalization, then it is to blame for the credibility problem and the failure of the reform. But causation can also run in the other direction from weak credibility to larger fiscal deficits. To take an especially simple case, drop money and saving from the model of Section 8.3.1 and allow lump-sum transfers G to differ from tariff revenues T. The trade surplus B is then

$$B = T - G, \tag{66}$$

where

$$T = h[D(P_m, E) - R'(P_m)].$$

Initially $G = T$, so when the government liberalizes

$$\frac{dG}{E} = \frac{dT}{E} = \gamma \left\{ \frac{Z}{D} - \frac{h}{1 + h\gamma_x}[\varepsilon + \eta(1 - Z/D)] \right\} \hat{P}_m \tag{67}$$

maintains a balanced budget. If

$$\varepsilon + \eta(1 - Z/D) > \frac{1 + h\gamma_x}{h} \frac{Z}{D}, \tag{68}$$

the tariff cut raises revenues and the government faces the pleasant task of deciding how to spend the windfall.

At first glance, these results are encouraging. Since the market share of competing imports (Z/D) is only 10–30% in countries that levy high tariffs on consumer goods, the term $Z(1 + h\gamma_x)/Dh$ on the right side in

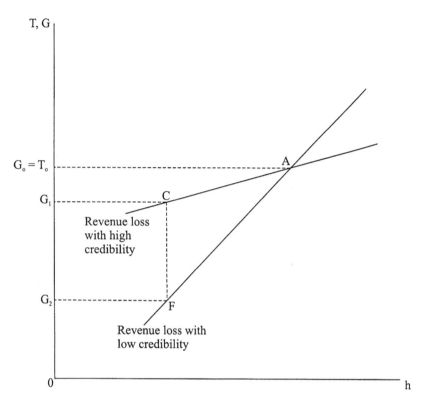

Figure 8.7. The connection between credibility, tariff revenues, and the *ex post* fiscal deficit.

(68) will often be well below unity. On the left side, ε tends to be small, but the sum $\varepsilon + \eta(1 - Z/D)$ is .4 or larger for normal values of the general equilibrium supply elasticity η. The condition in (68) is not therefore particularly stringent *if* domestic producers respond to the change in relative prices. This is what underpins Greenaway and Milner's conclusion that highly protective tariffs are likely to exceed the revenue-maximizing tariff. And even if revenues fall, they would not be expected to fall very much. For example, when $\gamma = .30$, $Z/D = .25$, $h = .50$, $\varepsilon = .25$, $\eta = .40$, and the import price falls 25%, the loss in revenues is only .35% of national income. Thus, a small cut in government expenditures suffices to sustain liberalization. This is shown in Figure 8.7 by the movement from point A to point C along the flat high-credibility schedule.

Unfortunately, there is an element of circular reasoning involved in appealing to a normal supply response to establish that a given cut in government expenditure preserves external balance and makes liberalization credible. A normal value for η *presumes* credibility. But this presumes too much, for the supply response, credibility, and the fiscal deficit are *jointly* determined. If firms fear a policy reversal, the supply response will be weak ($\eta \approx 0$),[23] imports will increase little and revenues will fall sharply. In this case, the economy moves along the steeply sloped low-credibility schedule in Figure 8.7. The expenditure cut $G_1 - G_o$ that maintains fiscal balance when liberalization is credible then leaves a large deficit of CF.[24] Both failure and success are thus self-fulfilling equilibria. Moreover, the bad equilibrium does not disappear unless expenditures are cut by $G_2 - G_o$. The indeterminancy problem can be overcome, but, as earlier in Section 8.3, there is a cost: to guarantee that expectation of success is the unique equilibrium, the government must cut expenditure much more than needed to sustain a permanent liberalization.

In Figure 8.7 expectations of a policy reversal worsen the fiscal deficit by weakening the supply response and reducing tariff collections. Weak credibility may also cause trouble, however, by creating pressures to increase spending. Suppose that: (i) adjustment costs are negligible so that firms respond in the same way to temporary and permanent price changes; (ii) workers laid off in the import sector do not seek work elsewhere when they believe the reform will be short-lived (see the discussion in Section 6.2.4 of Chapter 6); and (iii) the government pays out unemployment compensation. Under these assumptions, the low-credibility revenue schedule is almost as flat as the high-credibility schedule,[25] but the government will find it more difficult to make the requisite expenditure cuts when credibility is weak and outlays on unemployment compensation increase. Once again, the planned expenditure cuts that suffice when liberalization is credible fall short when it is not.

---

[23] There are several ways to motivate adjustment costs and a weak supply response to temporary price changes. Firms in the import sector may refrain from layoffs if they are obligated to make large severance payments or if training costs would increase because new workers have to be hired after the reform collapses. In the case of a lower export tax, firms will be reluctant to hire more workers if they doubt the reform will survive and the law prohibits layoffs. Even if the law is repealed during liberalization, firms may fear that it will be reimposed in the near future and that they will be saddled with too large a workforce after the government reverses the reform.

[24] In the example cited earlier, the revenue loss rises from .35% of national income when η equals .4 to 1.2% when η equals zero.

[25] The low-credibility schedule is a little flatter because an increase in unemployment lowers income and the demand for imports.

8.4.2   Inadequate Fiscal Adjustment Disguised as Fiscal Surpluses

Speculative import sprees triggered by weak credibility may allow inadequate fiscal adjustment to masquerade as a fiscal surplus. This is easy to demonstrate in a slightly modified version of the model employed in Section 8.3.1. The capital account is closed and the private agent solves the same optimization problem

$$Max \int_0^\infty [V(P_m, E) + \phi(M/P)]e^{-\rho t} dt, \tag{69}$$

subject to

$$E + S = R(P_m) + G, \tag{70}$$

$$\dot{M} = S, \tag{71}$$

but now lump-sum transfers may exeed tariff revenues. When they do, the resulting fiscal deficit is financed by printing money. The domestic component of the monetary base is called "central bank credit," or CBC for short. Thus

$$\dot{CBC} = G - h[D(P_m, E) - R'(P_m)]. \tag{72}$$

Subtracting (72) from (71) gives

$$\dot{M} - \dot{CBC} = S + h[D(P_m, E) - R'(P_m)] - G. \tag{73}$$

Central bank credit and reserve accumulation are the two sources of money growth, so

$$\text{reserve accumulation} = B = S + h[D(P_m, E) - R'(P_m)] - G. \tag{74}$$

Equation (74) is the accounting identity that the trade surplus equals the sum of private saving and the fiscal surplus.

For simplicity, assume supply is inelastic ($R'' = 0$) and that initially transfers equal revenues.[26] Starting from this situation, the government must cut transfers by the amount

$$dT_1 = \gamma E \left(\frac{Z}{D} - \frac{h\varepsilon}{1 - h\gamma_x} \right) \hat{P}_m$$

---

[26] The assumption of inelastic supply does not affect the results. An increase in demand for the importable good has the same effect on national income and tariff revenues as a decrease in domestic production of importable goods. Hence, positive values of η can be taken into account by increasing the value of ε.

if liberalization is to stand a chance of being credible. Suppose, however, that transfers decrease less, that they decrease only

$$dG = \alpha dT_1 = \alpha \gamma E \left(\frac{Z}{D} - \frac{h\varepsilon}{1 - h\gamma_x} \right) \hat{P}_m, \qquad 0 \leq \alpha < 1. \tag{75}$$

Liberalization is then doomed to fail because the trade balance would show a deficit in the steady state associated with a permanent tariff cut. The payments deficit is exactly equal to $(1 - \alpha)dT_1$, the shortfall in fiscal adjustment.

Since the private sector recognizes that liberalization is not sustainable, the dynamics can be worked out by following the same procedure as in Section 8.3.3. This produces the solutions[27]

$$\frac{1}{E} \frac{S(t)}{\hat{P}_m} = \frac{N + \Lambda \lambda_2 \mu}{(\lambda_1 - \lambda_2) e^{\lambda_1 t_1}} \lambda_1 e^{\lambda_1 t}$$

$$- \left[\Lambda \mu + \frac{N + \Lambda \lambda_2 \mu}{(\lambda_1 - \lambda_2) e^{\lambda_1 t_1}} \right] \lambda_2 e^{\lambda_2 t}, \qquad t \leq t_1, \tag{76}$$

$$\frac{1}{E} \frac{X(t)}{\hat{P}_m} = \frac{h}{1+h} \frac{\gamma}{E} \frac{S(t)}{\hat{P}_m} - \underbrace{\frac{(1-\alpha)\gamma}{1+h} \left[(1 + h\gamma_x) \frac{Z}{D} - h\varepsilon \right]}_{\text{shortfall in fiscal adjustment}}, \qquad t \leq t_1, \tag{77}$$

where

$$N \equiv \gamma \left[\tau - \frac{h\varepsilon}{1 + h\gamma_x} + (1 - \alpha) \left(\frac{h\varepsilon}{1 + h\gamma_x} - \frac{Z}{D} \right) \right],$$

$$\Lambda \equiv \gamma \left[1 - \frac{h\varepsilon}{1 + h\gamma_x} + (1 - \alpha) \left(\frac{h\varepsilon}{1 + h\gamma_x} - \frac{Z}{D} \right) \right],$$

$$\lambda_1, \lambda_2 = \frac{\rho \pm \sqrt{\rho^2 + 4\rho/\mu}}{2},$$

$X \equiv T - G$, the fiscal surplus, and t_1 is again the time at which the reform collapses. Note that $h\varepsilon < (1 + h\gamma_x)Z/D$ on the assumption that the tariff cut lowers revenues.

---

[27] The solutions in (76) and (77) assume that the cut in lump-sum transfers is fully reversed when the tariff is put back to its original level at time t_1. That is, the government returns to the preliberalization fiscal and trade policy regime at t_1.

The truth, that fiscal policy is incompatible with liberalization, resides in the second term in (77). But the truth may not be evident in the data. If

$$\tau > \rho + (1-\rho)\left[\alpha \frac{h\varepsilon}{1+h\gamma_x} + (1-\alpha)\frac{Z}{D}\right], \tag{78}$$

the rush to buy imports before the policy reversal pulls down private saving at $t = 0$ and tariff revenues are higher than on a sustainable equilibrium path.[28] This favorable effect on the budget is picked up by the first term. If it dominates the second term, the reform package produces a fiscal surplus and the government may conclude erroneously that it has made the necessary expenditure cuts and more. Nor are subsequent developments likely to cast doubt on this belief. The results to be presented shortly indicate that when $\tau \geq .50$ the initial downward jump in saving will often be followed by further decreases up to time t_1. The fiscal surplus may therefore rise steadily throughout the liberalization phase.

It is difficult to get more than suggestive results from the complicated solutions in (76) and (77). To go further, I set $VA_m = .20$, $\rho = .05$, $\gamma = .30$, $\beta = .50$, $h = .75$, and $\alpha = .80$ and calculate $X(t)/\hat{P}_m E$ and $-B(t)/\hat{P}_m E$ (semi-elasticities scaled by national income) at $t = 0$ and $t = t_1$ for alternative values of τ and t_1. The results, shown in Table 8.7, are somewhat mixed.[29] The semi-elasticity of the shortfall in fiscal adjustment is 1% of national income. For $\tau = .50$, the actual deficit is smaller during liberalization, but it does not disappear. When $\tau = .75 - 1$ and $t_1 \leq 1$, however, the fiscal surplus increases immediately and grows progressively larger until the reform collapses (see Figures 8.8 and 8.9).[30] If liberalization lasts two or

---

[28] The condition in (78) is sufficient, though not necessary, for saving to decrease at $t = 0$.

[29] If $\varepsilon h/(1 + h\gamma_x) < 1$, saving is lower on the transition path when liberalization is permanent and credible. Since the cut in transfers at $t = 0$ equals the decrease in tariff revenues in the new steady state, the economy runs a fiscal surplus on the transition path. The surplus, however, is very small because $S(t)/E\hat{P}_m = -\lambda_2\mu\Lambda e^{\lambda_2 t} < \rho\gamma\,(\Lambda < \gamma, e^{\lambda_2 t} < 1$ and $-\lambda_2\mu < \rho)$. Most of the discrepancy between the actual deficit and the shortfall in fiscal adjustment in Table 8.7 thus reflects the impact on tariff collections of imports purchased in anticipation of a policy reversal.

[30] Lump-sum transfers return to their original level when the reform collapses. Tariff revenues, however, are below their preliberalization level because saving is positive for $t \geq t_1$. In Figure 8.8, therefore, the fiscal surpluses during the liberalization phase are followed by temporary deficits after the reform is reversed. The results differ little if one assumes instead that transfers equal tariff revenues and the budget is balanced from t_1 onward.

fiscal surplus

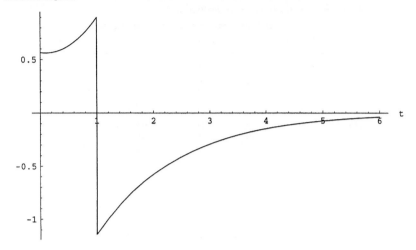

Figure 8.8. Path for the semi-elasticity of the fiscal surplus when $\tau = 1$ and $t_1 = 1$.

trade surplus

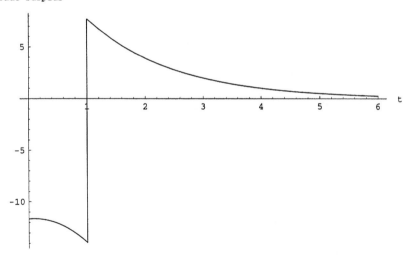

Figure 8.9. Path of the semi-elasticity of the trade surplus when $\tau = 1$ and $t_1 = 1$.

Table 8.7. *The fiscal surplus and trade surplus at* t = 0 *and*
t = t₁ *when fiscal adjustment is incomplete.**

τ	$X(0)$	$X(t_1)$	$B(0)$	$B(t_1)$	t_1
.50	−.17	−.17	−6.68	−6.66	.5
	−.36	−.32	−5.37	−5.63	1
	−.59	−.46	−3.84	−4.73	2
	−.70	−.50	−3.10	−4.42	3
.75	.50	.56	−11.21	−11.60	.5
	.10	.29	−8.52	−9.78	1
	−.37	.07	−5.35	−8.30	2
	−.59	.003	−3.82	−7.35	3
1	1.17	1.28	−15.75	−16.53	.5
	.57	.90	−11.66	−13.92	1
	−.14	.60	−6.86	−11.87	2
	−.48	.51	−4.55	−11.27	3

* X and B are the semi-elasticities of the fiscal surplus and the trade surplus with respect to the price of the import good. The semi-elasticities are expressed as a percentage of national income. The semi-elasticity of the shortfall in fiscal adjustment is 1% of national income.

three years, the fiscal account worsens before it improves. But this case is probably of limited relevance: since the payments deficits are very large, liberalization will not survive long unless the government is armed with a huge reserve cushion.

In Table 8.7 the shortfall in fiscal adjustment is .3–.4% of national income for a tariff cut that lowers the import price 33%. When the shortfall is substantially larger, temporary import binges do not mask the underlying fiscal problem. If α is lowered to .5, for example, the semi-elasticity of the shortfall in fiscal adjustment increases from 1% to 2.52% of national income and all of the numbers for $X(0)$ and $X(t_1)$ are negative, most being larger than unity in absolute value.[31] The larger fiscal deficits during liberalization reflect not only the larger shortfall in fiscal adjustment but also the greater weight of a factor that weakens the incentive to dissave. Real income of the private agent increases when the government cuts transfers less than tariff revenues. Since this income effect is temporary, it counteracts the incentive to substitute toward

[31] $X(t_1)$ is less than unity in absolute value only for $\tau = 1$ and $t_1 \leq 1$.

current consumption.[32] *Ceteris paribus*, therefore, dissaving by the private agent is smaller the larger the shortfall in fiscal adjustment [i.e., the first term in (77) decreases when the second becomes larger]. The underlying incompatibility of fiscal policy and trade reform will be obvious enough when fiscal adjustment is badly inadequate, though it may be difficult to discern in less extreme cases.

8.5　Concluding Observations on the General Nature of the Transition Problem

Weak credibility is the source of numerous difficulties. On the production side, lack of credibility makes it more difficult to extract wage concessions from workers in the import-competing sector and creates an incentive for workers who are laid off to sit tight and await the day that protectionist policies are reimposed and firms rehire. Open unemployment is likely to be higher and to last longer therefore when labor suspects that the trade reform will not survive. The problem does not arise if firms elect to keep workers on the payroll rather than incur the adjustment costs associated with temporary changes in employment. But the lack of a supply response may then lead to a sharp loss in tariff revenues and large fiscal deficits incompatible with external balance and sustained liberalization.

This chapter has focused mainly on how weak credibility distorts the choice of current vs. future consumption. Although current theory suggests that the welfare losses from this distortion tend to be small, the issue needs further investigation. The verdict is in, however, on another, more serious aspect of the problem: both theory and the evidence from numerous liberalization episodes argue that consumption booms can engender large payments deficits that threaten the viability of the reform. This problem cannot, in general, be overcome simply by accumulating in advance the reserves needed to make a permanent tariff cut financially feasible. Though a sustained reform then passes the test of financial feasibility, it may not be the only equilibrium when policy makers are unwilling to forswear using tariffs and quotas as instruments to regulate the balance of payments. If the capital account is closed and a modest degree of intertemporal substitution is possible, the failure to make a clear and unconditional commitment to the new policy regime often gives rise to equilibria where expectations of a policy reversal prove self-fulfilling. The government can always induce the private sector

---

[32] The income effect shows up in the negative term $(1 - \alpha)[\varepsilon h/(1 + h\chi_x) - Z/D]$ in the expressions for N and Λ listed after equations (76) and (77).

to coordinate on the permanent reform equilibrium by stockpiling enough reserves. This method of ensuring credibility, however, is likely to involve a considerable financial burden; frequently, the reserve cushion must be sufficient to cover payments deficits many times larger than those stemming from a successful, sustained reform.

The bottom line thus seems to be that everything can go wrong when past failures have damaged the government's reputation for seeing through difficult reforms. Weak credibility is partially or wholly responsible for slow adjustment in the labor market and transitory high unemployment, the distortion of intertemporal choice, and large payments deficits that quickly deplete the central bank's stock of foreign exchange reserves. Furthermore, all of these problems, which are bad enough on their own, become worse when they keep each other company. High unemployment and big payments deficits weaken credibility by increasing the likelihood that the government will either judge the liberalization program to be unsound or conclude that the price to be paid for future gains in allocative efficiency is too high. But fears of a future policy reversal lead to more unemployment and larger payments deficits, which further diminish credibility, and so on. A broad perspective on the transition problem thus favors a gradual approach to liberalization. The reserve cushion is more likely to hold out, the accompanying expenditure cuts are more likely to maintain fiscal balance, the losses from the intertemporal distortion are smaller relative to the gains from trade, and unemployment is less likely to rise to a socially intolerable level when the tariff cut is small. After consolidating the gains from a few modest successes, the credibility problem should be less severe and the government can consider more ambitious, deeper cuts in protection. The main argument against gradualism is that sudden, dramatic tariff cuts may enhance credibility by signaling to the private sector the government's intention to achieve a *complete* break with the old policy regime.[33] If the strategy works, it is superior to gradualism. But the potential losses are large and the risk of failure is high if the public does not go along with the proposition that the days of high protection are over for sure.

---

[33] In Auernheimer and George (1997), gradualism is inferior to shock liberalization because anticipation of future tariff cuts leads to excessive saving and inefficient asset accumulation. This conclusion, however, is special to the case of perfect credibility. If shock liberalization is not perfectly credible, then gradual tariff cuts lessen the intertemporal distortion by reducing the incentive to dissave. Moreover, even in the case of perfect credibility, the analysis here suggests that the losses from excessive saving induced by gradualism are likely to be small relative to the gains from trade.

CHAPTER 9

Direct Foreign Investment, Economic Development, and Welfare

In previous chapters I analyzed in detail the arguments for and against protection, the relationship between major factor market distortions and optimal trade policy, and the problems that arise in managing the transition to a more liberal trade regime. These issues are central to the conduct of commercial policy. They are not, however, the only issues that preoccupy minstries of trade in developing countries. The treatment of direct foreign investment is also an important aspect of trade policy. Foreign firms dominate the production of resource-intensive exports and account for a large share of investment and employment in manufacturing in Sub-Saharan Africa, in numerous island economies, and in parts of Latin America and Asia.[1] Nor is this likely to change anytime soon. The recent financial crisis in East Asia will no doubt make policy makers more cautious about accepting hot money and intensify the competition to attract direct foreign investment. If anything, foreign firms will be more important players in the near future.

Although most LDCs desire foreign investment (FI hereafter), they are also wary of its side effects. Policy makers want FI only on terms conducive to economic development. This leads, inevitably, to a certain amount of tension. If FI is valued as a source of employment, technology transfer, tax revenues, and marketing outlets, it is also feared as a powerful competitor that may discourage domestic investment.[2] The fear that FI will strongly crowd out domestic investment is a legitimate economic concern, not just raw xenophobia. When the return on capital exceeds the social time preference rate, crowding out of domestic invest-

---

[1] Maquiladoras employed 500,000 people and accounted for 25% of Mexico's industrial exports in 1993 (Brannon, James, and Lucker, 1994, p. 1935). Foreign firms supply 15–20% of all manufacturing jobs in Sri Lanka (Wanigatunga, 1987) and own a sizeable part of the aggregate capital stock in Fiji, Trinidad and Tobago, Barbados, Cote d'Ivoire, and Zimbabwe (Farrell, 1987; Riddell, 1987; Samy, 1987; Worrel et al., 1987; Harrison, 1996).
[2] Countries use many criteria to judge the desirability of FI. One of the most common is that FI should be complementary to rather than competitive with domestic investment (Page, 1987, p. 39).

293

ment is associated with a welfare loss that has to be set against the benefits of FI. Moreover, if crowding out is so great as to lower the aggregate capital stock, underemployment may worsen. It is not obvious, therefore, that LDCs benefit from FI or that the operations of foreign firms should not be regulated to minimize potential crowding out. Policy makers may be doing the sensible thing when they restrict FI to "priority sectors" (where domestic investment is judged deficient), allow only joint ventures, and require foreign firms to export a minimum share of their output.

This chapter analyzes the impact of FI on domestic capital accumulation, welfare, and underemployment in a two-sector general equilibrium model that shares many of the features of the model developed in Chapter 5. The economy consists of a high-wage manufacturing sector that produces for the home market and a low-wage primary export sector. FI may flow into either of these two sectors or into a distinct enclave sector. The central theme to emerge from the analysis is that a lot depends on the sector in which foreign firms invest and on how FI is packaged. In the benchmark variant of the model, foreign firms are free of performance requirements and utilize the same technology as domestic firms. When this "plain vanilla" type of foreign capital enters the high-wage manufacturing sector, underemployment decreases in the short run but worsens in the long run. Underemployment eventually worsens because, over time, foreign capital crowds out domestic capital on a greater than one-for-one basis, causing the *aggregate* capital stock, employment in manufacturing, and the real wage in the primary sector to decline. Despite the adverse long-run effects on domestic capital accumulation and underemployment, FI may produce a small welfare gain over the entire transition path when the social time preference rate coincides with the private rate. But if the social rate is a point or more below the private rate, welfare declines by a significant amount, the losses being equivalent to an annual return of -10–35% per dollar of FI. Overall, there is not much to be said for allowing plain vanilla FI in the branches of the manufacturing sector that serve the home market.

By contrast, a great deal can be said in favor of FI of the classical type. FI that develops an enclave sector or expands primary export production crowds in domestic capital and reduces underemployment in the long run. Furthermore, in the case of FI in the primary sector, manufacturing sector employment continuously exceeds its pre-FI level on the transition path between steady states. As no intertemporal tradeoff exists, FI is unambiguously welfare-improving. Exceptional cases aside, the same strong conclusion holds for FI in an enclave sector.

The results for plain vanilla FI are worked out in Sections 9.1–9.4.

In Sections 9.5–9.7 I adapt the model to analyze the repercussions of export requirements, joint venture provisions, and technology transfer. Adding one or more of these elements to the plain vanilla package enhances the prospects for a welfare gain. In the case of FI in manufacturing, however, joint ventures and technology transfer may cause the capital stock and high-wage employment to decrease more in the long run. The bottom line is thus quite simple: if the objective is to secure a discounted welfare gain, then access to the domestic manufactures market should be tied to some combination of technological spillovers, export requirements, and restrictions on foreign ownership; but if policy makers want more than this, if they want both a net welfare gain and more economic development, it is best to confine FI to the export sector or to impose very high export requirements on foreign firms that sell in the domestic market.

9.1 The Benchmark Model: Plain Vanilla Foreign Investment[3]

Consider an economy comprised of a foreign enclave, a primary export sector, and a manufacturing sector. The domestic manufacturing sector and the foreign enclave use labor L and capital K, while the primary export good is produced by means of labor and land T. The manufactured good is a "semitradable" or "quasi-nontradable" good whose price adjusts to clear the domestic market. Foreign firms own T_f units of land, K_f units of capital in the manufacturing sector, and K_s units of capital in the enclave sector. There is no direct competition with domestic firms in the enclave: foreign firms own the entire capital stock and all output is exported. Initially, $K_f = T_f = K_s = 0$; variations in returns do not therefore affect payments to inframarginal units of foreign-owned capital and land.[4]

The structure of the model is similar to but less complicated than the model of Chapter 5. Under the assumptions of perfect competition and constant returns to scale, the zero profit conditions link goods and factor prices:

---

[3] Much of the analysis of the benchmark model is based on E. Buffie, "Direct Foreign Investment, Crowding Out, and Underemployment in the Dualistic Economy," *Oxford Economic Papers* 45 (1993): 639–667. I thank Oxford University Press for permission to reproduce parts of this article.

[4] The capital rental is constant across steady states when FI occurs in the manufacturing sector, so payments to inframarginal units of foreign capital do not change (in the long run). FI in the primary sector does lower payments to inframarginal units of foreign capital. Allowing for this effect simply strengthens the results quantitatively by creating another channel besides taxation through which some of the foreign profits are distributed to the domestic economy.

$$P_m = C^m(w_m, r),\qquad(1)$$

$$1 = C^x(w_x, v),\qquad(2)$$

$$1 = C^s(w_x, z),\qquad(3)$$

where C^i is the unit cost function in sector i; r and z are the capital rentals in sectors m and s; v is the land rental; P_m is the domestic price of the manufactured good; and w_m and w_x are, respectively, the wage rates in the manufacturing sector and in the primary export sector. Neither export good is taxed or subsidized, so in equations (2) and (3) the domestic and world market prices coincide. The zero profit condition in the enclave is not enforced by any competitive mechanism and serves merely to define the quasi-rent earned by foreign capital.

Factories are built by combining a_o units of imported machinery with a_1 units of some component produced by the domestic manufacturing sector. The supply price of capital is thus

$$P_k = a_o + a_1 P_m,\qquad(4)$$

and the domestic manufactures market clears when

$$D^m(P_m, E) + a_1(I_d + I_i) = Q_m,\qquad(5)$$

where E is aggregate consumption spending, I_i is foreign investment ($i = f$ or s), I_d is domestic investment, $D^m(\cdot)$ is a Marshallian demand function, and Q_m is aggregate supply. There is no need to distinguish here between domestic and foreign production because domestic and foreign-owned firms operate with identical technology. In other variants of the model, this assumption will be relaxed and foreign and domestic supply will appear separately on the right side.

The labor market is dualistic in the usual way. In the high-wage manufacturing sector, w_m moves with exact consumer price index to preserve workers' real income. This implies

$$\hat{w}_m = c_m \hat{P}_m,\qquad(6)$$

as c_i, the marginal propensity to consume good i, equals its consumption share for homothetic preferences.

In the primary export sector and the foreign enclave, the wage adjusts to equate labor supply and labor demand at every point in time. Utilizing Shephard's lemma, the sectoral factor demands may be stated together with the full-employment conditions as

$$L_i = C^i_w Q_i,\qquad(7)$$

$$L = L_x + L_m + L_s, \tag{8}$$

$$T = C_v^x Q_x, \tag{9}$$

$$K_s = C_z^s Q_s, \tag{10}$$

$$K = C_r^m Q_m, \tag{11}$$

where L is the fixed supply of labor, $T \equiv T_d + T_f$, $K \equiv K_d + K_f$, and T_d and K_d are land and capital owned by domestic residents. In passing, it should be remarked that (11) is not really a "full-employment" condition; it serves, in conjunction with (1), (6), and (7), to fix the supply curve in the manufacturing sector – to determine Q_m as a function of K and P_m.

Domestic capital accumulation is driven by the solution to a standard Ramsey problem. The representative agent chooses E and I_d to maximize

$$\int_0^\infty V(P_m, E)e^{-\rho t} dt \tag{12}$$

subject to

$$E + P_k I_d = R(P_m, K, T, K_s, L_m) + J$$
$$\qquad - brK_d - rK_f - zK_s - vT_f, \tag{13}$$

$$\dot{K}_d = I_d - \delta K_d, \tag{14}$$

where b is the tax on gross earnings of capital in manufacturing and J is lump-sum transfers. The country can borrow only in the form of direct foreign investment. Consequently, the budget constraint (13) requires that consumption and domestic investment sum to national income each period. The tax contribution of foreign firms to national income shows up in J:

$$J = brK + b_f(zK_s + vT_f). \tag{15}$$

For reasons that will become clear later, I allow b_f, the tax on earnings in the enclave and the primary export sector, to differ from b. Substituting for J in (13) gives

$$E + P_k I_d = R(P_m, K, T, K_s, L_m) - (1 - b)rK_f$$
$$\qquad - (1 - b_f)(zK_s + vT_f). \tag{13'}$$

National income is thus the value of private sector output $R(\cdot)$ less after-tax payments to foreign capital and land.

Finally, I assume that the government exercises strict control over the level and sectoral destination of FI. I_i is therefore exogenous and the paths of K_f and K_s follow immediately from

$$\dot{K_i} = I_i - \delta K_i, \qquad i = f, s. \tag{16}$$

While the model in equations (1)–(16) is similar in many ways to the more elaborate model in Chapter 5, it differs in one important respect: the manufactured good resides in the nontradables sector. This is certainly the right place for the manufactured good when quotas keep out competing imports.[5] It may even be the right assignment under free trade. In previous chapters, I assumed that imported and domestically produced manufactures were perfect substitutes. A credible case can be made, however, for the view that manufactures lie somewhere between haircuts and wheat on the spectrum of tradability. The prevalence of cross-hauling in manufactures trade, the procyclical nature of manufactures prices in small open economies, and the strong expansion of the manufacturing sector in oil-exporting countries in the seventies all suggest that manufactures are heterogeneous, "semi-tradable" goods whose prices vary with domestic supply and demand (see de Melo, 1988; Devarajan, 1988; Benjamin, Devarajan, and Weiner, 1989; and Ocampo, 1994).

The distinction between semi-tradability and perfect tradability is critical in the present context. As will become apparent shortly, crowding in and crowding out work through induced changes in the price of the manufactured good. This causal connection disappears if the price is fixed on the world market.

9.1.1   The Transition Paths for Investment and the Capital Stock

Let π be the multiplier attached to the constraint (13) in the private agent's optimization problem. The optimal path for domestic investment then satisfies

$$\pi = V_E[R(P_m, K, T, K_s, L_m) - (1-b)rK_f$$
$$- (1-b_f)(zK_s + vT_f) - P_k I_d]P_k(P_m) \tag{17}$$

and the co-state equation

$$\dot{\pi} = (\rho + \delta)\pi - V_E r(1-b). \tag{18}$$

---

[5] Adding a fixed amount of quota-restricted imports to the right side in (5) does not alter the results. The precise level of the quota is immaterial because (unlike a tariff) under a quota there are no welfare effects associated with endogenous variations in the import volume.

Differentiating (17) with respect to time and making use of the relationship $V_{EPm}/V_{EE}D^m = \tau - 1$ leads to

$$V_{EE}P_k[r\dot{K}_d + br\dot{K}_f + b_f z\dot{K}_s + (w_m - w_x)\dot{L}_m - P_k\dot{I}_d]$$

$$+ V_E P_k(\alpha - c_m)\frac{\dot{P}_m}{P_m} = V_E[(\rho + \delta)P_k - r(1 - b)], \tag{19}$$

where $\alpha \equiv P_m a_1/P_k$ is the cost share of the domestic component in the production of capital and I have exploited the fact that $P_m(Q_m - a_1 I_d)/E = P_m D^m/E = c_m$ [$I_i = 0$ initially in (5)].

The variables in the dynamic system are I_d, K_d, and either K_f or K_s. We need to know therefore how r, L_m, and P_m relate to these three variables on the transition path. Looking ahead, since we are also interested in welfare, it will prove advantageous at this point to solve the quasi-static variant of the model for L_m, P_m, and current utility u as a function of I_s, I_f, I_d, K_d, K_f, T_f, and K_s. Toward that end, replace $D^m(P_m, E)$ and E by the compensated demand function $D^m(P_m, u)$ and the expenditure function $E(P_m, u)$. Equations (5) and (13) then yield

$$c_m du + P_k\alpha(dI_d + dI_i) = P_m Q_m \hat{Q}_m + P_m D^m \varepsilon \hat{P}_m, \tag{20}$$

$$du + P_k dI_d = rdK_d + brdK_f + b_f(zdK_s + vdT_f)$$

$$+ (1 - \psi)w_m L_m \hat{L}_m, \tag{21}$$

where $\psi \equiv w_x/w_m < 1$ and units have been chosen so that $E_u = 1$ initially. From (1), (6), (7), and (11),

$$\hat{r} = \frac{1 - \theta_L^m c_m}{\theta_K^m}\hat{P}_m, \tag{22}$$

$$\hat{L}_m = \frac{\sigma^m c_x}{\theta_K^m}\hat{P}_m + \hat{K}, \tag{23}$$

$$\hat{Q}_m = \frac{\sigma^m c_x \theta_L^m}{\theta_K^m}\hat{P}_m + \hat{K}. \tag{24}$$

The solutions for P_m and u are thus

$$\hat{P}_m = (P_m Q_m h_o)^{-1}[(\alpha - c_m)P_k dI_d + \alpha P_k dI_i$$

$$+ c_m b_f(zdK_s + vdT_f) - rh_1 dK_d - rh_2 dK_f], \tag{25}$$

$$du = r\left[1 + (1 - \psi)\frac{\theta_L^m}{\theta_K^m}\left(1 - \frac{\sigma^m c_x h_1}{h_o}\right)\right]dK_d$$

$$+ r\left[b + (1 - \psi)\frac{\theta_L^m}{\theta_K^m}\left(1 - \frac{\sigma^m c_x h_2}{h_o}\right)\right]dK_f$$

$$+ \frac{\sigma^m c_x (1 - \psi)\theta_L^m \alpha}{\theta_K^m h_o} P_k(dI_f + dI_s)$$

$$+ \left[\frac{\sigma^m c_x (1 - \psi)\theta_L^m}{\theta_K^m h_o}(\alpha - c_m) - 1\right]P_k dI_d$$

$$+ zb_f\left[1 + \frac{\sigma^m c_x c_m (1 - \psi)\theta_L^m}{\theta_K^m h_o}\right]dK_s$$

$$+ vb_f\left[1 + \frac{\sigma^m c_x c_m (1 - \psi)\theta_L^m}{\theta_K^m h_o}\right]dT_f, \tag{26}$$

where

$$h_o \equiv \varepsilon D^m / Q_m + \sigma^m c_x (c_x + c_m \psi)\, \theta_L^m / \theta_K^m,$$

$$h_1 \equiv c_x + (c_x + c_m \psi)\theta_L^m / \theta_K^m,$$

$$h_2 \equiv 1 - c_m b + (c_x + c_m \psi)\theta_L^m / \theta_K^m.$$

Returning to (19), substitute for $\dot{K}_d$, $\dot{K}_i$, $\dot{L}_m$, and $\dot{P}_m$ from (14), (16), (23), and (25). This gives

$$g_o \dot{I}_d = \frac{r}{P_k} g_1 (I_d - \delta K_d) + \frac{r}{P_k} g_2 (I_f - \delta K_f)$$

$$- \frac{zb_f}{P_k} g_3 (I_s - \delta K_s) + g_4, \tag{27}$$

where

$$g_o \equiv \frac{D^m}{Q_m c_m h_o}[\alpha - c_m(1 + f)](\alpha - c_m) + \frac{1}{\tau},$$

$$g_1 \equiv \frac{\theta_K^m + (1 - \psi)\theta_L^m}{\theta_K^m \tau} + \frac{D^m h_1}{Q_m c_m h_o}[\alpha - c_m(1 + f)],$$

$$g_2 \equiv \frac{b\theta_K^m + (1 - \psi)\theta_L^m}{\theta_K^m \tau} + \frac{D^m h_2}{Q_m c_m h_o}[\alpha - c_m(1 + f)],$$

$$g_3 \equiv \frac{D^m}{Q_m h_o}[\alpha - c_m(1+f)] - \frac{1}{\tau},$$

$$g_4 \equiv V_E[(\rho + \delta)P_k - r],$$

$$f \equiv \sigma^m \theta_L^m (1 - \psi) c_x Q_m / D^m \theta_K^m \tau.$$

Equations (14), (16), and (27) form a self-contained system of three nonlinear differential equations in I_d, K_d, and K_i. The linearized version of the system is

$$\begin{bmatrix} \dot{I}_d \\ \dot{K}_d \\ \dot{K}_i \end{bmatrix} = \begin{bmatrix} y_1 & y_2 & y_3^i \\ 1 & -\delta & 0 \\ 0 & 0 & -\delta \end{bmatrix} \begin{bmatrix} I_d - I_d^* \\ K_d - K_d^* \\ K_i - K_i^* \end{bmatrix}, \tag{28}$$

where

$$y_1 \equiv \frac{\rho + \delta}{(1-b)g_o} \left[\frac{D^m(\alpha - c_m)G}{Q_m c_m h_o} + g_1 \right],$$

$$y_2 \equiv -\frac{\rho + \delta}{(1-b)g_o} \left[g_1 \delta + \frac{(\rho+\delta)D^m h_1 G}{(1-b)Q_m c_m h_o} \right],$$

$$y_3^i \equiv \begin{cases} -\dfrac{\rho+\delta}{(1-b)g_o} \left[g_2 \delta + \dfrac{(\rho+\delta)D^m h_2 G}{(1-b)Q_m c_m h_o} \right] & \text{for } i = m, \\[3ex] \dfrac{b_f z}{g_o} \left[g_3 \delta + \dfrac{(\rho+\delta)D^m G}{(1-b)Q_m c_m h_o} \right] & \text{for } i = s, \end{cases}$$

$$G \equiv (1-b)\frac{\alpha \theta_K^m + c_m \theta_L^m - 1}{\theta_K^m},$$

and units have been chosen so that $V_E = P_k = 1$ initially.

For the steady state to be a saddle point with a unique convergent path, two of the system's three eigenvalues must have negative real parts. This is, in fact, the case. The characteristic equation is

$$(\lambda + \delta)[\lambda^2 - \lambda(y_1 - \delta) - (y_2 + y_1 \delta)] = 0.$$

Clearly, $-\delta$ is one eigenvalue. The other two eigenvalues depend on the subsystem involving I_d and K_d and will be real and opposite in sign iff $y_1 \delta + y_2 > 0$. This requires $g_o > 0$, or

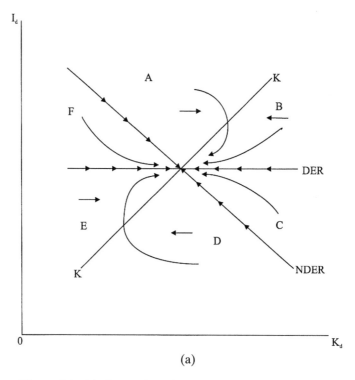

(a)

Figure 9.1. (a) Dynamics when the dominant eigenvector ray is horizontal.

$$\tau(\alpha - c_m)^2 + c_m\varepsilon + \frac{(1 + c_m\psi - \alpha)\sigma^m c_x c_m \theta_L^m Q_m}{D^m \theta_K^m} > 0,$$

which always holds since $\alpha \leq 1$. In what follows I designate

$$\lambda_2 = \frac{y_1 - \delta - \sqrt{(y_1 - \delta)^2 + 4(y_1\delta + y_2)}}{2} \qquad \text{and} \qquad \lambda_3 = -\delta$$

to be the system's two negative eigenvalues.

Figures 9.1a and b depict the transition paths for I_d and K_d. The KK schedule shows the set of points for which K_d is constant. KK has a positive slope of σ, to its right net investment is negative and K_d is falling, while to its left net investment is positive and K_d is increasing. The other

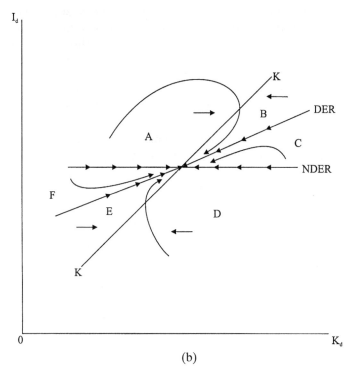

(b)

Figure 9.1. (b) Dynamics when the dominant eigenvector ray is positively sloped.

two schedules are *eigenvector rays* (see Section 4.1.3.1 of Chapter 4). Recall that

$$
\begin{bmatrix} y_1 & y_2 & y_3^i \\ 1 & -\delta & 0 \\ 0 & 0 & -\delta \end{bmatrix} \begin{bmatrix} X_{1j} \\ X_{2j} \\ X_{3j} \end{bmatrix} = \lambda_j \begin{bmatrix} X_{1j} \\ X_{2j} \\ X_{3j} \end{bmatrix},
$$

where $(X_{1j}, X_{2j}, X_{3j})'$ is the eigenvector associated with the eigenvalue λ_j. The second row of the above matrix equation provides two eigenvector rays in (I_d, K_d) space:

$$
X_{13}/X_{23} = \lambda_3 + \delta = 0,
$$

$$
X_{12}/X_{22} = \lambda_2 + \delta \gtreqless 0.
$$

The two eigenvector rays are, in essence, the two convergent paths that can be defined using one or the other of the system's two negative eigenvalues. In the case at hand, one ray is horizontal. This reflects the fact that the foreign-owned capital stock is a pure forcing variable: since neither domestic investment nor the domestic capital stock affect the path of the foreign-owned capital stock, the economy will converge to the steady-state equilibrium if I_d is kept at its steady-state level throughout the adjustment process.

The behavioral content of the dynamics is embodied in the nonhorizontal eigenvector ray. This second ray may be positively or negatively sloped. As usual, investment is more profitable the further the capital stock is from its equilibrium level.[6] The pure profit motive, therefore, is conducive to high levels of investment when the capital stock is small (i.e., the profit motive tends to produce a negatively sloped ray). Working against this effect is the private agent's desire, *ceteris paribus*, for the smoothest possible consumption path. The capital stock grows more slowly but the consumption path is smoother if investment increases when the capital stock and real income are rising. If this consumption smoothing effect proves stronger (weaker) than the profit effect, the second eigenvector ray is positively (negatively) sloped as in Figure 9.1b (9.1a).

The directional arrows are fixed by the KK schedule and the rules pertaining to the "pull" of the eigenvector rays when the two negative eigenvalues are real. Briefly, if the path starts out on either eigenvector ray, it follows that ray to the stationary equilibrium. Starting from any other point, the path never crosses either ray and as it approaches the equilibrium point it assumes the slope of the *dominant eigenvector ray* (DER).

9.1.2   The Steady-State Equilibrium

The structure of the steady-state equilibrium is very simple. Observe from (17) and (18) that the capital rental is tied down by the time preference rate ρ, the tax b, and the price of the manufactured good P_m: $r = (\rho + \delta)P_k(P_m)/(1 - b)$. It follows immediately from (1) and (6) that P_m, and hence r and w_m, are constant across steady states.

Since P_m does not change in the long run, the solutions for K_d and u can be obtained directly from (20), (21), (23), and (24) by setting $\hat{P}_m = 0$,

---

[6] A decrease in the capital stock raises the capital rental by driving up the price of the manufactured good.

$dI_d = \delta dK_d$, and $dI_i = \delta dK_i$. Focusing on K, the aggregate capital stock in manufacturing, we have

$$dK = \frac{(1-b)}{(\rho+\delta)\Delta}[(c_m z b_f + \delta\alpha)dK_s + c_m v b_f dT_f - c_m \rho dK_f], \tag{29}$$

$$du = \frac{\rho+\delta}{1-b}\left[\frac{\rho+\delta b}{\rho+\delta} + \frac{(1-\psi)\theta_L^m}{\theta_K^m}\right]dK - \rho dK_f$$
$$+ z b_f dK_s + v b_f dT_f, \tag{30}$$

where

$$\Delta \equiv \frac{c_x \rho}{\rho+\delta} + \frac{\delta}{\rho+\delta}[bc_x + (1-b)(1-\alpha)] + \frac{\theta_L^m}{\theta_K^m}(c_x + c_m \psi) > 0$$

and θ_j^m is the cost share of factor j in the manufacturing sector.

To characterize the long-run effects on poverty and the distribution of income, we need to know what happens to high-wage employment and the wage in the export sector. These variables are pinned down by the sectoral factor demands and the full-employment condition. From (7) and (9)–(11),

$$dL_m = \ell_m dK, \tag{31}$$

$$dL_x = -\frac{\sigma^x L_x}{\theta_T^x}\hat{w}_x + \ell_x dT_f, \tag{32}$$

$$dL_s = \ell_s dK_s, \tag{33}$$

where θ_T^x is the cost share of land in the export sector, ℓ_x is the ratio of labor to land in the primary export sector, and ℓ_m and ℓ_s are ratios of labor to capital in the manufacturing and enclave sectors.[7] Substituting the above solutions into (8) produces

$$\hat{w}_x = \frac{\theta_T^x}{\sigma^x L_x}(\ell_m dK + \ell_x dT_f + \ell_s dK_s). \tag{34}$$

Equations (29), (30), and (34) are a recursive system: (29) gives the solution for K which can then be substituted into (30) and (34) to determine u and w_x. Figure 9.2 illustrates the resulting steady-state equilib-

---

[7] The wage does not appear in (33) because $L_s = 0$ initially.

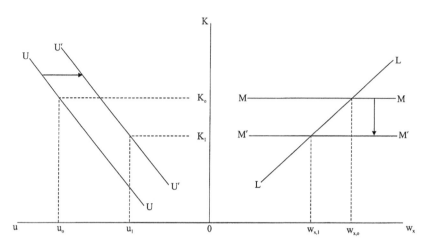

Figure 9.2. The long-run effects of foreign investment in the domestic manufacturing sector.

rium. The LL and MM schedules in the first quadrant represent the combinations of K and w_x consistent with equilibrium in the labor and manufactures markets. MM is horizontal as w_x affects neither manufactures supply nor manufactures demand. LL, on the other hand, is upward-sloping: when capital accumulation increases the number of jobs in manufacturing, labor leaves the primary sector and competitive pressures push up the wage paid to those who stay behind.

The UU schedule in the adjoining quadrant is derived from (30). This schedule is defined for given values of K_f, K_s, and T_f. It thus captures the positive relationship between domestic capital accumulation and steady-state utility.

9.1.3   Model Calibration

Most of the parameter values that underlie the numerical solutions will be familiar by now. In some runs, however, the consumption share for manufactures, c_m, and the elasticity of substitution in consumption between nontradables and tradables, β, will take higher values than in earlier chapters. I allow β to vary from .15 to 1.5 to accommodate the alternative interpretations of manufactures as nontraded goods. The cases where $\beta \leq .5$ assume quotas are in place, so that consumers substitute only between manufactures and primary goods. When the manufacturing sector is not protected by quotas, a much larger value is appropriate since consumers can then substitute not only between broad commodity groups but also between domestic and imported manufactures. In this case, I set β at 1.5, a value in line with CGE model builders' guesstimates of what "semi-tradability" of manufactures means.[8]

The other parameters that need to be interpreted more flexibly are those that bear on the size and the characteristics of the high-wage sector. In Chapter 5 I put all services and domestic capital goods production in the low-wage informal sector. But this is not the only relevant case. In more advanced, semi-industrialized economies, the high-wage sector may comprise manufacturing and a significant part of services and construction. I wish to include runs for these economies without adding a second nontradables sector that would make the model analytically intractable. The values assigned to c_m, α, and θ_L^m will differ therefore depending on whether the high-wage sector is large or small. When it is small, $c_m = \alpha = .25$ and $\theta_L^m = .30$; when it is large, $c_m = \alpha = .50$ and $\theta_L^m = .40$. The value for θ_L^m is higher in the latter case because the nontradables high-wage sector encompasses construction and part of services, which are labor-intensive relative to manufacturing.

9.2 Plain Vanilla Foreign Investment in the Domestic Manufacturing Sector

The share of FI going into the manufacturing sector has increased substantially in the last 40 years. Much of the investment is motivated by the desire to gain access to a sizeable and/or highly protected domestic market (Page, 1987; Helleiner, 1989; Greenaway, 1992). Foreign firms are heavily involved in producing consumer durables for the domestic market throughout the Third World.[9] In some countries, they even run a large part of the manufacturing sector. Forty percent of the capital stock in the manufacturing sector of Cote d'Ivoire is owned by foreign firms (Harrison, 1996); if crude estimates are believable, the corresponding figure for Zimbabwe is 70% (Riddell, 1987).

Over the long haul, this type of FI is inimical to development. Figure 9.2 shows the steady-state outcome and provides

[8] The elasticity of substitution between imported and domestic manufactured goods is 1.2 in Devarajan and Sussangkarn (1992); 1.25 in Benjamin, Devarajan, and Weiner (1989); and 2 in Devarajan, Lewis, and Robinson (1990). Devarajan and de Melo (1987) allow the substitution elasticity to vary from .2 to 100, but consider .5–2 to be the most plausible range.

[9] This is true not only in Latin America but also in much of East Asia (Hughes and Dorrance, 1987; Vera-Vasallo, 1996).

Proposition 1 *Across steady states, FI in the high-wage manufacturing sector lowers utility, the aggregate capital stock, the level of manufacturing sector employment, and the real wage paid to labor in the primary sector.*

An increase in foreign-owned capital K_f shifts the MM schedule downward and the UU schedule to the right but does not affect the position of the LL schedule. The *aggregate* capital stock falls, reflecting greater than one-for-one crowding out of domestic capital by foreign capital. Since the decrease in the aggregate capital stock produces a proportionate decrease in manufacturing sector employment, more labor is released to the primary sector, depressing w_x. Total real wage income declines both because the share of employment in the high-wage manufacturing sector decreases and because the real wage in the primary sector falls.

Some crowding out of domestic investment is hardly surprising given that domestic and foreign capital compete on the supply side: for a given level of K_d, an increase in K_f produces a greater supply of manufactures, a lower value of P_m, and a lower return on capital. What underlies the striking result of greater than one-for-one crowding out, however, is a simple income effect. Consider the nature of the equilibrium when K_d has fallen by an amount equalling the increase in K_f. This does not disturb the equilibrium on the supply side (which is why the LL curve does not shift). On the demand side, however, the replacement of domestically owned capital by foreign-owned capital reduces national income and thereby lowers the demand for manufactures. Hence, at an unchanged aggregate capital stock, there is still an excess supply of manufactures that depresses P_m and the profitability of investment. Capital decumulation must proceed further before supply contracts enough to clear the manufactures market at its pre-FI price.

9.2.1   Short- vs. Long-Run Effects on Underemployment

Although the aggregate capital stock falls and underemployment worsens in the long run, these adverse effects may not become apparent until the later stages of the adjustment process. In the short run, FI may appear to promote domestic development. The dynamics for underemployment are particularly deceiving in this respect. Since the domestic- and foreign-owned capital stocks are fixed at time $t = 0$, the change in P_m alone determines whether manufacturing sector employment initially rises or falls. The impact on P_m depends, in turn, on how higher FI and the induced rise or fall in domestic investment alter the overall demand for manufactures. From (25),

$$\hat{L}_m\big|_{t=0}, \hat{P}_m\big|_{t=0} \gtreqless 0 \quad \text{as} \quad (\alpha - c_m)dI_d + \alpha dI_f \gtreqless 0. \tag{35}$$

FI bolsters demand to the extent that domestic components are used in the production of capital goods. Domestic investment does the same but is paid for by a reduction in consumption spending that lowers purchases of manufactured consumer goods by $c_m dI_d$. The first term is negative therefore whenever $\alpha - c_m$ and dI_d are opposite in sign. It is rarely large enough, however, to lower P_m. As will be explained below, if domestic investment increases, it does so only in *response to* an increase in P_m. The case where $dI_d > 0$ and $\alpha < c_m$ is thus incompatible with a fall in L_m. The other possibility is that $\alpha > c_m$ and I_d decreases. In this case, P_m decreases only if immediate massive crowding out of domestic investment produces a steep drop in total investment spending. But this will seldom be consistent with optimizing behavior; the representative agent's desire, *ceteris paribus*, for the smoothest possible consumption path usually rules out sharp swings in investment spending.

Proceeding more formally, it is easy to demonstrate that P_m must rise if domestic investment undershoots its steady-state value as in Figure 9.3.[10] Hence, to establish a strong presumption that underemployment will diminish in the short run, it is necessary only to establish that, normally, domestic investment will not overshoot its new steady-state level. Calculating the initial jump in I_d in the usual fashion shows that

$$1 + \frac{\rho}{\delta} > \frac{(\alpha - c_m)\theta_K^m}{\theta_K^m (1-\alpha) + \theta_L^m c_x} \tag{36}$$

is sufficient to ensure undershooting. This is an exceedingly weak condition that will fail to hold only for unbelievably large values of the cost share of domestically produced capital goods (α). The term on the right side will exceed unity only if

$$\alpha > \frac{1 + c_m + c_x \theta_L^m / \theta_K^m}{2},$$

which will typically require α itself to be close to unity. (For $\theta_L^m >> \theta_K^m$, $\alpha > 1$ is required.) And even should the above condition be satisfied, it is

---

[10] Set $dI_f/dK_f = \sigma$ and $dI_d/dK_f = \sigma dK_d/dK_f$ in (35), where the solution for dK_d/dK_f is obtained from (29).

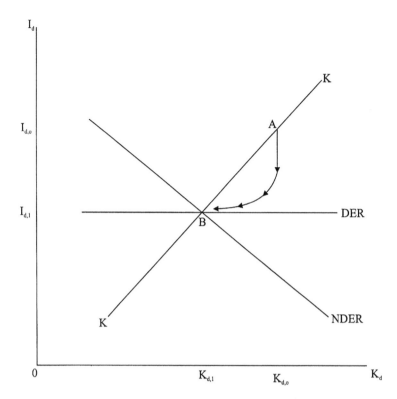

Figure 9.3. Dynamics when domestic investment decreases on impact and undershoots its steady-state level.

difficult to believe that α could be large enough in any economy, let alone an LDC, to make the right-side term in (36) exceed unity by a factor of more than ρ/σ.

9.2.2   The Dynamics of Domestic Capital Accumulation

The demonstration that FI usually reduces underemployment in the short run was one and the same as the demonstration that the price of the manufactured good invariably rises on impact. It is a small step from this to the result that the short- and long-run effects on domestic capital accumulation may also differ. Since the return on capital r/P_k moves in sync with P_m, the profitability of investment is higher in the short run but lower in the long run. The temporary increases in P_m and r are larger and last longer when demand and supply elasticities are small in the

Table 9.1. *The impact effect on domestic investment* (dI_d/dI_f *at* t = 0) *of plain vanilla FI in the manufacturing sector.**

			$c_m = .25,\ \alpha = .25,\ \theta_L^m = .30$			
			Value of τ			
β	.25	.5	.75	1	1.5	σ^m
.15	−.41	−.28	−.17	−.06	.13	.25
	−.42	−.34	−.26	−.18	−.03	.50
	−.42	−.39	−.34	−.29	−.18	1
.50	−.47	−.44	−.39	−.33	−.23	.25
	−.46	−.44	−.40	−.36	−.27	.50
	−.44	−.44	−.42	−.39	−.32	1
1.50	−.46	−.48	−.48	−.47	−.44	.25
	−.45	−.47	−.48	−.47	−.44	.50
	−.43	−.46	−.47	−.46	−.44	1

			$c_m = .50,\ \alpha = .50,\ \theta_L^m = .40$			
			Value of τ			
β	.25	.5	.75	1	1.5	σ^m
.15	−.24	−.07	.10	.25	.52	.25
	−.26	−.16	−.05	.06	.26	.50
	−.25	−.22	−.16	−.10	.03	1
.50	−.35	−.29	−.21	−.12	.03	.25
	−.33	−.29	−.23	−.17	−.04	.50
	−.30	−.29	−.26	−.22	−.12	1
1.50	−.39	−.39	−.37	−.34	−.28	.25
	−.37	−.38	−.36	−.34	−.28	.50
	−.34	−.35	−.35	−.33	−.29	1

* $\rho = .08$, $\delta = .05$, $b = .20$, and $\psi = .67$.

manufacturing sector. If the small elasticities join forces with a private agent who is willing to substitute intertemporally, then investment may increase in the short run even though the fundamentals call for substantial capital decumulation in the long run. Temporary *crowding in* of domestic investment is most likely therefore when τ is large and σ^m and β are small. This pattern is evident in Table 9.1. In the upper panel, the impact effect on domestic investment is positive only when $\beta = .15$, $\sigma^m = .25$, and $\tau = 1.5$. In the lower panel, there are more positive entries, but, with one exception, they are confined to the columns in which $\tau \geq 1$.

While domestic investment may increase initially, it does not remain positive for very long. In the eight cases where the impact coefficient is positive, the domestic capital stock falls below its pre-FI level within 1.5 years. This does not mean, however, that the conflicting short- and long-run effects on profitability are irrelevant to the dynamics and the normative conclusions. On the contrary, they are very relevant. The important feature of Table 9.1 is that, due to the temporary increase in profitability, the numbers are generally small. Since the small numbers imply *gradual* crowding out, the aggregate capital stock and high-wage employment are often higher for an extended period of time. In many of the cases covered by Table 9.2, it takes 15–40 years before these variables drop below their pre-FI levels.[11]

9.2.3   Welfare

Table 9.2 has important normative implications. Over the short/medium run, before the repercussions of crowding out domestic capital are fully felt, the host country benefits from higher employment in manufacturing and from taxes collected on profits of foreign firms. These gains have to be balanced against the losses that occur further out on the transition path as the economy moves toward a steady state where underemployment is greater and utility is lower; a very difficult intertemporal trade-off is thus involved in judging the desirability of FI.

In calculating the welfare gain/loss, I allow for the possibility that the social time preference rate ρ_1 may be lower than the private rate ρ. Accordingly, the social welfare function is

$$W = \int_0^\infty u(t)e^{-\rho_1 t}dt.$$

Since $V_E = P_k = 1$ initially,

$$\frac{W - W_o}{dI_f} = \int_0^\infty \frac{u(t) - u_o}{dI_f} e^{-\rho_1 t}dt$$

[11] The relationship between τ and crowding out of domestic investment is negative in the short run but positive in the medium run. (The larger is τ the more rapidly domestic investment declines as the return falls further out on the transition path.) This is why higher values of τ cause the aggregate capital stock to drop below its pre-FI level sooner.

Table 9.2. *Length of time that the aggregate capital stock and high-wage employment exceed their pre-FI levels (plain vanilla FI in the manufacturing sector).*[*]

	$c_m = .25, \alpha = .25, \theta_L^m = .30$						
	K			L_m			
β	$\tau = .25$	$\tau = .5$	$\tau = 1$	$\tau = .25$	$\tau = .5$	$\tau = 1$	σ^m
.15	15.7	12.9	11.4	8.6	9.1	9.4	.25
	17.8	14.1	12.0	5.8	6.9	8.1	.50
	21.6	16.3	13.2	4.2	5.0	6.1	1
.50	22.5	16.8	13.5	16.5	13.4	11.6	.25
	24.2	17.8	14.1	11.9	10.9	10.4	.50
	27.4	19.8	15.2	6.2	7.1	8.0	1
1.50	37.2	25.9	18.8	33.5	23.4	17.2	.25
	38.5	26.7	19.3	30.7	21.5	16.1	.50
	40.8	28.2	20.2	23.4	17.3	13.8	1

	$c_m = .50, \alpha = .50, \theta_L^m = .40$						
	K			L_m			
β	$\tau = .25$	$\tau = .5$	$\tau = 1$	$\tau = .25$	$\tau = .5$	$\tau = 1$	σ^m
.15	16.9	13.6	11.8	10.0	9.9	9.8	.25
	20.1	15.3	12.7	8.0	8.5	8.9	.50
	25.6	18.6	14.5	6.4	7.1	7.8	1
.50	23.8	17.4	13.9	17.2	13.8	12.0	.25
	26.5	19.0	14.7	13.6	12.0	11.0	.50
	31.5	22.0	16.4	9.2	9.3	9.5	1
1.50	39.9	26.9	19.2	35.1	23.9	17.4	.25
	42.0	28.2	19.9	32.2	22.1	16.5	.50
	46.0	30.7	21.4	25.4	18.4	14.6	1

[*] $\rho = .08, \delta = .05, b = .20,$ and $\psi = .67$.

measures the present value welfare gain per dollar of FI. To express the gain in more familiar terms, note that the constant stream y yields a total welfare gain of y/ρ_1. Hence

$$\rho_1 \frac{W - W_o}{dI_f} = \rho_1 \int_0^\infty \frac{u(t) - u_o}{dI_f} e^{-\rho_1 t} dt \tag{37}$$

measures the welfare gain/loss in terms of the annual equivalent return per dollar of FI (i.e., the return on I_f, the flow, not K_f, the stock). For purposes of comparison, it is also useful to calculate what the return would be if K_d and L_m were constant and the gain to the economy were simply the taxes paid by foreign capital. Under this hypothetical scenario,

$$W - W_o = \int_o^\infty rbK_f(t)e^{-\rho_1 t} dt$$

$$\Rightarrow \rho_1 \frac{W - W_o}{dI_f} = \frac{\rho + \delta}{\rho_1 + \delta} \frac{1}{1 - b}.$$

In the numerical solutions, $b = .20$, $\rho = .08$, $\delta = .05$, and $\rho_1 = .05 - .08$. Thus, the annual equivalent return lies between .25 and .325 when FI does not adversely affect either underinvestment or underemployment.

Table 9.3 shows the results of calculating (37) when $\sigma^m = .50$ and all other parameters take the same values as in Table 9.1.[12] There is not much in the numbers to get excited about. For $\rho_1 = \rho$, the impact on welfare is positive, but the gains are trivial: half of the positive returns are less than 2% (i.e., less than .1% per unit of foreign capital) and only four exceed 5%.[13] Moreover, all of the returns become negative when the social time preference rate is slightly below the private time preference rate, with the losses being quite large for $\rho_1 = .05 - .06$.

The conclusion one draws here depends on what one judges to be a sensible value of ρ_1, viz., on one's view about the extent to which economic development should be treated as an objective in its own right. Clearly, however, there is no compelling case in Table 9.3 for trying to attract foreign capital. LDCs have little to gain and run the risk of large losses from opening up the domestic market to plain vanilla FI.

9.3   Plain Vanilla FI in an Enclave

Foreign firms are said to operate an enclave if there is no overlap between the goods they produce and those produced by domestic firms. The foreign enclave may export a manufactured good, but in behavioral terms it is part of the primary sector: FI is attracted by the opportunity to pay the low primary sector wage. The maquiladora plants operating in northern Mexico and the multinational corporations Malaysia, Sri

---

[12] The results are insensitive to σ^m and ψ. Most of the numbers in Table 9.3 change by less than one percentage point when either $\psi = .5, \sigma^m = .25$, or $\sigma^m = 1$.
[13] It should also be noted here that Table 9.1 assumes a tax of 20% on gross profits (32.5% on profits net of depreciation charges). Tax holidays of 10+ years are often used, however, to lure FI. This might cause many of the numbers in the $\rho_1 = .08$ column to change signs. (The outcome for a temporary tax holiday could be analyzed by using the methods in Chapter 7.)

Table 9.3. *Impact on domestic welfare measured as the annual equivalent return per dollar of foreign investment (plain vanilla FI in the manufacturing sector).**

β	$c_m = .25, \alpha = .25, \theta_L^m = .30$				τ
	$\rho_1 = .05$	$\rho_1 = .06$	$\rho_1 = .07$	$\rho_1 = .08$	
.15	−31.5	−18.5	−8.0	.65	.25
	−32.6	−19.4	−8.6	.27	.50
	−33.1	−19.8	−8.9	.08	1
.50	−28.2	−15.6	−5.5	2.7	.25
	−30.8	−17.8	−7.3	1.3	.50
	−32.3	−19.0	−8.3	.56	1
1.50	−20.7	−9.0	.05	7.2	.25
	−26.3	−13.8	−3.8	4.2	.50
	−29.7	−16.8	−6.4	2.1	1

β	$c_m = .50, \alpha = .50, \theta_L^m = .40$				τ
	$\rho_1 = .05$	$\rho_1 = .06$	$\rho_1 = .07$	$\rho_1 = .08$	
.15	−33.9	−19.2	−7.6	1.7	.25
	−36.5	−21.3	−9.2	.64	.50
	−37.9	−22.4	−10.0	.08	1
.50	−27.8	−13.9	−3.2	5.3	.25
	−33.1	−18.4	−6.8	2.5	.50
	−36.2	−21.0	−8.9	.86	1
1.50	−15.2	−3.3	5.5	12.3	.25
	−24.8	−11.2	−.78	7.4	.50
	−31.4	−16.8	−5.4	3.7	1

* $\rho = .08, \delta = .05, b = .20, \psi = .67,$ and $\sigma^m = .50.$

Lanka, the southern provinces of China (Guangdong and Fujian), and Mauritius have attracted into their export processing zones come to mind as examples of such low-wage manufacturing enclaves.[14]

Figure 9.4 shows what happens after the economy arrives at the new steady state. FI raises the demand for labor in the low-wage sector, shifting the LL schedule to the right. If any domestic components are used in constructing capital ($\alpha > 0$), or if any part of foreign earnings are taxed

[14] This type of FI has become increasingly common (Casson and Pearce, 1987). Zhang (1994) and Wanigatunga (1987) provide good accounts of the export processing zones in southern China and Sri Lanka.

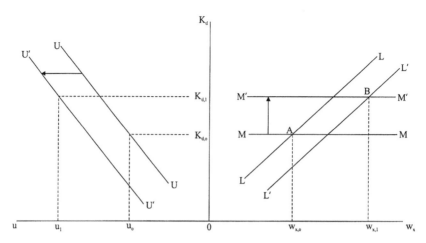

Figure 9.4. The long-run effects of foreign investment in an export enclave.

$(b_f > 0)$, the demand for manufactures increases and the resulting rise in profitability spurs domestic capital accumulation. The MM schedule therefore shifts upward and the economy moves to the equilibrium B. Domestic capital accumulation further strengthens labor demand, bidding up the wage w_x to the point where the primary sector releases enough labor to enable employment in both the foreign enclave and the manufacturing sector to increase. Summarizing, we have

Proposition 2 *Across steady states, FI in an enclave sector crowds in domestic capital, raises the real wage in the primary sector, and increases employment in the high-wage manufacturing sector if either $\alpha > 0$ or $b_f > 0$.*

Interestingly, this very classical type of FI accomplishes everything that FI in the high-wage manufacturing sector does not. In the long run, the indirect approach of allowing foreign firms to develop a low-wage enclave succeeds in promoting capital accumulation and employment in the high-wage manufacturing sector, whereas the direct, commonsensical approach of attracting FI into the manufacturing sector itself fails.

9.3.1   The Adjustment Process and Domestic Welfare

FI has highly favorable effects on domestic capital accumulation, under-employment, and the distribution of income in the long run. There is

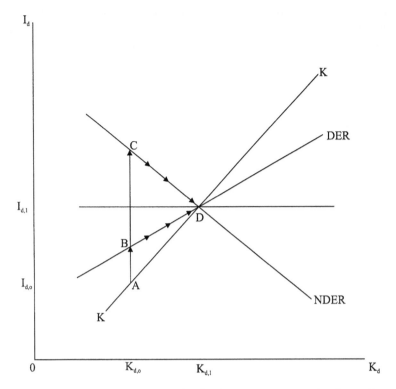

Figure 9.5. Dynamics when foreign investment occurs in the enclave sector and foreign profits are untaxed.

much more than this, however, to the argument for allowing foreign capital to build an enclave. It can be established as well that FI is virtually certain to be welfare-improving and that the transition path will usually be free of difficulties. Take the case where earnings of foreign capital are untaxed. The impact effect on domestic investment is then

$$I_d(0) - I_{d,o} = \lambda_2 \left(K_{d,o} - K_d^* \right) > 0. \tag{38}$$

Since FI increases the demand for domestically produced capital goods (assuming $\alpha > 0$), P_m jumps upward on impact (see the appendix at the end of this chapter). The jump in P_m raises the return on capital, eliciting an immediate increase in domestic investment.

To connect (38) with Figure 9.5, rewrite the solution as

$$I_d(0) - I_d^* = (\lambda_2 + \delta) \left(K_{d,o} - K_d^* \right).$$

This is the equation for the eigenvector ray associated with λ_2. Thus, domestic investment jumps onto the nonhorizontal ray. Following the jump from point A to point B or point C, the economy traverses the nonhorizontal ray to the new stationary equilibrium D. As the capital stock rises monotonically toward its steady-state level, the supply of manufactures expands enough to swamp any increases in demand associated with rising or falling investment. Hence, after jumping upward initially, P_m falls steadily until it returns to its previous level. (Recall that P_m is unchanged across steady states.) Since both the capital stock and the price of the manufactured good are higher throughout the adjustment process, high-wage employment always exceeds its pre-FI level; ongoing contraction in the primary export sector, brought about by a steadily rising wage, makes possible the simultaneous expansion of employment in the manufacturing and enclave sectors. This and the monotonic path for the domestic capital stock ensure that the LDC reaps a welfare gain:

Proposition 3 *When foreign profits are untaxed, FI in an enclave is welfare-improving.*

The qualification in Proposition 3 that foreign profits are not taxed is counterintuitive. It is needed, however, to guarantee an immediate increase in domestic investment. A higher tax rate implies that national income will be higher in the future (as K_s increases, foreign firms pay more taxes and domestic residents receive more transfers). If the tax rate is sufficiently large, the forward-looking representative agent finds it optimal to consume part of his/her higher future income today by lowering current investment. The ensuing bout of temporary capital decumulation worsens underemployment when technology exhibits fixed coefficients. It is impossible therefore to get a completely clean result – to prove that FI is welfare-improving for all parameter values.

Although purely analytical methods do not suffice in this situation, one can conduct an extensive search of the relevant parameter space to determine whether the dynamics are ever perverse enough to produce perverse welfare conclusions. In keeping with this strategy, I expanded the solution grids to include runs where σ^m and τ are extremely small. Also, to handle the case where FI is needed to exploit some natural resource, I set $z = \eta r$ and assumed that for $\eta > 1$ the government adjusts the tax b_f on foreign earnings so that $z(1 - b_f) = r(1 - b)$. That is, the government claims all of the rents from exploitation of the country's natural resources. This is unrealistic but also unimportant. From an analytical

Table 9.4a. *Impact effect on domestic investment* $(dI_d/dI_s$ *at* t = 0) *of plain vanilla FI in an export enclave when* $\eta = 1, 1.2$.*

	$c_m = .25, \alpha = .25, \theta_L^m = .30$								
	$\eta = 1$				$\eta = 1.2$				
β	$\tau = .1$	$\tau = .25$	$\tau = .50$	$\tau = 1$	$\tau = .1$	$\tau = .25$	$\tau = .50$	$\tau = 1$	σ^m
.15	.17	.39	.61	.92	.10	.35	.59	.91	.25
	.12	.30	.50	.76	.02	.25	.47	.75	.50
	.04	.20	.37	.58	−.07	.13	.32	.56	1
.50	.03	.18	.33	.54	−.07	.11	.29	.52	.25
	.01	.15	.30	.49	−.10	.08	.25	.46	.50
	−.02	.11	.24	.42	−.15	.02	.18	.38	1
1.50	−.07	.02	.13	.26	−.20	−.08	.05	.21	.25
	−.08	.02	.12	.25	−.21	−.09	.04	.19	.50
	−.09	≈0	.10	.23	−.23	−.11	.01	.17	1

	$c_m = .50, \alpha = .50, \theta_L^m = .40$								
	$\eta = 1$				$\eta = 1.2$				
β	$\tau = .1$	$\tau = .25$	$\tau = .50$	$\tau = 1$	$\tau = .1$	$\tau = .25$	$\tau = .50$	$\tau = 1$	σ^m
.15	.23	.53	.85	1.30	.13	.48	.83	1.31	.25
	.13	.39	.66	1.03	.01	.32	.62	1.02	.50
	.03	.24	.46	.75	−.13	.13	.39	.72	1
.50	.06	.26	.48	.79	−.06	.18	.44	.78	.25
	.02	.21	.41	.70	−.11	.11	.35	.67	.50
	−.03	.13	.32	.56	−.19	.02	.24	.52	1
1.50	−.06	.05	.19	.39	−.20	−.06	.11	.34	.25
	−.07	.04	.17	.36	−.22	−.08	.08	.31	.50
	−.08	.01	.14	.32	−.25	−.12	.04	.25	1

* $\rho = .08$, $\delta = .05$, $b = .20$, and $\psi = .67$.

standpoint, all that matters is total taxes paid by foreign capital; the results are the same for any combination of z and b_f that yields the same amount of tax revenue.

A quick scan of Tables 9.4–9.6 reveals that the dynamics are somewhat sensitive to the tax on foreign capital (which rises from .2 at $\eta = 1$ to .6 at $\eta = 2$). A lot depends on just how small τ is and on just how much the government collects in rents from the foreign enclave. Domestic investment increases immediately in all but two of the 96 cases where $\tau \geq .5$

Table 9.4b. *Impact effect on domestic investment* (dI_d/dI_s *at* t = 0) *of plain vanilla FI in an export enclave when* $\eta = 1.6, 2.$*

	$c_m = .25, \alpha = .25, \theta_L^m = .30$								
	$\eta = 1.6$				$\eta = 2$				
β	$\tau = .1$	$\tau = .25$	$\tau = .50$	$\tau = 1$	$\tau = .1$	$\tau = .25$	$\tau = .50$	$\tau = 1$	σ^m
.15	−.05	.26	.55	.90	−.20	.18	.51	.90	.25
	−.16	.14	.40	.72	−.34	.03	.34	.70	.50
	−.30	−.02	.23	.51	−.53	−.17	.13	.46	1
.50	−.28	−.03	.20	.47	−.49	−.17	.11	.42	.25
	−.33	−.08	.14	.40	−.55	−.23	.04	.34	.50
	−.40	−.16	.06	.30	−.66	−.34	−.07	.23	1
1.50	−.47	−.28	−.11	.10	−.74	−.49	−.26	−.01	.25
	−.49	−.30	−.13	.08	−.76	−.52	−.29	−.03	.50
	−.52	−.34	−.16	.04	−.81	−.57	−.34	−.08	1

	$c_m = .50, \alpha = .50, \theta_L^m = .40$								
	$\eta = 1.6$				$\eta = 2$				
β	$\tau = .1$	$\tau = .25$	$\tau = .50$	$\tau = 1$	$\tau = .1$	$\tau = .25$	$\tau = .50$	$\tau = 1$	σ^m
.15	−.05	.38	.80	1.33	−.24	.29	.77	1.35	.25
	−.23	.17	.55	1.01	−.47	.03	.48	1.00	.50
	−.43	−.07	.26	.66	−.74	−.28	.14	.61	1
.50	−.30	.02	.34	.74	−.53	−.13	.25	.71	.25
	−.38	−.07	.24	.62	−.65	−.25	.12	.56	.50
	−.50	−.21	.08	.43	−.81	−.43	−.07	.35	1
1.50	−.48	−.28	−.06	.23	−.76	−.50	−.23	.12	.25
	−.51	−.32	−.10	.19	−.81	−.55	−.28	.07	.50
	−.57	−.38	−.16	.11	−.89	−.64	−.37	−.03	1

* $\rho = .08, \delta = .05, b = .20,$ and $\psi = .67.$

and $\beta = .15, .50$; moreover, the crowding-in coefficient often exceeds .5, and is sometimes even larger than unity. At lower values of τ, however, FI crowds out (temporarily) domestic investment strongly when rents are sizeable ($\eta = 1.6$–2) and manufactures are semitradable ($\beta = 1.50$). Consequently, the domestic capital stock may spend a long time below its pre-FI level. In the runs where $\beta = 1.50$, $\tau = .50$, and $\eta = 1.6, 2$, K_d recovers to its previous level within ten years. But if $\tau = .25$, the domes-

Table 9.5. *Time it takes for the domestic capital stock to regain its pre-FI level (plain vanilla FI in an export enclave).**

	$c_m = .25, \alpha = .25, \theta_L^m = .30$						
	$\sigma^m = .5$			$\sigma^m = 1$			
β	$\tau = .1$	$\tau = .25$	$\tau = .5$	$\tau = .1$	$\tau = .25$	$\tau = .5$	η
.15	—	—	—	6.4	—	—	1.2
	6.7	—	—	13.9	.70	—	1.6
	9.6	—	—	16.6	4.1	—	2
.50	10.7	—	—	16.1	—	—	1.2
	18.1	3.4	—	23.4	7.0	—	1.6
	20.9	6.5	—	26.1	9.9	1.7	2
1.50	32.6	9.9	—	36.0	12.3	—	1.2
	40.4	17.5	5.9	43.9	19.8	7.6	1.6
	43.5	20.3	8.9	47.0	22.5	10.5	2

	$c_m = .50, \alpha = .50, \theta_L^m = .40$						
	$\sigma^m = .5$			$\sigma^m = 1$			
β	$\tau = .1$	$\tau = .25$	$\tau = .5$	$\tau = .1$	$\tau = .25$	$\tau = .5$	η
.15	—	—	—	9.9	—	—	1.2
	8.3	—	—	18.3	2.2	—	1.6
	11.6	—	—	21.4	5.7	—	2
.50	10.6	—	—	18.8	—	—	1.2
	19.2	2.4	—	27.4	7.7	—	1.6
	22.5	5.9	—	30.7	11.0	1.48	2
1.50	33.1	7.7	—	38.9	11.5	—	1.2
	42.9	16.5	3.7	49.0	20.2	6.5	1.6
	46.8	19.8	17.2	53.0	23.5	9.8	2

* $\rho = .08$, $\delta = .05$, $b = .20$, and $\psi = .67$. A dash indicates that the capital stock increases continuously.

tic capital stock is lower for 16–24 years, and when $\tau = .1$ it remains depressed for 43–53 years. In this latter case, high-wage employment may also contract for two or three decades (see Table 9.6).

Fortunately, none of this affects the qualitative conclusions in Table 9.7. While FI may crowd out domestic investment and worsen underemployment for a period of 20–40 years, K_d and L_m do not decrease

Table 9.6. *Time it takes for high-wage employment to rise permanently above its pre-FI level when* $\beta = 1.50$, $c_m = .50$, $\alpha = .50$, *and* $\theta_L^m = .40$ *(plain vanilla FI in an export enclave).**

	Value of σ^m			
τ	.1	.25	.5	η
.1	22.8	14.3	+	1.2
	33.3	28.4	16.1	1.6
	37.3	32.8	23.4	2
.25	+	+	+	1.2
	9.6	+	+	1.6
	13.6	9.7	+	2

* $\rho = .08$, $\delta = .05$, $b = .20$, and $\psi = .67$. A plus sign indicates that employment in manufacturing increases continuously.

Table 9.7. *Impact on domestic welfare measured as the annual equivalent return per dollar of foreign investment when the high-wage sector is large (plain vanilla FI in an export enclave).**

	$\tau = .1$			$\tau = .25$			
β	$\sigma^m = .1$	$\sigma^m = .25$	$\sigma^m = .5$	$\sigma^m = .1$	$\sigma^m = .25$	$\sigma^m = .5$	η
.15	42.3	43.6	44.9	45.2	45.9	46.6	1
	69.9	71.5	73.0	74.0	74.8	75.6	1.2
	125.3	127.3	129.4	131.6	132.6	133.6	1.6
	180.7	183.1	185.7	189.3	190.4	191.6	2
.50	34.8	36.2	37.9	40.0	40.7	41.8	1
	59.6	61.3	63.4	67.0	67.9	69.1	1.2
	109.1	111.4	114.4	120.9	122.1	123.7	1.6
	158.7	161.2	165.3	175.0	176.4	178.3	2
1.50	27.0	27.9	29.3	32.9	33.5	34.4	1
	48.4	49.5	51.3	57.0	57.7	58.8	1.2
	91.0	92.7	95.2	105.2	106.2	107.7	1.6
	133.7	135.9	139.1	153.3	154.6	156.5	2

* $\rho = \rho_1 = .08$, $\delta = .05$, $b = .20$, $\psi = .67$, $c_m = .50$, $\alpha = .50$, and $\theta_L^m = .40$.

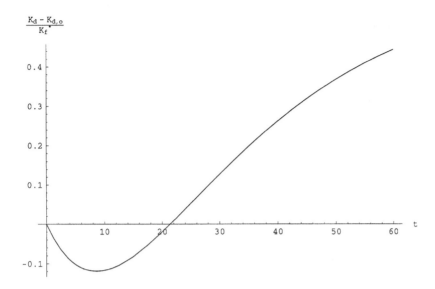

Figure 9.6. Path of K_d when the formal sector is large, $\sigma^m = 1$, $\tau = .25$, $\beta = 1.5$, and $\eta = 2$.

very much when either $\tau \geq .25$ or $\beta \geq .25$. (See Figures 9.6 and 9.7.)[15] The qualification in Proposition 3 that $b_f = 0$ is not, therefore, really necessary. For believable parameter values, the LDC always rakes in a hefty welfare gain. Indeed, the gain is much larger in the panels where $\eta > 1$ and $b_f > b$. The direct and indirect benefits of higher tax payments (which include more capital accumulation and more high-wage employment across steady states) invariably far outweigh the losses from temporarily lower investment and employment in the high-wage manufacturing sector.

9.4   Plain Vanilla FI in the Primary Export Sector

Since the stock of domestically owned land is fixed, the variable T_f can be interpreted in several ways. When domestic- and foreign-owned land

---

[15] Since $c_m = \alpha$, employment in manufacturing always increases on impact. It takes a couple of years before disinvestment lowers the capital stock enough to reduce labor demand. The results are similar for ($c_m = .25$, $\alpha = .50$) and ($\alpha = .25$, $c_m = .50$). L_m always increases in the short run and FI always produces large welfare gains.

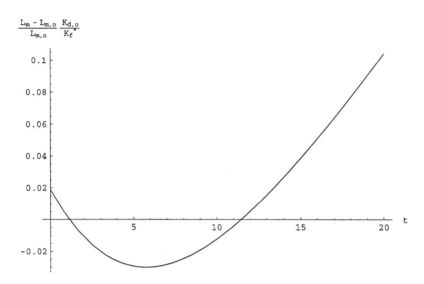

Figure 9.7. Path of L_m when the formal sector is large, $\sigma^m = .25$, $\beta = 1.5$, and $\eta = 2$.

are treated as homogeneous factors, the increase in T_f reflects expansion along existing export lines through more extensive exploitation of the country's natural resource base (e.g., reclamation of land, development of new mineral sites, etc.). Alternatively, T_d and T_f can be viewed as entirely distinct factors. On this interpretation, T_f represents any type of service provided by foreign firms that expands productive capacity in the primary export sector.

FI in this case has effects similar to FI in an export enclave. Figure 9.4 again portrays the steady-state outcome. If any part of foreign earnings are taxed, the domestic capital stock, employment in the manufacturing sector, and the primary sector real wage all increase across steady states. Furthermore, it is easily shown via the same reasoning as in Section 9.3 that manufacturing sector employment and the domestic capital stock are always higher on the transition path to the new steady state. FI is thus welfare-improving for any positive tax rate.[16]

---

[16] The same results hold if foreign capital is forced to pay a wage higher than w_x. All that matters is that the domestic economy claim some fraction of foreign profits. This can be accomplished either by taxing foreign profits or by setting a higher wage for foreign firms.

The next three sections dress up the benchmark model with export requirements, joint ventures, and technological spillovers.[17] The analysis will focus mainly on how these departures from plain vanilla FI change the results for crowding out, underemployment, and welfare when foreign firms produce for the domestic manufacturing market: Do the terms of the deal improve enough to make FI desirable? In the case of joint ventures in the export sector, I also investigate whether the dynamics look different, in particular, whether the high-wage manufacturing sector may undergo a prolonged slump before expanding more strongly than in the benchmark model.

9.5   Export Requirements

The rationale for export requirements is straightforward in static trade models where a tariff is the only distortion in the economy. FI in the protected manufacturing sector worsens the trade distortion by displacing imports. Domestic welfare falls because, in effect, foreign firms capture some of the tariff revenues that were previously rebated to the public. Export requirements reduce the transfer of revenue to foreign firms and thereby increase the likelihood of a welfare gain (or at least reduce the welfare loss).[18]

The relationship between FI and the trade distortion is completely different when protection takes the form of a quota instead of a tariff. Since the quota fixes the import volume, production by foreign firms in the protected sector does not exacerbate the trade distortion. Consequently, in the absence of other distortions, a small increase in FI leaves domestic welfare unchanged when $K_f = 0$ initially and foreign profits are untaxed. And if foreign firms pay taxes or create more high-wage jobs, they make a positive contribution to domestic welfare. In the static variant of the current model (where K_d is exogenous),

$$dL_m/dK_f > 0 \qquad \text{iff} \qquad \beta > \sigma^m (1 - c_m b), \tag{39}$$

$$du/dK_f > 0 \qquad \text{iff} \qquad \beta(1 + b\theta_K^m/\theta_L^m - \psi) \tag{40}$$
$$> \sigma^m [1 - (c_x + c_m\psi) - \psi].$$

---

[17] Export requirements, joint ventures, employment targets (especially in managerial positions), local content requirements, and other performance requirements are called TRIMs (short for trade-investment related measures). There is very little rigorous welfare analysis of TRIMs. See Greenaway (1992) for a survey of the literature.   [18] See Rodrik (1987).

Since the term multiplying σ^m in (40) is ambiguous in sign and much smaller than the term multiplying β, there is a very strong presumption that FI raises domestic welfare. If β is close to or greater than σ^m, part of the welfare gain stems from lower underemployment. This provides support for the view expressed in development textbooks that the private return on FI understates its social return in dualistic, labor-surplus economies. In the words of Meier (1976, p. 373),

> If, as was contended in the discussion of dualistic development in Chapter III, a shortage of capital in heavily populated poor countries limits the employment of labor from the rural sector in the advanced sector where wages are higher, an inflow of foreign capital may then make it possible to employ more labor in the advanced sector. The international flow of capital can thus be interpreted as an alternative to labor migration from the poor country. . . . The social benefit from the foreign investment in the advanced sector is then greater than the profits on this investment, for the wages received by the newly employed exceed their former real wage in the rural sector, and this excess should be added as a national benefit.

These optimistic conclusions are special to static models. In the present dynamic model, underemployment and underinvestment always worsen in the long run when domestic and foreign firms compete head-to-head in the domestic manufactures market. Moreover, the losses from exacerbating the two factor market distortions overwhelm the tax contributions of foreign capital when the social time preference rate is a point or two below the private rate. This result gets reversed if the private and social time preference rates coincide. FI then delivers a welfare gain viewed over the entire transition path; but the gain is small and is purchased at the price of less economic development and lower real income in the long run. In general, FI in the domestic manufactures market is a bad gamble.

The pessimistic results for inward-looking FI are in marked contrast to the very favorable results for FI in the export sector. Policy makers get everything they want from foreign capital in the export sector: greater domestic capital accumulation, less underemployment, and a better distribution of income. The obvious corollary for policy is that a welfare gain can be secured by using export requirements to limit the sales of foreign firms in the domestic market. A 100% export requirement does the job since foreign firms then operate a high-wage enclave. But this assumes away the problem when the protected domestic market is what attracts FI in the first place. The critical issue is whether much smaller export requirements suffice to make FI desirable. Is FI welfare-improving and conducive to domestic development if the highest feasible export requirment is 40%?

In adapting the model, I treat the manufactured good as a homogeneous good that can be exported at a price of unity or sold in the protected domestic market at the higher price P_m.[19] ($P_m - 1$ is the implicit tariff associated with the ban on consumer imports.) Foreign firms are required to export κ% of their output. The price they receive per unit of output is thus

$$P_f = (1-\kappa)P_m + \kappa. \tag{41}$$

Since $P_f < P_m$, foreign firms earn a lower return and face a higher product wage than domestic firms (i.e., $w_m/P_f > w_m/P_m$). Foreign and domestically owned capital have different effects therefore on supply and labor demand. This brings some extra variables and equations into the model. Let Q_m, L_m, and r refer now to production, employment, and the capital rental at domestic manufacturing plants and denote the foreign counterparts by Q_f, L_f, and r_f. Equations (5), (8), (11), (13), and (15) then change to

$$D^m(P_m, E) + a_1(I_d + I_f) = Q_m + (1-\kappa)Q_f, \tag{5'}$$

$$L = L_x + L_m + L_f, \tag{8'}$$

$$K_d = C_r^m(w_m, r)Q_m, \tag{11'}$$

$$E + P_k I_d = R(P_m, K_d, K_f, L_m, L_f) \\ + J - brK_d - r_f K_f, \tag{13'}$$

$$J = b(rK_d + r_f K_f), \tag{15'}$$

while

$$P_f = C_r^f(w_m, r_f)Q_f, \tag{42}$$

$$L_f = C_w^f(w_m, r_f)Q_f, \tag{43}$$

$$K_f = C_r^f(w_m, r_f)Q_f \tag{44}$$

pin down the three new variables Q_f, L_f, and r_f.

---

[19] There is a high correlation between export requirements and protection (Balasubramanyam, 1991; Greenaway, 1992).

9.5.1   Long-Run Effects on Capital Accumulation and Underemployment

The model can be solved by following the same procedure as before. For the long-run effect on the aggregate capital stock, we now get

$$
\Delta \frac{dK}{dK_f} = \underbrace{(1 - r_f/r)(1 - bc_m)}_{\text{effect of lower payments to foreign capital}} + \underbrace{\frac{\kappa a_f(1-b)}{P_f(\rho+\delta)}}_{\text{effect of diverting sales to the world market}}
$$

$$
+ \underbrace{\frac{\theta_L^m}{\theta_K^m}\left(1 - \frac{\ell_f}{\ell_m}\right)(c_x + c_m\psi)}_{\text{effect of foreign firms reducing employment}} - \underbrace{\frac{c_m\rho(1-b)}{\rho+\delta}}_{\text{outcome in the benchmark model}}, \tag{45}
$$

where $a_f \equiv P_f Q_f/K_f$ and $\ell_f \equiv L_f/K_f$ are the output–capital and labor–capital ratios at the foreign plant.[20] The first term reflects the favorable impact on national income and the demand for manufactures of lower payments to foreign capital ($r_f < r$). The second and third capture direct and indirect supply effects: when faced with an export requirement, foreign firms not only sell less in the domestic market, they also hire fewer workers and produce less total output. The cutback in employment shows up in the third term ($w_m/r_f > w_m/r$ implies $\ell_f/\ell_m < 1$).

The extra positive terms that appear in (45) make a difference. Note that the direct supply effect dominates the single negative term when $\kappa > c_m\rho P_f/a_f$. A value of κ of .20 is sufficient therefore to prevent a decrease in the aggregate capital stock. The condition for high-wage employment to increase is more stringent because the export requirement induces foreign firms to utilize less labor-intensive technology. But this effect is not quantitatively strong unless the elasticity of substitution between capital and labor is extremely large. In the numerical solutions to be presented shortly, the export requirement that ensures a reduction in underemployment is only five to six points higher than the one that prevents a decrease in the aggregate capital stock. Thus, modest export requirements of 15–30% will normally produce the outcome shown in Figure 9.8. FI shifts the MM schedule upward and the LL schedule to the left (because $\ell_f < \ell_m$), but the new equilibrium is northeast rather than northwest of point A.

While export requirements help counteract the pressures that crowd out domestic capital, they cannot eliminate them altogether unless the

---

[20] $P_f Q_f/K_f$ is the output–capital ratio because $P_k = 1$ initially and the analysis is confined to small changes.

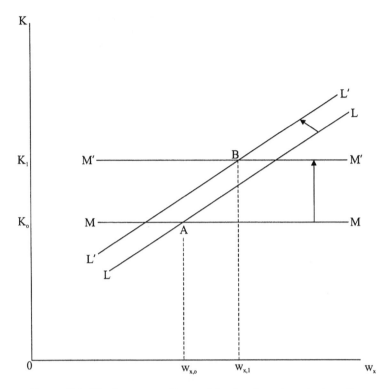

Figure 9.8. The long-run effects of foreign investment when the government imposes a minimum export requirement.

greater part of what foreign firms produce is diverted to world markets. The solution in (45) implies

$$\frac{dK_d}{dK_f} > 0 \qquad \text{iff} \qquad \kappa > P_f\left(1 - bc_m\theta_K^f - \delta\alpha a_f\right), \tag{46}$$

where θ_K^f is the cost share of capital at the foreign plant. As can be seen from Table 9.8, the value of κ that satisfies this condition is usually well above .70. By contrast, export requirements of just 8–20% guarantee an increase in the aggregate capital stock and more high-wage jobs.[21]

---

[21] In the numerical solutions, the values for r_f, l_f, and θ_j^f are determined by setting the distribution parameters in a CES production function so that initial cost shares are the same for domestic and foreign firms when they face the same factor prices.

Table 9.8. *Value of the export share requirement (κ) for which the domestic capital stock, high-wage employment, and the aggregate capital stock are unchanged across steady states.**

	$c_m = .25, \alpha = .25, \theta_L^m = .30$		
σ^m	K_d	L_m	K
.25	.900	.094	.085
.50	.898	.101	.082
1	.895	.119	.078
	$c_m = .50, \alpha = .50, \theta_L^m = .40$		
σ^m	K_d	L_m	K
.25	.804	.161	.147
.50	.800	.171	.141
1	.794	.192	.131

* $\rho = .08$, $\delta = .05$, $b = .20$, and $\psi = .67$. The implicit tariff is .50.

9.5.2   The Transition Path

The most interesting new twist in the dynamics is that domestic investment often increases in the short run even though the capital stock falls in the long run. Tables 9.9a and 9.9b show the initial jump in I_d when $\kappa = .25, .50$. Domestic investment increases in 78 of the 180 cases, including numerous cases where $\tau = .25, .50$. The transition path in Figure 9.9 is therefore not at all atypical. I_d jumps upward on impact and the domestic capital stock increases steadily over the phase BC. But this is merely the preliminary phase of an adjustment process that eventually entails strong crowding out of domestic capital. In the cases where $\kappa = .50$ and the formal sector is large, the economy spends two to six years completing the half-circle trek from A to D.

9.5.3   Welfare

The welfare results in Table 9.10 are, on the whole, encouraging. For $\rho_1 = .05$, the net pre-tax return ($r - \delta P_k$) is more than double the social time preference rate (.1125 vs. .05) and the losses from crowding out domestic capital are considerable. Nevertheless, lower underemployment plus the taxes paid by foreign capital are sufficient to produce a welfare gain when $\kappa = .19-.38$. It is a bit disconcerting, however, that

Table 9.9a. *Impact effect on domestic investment (dI$_d$/dI$_f$ at t = 0) when foreign firms are required to export 25% of their output.**

	$c_m = .25, \alpha = .25, \theta_L^m = .30$					
	Value of τ					
β	.25	.5	.75	1	1.5	σ^m
.15	−.20	−.05	.08	.19	.39	.25
	−.23	−.12	−.02	.07	.23	.50
	−.25	−.18	−.11	−.05	.08	1
.50	−.31	−.24	−.18	−.11	.004	.25
	−.30	−.25	−.19	−.14	−.03	.50
	−.29	−.25	−.21	−.17	−.08	1
1.50	−.34	−.33	−.31	−.28	−.23	.25
	−.33	−.32	−.30	−.28	−.23	.50
.	−.31	−.31	−.29	−.27	−.23	1

	$c_m = .50, \alpha = .50, \theta_L^m = .40$					
	Value of τ					
β	.25	.5	.75	1	1.5	σ^m
.15	−.04	.17	.36	.52	.81	.25
	−.09	.06	.20	.32	.55	.50
	−.11	−.03	.07	.15	.31	1
.50	−.20	−.09	.02	.11	.29	.25
	−.19	−.11	−.02	.07	.22	.50
	−.18	−.12	−.05	.01	.13	1
1.50	−.29	−.24	−.20	−.15	−.07	.25
	−.27	−.23	−.19	−.15	−.07	.50
.	−.24	−.21	−.18	−.14	−.07	1

* $\rho = .08, \delta = .05, b = .20$, and $\psi = .67$.

steady-state utility does not increase until the export requirement reaches 55–65%. The short-run/long-run tradeoff is still there when foreign firms export half of their output.

9.6 Joint Ventures

Joint ventures are appealing for at least three reasons. First, they are a natural way to address the concern that foreign capital might strongly

Table 9.9b. *Impact effect on domestic investment when foreign firms are required to export 50% of their output.**

	$c_m = .25, \alpha = .25, \theta_L^m = .30$					
			Value of τ			
β	.25	.5	.75	1	1.5	σ^m
.15	−.004	.17	.31	.44	.65	.25
	−.05	.09	.21	.31	.49	.50
	−.08	.02	.10	.18	.32	1
.50	−.15	−.05	.04	.11	.24	.25
	−.15	−.06	.01	.08	.20	.50
	−.14	−.07	−.01	.05	.15	1
1.50	−.22	−.18	−.14	−.10	−.03	.25
	−.21	−.17	−.13	−.10	−.03	.50
	−.20	−.16	−.13	−.09	−.03	1

	$c_m = .50, \alpha = .50, \theta_L^m = .40$					
			Value of τ			
β	.25	.5	.75	1	1.5	σ^m
.15	.15	.40	.61	.79	1.10	.25
	.07	.27	.43	.57	.82	.50
	.01	.15	.27	.38	.56	1
.50	−.05	.10	.23	.35	.54	.25
	−.06	.07	.19	.29	.46	.50
	−.06	.04	.13	.22	.36	1
1.50	−.18	−.11	−.04	.03	.14	.25
	−.17	−.10	−.03	.03	.13	.50
	−.15	−.08	−.03	.03	.12	1

* $\rho = .08, \delta = .05, b = .20$, and $\psi = .67$.

crowd out domestic capital. A priori, it is sensible to hope that the local equity contribution will not come entirely at the expense of domestic investment elsewhere in the economy. If so, joint ventures diminish crowding out. Second, when foreign capital earns a higher return than domestic capital, a joint venture ensures that domestic residents get a share of the rents. In principle, this can also be accomplished through taxation. But taxation will be ineffective if foreign

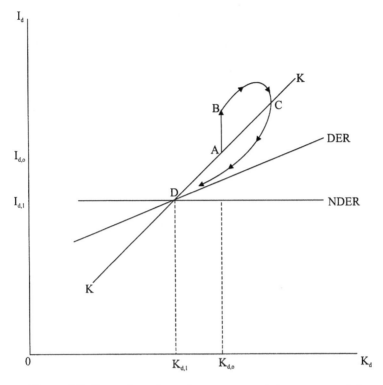

Figure 9.9. Dynamics when the government imposes a minimum export requirement and domestic investment increases initially.

firms can conceal profits through transfer pricing and other accounting tricks.[22] Third, joint ventures may serve as a vehicle for technology transfer. I ignore this because my aim is to isolate the effects of different ownership arrangements. Technology transfer will be analyzed in the next section.

[22] Greenaway emphasizes that local equity requirements can capture rents that would otherwise escape through transfer pricing (1992, pp. 154–155). Fried and Falvey (1986) analyze the connection between rent-shifting and local equity participation in a static model where control is assumed to change hands when the foreign subsidiary takes a domestic partner on board. (The foreign subsidiary maximizes its own profits when it is a joint venture. The parent company calls the shots, however, when it owns the entire operation.)

Table 9.10. *Value of the export requirement that leaves steady-state utility or welfare unchanged.**

		$c_m = .25, \alpha = .25, \theta_L^m = .30$			
β	Steady-state utility	$\rho_1 = .05$	$\rho_1 = .06$	$\rho_1 = .07$	τ
.15	.63	.37	.28	.16	.25
		.38	.29	.17	.50
		.38	.29	.17	1
.50	.63	.36	.26	.12	.25
		.37	.28	.15	.50
		.38	.28	.16	1
1.50	.63	.31	.18	—	.25
		.35	.24	.09	.50
		.37	.27	.13	1

		$c_m = .50, \alpha = .50, \theta_L^m = .40$			
β	Steady-state utility	$\rho_1 = .05$	$\rho_1 = .06$	$\rho_1 = .07$	τ
.15	.55	.28	.20	.10	.25
		.29	.21	.11	.50
		.29	.22	.12	1
.50	.55	.26	.17	.05	.25
		.28	.20	.09	.50
		.29	.21	.11	1
1.50	.55	.19	.05	—	.25
		.25	.15	.01	.50
		.28	.19	.08	1

* $\rho = .08$, $\delta = .05$, $b = .20$, $\psi = .67$, and $\sigma^m = .50$. In the two cases where $\beta = 1.5$, $\tau = .25$, and $\rho_1 = .07$, there is no entry because welfare improves in the absence of an export requirement.

9.6.1   Joint Ventures in the Domestic Manufacturing Sector

There is no point in a joint venture if the isoquant map is the same for domestic and foreign firms. I assume therefore that foreign technology is superior.[23] The return on foreign capital is $r_f > r$ and the labor inten-

[23] Estimates from panel data sets show multifactor productivity to be higher in joint ventures than in domestically owned plants in Morocco and Venezuela (Haddad and Harrison, 1993; Harrison, 1996).

sity and capital–output ratios may differ at domestic and foreign plants. Many of the changes in the model are thus the same as in the case where the government imposes an export requirement (which results in $r_f < r$, $a_f \neq a_m$, and $l_f \neq l_m$ even though foreign and domestic firms operate with the same technology set). The new element in the analysis is that part of domestic investment is tied to foreign investment in the joint venture. This can be handled by altering the definitions for a few variables. Let μ be the ratio of domestic to foreign equity in the joint venture, I_d and K_d be investment and capital in plants owned *entirely* by domestic residents, I_f and K_f be investment and capital owned by foreign firms, and Q_f be output at the jointly owned plant. The model is then virtually the same as in Section 9.5. The only changes occur in (5′), (13′), (15′), and (44). Total investment and capital in the joint venture are $(1 + \mu)I_f$ and $(1 + \mu)K_f$, and investment and capital owned by domestic residents are $I_d + \mu I_f$ and $K_d + \mu K_f$, so these equations are replaced by

$$D^m(P_m, E) + a_1[I_d + (1+\mu)I_f] = Q_m + Q_f, \tag{5″}$$

$$E + P_k(I_d + \mu I_f) = R[P_m, K_d, (1+\mu)K_f, L_m + L_f] + J \\ - b(rK_d + r_f \mu K_f) - r_f K_f, \tag{13″}$$

$$J = b[rK_d + r_f(1+\mu)K_f], \tag{15″}$$

$$(1+\mu)K_f = C_r^f(w_m, r_f)Q_f. \tag{44′}$$

9.6.1.1   THE STEADY-STATE OUTCOME

At the new stationary equilibrium,

$$\Delta\frac{dK}{dK_f} = (1+\mu)\frac{\theta_L^m}{\theta_K^m}\left(1 - \frac{\ell_f}{\ell_m}\right)(c_x + c_m\psi) - (r_f/r - 1)$$

$$(1+\mu c_x - c_m b) - \frac{c_m\rho(1-b)}{\rho+\delta}, \tag{47}$$

$$\frac{du}{r} = \left[\mu\left(\frac{r_f}{r} - 1\right) + \frac{r_f}{r}b + (1+\mu)(1-\psi)\frac{\theta_L^m}{\theta_K^m}\left(\frac{\ell_f}{\ell_m} - 1\right)\right. \\ \left. - \frac{\rho+\delta b}{\rho+\delta}\right]dK_f + \left[\frac{\rho+\delta b}{\rho+\delta} + (1-\psi)\frac{\theta_L^m}{\theta_K^m}\right]dK. \tag{48}$$

The terms involving $(r_f/r - 1)$ and $(\ell_f/\ell_m - 1)$ are related. Note from the zero-profit conditions

$$P_m Q_m = rK_d + w_m L_m$$

$$P_m Q_f = r_f(1+\mu)K_f + w_m L_f$$

that

$$\frac{r_f}{r} - 1 = \frac{a_f - a_m}{r} - \frac{\theta_L^m}{\theta_K^m}\left(\frac{\ell_f}{\ell_m} - 1\right), \tag{49}$$

where, to repeat, a_f and a_m are the output–capital ratios in the joint venture and domestic manufacturing. Equation (49) indicates that the higher return on foreign capital reflects either $a_f > a_m$ or $\ell_f < \ell_m$. To highlight the key points while avoiding excessive taxonomy, I restrict the analysis to the cases where $a_f = a_m$, $\ell_f = \ell_m$, or $\ell_f > \ell_m$.

Domestic and Foreign Technology are Equally Labor Intensive ($\ell_f = \ell_m$)[24]

Consider first the case in which domestic and joint venture plants are equally labor-intensive. The first term in (47) then drops out and

$$\Delta\frac{dK}{dK_f} = -(r_f/r - 1)(1 + \mu c_x - c_m b) - \frac{c_m \rho(1-b)}{\rho + \delta}. \tag{47'}$$

There is *more* crowding out than in the benchmark case because foreign capital produces more output than domestic capital ($a_f > a_m$): replacing one unit of domestic capital by one unit of foreign capital increases supply and drives down P_m and r. (Both supply and demand effects shift the MM curve downward in Figure 9.2.) For the same reason, crowding out is greater per unit of foreign capital when domestic and foreign firms collaborate in a joint venture. This result, however, is somewhat artificial, for while the stock of domestically owned capital decreases more, ownership of capital *services* ($r_d K_d + \mu r_f K_f$) decreases less.

The distinction between the capital stock and the services it provides is relevant to the interpretation of crowding out but not to the impact of joint ventures on labor demand in manufacturing. Since the aggregate

---

[24] The empirical evidence on ℓ_f vs. ℓ_m is mixed. There is certainly no systematic tendency for production at foreign-owned plants to be more capital-intensive than production at domestically owned plants (Pack, 1979; Casson and Pearce, 1987). Pack argues that, *ceteris paribus*, foreign firms would be expected to use more labor-intensive technology than domestic firms and points out that plant-level studies support this conjecture.

capital stock falls more, so also does high-wage employment. Despite this, participation in the joint venture is welfare-improving. The solution for steady-state utility,

$$
\begin{aligned}
\frac{du}{dK_f} = & -\left[\frac{\rho+\delta b}{\rho+\delta}+(1-\psi)\frac{\theta_L^m}{\theta_K^m}\right]\left[\frac{c_m\rho(1-b)}{\rho+\delta}+(r_f/r-1)(1-c_m b)\right] \\
& +\left(\frac{r_f b}{r}-\frac{\rho+\delta b}{\rho+\delta}\right)\left[c_x+\frac{\delta}{\rho+\delta}(1-b)(c_m-\alpha)+\frac{\theta_L^m}{\theta_K^m}(c_x+c_m\psi)\right] \\
& +\mu\left(\frac{r_f}{r}-1\right)\left[\frac{\delta(1-b)}{\rho+\delta}(1-\alpha)+\frac{\theta_L^m}{\theta_K^m}\psi\right],
\end{aligned}
\tag{50}
$$

is increasing in μ; thus, the direct gain from partnership in the high-return project always dominates the losses from greater underemployment.[25]

Same Output–Capital Ratio at Domestic and Foreign Plants ($a_f = a_m$)
For $a_f = a_m$, equations (47) and (49) give

$$
\frac{dK}{dK_f} = \frac{c_m}{\Delta}\left\{\left(\frac{r_f}{r}-1\right)[b+\psi(1+\mu)-1]-\frac{\rho(1-b)}{\rho+\delta}\right\}.
\tag{51}
$$

In this case, foreign technology is superior because it uses less labor per unit of output. When one unit of capital in the joint venture replaces one unit of domestic capital, the supply of manufactures does not change but labor demand contracts ($\ell_f < \ell_m$). This benefits the home economy to the extent that labor released from manufacturing finds productive employment in the primary export sector. The first term is most likely to be positive therefore when the sectoral wage gap is small (when ψ is large). Moreover, the joint venture requirement works to reduce crowding out. In fact, it will often determine whether there is more or less crowding out than in the benchmark case. For $\mu = 0$, the first term is positive if $\psi > 1 - b$. This condition would *not* be expected to hold as estimates of the formal sector wage premium place ψ somewhere between .5 and .8. But when the share of local equity in the joint venture is 50% ($\mu = 1$), the condition is $\psi > (1 - b)/2$, which holds even for values of ψ below .5. Thus, the gain from saving

---

[25] The solution in (50) is for steady-state utility. But since the private agent eats part of the capital stock on the way to the steady state, there is also a positive relationship between welfare and the local equity requirement. This will be confirmed later by the welfare results in Tables 9.13 and 9.14.

Table 9.11. *Value of γ for which the aggregate capital stock is unchanged across steady states when the capital–output ratio is the same at domestic and foreign plants.* *

ψ	$\mu = 1$	$\mu = 2$	$\mu = 3$
.50	Decreases always	Decreases always	1.59
.67	Decreases always	1.59	1.38
.80	1.89	1.44	1.30

* $\rho = .08$, $\delta = .05$, $\theta_L^m = .40$, and $b = .20$. The cost share of labor affects the solution only insofar as it limits the range of values for γ that are consistent with $\ell_f > 0$. "Decreases always" means that the value of γ that leaves the aggregate capital stock unchanged is inconsistent with positive employment in the joint venture.

on labor use in manufacturing will normally exceed the cost of making higher payments to foreign capital. [When $\psi = 0$, there is no benefit from labor saving and the extra income loss relative to the benchmark case is $(r_f/r - 1)(b - 1)$.]

While the gain from labor saving helps, it is not large enough to prevent a decrease in the aggregate capital stock unless foreign capital earns a much higher return than domestic capital and the share of local equity $[1/(1 + \mu)]$ is large. Table 9.11 shows the ratio of the net pre-tax return on foreign vs. domestic capital $[\gamma \equiv (r_f - \delta P_k)/(r - \delta P_k)]$ for which K is unchanged.[26] The ratio lies between 1.3 and 1.89 in six cases, and in the other three cases K always decreases. More than 100% crowding out is still the rule, not the exception.

The long-run effects on underemployment and utility are qualitatively similar to the effects in the case where domestic plants and joint ventures are equally labor-intensive. Across steady states,

[26] In this and later tables, μ lies between one and three. These are the values most commonly observed. India has long restricted the share of foreign ownership to 40%. In Malaysia, most FI takes the form of joint ventures, with majority local ownership required for investment in the domestic market and a local equity share of at least 70% for projects involving exploitation of natural resources (Ariff and Lim, 1987, p. 109). (Recently, restrictions on foreign ownership have been relaxed somewhat in both India and Malaysia.) Sri Lanka requires 75% local ownership for FI outside the free trade zone (Wanigatunga, 1987, p. 148). Joint ventures that call for domestic and foreign partners to put up equal shares are also fairly common.

$$\frac{\Delta}{\ell_m}\frac{d(L_m+L_f)}{dK_f} = -\frac{c_m(1-b)}{\rho+\delta}[r_f(1-b)-\delta]-(1+\mu)(r_f/r-1)$$

$$\times\left\{\frac{\theta_K^m}{\theta_L^m(\rho+\delta)}(c_x\rho+\delta[bc_x+(1-b)(1-\alpha)])+c_x\right\}, \quad (52)$$

$$\frac{\Delta}{r}\frac{du}{dK_f} = \underbrace{\left\{(r_f/r-1)[b+\psi(1+\mu)-1]-\frac{\rho(1-b)}{\rho+\delta}\right\}}_{\text{sign of } dK/dK_f}$$

$$\times\left\{1+\frac{c_m}{\Delta}\left[\frac{\rho+\delta b}{\rho+\delta}+(1-\psi)\frac{\theta_L^m}{\theta_K^m}\right]\right\} \quad (53)$$

Once again, high-wage employment decreases more than in the benchmark case, but the joint venture requirement exerts a positive effect on welfare.

Foreign Technology Is More Labor-Intensive ($\ell_f > \ell_m$)

Swapping one unit of domestic capital for one unit of foreign capital increases employment in the formal sector when $\ell_f > \ell_m$. More labor-intensive foreign technology also goes together with higher output per unit of capital at foreign plants and more crowding out of domestic investment [see (47)]. This weakens but does not fully offset the direct favorable effect on labor demand:

$$\frac{\Delta}{\ell_m}\frac{d(L_m+L_f)}{dK_f} = \frac{(\ell_f/\ell_m-1)(1+\mu)}{\rho+\delta}[(\rho+\delta b)c_x+\delta(1-b)(1-\alpha)]$$

$$-(r_f/r-1)(1+\mu c_x-c_mb)-\frac{c_m\rho(1-b)}{\rho+\delta}. \quad (54)$$

For any given spread between the returns on foreign and domestic capital, there is a positive relationship between ℓ_f/ℓ_m and the number of jobs in the formal sector. Consequently, FI may reduce underemployment in both the short and the long run. This requires, however, fairly large values for ℓ_f/ℓ_m, especially when foreign capital earns a high return and the equity share of the domestic partner is small. Table 9.12 shows how these two variables affect the value of ℓ_f/ℓ_m that keeps L_m at its pre-FI level. The borderline value jumps from 1.29 for $\mu = 3$ and $\gamma = 1.2$ to 1.53–1.83 when $\gamma = 1.4 - 1.6$ and $\mu = 1$. The latter numbers seem discouragingly high.[27]

[27] Unlike in the previous two cases, it cannot be proven that participation in the joint venture raises steady-state utility. There is, nevertheless, a strong presumption that the joint venture is in the national interest. In the results presented later in Table 9.16c, welfare always increases with the local equity share μ.

Table 9.12. *Value of ℓ_t/ℓ_m for which high-wage employment is unchanged across steady states when the high-wage sector is large.**

γ	$\mu = 1$	$\mu = 2$	$\mu = 3$
1.2	1.44	1.33	1.29
1.4	1.63	1.51	1.46
1.6	1.83	1.69	1.62
1.8	2.02	1.87	1.79

* $\rho = .08$, $\delta = .05$, and $b = .20$.

9.6.1.2   THE TRANSITION PATH

The transition path looks much like the path in the benchmark case of plain vanilla FI. A few differences are worth noting, however:

- Temporary crowding in virtually disappears when $\ell_f \geq \ell_m$ and the net return in the joint venture is 20% or more above the net domestic return ($\gamma \geq 1.2$). This is to be expected. The paths for the price of the manufactured good and the capital rental are continuously lower and the private agent anticipates higher future income relative to the benchmark case. Both factors increase the likelihood of an immediate decrease in domestic investment spending ($I_d + \mu I_f$).
- In the case where the superiority of foreign technology derives from labor saving ($\ell_f < \ell_m$ and $a_f = a_m$), the aggregate capital stock may exceed its pre-FI level for a much longer period of time, but the initial phase of higher employment in manufacturing is always very short-lived. Compare the results in Table 9.13 with those in Table 9.2 for $c_m = \alpha = .50$, $\theta_L^m = .40$, and $\sigma^m = .50$. Although K is higher for an additional 7–20 years when $\mu = 2, 3$, crowding out of labor-intensive domestic production by capital-intensive production in the joint venture worsens underemployment in just one to four years. By contrast, employment in manufacturing is higher for 16–32 years when $\beta = .5$, 1.5 and FI is the plain vanilla variety.
- The opposite pattern of short-lived increases in the aggregate capital stock and longer lived decreases in underemployment obtains when foreign plants are significantly more labor-intensive than domestic plants. In 26 of the 27 cases in Table 9.14, the aggregate capital stock falls below its initial level within six years. Nevertheless, employment is higher in the formal sector for 11–24 years when $\beta = .50$ and for 19–54 years when $\beta = 1.50$.

Table 9.13. *Length of time that the aggregate capital stock and high-wage employment exceed their pre-FI levels when γ = 1.3, the high-wage sector is large, and the capital–output ratio is the same at domestic and foreign plants.*

	K			L_m			
β	$\tau = .25$	$\tau = .5$	$\tau = 1$	$\tau = .25$	$\tau = .5$	$\tau = 1$	μ
.15	22.5	17.7	15.0	3.44	3.44	3.41	1
	27.6	22.5	19.6	2.84	2.81	2.77	2
	39.5	34.1	31.0	2.42	2.39	2.34	3
.50	29.1	21.5	17.1	3.15	3.14	3.16	1
	34.6	26.6	21.9	2.25	2.27	2.31	2
	47.4	38.5	33.4	1.74	1.76	1.81	3
1.50	45.1	30.9	22.5	2.63	2.53	2.54	1
	51.6	36.6	27.7	1.37	1.39	1.46	2
	66.8	49.7	39.8	.92	.94	1.00	3

* $\rho = .08$, $\delta = .05$, $b = .20$, $\psi = .67$, and $\sigma^m = .50$. For $\gamma = 1.3$, $\ell_f/\ell_m = .688$.

Table 9.14. *Length of time that the aggregate capital stock and high-wage employment exceed their pre-FI levels when γ = 1.3, the high-wage sector is large, and foreign technology is 30% more labor-intensive than domestic technology ($\ell_f/\ell_m = 1.3$).*

	K			L_m			
β	$\tau = .25$	$\tau = .5$	$\tau = 1$	$\tau = .25$	$\tau = .5$	$\tau = 1$	μ
.15	4.4	3.4	3.2	7.6	8.3	9.0	1
	1.0	1.1	1.6	8.5	9.6	10.5	2
	0	0	.4	9.8	11.4	12.8	3
.50	5.6	3.7	3.1	15.8	13.3	11.8	1
	.7	.5	.9	19.4	16.0	14.1	2
	0	0	0	24.3	19.8	17.3	3
1.50	10.1	5.5	3.5	39.7	26.8	19.3	1
	1.3	0	0	46.4	31.7	22.9	2
	0	0	0	54.5	37.8	27.7	3

* $\rho = .08$, $\delta = .05$, $b = .20$, $\psi = .67$, and $\sigma^m = .50$. The zeroes in some of the entries for K indicate that greater than 100% crowding out of domestic investment occurs immediately at time $t = 0$.

9.6.1.3   WELFARE

Joint ventures may be the difference between FI that helps and FI that hurts. Turning back to the solutions in (47′), (51), and (52), note that when $\mu = 0$ (no local equity contribution) high-wage employment and the aggregate capital stock decrease more the more productive is FI.[28] The welfare losses in Table 9.15 are often therefore considerably larger than in the benchmark variant of the model. But if the LDC gets a decent share of the high returns produced by superior foreign technology, these large losses may be replaced by gains. Tables 9.16a–9.16c show the value of γ (the ratio of the net pre-tax return in the joint venture to the net pre-tax return on domestic capital) that leaves welfare unchanged when domestic residents subscribe 50–75% of the capital in the joint venture. The prospects for an overall welfare gain are quite good when the social time preference rate lies within three percentage points of the private rate, the labor market is not too highly distorted ($\psi = .67$), and the local equity share is 67–75% ($\mu = 2, 3$). Elsewhere, however, the results are less favorable. The borderline value of γ is frequently 1.4 or larger when $\mu = 1$ and (i) $\rho_1 \leq .06$ or (ii) $\psi = .50$ and $a_f = a_m$ (the lower panel in Table 9.16b). And regardless of the panel and the table, there is not much hope of avoiding a decrease in steady-state utility.

9.6.2   *Joint Ventures in an Export Enclave*

Employment in the high-wage manufacturing sector and the domestic capital stock both increase more in the long run when the export enclave is a joint venture instead of a wholly foreign-owned operation. (The upward shift of the *MM* schedule is larger in Figure 9.4.) The numerical solutions also confirm that the welfare gains are invariably larger for the joint venture. What needs investigation is the dynamics. In the short run, is domestic investment in the export enclave financed by higher saving or by lower investment in the high-wage manufacturing sector? If investment in the enclave temporarily crowds out investment in manufacturing, how long does the capital stock in the manufacturing sector remain depressed? Might temporary capital decumulation in manufacturing result in a lengthy period of higher underemployment?

Before looking at the answers in Tables 9.17 and 9.18 it will be helpful to review the factors that influence domestic investment in the benchmark case. Recall that the tension in the dynamics centers around two conflicting effects: the higher profit stream, which tends to increase

---

[28] This statement assumes that $\psi < 1 - b$ in the case where $a_f = a_m$.

Table 9.15. *Impact on domestic welfare measured as the annual equivalent return per dollar of FI when foreign firms earn a higher return than domestic firms and there is no joint venture (FI in manufacturing).**

	Domestic and foreign plants are equally labor-intensive ($\ell_f = \ell_m$)								
	$\gamma = 1.3$				$\gamma = 1.5$				
β	$\rho_1 = .05$	$\rho_1 = .06$	$\rho_1 = .07$	$\rho_1 = .08$	$\rho_1 = .05$	$\rho_1 = .06$	$\rho_1 = .07$	$\rho_1 = .08$	τ
.15	−43.3	−26.3	−12.7	−1.9	−49.6	−31.0	−16.2	−4.3	.25
	−46.4	−28.8	−14.6	−3.1	−53.1	−33.8	−18.3	−5.7	.50
	−48.1	−30.1	−15.7	−3.8	−55.0	−35.3	−19.4	−6.4	1
.50	−36.0	−19.8	−7.3	2.6	−41.4	−23.8	−10.0	.9	.25
	−42.3	−25.1	−11.6	−.7	−48.4	−29.6	−14.7	−2.8	.50
	−46.0	−28.3	−14.2	−2.7	−52.6	−33.2	−17.7	−5.1	1
1.50	−20.9	−7.1	3.3	11.3	−24.7	−9.6	1.8	10.6	.25
	−32.2	−16.4	−4.2	5.4	−37.2	−19.9	−6.5	4.0	.50
	−40.1	−23.2	−9.8	.9	−45.9	−27.4	−12.7	−.9	1

	Domestic and foreign plants have the same capital output ratio ($a_f = a_m$)								
	$\gamma = 1.3$				$\gamma = 1.5$				
β	$\rho_1 = .05$	$\rho_1 = .06$	$\rho_1 = .07$	$\rho_1 = .08$	$\rho_1 = .05$	$\rho_1 = .06$	$\rho_1 = .07$	$\rho_1 = .08$	τ
.15	−39.2	−24.0	−11.9	−2.2	−42.8	−27.1	−14.8	−4.9	.25
	−41.9	−26.1	−13.5	−3.3	−45.6	−29.4	−16.5	−6.0	.50
	−43.4	−27.3	−14.4	−3.9	−47.1	−30.6	−17.4	−6.6	1
.50	−32.8	−18.4	−7.2	1.6	−36.2	−21.4	−9.9	−.9	.25
	−38.4	−23.1	−11.0	−1.3	−41.9	−26.2	−13.8	−3.8	.50
	−41.7	−25.8	−13.2	−3.1	−45.3	−29.1	−16.1	−5.7	1
1.50	−19.6	−7.3	2.0	9.0	−22.6	−9.9	−.4	6.8	.25
	−29.6	−15.5	−4.7	3.8	−32.9	−18.4	−7.3	1.5	.50
	−36.6	−21.4	−9.5	−.04	−40.0	−24.5	−12.3	−2.5	1

	Foreign technology is 30% more labor-intensive than domestic technology ($\ell_f = 1.3\,\ell_m$)								
	$\gamma = 1.3$				$\gamma = 1.5$				
β	$\rho_1 = .05$	$\rho_1 = .06$	$\rho_1 = .07$	$\rho_1 = .08$	$\rho_1 = .05$	$\rho_1 = .06$	$\rho_1 = .07$	$\rho_1 = .08$	τ
.15	−47.3	−28.5	−13.6	−1.5	−53.6	−33.2	−17.0	−3.9	.25
	−50.8	−31.3	−15.7	−3.0	−57.4	−36.3	−19.3	−5.5	.50
	−52.7	−32.8	−16.8	−3.8	−59.5	−38.0	−20.6	−6.4	1
.50	−39.0	−21.2	−7.3	−3.7	−44.4	−25.1	−10.0	1.9	.25
	−46.0	−27.1	−12.1	−.03	−52.1	−31.6	−15.3	−2.2	.50
	−50.2	−30.7	−15.1	−2.4	−56.8	−35.6	−18.6	−4.7	1
1.50	−22.2	−6.9	4.6	13.5	−26.0	−9.4	3.2	12.8	.25
	−34.7	−17.3	−3.8	6.9	−39.7	−20.8	−6.1	5.5	.50
	−43.5	−24.8	−10.0	1.8	−49.4	−29.0	−13.0	−.04	1

* $\rho = .08$, $\delta = .05$, $b = .20$, $\psi = .67$, and $\sigma^m = .50$.

Table 9.16a. *Value of γ for which steady-state utility (u$_{ss}$) and welfare are unchanged when the high-wage sector is large and domestic and foreign plants are equally labor-intensive (joint venture in manufacturing).**

ψ = .67

β	u$_{ss}$	μ = 1 ρ$_1$ = .05	μ = 1 ρ$_1$ = .06	μ = 1 ρ$_1$ = .07	u$_{ss}$	μ = 2 ρ$_1$ = .05	μ = 2 ρ$_1$ = .06	μ = 2 ρ$_1$ = .07	u$_{ss}$	μ = 3 ρ$_1$ = .05	μ = 3 ρ$_1$ = .06	μ = 3 ρ$_1$ = .07	τ
.15	↓always	1.72	1.38	1.14	2.82	1.27	1.15	1.06	1.90	1.17	1.10	1.04	.25
		1.79	1.42	1.17		1.29	1.17	1.07		1.18	1.11	1.05	.50
		1.83	1.45	1.19		1.30	1.18	1.08		1.18	1.11	1.05	1
.50	↓always	1.57	1.26	1.06	2.82	1.22	1.11	1.03	1.90	1.14	1.07	1.02	.25
		1.70	1.36	1.12		1.26	1.15	1.05		1.16	1.09	1.03	.50
		1.78	1.42	1.17		1.29	1.17	1.07		1.18	1.11	1.05	1
1.50	↓always	1.29	1.06	+	2.82	1.12	1.03	+	1.90	1.08	1.02	+	.25
		1.49	1.21	1.01		1.20	1.09	1.01		1.12	1.06	1.004	.50
		1.65	1.32	1.10		1.25	1.13	1.04		1.16	1.08	1.03	1

ψ = .50

β	u$_{ss}$	μ = 1 ρ$_1$ = .05	μ = 1 ρ$_1$ = .06	μ = 1 ρ$_1$ = .07	u$_{ss}$	μ = 2 ρ$_1$ = .05	μ = 2 ρ$_1$ = .06	μ = 2 ρ$_1$ = .07	u$_{ss}$	μ = 3 ρ$_1$ = .05	μ = 3 ρ$_1$ = .06	μ = 3 ρ$_1$ = .07	τ
.15	↓always	2.48	1.67	1.24	5.28	1.38	1.21	1.08	2.46	1.22	1.13	1.05	.25
		2.65	1.76	1.28		1.41	1.23	1.10		1.23	1.14	1.06	.50
		2.76	1.81	1.30		1.42	1.24	1.11		1.24	1.14	1.06	1
.50	↓always	1.98	1.40	1.07	5.28	1.29	1.14	1.03	2.46	1.17	1.08	1.02	.25
		2.32	1.58	1.18		1.36	1.19	1.07		1.21	1.11	1.04	.50
		2.57	1.71	1.25		1.40	1.22	1.09		1.23	1.13	1.06	1
1.50	↓always	1.34	1.01	+	5.28	1.12	1.005	+	2.46	1.08	1.003	+	.25
		1.75	1.26	+		1.24	1.10	+		1.14	1.06	+	.50
		2.15	1.49	1.12		1.33	1.17	1.05		1.19	1.10	1.03	1

* ρ = .08, δ = .05, b = .20, ψ = .67, and σ^m = .50. A plus sign indicates that welfare increases in the benchmark model.

Table 9.16b. *Value of γ for which steady-state utility (u$_{ss}$) and welfare are unchanged when the high-wage sector is large and domestic and foreign plants have the same capital–output ratio (joint venture in manufacturing).*

ψ = .67

β	u$_{ss}$	μ = 1 ρ₁ = .05	ρ₁ = .06	ρ₁ = .07	u$_{ss}$	μ = 2 ρ₁ = .05	ρ₁ = .06	ρ₁ = .07	u$_{ss}$	μ = 3 ρ₁ = .05	ρ₁ = .06	ρ₁ = .07	τ
.15	↓always	1.46	1.29	1.13	1.59	1.20	1.13	1.06	1.38	1.13	1.08	1.04	.25
		1.48	1.32	1.15		1.21	1.14	1.07		1.14	1.09	1.04	.50
		1.49	1.33	1.16		1.22	1.15	1.07		1.14	1.09	1.05	1
.50	↓always	1.40	1.22	1.06	1.59	1.18	1.10	1.03	1.38	1.11	1.06	1.02	.25
		1.45	1.28	1.12		1.20	1.13	1.05		1.13	1.08	1.03	.50
		1.48	1.31	1.15		1.21	1.14	1.07		1.14	1.09	1.04	1
1.50	↓always	1.25	1.06	+	1.59	1.11	1.03	+	1.38	1.07	1.02	+	.25
		1.37	1.19	1.01		1.16	1.08	1.01		1.11	1.05	1.004	.50
		1.44	1.26	1.10		1.20	1.12	1.04		1.13	1.08	1.03	1

ψ = .50

β	u$_{ss}$	μ = 1 ρ₁ = .05	ρ₁ = .06	ρ₁ = .07	u$_{ss}$	μ = 2 ρ₁ = .05	ρ₁ = .06	ρ₁ = .07	u$_{ss}$	μ = 3 ρ₁ = .05	ρ₁ = .06	ρ₁ = .07	τ
.15	↓always	↓always	1.80	1.36	↓always	1.36	1.23	1.10		1.21	1.13	1.06	.25
			1.86	1.41		1.37	1.24	1.12		1.22	1.14	1.07	.50
			1.88	1.44		1.38	1.25	1.13		1.22	1.15	1.07	1
.50	↓always	↓always	1.58	1.12	↓always	1.30	1.16	1.03		1.18	1.10	1.02	.25
			1.75	1.30		1.35	1.21	1.08		1.20	1.12	1.05	.50
			1.84	1.40		1.37	1.24	1.11		1.22	1.14	1.07	1
1.50	↓always	1.55	1.02	+	↓always	1.16	1.01	+		1.09	1.004	+	.25
		1.93	1.43	+		1.27	1.12	+		1.16	1.07	+	.50
		↓always	1.68	1.22		1.33	1.19	1.06		1.19	1.11	1.04	1

* ρ = .08, δ = .05, b = .20, ψ = .67, and σᵐ = .50. A plus sign indicates that welfare increases in the benchmark model.

345

Table 9.16c. Value of γ for which steady-state utility (u_{ss}) and welfare are unchanged when the high-wage sector is large and foreign technology is 30% more labor-intensive than domestic technology ($\ell_f = 1.3\ell_m$; joint venture in manufacturing).*

$\psi = .67$

β	u_{ss}	$\mu = 1$ $\rho_1 = .05$	$\rho_1 = .06$	$\rho_1 = .07$	u_{ss}	$\mu = 2$ $\rho_1 = .05$	$\rho_1 = .06$	$\rho_1 = .07$	u_{ss}	$\mu = 3$ $\rho_1 = .05$	$\rho_1 = .06$	$\rho_1 = .07$	τ
.15	↓always	1.89	1.47	1.17	3.42	1.37	1.21	1.08	2.30	1.24	1.14	1.06	.25
		1.98	1.53	1.21		1.39	1.23	1.10		1.26	1.16	1.07	.50
		2.03	1.56	1.23		1.41	1.24	1.11		1.27	1.17	1.07	1
.50	↓always	1.69	1.32	1.06	3.42	1.29	1.14	1.03	2.30	1.20	1.10	1.02	.25
		1.86	1.44	1.14		1.35	1.19	1.07		1.24	1.13	1.05	.50
		1.97	1.51	1.20		1.39	1.23	1.09		1.26	1.15	1.06	1
1.50	↓always	1.33	1.05	+	3.42	1.15	1.02	+	2.30	1.10	1.01	+	.25
		1.59	1.24	1		1.26	1.11	1		1.17	1.07	1	.50
		1.80	1.39	1.11		1.33	1.17	1.05		1.22	1.12	1.03	1

$\psi = .50$

β	u_{ss}	$\mu = 1$ $\rho_1 = .05$	$\rho_1 = .06$	$\rho_1 = .07$	u_{ss}	$\mu = 2$ $\rho_1 = .05$	$\rho_1 = .06$	$\rho_1 = .07$	u_{ss}	$\mu = 3$ $\rho_1 = .05$	$\rho_1 = .06$	$\rho_1 = .07$	τ
.15	↓always	2.53	1.63	1.14	6.21	1.40	1.19	1.03	2.88	1.24	1.11	1.01	.25
		2.73	1.72	1.19		1.44	1.22	1.05		1.26	1.12	1.02	.50
		2.86	1.78	1.21		1.46	1.23	1.06		1.27	1.13	1.03	1
.50	↓always	1.96	1.31	1	6.21	1.28	1.09	1	2.88	1.16	1.05	1	.25
		2.35	1.52	1.06		1.37	1.16	1		1.22	1.09	1	.50
		2.63	1.67	1.15		1.42	1.20	1.04		1.25	1.12	1.01	1
1.50	↓always	1.23	1	+	6.21	1.07	1	+	2.88	1.03	1	+	.25
		1.70	1.15	+		1.22	1.03	+		1.12	1.01	+	.50
		2.14	1.40	1		1.33	1.12	1		1.19	1.07	1	1

* $\rho = .08$, $\delta = .05$, $b = .20$, $\psi = .67$, and $\sigma^m = .50$. A plus sign indicates that welfare increases in the benchmark model.

Table 9.17a. *Impact effect on total domestic investment spending when η = 1 (joint venture in an export enclave).**

$c_m = .25$, $\alpha = .25$, $\theta_L^m = .30$

β		μ = 1				μ = 2				μ = 3			σ^m
	τ = .25	τ = .50	τ = .75	τ = 1	τ = .25	τ = .50	τ = .75	τ = 1	τ = .25	τ = .50	τ = .75	τ = 1	
.15	1.18	1.51	1.72	1.90	1.97	2.40	2.67	2.87	2.77	3.30	3.62	3.85	.25
	1.03	1.34	1.54	1.70	1.76	2.18	2.44	2.63	2.48	3.03	3.34	3.57	.50
	.83	1.13	1.32	1.46	1.46	1.89	2.15	2.33	2.09	2.66	2.98	3.21	1
.50	.83	1.11	1.28	1.42	1.48	1.88	2.12	2.29	2.14	2.65	2.96	3.17	.25
	.77	1.04	1.21	1.34	1.38	1.78	2.02	2.20	2.00	2.52	2.83	3.05	.50
	.66	.93	1.10	1.23	1.21	1.62	1.86	2.03	1.76	2.30	2.62	2.84	1
1.50	.51	.74	.88	.99	.99	1.34	1.56	1.72	1.48	1.95	2.25	2.45	.25
	.48	.71	.86	.97	.95	1.30	1.52	1.68	1.41	1.90	2.19	2.40	.50
	.43	.66	.81	.92	.86	1.23	1.45	1.61	1.29	1.79	2.09	2.30	1

$c_m = .25$, $\alpha = .50$, $\theta_L^m = .30$

β		μ = 1				μ = 2				μ = 3			σ^m
	τ = .25	τ = .50	τ = .75	τ = 1	τ = .25	τ = .50	τ = .75	τ = 1	τ = .25	τ = .50	τ = .75	τ = 1	
.15	1.77	2.21	2.45	2.59	2.96	3.65	4.00	4.22	4.16	5.08	5.55	5.85	.25
	1.54	2.00	2.26	2.42	2.60	3.32	3.71	3.96	3.66	4.64	5.16	5.50	.50
	1.23	1.70	1.97	2.16	2.11	2.85	3.27	3.56	2.99	3.99	4.57	4.95	1
.50	1.21	1.65	1.91	2.10	2.10	2.79	3.19	3.47	2.99	3.93	4.47	4.85	.25
	1.11	1.54	1.81	2.00	1.94	2.62	3.04	3.32	2.76	3.70	4.26	4.65	.50
	.95	1.38	1.65	1.84	1.67	2.35	2.77	3.07	2.39	3.33	3.90	4.30	1
1.50	.69	1.05	1.29	1.47	1.28	1.85	2.23	2.51	1.88	2.66	3.17	3.55	.25
	.66	1.01	1.25	1.43	1.22	1.79	2.16	2.44	1.79	2.57	3.08	3.46	.50
	.59	.94	1.18	1.35	1.10	1.67	2.04	2.32	1.62	2.40	2.91	3.30	1

347

Table 9.17a. (cont.)

$c_m = .50$, $\alpha = .25$, $\theta_L^m = .40$

β	μ=1				μ=2				μ=3				σ^m
	τ=.25	τ=.50	τ=.75	τ=1	τ=.25	τ=.50	τ=.75	τ=1	τ=.25	τ=.50	τ=.75	τ=1	
.15	.68	.80	.85	.88	1.09	1.18	1.20	1.19	1.51	1.57	1.54	1.50	.25
	.58	.73	.80	.84	.97	1.13	1.17	1.19	1.37	1.53	1.55	1.54	.50
	.44	.62	.70	.76	.77	1.01	1.10	1.14	1.11	1.39	1.49	1.53	1
.50	.53	.68	.75	.79	.95	1.11	1.17	1.19	1.36	1.54	1.59	1.59	.25
	.47	.63	.71	.76	.85	1.05	1.13	1.17	1.23	1.47	1.55	1.57	.50
	.37	.54	.64	.70	.69	.94	1.05	1.11	1.02	1.33	1.45	1.52	1
1.50	.35	.50	.58	.64	.71	.91	1.02	1.08	1.07	1.33	1.45	1.52	.25
	.32	.47	.56	.62	.65	.87	.98	1.05	.99	1.27	1.41	1.49	.50
	.26	.42	.51	.58	.55	.79	.91	.99	.85	1.16	1.32	1.41	1

$c_m = .50$, $\alpha = .50$, $\theta_L^m = .40$

β	μ=1				μ=2				μ=3				σ^m
	τ=.25	τ=.50	τ=.75	τ=1	τ=.25	τ=.50	τ=.75	τ=1	τ=.25	τ=.50	τ=.75	τ=1	
.15	1.29	1.77	2.09	2.35	2.05	2.69	3.09	3.40	2.82	3.61	4.09	4.45	.25
	1.03	1.48	1.77	2.00	1.67	2.30	2.68	2.97	2.32	3.11	3.59	3.94	.50
	.72	1.14	1.40	1.61	1.21	1.81	2.18	2.46	1.70	2.49	2.97	3.31	1
.50	.87	1.25	1.51	1.71	1.48	2.02	2.36	2.62	2.09	2.79	3.22	3.54	.25
	.75	1.12	1.37	1.56	1.29	1.83	2.17	2.43	1.83	2.53	2.97	3.29	.50
	.57	.93	1.16	1.34	1.00	1.53	1.87	2.12	1.43	2.14	2.58	2.90	1
1.50	.50	.77	.97	1.12	.94	1.35	1.63	1.85	1.38	1.93	2.30	2.58	.25
	.45	.72	.92	1.07	.86	1.27	1.55	1.77	1.26	1.82	2.19	2.47	.50
	.36	.63	.83	.97	.71	1.13	1.41	1.63	1.06	1.62	2.00	2.28	1

* $\rho = .08$, $\delta = .05$, $b = .20$, and $\psi = .67$. Total domestic investment is the sum of investment in the manufacturing sector plus investment by the domestic partner in the joint venture.

348

Table 9.17b. *Impact effect on total domestic investment spending when η = 3 (joint venture in an export enclave).**

$c_m = .25$, $\alpha = .25$, $\theta_L^m = .30$

β	μ=1				μ=2				μ=3				σ^m
	τ=.25	τ=.50	τ=.75	τ=1	τ=.25	τ=.50	τ=.75	τ=1	τ=.25	τ=.50	τ=.75	τ=1	
.15	.68	1.26	1.60	1.84	1.06	1.94	2.43	2.78	1.43	2.63	3.27	3.71	.25
	.37	.96	1.30	1.55	.55	1.49	2.01	2.36	.73	2.02	2.71	3.17	.50
	-.06	.56	.91	1.16	-.17	.85	1.40	1.78	-.29	1.14	1.89	2.40	1
.50	≈0	.56	.89	1.12	-.04	.88	1.40	1.75	-.08	1.20	1.91	2.38	.25
	-.16	.42	.75	.99	-.31	.64	1.18	1.54	-.47	.87	1.60	2.10	.50
	-.42	.18	.52	.76	-.77	.24	.80	1.19	-1.12	.30	1.08	1.61	1
1.50	-.73	-.20	.12	.35	-1.28	-.38	.16	.54	-1.83	-.55	.21	.73	.25
	-.80	-.27	.06	.29	-1.41	-.49	.06	.44	-2.01	-.71	.06	.59	.50
	-.93	-.39	-.06	.18	-1.64	-.70	-.14	.26	-2.35	-1.01	-.22	.33	1

$c_m = .25$, $\alpha = .50$, $\theta_L^m = .30$

β	μ=1				μ=2				μ=3				σ^m
	τ=.25	τ=.50	τ=.75	τ=1	τ=.25	τ=.50	τ=.75	τ=1	τ=.25	τ=.50	τ=.75	τ=1	
.15	1.52	2.32	2.73	2.98	2.50	3.85	4.52	4.94	3.49	5.37	6.31	6.89	.25
	1.06	1.93	2.39	2.68	1.73	3.18	3.95	4.43	2.39	4.44	5.50	6.18	.50
	.43	1.35	1.86	2.20	.63	2.20	3.06	3.62	.84	3.05	4.26	5.05	1
.50	.50	1.33	1.81	2.14	.79	2.21	3.01	3.55	1.09	3.08	4.21	4.96	.25
	.27	1.12	1.62	1.96	.40	1.84	2.68	3.24	.53	2.57	3.74	4.53	.50
	-.10	.77	1.29	1.64	-.25	1.24	2.11	2.71	-.40	1.71	2.93	3.77	1
1.50	-.53	.20	.67	1.01	-.96	.29	1.09	1.66	-1.39	.39	1.51	2.32	.25
	-.62	.11	.58	.92	-1.12	.13	.94	1.52	-1.62	.16	1.29	2.11	.50
	-.79	-.06	.42	.76	-1.43	-.16	.65	1.24	-2.06	-.26	.89	1.72	1

349

Table 9.17b. (cont.)

$c_m = .50, \alpha = .25, \theta_L^m = .40$

β	μ=1				μ=2				μ=3				σ^m
	τ=.25	τ=.50	τ=.75	τ=1	τ=.25	τ=.50	τ=.75	τ=1	τ=.25	τ=.50	τ=.75	τ=1	
.15	.04	.40	.56	.65	-.08	.45	.66	.77	-.20	.50	.76	.88	.25
	-.25	.19	.39	.51	-.56	.13	.43	.59	-.86	.08	.47	.67	.50
	-.68	-.15	.11	.27	-1.28	-.40	.01	.25	-1.88	-.65	-.09	.24	1
.50	-.40	.03	.25	.38	-.77	-.08	.25	.44	-1.13	-.18	.25	.50	.25
	-.59	-.12	.12	.27	-1.09	-.32	.06	.28	-1.59	-.52	-.01	.29	.50
	-.90	-.37	-.09	.09	-1.63	-.74	-.29	-.01	-2.36	-1.11	-.49	-.11	1
1.50	-.95	-.51	-.26	-.08	-1.67	-.94	-.52	-.24	-2.40	-1.36	-.78	-.40	.25
	-1.05	-.60	-.33	-.15	-1.85	-1.08	-.65	-.36	-2.65	-1.57	-.96	-.56	.50
	-1.22	-.75	-.47	-.27	-2.16	-1.35	-.88	-.56	-3.11	-1.95	-1.29	-.85	1

$c_m = .50, \alpha = .50, \theta_L^m = .40$

β	μ=1				μ=2				μ=3				σ^m
	τ=.25	τ=.50	τ=.75	τ=1	τ=.25	τ=.50	τ=.75	τ=1	τ=.25	τ=.50	τ=.75	τ=1	
.15	.72	1.57	2.09	2.47	1.01	2.33	3.08	3.62	1.30	3.08	4.08	4.76	.25
	.18	1.04	1.55	1.92	.12	1.50	2.28	2.83	.05	1.95	3.01	3.74	.50
	-.51	.36	.88	1.25	-1.05	.40	1.23	1.81	-1.59	.44	1.58	2.36	1
.50	-.06	.70	1.16	1.51	-.23	1.00	1.74	2.25	-.40	1.31	2.31	3.00	.25
	-.35	.42	.89	1.24	-.73	.54	1.29	1.83	-1.11	.66	1.70	2.42	.50
	-.80	-.01	.47	.82	-1.50	-.19	.60	1.16	-2.21	-.36	.73	1.50	1
1.50	-.84	-.24	.17	.47	-1.52	-.50	.17	.66	-2.19	-.76	.17	.85	.25
	-.97	-.36	.05	.35	-1.75	-.71	-.04	.46	-2.52	-1.07	-.12	.57	.50
	-1.20	-.58	-.17	.14	-2.15	-1.10	-.41	.10	-3.11	-1.62	-.65	.06	1

* $\rho = .08$, $\delta = .05$, $b = .20$, and $\psi = .67$. Total domestic investment is the sum of investment in the manufacturing sector plus investment by the domestic partner in the joint venture.

Table 9.18. *Length of time it takes the capital stock in manufacturing to regain its pre-FI level when the formal sector is large (joint venture in an export enclave).*

	$\sigma^m = .5$				$\sigma^m = 1$				
β	$\tau = .25$	$\tau = .50$	$\tau = .75$	$\tau = 1$	$\tau = .25$	$\tau = .50$	$\tau = .75$	$\tau = 1$	μ
.15	—	—	—	—	5.70	—	—	—	1
	3.12	—	—	—	8.90	1.65	—	—	2
	4.46	—	—	—	10.12	3.05	.17	—	3
.50	5.91	—	—	—	11.00	1.48	—	—	1
	9.18	1.69	—	—	14.13	4.96	1.17	—	2
	10.43	3.10	.17	—	15.34	6.26	2.60	.54	3
1.50	19.77	7.21	1.86	—	23.51	9.81	3.98	.53	1
	23.00	10.48	5.36	2.46	26.76	13.01	7.34	4.12	2
	24.28	11.75	6.67	3.84	28.04	14.25	8.61	5.45	3

$\eta = 3$

	$\sigma^m = .5$				$\sigma^m = 1$				
β	$\tau = .25$	$\tau = .50$	$\tau = .75$	$\tau = 1$	$\tau = .25$	$\tau = .50$	$\tau = .75$	$\tau = 1$	μ
.15	4.79	—	—	—	10.42	3.38	.55	—	1
	5.97	1.22	—	—	11.53	4.60	1.90	.43	2
	6.41	1.73	—	—	11.94	5.05	2.39	.96	3
.50	10.74	3.44	.55	—	15.64	6.58	2.94	.91	1
	11.88	4.67	1.90	.41	16.75	7.74	4.18	2.24	2
	12.31	5.13	2.40	.95	17.18	8.17	4.64	2.73	3
1.50	24.60	12.06	7.00	4.18	28.36	14.56	8.93	5.78	1
	25.78	13.21	8.17	5.41	29.55	15.69	10.08	6.97	2
	26.23	13.64	8.62	5.87	30.00	16.13	10.52	7.41	3

The top section is headed $\eta = 1$.

* $\rho = .08$, $\delta = .05$, $b = .20$, and $\psi = .67$. A dash indicates that the capital stock in the manufacturing sector increases continuously.

domestic investment, vs. the anticipation of higher future income from taxation of foreign capital, which creates an incentive to smooth the path of consumption by investing less in the short term. When foreign capital is heavily taxed and the intertemporal elasticity of substitution is small, the consumption-smoothing effect proves stronger than the positive pull of the long-run fundamentals and the domestic capital stock decreases for a period before starting the long ascent to its higher steady-state level. The initial period of capital decumulation lasts 2–11 years and is shallow if either $\beta \le .50$ or $\tau \ge .50$.

The same forces are at work when the export enclave is developed through a joint venture, but they pack a much more powerful punch. Consequently, there is tremendous variation in the initial response of total domestic investment spending $(I_d + \mu I_s)$ and its division between the enclave and the manufacturing sector. In Table 9.17a, where capital in the enclave fetches the same return as capital in domestic manufacturing, the short-run crowding-in coefficient ranges from .26 to 5.85 for total domestic investment and from −1.94 to 2.85 for investment in manufacturing. Thus, investment in manufacturing may contract sharply or increase more than domestic investment in the enclave. The outcome is sensitive not only to τ, but also to $\alpha - c_m$, which determines whether higher domestic investment raises or lowers demand for manufactures [see (25)]. Observe that in the panel ($\alpha = .50$, $c_m = .25$) the crowding-in coefficient for I_d is positive in 84 of 108 cases and *exceeds unity* in 36 cases; but when the values for c_m and α are reversed in the third panel, dI_d/dI_f is negative in every single case.[29]

The variation in the results is even more extreme in Table 9.17b, where FI is instrumental in bringing about a resource boom.[30] For $\eta = 3$, the gains from participating in the joint venture are very large; when this combines with $\tau \le .5$, the incentive to smooth consumption is so powerful that total domestic investment spending *decreases* in 123 of 216 cases. More striking still, in the last two panels a dollar of FI crowds out more than one dollar of domestic investment in 24 of the 36 cases where $\tau = .25$ and $\mu = 2, 3$. This may cause significant and much greater underemployment and capital decumulation in the first phase of the adjustment process. In some parts of the parameter space, the capital stock in the domestic manufacturing sector decreases by more than 100% of the eventual increase in K_s and does not recover to its pre-FI level until 25–30 years have passed (see Table 9.18 and Figures 9.10a and b). The numbers for underemployment may also be quite bad for believably low values of σ^m and τ: in Table 9.19, high-wage employment stays depressed for a decade or more in half of the cases where one of the two

---

[29] In the previous cases the solution grids did not include panels for ($c_m = .25$, $\alpha = .50$) and ($c_m = .50$, $\alpha = .25$) because the dynamics were not especially sensitive to differences between c_m and α.

[30] Recall that in Tables 9.4–9.6 the government adjusts the tax b_f so as to capture all of the rents when $\eta > 1$. A value of 1.4 for η in Tables 9.4–9.6 is equivalent therefore to $\eta = 3$ in Tables 9.17–9.19. (That is, in the absence of a joint venture, the results are the same for $b_f = .2$ and $\eta = 3$ and for $b_f = .4286$ and $\eta = 1.4$.)

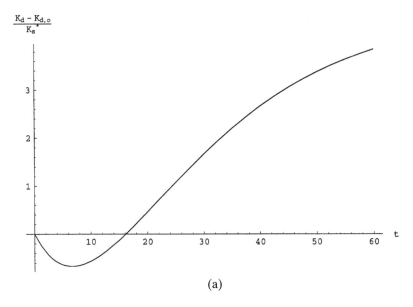

(a)

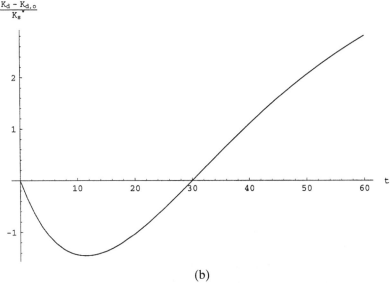

(b)

Figure 9.10. (a) Path of K_d when the high-wage sector is large, $\sigma^m = 1$, $\tau = .50$, $\beta = 1.50$, $\eta = 3$, and $\mu = 3$. (b) Path of K_d when the high-wage sector is large, $\sigma^m = 1$, $\tau = .25$, $\beta = 1.50$, $\eta = 3$, and $\mu = 3$.

Table 9.19. *Time it takes for high-wage employment to rise permanently above its pre-FI level when $\beta = 1.50$, $c_m = .50$, $\alpha = .50$, and $\theta_L^m = .40$ (joint venture in an export enclave).***

	$\eta = 1$		
τ	$\sigma^m = .25$	$\sigma^m = .50$	μ
.25	9.73	+	1
	14.28	7.15	2
	15.86	10.17	3
.50	+	+	1
	+	+	2
	5.33	+	3
	$\eta = 3$		
τ	$\sigma^m = .25$	$\sigma^m = .50$	μ
.25	16.24	10.75	1
	17.64	12.68	2
	18.16	13.36	3
.50	5.84	+	1
	7.49	+	2
	8.06	4.28	3

* $\rho = .08$, $\delta = .05$, $b = .20$, and $\psi = .67$. A plus sign indicates that high-wage employment is continuously higher.

parameters is smaller than .50; moreover, when $\tau = .25$, $\mu = 3$, and $\sigma^m = .25, .50$, the employment cuts are severe (see Figures 9.11a and b). Ironically, these are also the scenarios in which the capital stock and high-wage employment increase the most across steady states. For low values of τ, strong crowding out and higher underemployment in the short run go together with strong crowding in and much lower underemployment over the long run (Figures 9.12a and b).

Prolonged, deep contraction in manufacturing does not call into question the desirability of FI. Domestic investment plunges in the short run only because future income is expected to be so much higher. Temporary capital decumulation, when it occurs, is simply the response to a very favorable wealth shock. Viewed from this angle, it comes as no surprise that the welfare gain is increasing in η and greater in the joint venture than in the benchmark case.

Joint Ventures

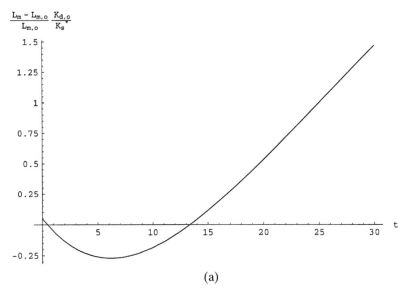

(a)

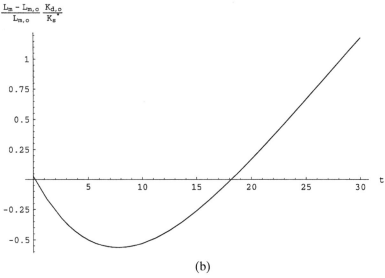

(b)

Figure 9.11. (a) Path of L_m when the high-wage sector is large, $\sigma^m = .50$, $\tau = .25$, $\beta = 1.50$, $\eta = 3$, and $\mu = 3$. (b) Path of L_m when the high-wage sector is large, $\sigma^m = .25$, $\tau = .25$, $\beta = 1.50$, $\eta = 3$, and $\mu = 3$.

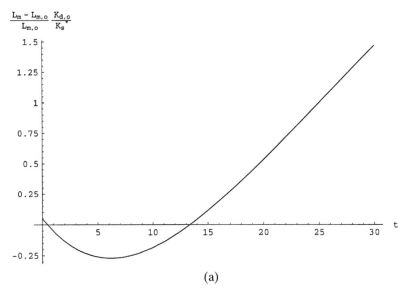

(a)

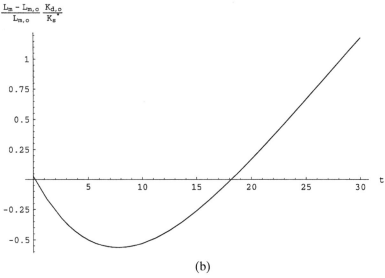

(b)

Figure 9.11. (a) Path of L_m when the high-wage sector is large, $\sigma^m = .50$, $\tau = .25$, $\beta = 1.50$, $\eta = 3$, and $\mu = 3$. (b) Path of L_m when the high-wage sector is large, $\sigma^m = .25$, $\tau = .25$, $\beta = 1.50$, $\eta = 3$, and $\mu = 3$.

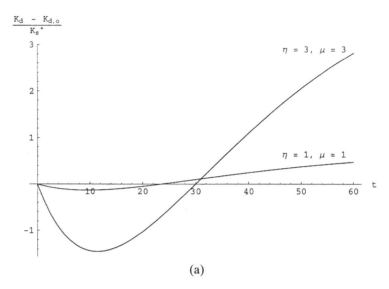

(a)

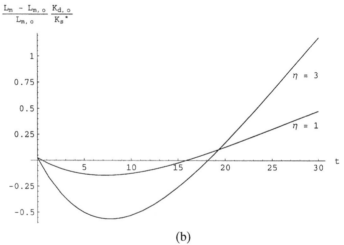

(b)

Figure 9.12. (a) Paths of K_d when the high-wage sector is large, $\sigma^m = 1$, $\tau = .25$, $\beta = 1.50$, and either (i) $\eta = 3$ and $\mu = 3$ or (ii) $\eta = 1$ and $\mu = 1$. (b) Paths of L_m when the high-wage sector is large, $\sigma^m = .25$, $\tau = .25$, $\beta = 1.50$, $\mu = 3$, and either $\eta = 1$ or $\eta = 3$.

9.7   Technology Transfer

Policy makers seek out FI not only to reduce underemployment but also to enhance domestic productivity. It is natural to conjecture therefore that technology transfer will at least soften and possibly reverse the pessimistic results obtained earlier for FI in the domestic manufacturing sector. This is not invariably the case, however; much depends on the precise characteristics of the technology transfer and on the values assumed by certain key demand and supply parameters.

For illustrative purposes, suppose FI brings about a Hicks-neutral improvement in technology so that the production function in the manufacturing sector reads $Q_m = \phi(K_f)F(K, L_m)$, where $\phi(0) = 1$ and $\phi' > 0$. Since an increase in ϕ acts like a reduction in the input–output coefficients for labor and capital, the zero-profit condition and factor demands in manufacturing are

$$P_m = C^m(w_m, r)/\phi(K_f), \tag{1'}$$

$$L_m = C_w^m(w_m, r)Q_m/\phi(K_f), \tag{55}$$

$$K = C_w^m(w_m, r)Q_m/\phi(K_f), \tag{56}$$

and the revenue function is $R[\phi(K_f)P_m, K, T, L_m]$. Otherwise, the model is the same as in the benchmark case of plain vanilla FI.[31]

Now consider again the nature of the temporary equilibrium when manufacturing sector employment and the aggregate capital stock are unchanged. The replacement of domestic capital by foreign capital lowers the demand for manufactures while the improvement in technology generates greater supply. Due to the increase in supply, the price of the manufactured good is lower than when no technology transfer occurs. On the other hand, the introduction of superior technology also raises the marginal physical productivity of capital and labor in the manufacturing sector. If the demand curve is steeply sloped (i.e., the compensated demand elasticity ε is small), the price fall is large and, notwithstanding the favorable effect on productivity, FI may reduce

---

[31] For simplicity, I assume that $r_f \simeq r$ even though foreign capital generates favorable technological spillovers. (Strictly speaking, r_f is infinitesimally larger than r. This does not rule out relatively large spillovers because the spillovers affect the productivity of all domestic firms in the manufacturing sector.) When $r_f > r$, extra terms appear involving r_f/r that are the same as in the case of a joint venture where foreign technology is Hicks-neutral superior to domestic technology (i.e., the case where $l_f = l_m$).

manufacturing sector employment and crowd out domestic capital to a greater extent. Across steady states,

$$K_d \frac{\hat{L}_m}{dK_f} = \frac{c_m - \alpha}{N} \sigma^m \theta_K^m q + \frac{dK}{dK_f}, \tag{57}$$

$$\Delta \frac{dK}{dK_f} = \left[\frac{\varepsilon D^m / Q_m + \sigma^m (\alpha - c_m) \theta_L^m (c_x + c_m \psi)}{N} - c_x \right] q$$

$$\qquad - \frac{c_m \rho (1 - b)}{\rho + \delta}, \tag{58}$$

$$\frac{\hat{P}_m}{dK_f} = -\phi' / N, \tag{59}$$

$$\frac{\hat{w}_m - \hat{r}}{dK_f} = (\alpha - c_m) \phi' / N, \tag{60}$$

where $N \equiv \theta_L^m c_x + \theta_K^m (1 - \alpha)$ and $q \equiv P_m Q_m \phi' / r$ measures the real income gain from technological spillovers as a percentage of the gross capital rental. The terms involving $(\alpha - c_m)$ in (57) and (58) reflect movement along the production isoquant induced by the change in the wage–rental ratio. To isolate the conflicting price and productivity effects discussed above, set $\alpha = c_m$. Then $\hat{L}_m = \hat{K}$ and

$$\Delta \frac{dK}{dK_f} = (\beta D^m / Q_m - c_x) q - \frac{c_m \rho (1 - b)}{\rho + \delta}. \tag{58'}$$

Thus, if $\beta < c_x Q_m / D^m$, both K and L_m fall *more* when FI is a conduit for technology transfer.

This is a case where quotas are potentially very harmful. If consumers can substitute freely between domestic and imported manufactures, then β is probably large (i.e., >1) and there is a presumption that the productivity effect outweighs the price effect. The presumption goes the other way, however, if imported manufactures are kept out by quotas: domestic manufactures become nontradable as opposed to semitradable, β drops to .5 or less, and the price effect wins with margin to spare. (In the condition $\beta < c_x Q_m / D^m$, c_x should be interpreted as the consumption share of nonmanufactured goods.) When $c_m \neq \alpha$, demand for one of the two factors will be strengthened by the shift to more capital- or labor-intensive technology. But the elasticity of substitution σ^m has to be very large for the substitution and productivity effects to prevent a decrease in K or L_m. In Table 9.20, one or both variables often increase when manufactures are semitradable (i.e., $\beta = 1.5$) and $\sigma^m = .5 - 1$. But in the cases

Table 9.20. *Change in the aggregate capital stock and high-wage employment across steady states (technology transfer).* *

| | | $c_m = .25, \alpha = .25, \theta_L^m = .30$ | | | | | |
| | K | | | L_m | | | |
β	$\sigma^m = .5$	$\sigma^m = 1$	$\sigma^m = 3$	$\sigma^m = .5$	$\sigma^m = 1$	$\sigma^m = 3$	q
.15		-.24			-.24		.25
		-.51			-.51		.75
.50		-.17			-.17		.25
		-.29			-.29		.75
1.50		.04			.04		.25
		.33			.33		.75

| | | $c_m = .25, \alpha = .50, \theta_L^m = .30$ | | | | | |
| | K | | | L_m | | | |
β	$\sigma^m = .5$	$\sigma^m = 1$	$\sigma^m = 3$	$\sigma^m = .5$	$\sigma^m = 1$	$\sigma^m = 3$	q
.15	-.24	-.22	-.17	-.27	-.30	-.39	.25
	-.48	-.44	-.27	-.59	-.66	-.95	.75
.50	-.14	-.13	-.07	-.18	-.20	-.30	.25
	-.19	-.15	.02	-.31	-.38	-.67	.75
1.50	.13	.15	.20	.09	.07	-.03	.25
	.63	.67	.84	.51	.44	.15	.75

| | | $c_m = .50, \alpha = .25, \theta_L^m = .40$ | | | | | |
| | K | | | L_m | | | |
β	$\sigma^m = .5$	$\sigma^m = 1$	$\sigma^m = 3$	$\sigma^m = .5$	$\sigma^m = 1$	$\sigma^m = 3$	q
.15	-.32	-.33	-.39	-.29	-.27	-.22	.25
	-.52	-.56	-.73	-.43	-.39	-.21	.75
.50	-.26	-.27	-.33	-.23	-.22	-.16	.25
	-.35	-.39	-.56	-.26	-.22	-.41	.75
1.50	-.10	-.11	-.17	-.07	-.06	.003	.25
	.14	.01	-.07	.22	.27	.44	.75

| | | $c_m = .50, \alpha = .50, \theta_L^m = .40$ | | | | | |
| | K | | | L_m | | | |
β	$\sigma^m = .5$	$\sigma^m = 1$	$\sigma^m = 3$	$\sigma^m = .5$	$\sigma^m = 1$	$\sigma^m = 3$	q
.15		-.32			-.32		.25
		-.49			-.49		.75
.50		-.24			-.24		.25
		-.27			-.27		.75
1.50		-.03			-.03		.25
		.38			.38		.75

* $\rho = .08$, $\delta = .05$, $b = .20$, and $\psi = .67$. The numbers in the column for K are dK/dK_f, while those in the column for L_m are $(dL_m/dK_f)/\ell_m$ (the elasticity of employment in manufacturing with respect to the direct percentage change in the capital stock brought about by the increase in K_f).

where quotas reduce β to .15–.50, neither K nor L_m increases until σ^m becomes unbelievably large.

9.7.1   Welfare

In Section 9.6, I was able to demonstrate that joint ventures exert a positive effect on steady-state utility despite potentially adverse effects on underemployment and underinvestment. This is not possible in the present case. In the long run,

$$
\frac{1}{r}\frac{du}{dK_f} = \left\{ 1 + \frac{\sigma^m(1-\psi)(c_m - \alpha)\theta_L^m}{N} + \Delta^{-1}\left[\frac{\rho + \delta b}{\rho + \delta} + (1-\psi)\frac{\theta_L^m}{\theta_K^m} \right] \right.
$$
$$
\times \left[\frac{\varepsilon D^m/Q_m + \sigma^m(\alpha - c_m)\theta_L^m(c_x + c_m\psi)}{N} - c_x \right] \Bigg\} q
$$
$$
\left. - \frac{\rho(1-b)}{\rho+\delta}\left\{ 1 + \frac{c_m}{\Delta}\left[\frac{\rho + \delta b}{\rho + \delta} + (1-\psi)\frac{\theta_L^m}{\theta_K^m} \right] \right\}. \right.
$$
(61)

It is readily shown that the coefficient on q is positive iff

$$
\frac{\varepsilon D^m}{NQ_m}\left[\frac{\rho + \delta b}{\rho + \delta} + (1-\psi)\frac{\theta_L^m}{\theta_K^m} \right] + \frac{\theta_L^m}{\theta_K^m}\psi + \frac{\delta}{\rho+\delta}(1-b)(1-\alpha)
$$
$$
\frac{\sigma^m(c_m - \alpha)\theta_L^m}{(\rho+\delta)N}[\delta(1-\alpha)(1-b)(1-\psi) - (\rho + \delta b)\psi] > 0.
$$
(62)

The first three terms are positive but the fourth is ambiguous in sign. A completely unqualified result is out of reach because when σ^m is very large and $c_m \neq \alpha$ very strong substitution effects lead to very large decreases in either K_d or L_m. But this is only an aesthetic disappointment. Observe that (62) always holds when

$$
\sigma^m < Max\left\{ \frac{\rho + \delta}{\rho + \delta b}\frac{\theta_L^m c_x + \theta_K^m(1-\alpha)}{\theta_K^m(c_m - \alpha)}, \frac{\theta_L^m c_x + \theta_K^m(1-\alpha)}{\theta_L^m(1-\psi)(\alpha - c_m)} \right\}.
$$
(63)

Both terms inside the braces are far above unity (for either $\alpha > c_m$ or $c_m > \alpha$). Moreover, (63) is merely a sufficient condition. In Table 9.21, the borderline value of σ^m that satisfies (62) usually exceeds five and is never smaller than three. There is not much doubt that technology transfer makes a positive contribution to long-run real income (or utility) for parameter values in the empirically relevant range.

Might the contribution be large enough to generate an overall welfare gain? The numbers in Table 9.22 suggest that the answer will often be

Table 9.21. *Value of σ^m above which the technological spillover exerts an adverse effect on steady-state utility.* *

β	$\alpha = 0$	$\alpha = .25$	$\alpha = .50$	$\alpha = .75$	ψ
		$c_m = .25$ and $\theta_L^m = .30$			
.15	+	+	15.0	4.4	.50
	+	+	10.9	3.4	.67
	+	+	9.3	3.0	.80
.50	+	+	25.5	8.7	.50
	+	+	17.2	6.2	.67
	+	+	13.9	5.1	.80
		$c_m = .50$ and $\theta_L^m = .40$			
.15	+	+	+	6.8	.50
	+	+	+	5.5	.67
	+	+	+	5.0	.80
.50	+	+	+	11.8	.50
	+	+	+	8.7	.67
	+	+	+	7.3	.80

* $\rho = .08$, $\delta = .05$, and $b = .20$. A plus sign indicates that the impact on steady-state utility is always positive.

yes. Remarkably, when $\beta \le .5$ and the private and social time preference rates coincide, the return per dollar FI equals or exceeds q itself. (For $\beta = 1.5$, it is 70–100% greater than q.) This implies the conclusion in Table 9.23 that modest values of q make FI welfare-improving when the social time preference rate is one to three points below the private rate. Steady-state utility does not increase, however, until q gets up around .4 or higher. While there are no reliable empirical estimates of q, this strikes me as a large number.[32] The technological spillovers have to be

[32] The evidence on technological spillovers is thin and hard to evaluate (Helleiner, 1989). There is some evidence of negative spillovers in the time series data for Morocco and Venezuela, but the positive correlation in the cross-section data may be consistent with positive long-run effects on domestic productivity (Harrison, 1996). The estimates for Mexico by Blomstrom and Persson (1983) suggest that FI generates favorable intraindustry spillovers but does not shed light on their magnitude. Aitken, Hanson, and Harrison (1997) find that multi-

Table 9.22. *Impact on domestic welfare measured as the annual equivalent return per dollar of foreign investment (FI in the manufacturing sector generates technological spillovers).* *

	$c_m = .25, \alpha = .25, \theta_L^m = .30$			
β	$q = .10$	$q = .25$	$q = .50$	τ
.15	11.0	26.4	52.2	.25
	10.5	26.0	51.6	.50
	10.3	25.7	51.3	1
.50	14.3	31.8	60.8	.25
	12.9	30.2	59.1	.50
	12.1	29.3	58.1	1
.50	21.6	43.2	79.2	.25
	18.8	40.7	77.2	.50
	16.9	39.1	76.0	1

	$c_m = .50, \alpha = .50, \theta_L^m = .40$			
β	$q = .10$	$q = .25$	$q = .50$	τ
.15	12.5	28.8	56.0	.25
	11.4	27.6	54.6	.50
	10.8	26.9	53.8	1
.50	17.7	36.3	67.3	.25
	14.9	33.4	64.3	.50
	13.2	31.7	62.5	1
.50	27.6	50.4	88.5	.25
	23.1	46.7	86.0	.50
	19.8	44.0	84.3	1

* $\rho = .08, \delta = .05, b = .20, \psi = .67,$ and $\sigma^m = .50$.

half as large as the direct contribution of FI to output (i.e., r) to escape the tradeoff between welfare and long-run development.

national enterprises in Mexico are a valuable source of information about international marketing channels and foreign consumer tastes; the informational externality associated with FI makes it easier for domestic firms to break into export markets. (The informational externality is confined to multinational exporters. The probability that a domestic plant will export is uncorrelated with local export activity.)

Table 9.23. *Value of the technology transfer coefficient that leaves domestic welfare unchanged.**

		$c_m = .25, \alpha = .25, \theta_L^m = .30$			
β	Steady-state utility	$\rho_1 = .05$	$\rho_1 = .06$	$\rho_1 = .07$	τ
.15	1.05	.265	.164	.074	.25
		.276	.173	.080	.50
		.282	.177	.083	1
.50	.73	.196	.117	.044	.25
		.215	.134	.059	.50
		.226	.144	.068	1
1.50	.39	.102	.050	—	.25
		.127	.075	.024	.50
		.142	.091	.039	1

		$c_m = .50, \alpha = .50, \theta_L^m = .40$			
β	Steady-state utility	$\rho_1 = .05$	$\rho_1 = .06$	$\rho_1 = .07$	τ
.15	1.03	.256	.156	.066	.25
		.279	.175	.080	.50
		.292	.185	.088	1
.50	.73	.173	.095	.024	.25
		.207	.126	.051	.50
		.228	.145	.067	1
1.50	.40	.070	.017	—	.25
		.109	.056	.004	.50
		.135	.082	.030	1

* $\rho = .08$, $\delta = .05$, $b = .20$, $\psi = .67$, and $\sigma^m = .50$. A dash indicates that welfare increases in the absence of any favorable technological spillovers.

9.8 Allowing for Capital Accumulation in Other Sectors

The main insight developed in the benchmark model was that, at the existing aggregate capital stock, the demand for manufactures is increased by FI in the export sector and decreased by FI in the manufacturing sector. The change in demand induced expansion or contraction in the manufacturing sector with a corresponding impact on the aggregate domestically owned capital stock because the manufacturing sector was the only domestic sector that utilized capital. When other sectors besides manufacturing use capital, a similar mechanism operates but, as should be expected, sectoral factor intensity rankings also play a critical role in determining the outcome.

Take first the easiest case where the exportable is a processed primary good produced by means of capital, labor, and land. All of the previous steady-state results then go through provided the capital–labor ratio in the export sector is lower than in the manufacturing sector, a weak condition that casual observation and empirical studies suggest will usually be satisfied. (See the discussion of the empirical literature in Chapter 5.) The intuition in this case differs little from that in Sections 9.2–9.4. As before, FI in the manufacturing (primary or enclave export) sector causes manufacturing output to contract (rise). This shift in the composition of output raises or lowers the aggregate capital stock, depending on whether the manufacturing sector is relatively capital- or labor-intensive.

The results differ more substantively when a sizeable tradables manufactures sector exists. If we confine our attention to economies where protection is provided largely through quotas, the tradables manufactures sector is necessarily a second distinct export sector. Furthermore, in view of the findings of the NBER study (Krueger et al., 1982), it can be safely assumed that the manufactures export sector, like the primary export sector, pays the low wage w_x. Since FI in the primary sector and the enclave sector have qualitatively similar effects on the steady-state equilibrium, I drop the enclave good from the model and economize on notation by treating good s as the domestically produced manufactured exportable.[33]

In an economy having this structure, all goods and factor prices remain constant across steady states. The three zero-profit conditions read

$$P_m = C^m[w_m(P_m),(\rho+\delta)P_k(P_m)], \tag{1''}$$

$$1 = C^x(w_x, v), \tag{2''}$$

$$1 = C^s[w_x, (\rho+\delta)P_k(P_m)]. \tag{3''}$$

Equations (1'') and (3'') imply that P_m and w_x are invariant across steady states. It then follows from (2'') that v is constant as well.

Letting K_f denote foreign capital located either in sector m or sector s and following manipulations similar to those in Section 9.1.2 yields

---

[33] L_s is now positive initially, so labor demand in sector s depends on the wage. It turns out, however, that w_x is unchanged in the long run. Equation (33), therefore, still gives the correct solution for the change in L_s across steady states.

$$\frac{dK}{dK_f} = \frac{c_m \rho (1-b)(\ell_m - \ell_s)}{(\rho+\delta)H}, \tag{64}$$

$$\frac{dL_m}{dK_f} = -\frac{c_m \rho (1-b)\ell_s \ell_m}{(\rho+\delta)H} < 0, \tag{65}$$

$$\frac{dK}{dT_f} = \frac{c_m v b_f (1-b)(\ell_s - \ell_m) - \ell_x (\rho+\delta)\Lambda}{(\rho+\delta)H}, \tag{66}$$

$$\frac{dL_m}{dT_f} = \frac{c_m \ell_m}{(\rho+\delta)H}[v(1-b)b_f \ell_s - \ell_x \{\rho+\delta[b+(1-b)\alpha/c_m]\}], \tag{67}$$

where

$$H \equiv \ell_m \frac{c_m \rho + \delta[(1-b)\alpha + c_m b]}{\rho+\delta} + \left[\ell_s \frac{\rho(1-c_m) + \delta[(1-b)(1-\alpha) + b(1-c_m)]}{\rho+\delta}\right.$$

$$\left. + \frac{\theta_L^m}{\theta_K^m}(c_x + c_s + c_m \psi)\right] > 0,$$

$$\Lambda \equiv 1 + (c_x + c_s + c_m \psi)\theta_L^m/\theta_K^m > 0.$$

FI in the manufacturing sector (either sector m or sector s) reduces the aggregate capital stock on the weak condition that sector m is capital-intensive relative to sector s. The level of high-wage employment declines regardless of sectoral factor intensity rankings because sector m output always decreases.[34]

The unfavorable evaluation of FI in the manufacturing sector may also now apply to FI in the primary export sector. It is evident from (66) and (67) that with greater diversification in export production FI may neither stimulate aggregate capital accumulation nor lessen underemployment. The reason lies in the different impact on primary sector employment. In an economy specializing in primary exports, FI drives up the wage w_x so strongly that total primary sector employment contracts, freeing labor to move into the high-wage manufacturing sector. By contrast, in an economy with a more diversified export base, w_x is fixed and primary

---

[34] Employment in the primary sector is unchanged by FI in the manufacturing sector. Sectors m and s, therefore, form a Heckscher–Ohlin subsector. If sector m is relatively capital-intensive, the aggregate capital stock declines and, by the Rybczynski theorem, Q_m decreases. Similarly, if sector m is relatively labor-intensive, the aggregate capital stock increases and again the Rybczynski theorem ensures that Q_m will fall.

sector employment increases by an amount proportional to the increase in the stock of land $(dL_x = \ell_x dT_f)$. The withdrawal of labor from the capital-using manufacturing sectors exerts pressure toward capital decumulation and lower sector m employment as reflected in the l_x terms in (66) and (67). Working against this adverse labor withdrawal effect is the increase in demand for good m derived from taxation of foreign profits. For $l_m < l_s$ and a sufficiently high value of b_f, a favorable impact on sector m employment and aggregate capital accumulation can be guaranteed. Routine manipulations show that K rises when

$$b_f > \frac{\theta_K^s \theta_L^x [\theta_K^m + \theta_L^m (c_x + c_s + c_m \psi)]}{\underbrace{c_m \theta_T^x (\theta_L^s \theta_K^m - \theta_L^m \theta_K^s \psi)}_{\text{sign of } \ell_s - \ell_m}}$$

and that for

$$b_f > \frac{\{\rho + \delta[b + (1-b)\alpha/c_m]\}\theta_L^x \theta_K^s}{(\rho + \delta)\theta_L^s \theta_T^x}$$

L_m increases. The more resource-intensive is the primary product, the weaker is the labor withdrawal effect and the lower is the required tax rate b_f. In the limiting case of a pure resource good $(L_x = 0)$, any positive tax ensures that high-wage employment and the aggregate capital stock will increase.

9.9   Summary and Guidelines for Policy

The stimulus that FI provides to domestic development depends very much on the sector in which foreign firms invest, the strength of technological spillovers, restrictions on ownership and sales in the domestic market, and the structural characteristics of the economy. Six useful guidelines for policy can be extracted from the preceding results:

1. FI in the domestic manufacturing sector is likely to reduce domestic welfare when the social time preference rate is slightly below the private rate. While underemployment normally decreases in the short run, it always rises in the long run. If exports are pure primary goods whose production requires largely labor and some natural resource, FI crowds out domestic capital so strongly that in the end the aggregate capital stock and employment in the high-wage manufacturing sector decline. In economies where capital is a significant factor of

production in the export sector, the same outcome obtains whenever the capital-using part of the export sector has a lower capital–labor ratio than the quota protected manufacturing sector.

2. Modest export requirements can reverse some of the adverse effects of FI in the domestic manufacturing sector. The aggregate capital stock increases and underemployment diminishes when foreign firms are required to export 10–20% of their output. Higher export requirements of 20–40% produce an overall welfare gain provided the social time preference rate is not more than two to three points below the private rate. However, due to strong crowding out of domestic capital, steady-state utility declines. FI is not compatible with a long-run improvement in the standard of living unless the export requirement can be pushed far enough above 50% (usually to somewhere between 55 and 70%).

3. FI in the manufacturing sector is more likely to be welfare-improving when some of the rents associated with superior foreign technology accrue to the domestic economy via joint ventures or technological spillovers. Unfortunately, the efficiency gains often come with more crowding out of domestic capital and greater job losses in the high-wage manufacturing sector. As a result, the efficiency gains have to be very large to avert a decrease in steady-state utility. The chances for a welfare gain are best when the manufacturing sector is not protected by quotas and when the share of local equity is high in joint ventures.

4. FI in an export enclave is strongly welfare-improving when a country specializes in production of primary exports. Underemployment declines and the domestically owned capital stock expands across steady states if the exportable is either a pure primary good or a processed primary good whose capital–labor ratio is lower than that of the manufactured good. Moreover, while the manufacturing sector may contract in the first phase of the adjustment process, the "recession" is mild for believably small values of the intertemporal elasticity of substitution. If τ is around .25 or larger, the downturn that precedes expansion in the manufacturing sector is akin to a lengthy pause.

5. The overall welfare gain and the favorable long-run effects on domestic capital accumulation and underemployment are much greater when the export enclave is developed as a joint venture. Joint ventures may, however, give rise to fairly long-lived Dutch Disease–type problems – the capital stock and employment in the high-wage manufacturing sector may be lower for several decades when the intertemporal elasticity of substitution and the elasticity of substitution between capital and labor take believably low values (i.e., σ^m, $\tau = .25 - .50$).

6. In diversified economies that export substantial amounts of both primary goods and manufactures, the presumption that FI in an export enclave (or the primary sector) will be welfare-improving is substantially weakened. FI crowds in domestic capital and reduces underemployment only if foreign profits are taxed at a sufficiently high rate. *Ceteris paribus*, the required tax rate is lower the more resource/capital-intensive is the export product.

In closing, one final point should be discussed. Although FI in the manufacturing sector is often welfare-improving when export requirements, joint ventures, and technological spillovers add to the credit side of the ledger, steady-state utility usually declines. This is the source of the statement in the introduction that policy makers who aim for both a net welfare gain and more economic development should confine FI to the export sector (or impose very high export requirements, which amounts to much the same thing). This conclusion may, however, be overly cautious. The extra revenues that the government obtains from taxation of foreign firms need not be returned to the general public as lump-sum transfers. They could and probably should be dedicated instead to the objective of promoting long-run development. The government could, for example, use the additional revenues to underwrite subsidies to high-wage employment or to pay for a cut in the tax on domestic profits. FI in the manufacturing sector might then stimulate domestic capital accumulation and/or reduce underemployment. The issue needs further investigation.[35]

Appendix

The price of the manufactured good is continuously higher when foreign firms build an export enclave and $b_f = 0$. In this case,

$$\frac{P_m(t) - P_m^*}{P_m^*} \quad \text{sign of} \quad (\alpha - c_m)P_k\left[I_d(t) - I_d^*\right] - rh_1\left[K_d(t) - K_d^*\right]$$

[35] The results do not change qualitatively for plain vanilla FI in the manufacturing sector because tax revenues are unchanged when the aggregate capital stock is unchanged and domestic and foreign profits are taxed at the same rate. The results might differ, however, when (i) the tax rate on foreign profits is higher, (ii) foreign firms earn a higher return, or (iii) there are favorable technological spillovers. In each of these cases, tax revenues will be higher at an unchanged aggregate capital stock.

and the transition path coincides with the nondominant eigenvector ray

$$I_d(t) - I_d^* = (\lambda_2 + \delta)\left[K_d(t) - K_d^*\right].$$

Thus

$$\frac{P_m(t) - P_m^*}{P_m^*} \quad \text{sign of} \quad [(\alpha - c_m)P_k(\lambda_2 + \delta) - rh_1][K_d(t) - K_d^*].$$

Note that $\sigma(\alpha - c_m)P_k - rh_1 = (y_1\delta + y_2)h_o g_o P_k^2 Q_m/(D^m rG) > 0$ as $(y_1\delta + y_2)$, h_o and g_o are all positive, while G is negative. Since P_m is unchanged across steady states and K_d approaches its steady-state level monotonically, P_m will be higher everywhere on the transition path if and only if

$$(\alpha - c_m)\lambda_2 + \frac{(y_1\delta + y_2)h_o g_o P_k Q_m}{rGD^m} < 0.$$

This condition obviously holds when $\alpha > c_m$. To see that it also holds when $\alpha < c_m$, substitute for λ_2 to get

$$\sqrt{(y_1 - \delta)^2 + 4(y_1\delta + y_2)} < y_1 - \delta - \frac{2(y_1\delta + y_2)h_o g_o P_k Q_m}{(c_m - \alpha)rGD^m}.$$

It is easily shown that the expression on the right side is positive when $c_m > \alpha$. One can square both sides, therefore, without reversing the inequality sign. After doing this and canceling terms, the above condition reduces to

$$1 + (1 - \psi)\frac{\theta_L^m}{\theta_K^m} + \frac{h_1}{c_m - \alpha} > 0,$$

which holds since $h_1 > 0$ and $c_m > \alpha$.

CHAPTER 10

Suggestions for Future Research

The concluding sections of Chapters 3, 5, 6, 8, and 9 summarize what the book has to say about various aspects of the trade policy debate in developing countries. Rather than cover that ground again in slightly different language, I will bring matters to a close by emphasizing that a good deal of additional work is needed in the areas of optimal commercial policy, liberalization, and direct foreign investment to complete the research program started here.

Optimal Commercial Policy

The analysis of optimal commercial policy in Chapter 5 assumed that exports were primary products (or lightly processed manufactured goods) and that high-wage employment was confined to the import-competing sector. It is desirable to relax these two assumptions. A significant minority of LDCs are now proficient exporters of manufactured goods, and in some parts of Latin America the high-wage sector includes large sections of the export sector and services in addition to import-competing manufacturing production.

No special adaptations of the model in Chapter 5 are required to analyze optimal commercial policy when the manufacturing export sector resides in the low-wage informal sector. This case can be handled simply by marking down the cost share of land and marking up the cost shares of labor and capital. I doubt if it would produce results appreciably different from those in Chapter 5.

The more challenging and more interesting case places manufactured exports in the high-wage formal sector. Since agriculture still produces 10–25% of GDP in most semi-industrial countries, a proper analysis of this case requires a four-sector model. The solutions for optimal policy would, *inter alia*, tell us whether nontraditional exports deserve more encouragement than traditional exports. I suspect the answer is yes, that optimal policy will be characterized by a fairly balanced combination of protection and export promotion in the manufacturing sector together with small export subsidies or relatively low protection for agriculture (if it is an import-competing sector).[1]

---

[1] Distributional concerns may justify more protection for agriculture.

On a more speculative note, it might be worthwhile to investigate how externalities associated with exports, imports of capital goods, or total manufacturing production affect optimal policy. I have misgivings about this suggestion because there is no evidence thus far that such externalities are important. But future empirical studies may overturn this conclusion. And even now the policy debate may benefit from a rigorous analysis of the case where export sales generate some type of production externality. The objective would be to determine the "disagreement point," that is, to determine how large externalities have to be in order to reverse the conclusion in Chapter 5 that the optimal trade regime has a moderate protectionist bias.

Liberalization

The problem of transitory unemployment should be revisited in a more elaborate dynamic model that allows for sector-specific capital accumulation. The results in Chapter 5 provide the reason: lower tariffs on consumer goods and higher tariffs on intermediates (both decrease the effective rate of protection) would be expected to cause *large* reductions in the aggregate capital stock, the number of high-wage jobs, and the market-clearing wage in the informal sector. Although the paths of these three variables are loosely correlated in the short run, they tend to move in the same direction over the medium run because reductions in the aggregate capital stock and lower purchases of intermediates shift labor demand curves to the left. Consequently, capital decumulation may significantly lengthen and deepen the phase of transitory unemployment following liberalization. In this event, the losses during the adjustment process will be larger relative to the permanent gains from trade and the optimal stopping point will lie further away from the ex ante optimum than in a model that assumes fixed capital stocks. The results in the first half of Chapter 6 may therefore understate the costs of adjustment and overstate the optimal amount of liberalization.

The analysis of liberalization in Chapters 6 and 8 is wanting in other respects. In fact, several issues that figure prominently in the policy debate were ignored altogether. The most important concerns the optimal speed of policy adjustment. The question of whether liberalization should be gradual or cold turkey has been around for some time; it has not, however, been the object of much formal theoretical analysis.[2] No doubt this reflects the daunting technical problems that arise when policy instruments are freely chosen at every point in time. But simpler

[2] Surprisingly, nobody has followed up on the promising start in Mussa (1986).

formulations probably capture most of the relevant insights while keeping the worst technical dragons at bay. A lot could be learned, for example, from analysis of the case where policy instruments evolve according to $x(t) = x^* + [k - (x^* - x_o)]e^{-\beta t}$. If the context is optimal liberalization, the task is to solve jointly for x^*, the optimal stopping point, and for the values of k and β, the two parameters that define the optimal path that leads from x_o to x^*. (k is the initial jump in x at $t = 0$ and β determines the speed of policy adjustment thereafter.) Alternatively, one might be interested in how the values of k and β influence the path of the payments deficit and the likelihood of a policy reversal when credibility is weak. x^* is then the target value of the tariff and the analysis focuses on whether liberalization is more or less vulnerable to self-fulfilling failures when tariff cuts are phased-in slowly.

Direct Foreign Investment

Chapter 9 investigated how export requirements, profits taxes, and joint venture provisions alter the net benefits LDCs receive from foreign investment. There was no analysis, however, of local content requirements that force foreign firms to purchase more inputs from domestic suppliers. Policy makers like content requirements because they believe that more linkages to domestic industry translate directly into more economic development. This is simplistic. It is not clear whether more employment in the domestic intermediates sector comes at the price of less job creation by foreign firms or what the impact is on aggregate capital accumulation, underemployment, and welfare when this possibly inefficient sector attracts resources away from the rest of the economy. The issue is ripe for some careful general equilibrium analysis.

Among the other items that rank high on the research agenda, I would give priority to the analysis of foreign investment in more general dynamic models that distinguish between skilled and unskilled labor. There is evidence in some cases that foreign firms use more skilled labor per unit of output (or capital) than domestic firms.[3] This raises all sorts of questions. The stronger demand for skilled labor associated with foreign investment is likely to worsen the distribution of wage income in the short run (Hanson and Feenstra, 1996, 1997), but is this also true in the long run and, if so, do unskilled workers suffer an absolute loss or just a decrease in their relative wage? Does recruitment of skilled labor away from local firms reduce the return on capital and cause more crowding out of domestic investment? And how do the answers to these

---

[3] See Hanson and Feenstra (1997) and Pitt and Lee (1984).

and other questions (e.g., the impact on welfare and high-wage employment) change when the government requires foreign firms to train local workers for skill positions?

In assessing the contribution economists make to practical affairs, Robert Lucas wrote "As an advice-giving profession, we are in way over our heads" (1980, p. 209). I am not in complete agreement with this or with the sentiments of the theorist who bragged that he does not allow students in his courses to use the word policy. But Lucas has a point, and trade and development economists would do well to contemplate it. There is often an embarrassing disparity between the information policy makers need to make intelligent, well-informed choices and what economics can provide. The present case is, regrettably, no exception: we are far away from a reasonably complete analysis of trade policy based on models that do justice to the structural diversity of LDC economies.

References

Abel, A. and O. Blanchard, 1986. "The Present Value of Profits and Cyclical Movements in Investment." *Econometrica* 54: 249–276.

Ademola Oyejide, T., 1997. "Regional Integration and Trade Liberalization in Sub-Saharan Africa: Sumary Report 1996." *Special Paper No. 28* (African Economic Research Consortium).

African Development Bank, 1995, 1998. *African Development Report 1995, 1998* (Oxford University Press, New York).

Agha, A. and J. Haughton, 1996. "Designing VAT Systems: Some Efficiency Considerations." *Review of Economics and Statistics* 78: 303–308.

Aitken, B., G. Hanson, and A. Harrison, 1997. "Spillovers, Foreign Investment and Export Behavior." *Journal of International Economics* 43: 103–132.

Akrasanee, N., 1981. "Trade Strategy for Employment Growth in Thailand." In A. Krueger, ed., *Trade and Employment in Developing Countries: Individual Studies, Vol. I* (University of Chicago Press for the National Bureau of Economic Research, Chicago).

Akrasanee, N. and P. Wiboonchutikula, 1994. "Trade and Industrialization Policy and Productivity Growth in Thailand." In G. Helleiner, ed., *Trade Policy and Industrialization in Turbulent Times* (Routledge, New York).

Alonso-Borrego, C. and S. Bentolila, 1994. "Investment and Q in Spanish Manufacturing." *Oxford Bulletin of Economics and Statistics* 56: 49–66.

Ahmad, J. and A. Kwan, 1991. "Causality Between Exports and Economic Growth: Empirical Evidence from Africa." *Economics Letters* 37: 243–248.

Alderman, H. and V. Kozel, 1989. "Formal and Informal Sector Wage Determination in Low-Income Neighborhoods in Pakistan." *LSMS Working Paper No. 65* (World Bank).

Allen, R., 1938. *Mathematical Analysis for Economists* (MacMillan, London).

Aravena, O., 1996. "Controlling Hyperinflation and Structural Adjustment in Nicaragua." In A. Jilberto and A. Mommen, eds., *Liberalization in the Developing World* (Routledge, New York).

374

Arift, M. and C. Lim, 1987. "Foreign Investments in Malaysia." In V. Cable and B. Persaud, eds., *Developing with Foreign Investment* (Croom Helm, New York).

Arrow, K. and M. Kurz, 1970. *Public Investment, the Rate of Return, and Optimal Fiscal Policy* (Johns Hopkins Press, Baltimore, MD).

Arulpragasam, J. and C. del Ninno, 1996. "Do Cheap Imports Harm the Poor? Rural-Urban Tradeoffs in Guinea." In D. Sahn, ed., *Economic Reform and the Poor in Africa* (Oxford University Press, New York).

Auernheimer, L. and S. George, 1997. "Shock versus Gradualism in Models of Rational Expectations: The Case of Trade Liberalization." *Journal of Development Economics* 54: 307–322.

Aw, B., S. Chung, and M. Roberts, 1998. "Productivity and the Decision to Export: Micro Evidence from Taiwan and South Korea." National Bureau of Economic Research Working Paper 6558 (forthcoming in *World Bank Economic Review*).

Baer, W. and M. Fonseca, 1987. "Structural Change in Brazil's Industrial Economy, 1960–1980." *World Development* 15: 275–286.

Bahmani-Oskooee, M., H. Mohtadi, and G. Shabsigh, 1991. "Exports, Growth and Causality in LDCs: A Re-examination." *Journal of Development Economics* 36: 405–415.

Balassa, B. and Associates, 1971. *The Structure of Protection in Developing Countries* (Johns Hopkins University; Baltimore, MD).

Balasubramanyan, V., 1991. "Putting TRIMs to Good Use." *World Development* 19: 1215–1224.

Baldwin, R., 1975. *Foreign Trade and Economic Development: The Philippines* (Columbia University Press, New York).

Bardhan, P., 1995. "The Contributions of Endogenous Growth Theory to the Analysis of Development Problems: An Assessment." In J. Behrman and T. N. Srinivasan, eds., *Handbook of Development Economics, Volume 3b* (North-Holland, New York).

Baumol, W., 1965. *Welfare Economics and the Theory of the State* (G. Bell and Sons, London).

Becker, R. and J. Boyd, 1997. *Capital Theory, Equilibrium Analysis, and Recursive Utility* (Blackwell, Malden, MA).

Behrman, J., 1976. *Foreign Trade and Economic Development: Chile* (Columbia University Press, New York).

———, 1982. "Country and Sector Variations in Manufacturing Elasticities of Substitution Between Capital and Labor." In A. Krueger, ed., *Trade and*

Employment in Developing Countries, Vol. 2: Factor Supply and Substitution (University of Chicago Press for the National Bureau of Economic Research, Chicago).

Bell, M., B. Ross-Larsen, and L. Westphal, 1984. "Assessing the Performance of Infant Industries." *Journal of Development Economics* 16: 101–128.

Ben-David, D., 1993. "Equalizing Exchange: Trade Liberalization and Income Convergence." *Quarterly Journal of Economics* 108: 653–679.

Benjamin, N., S. Devarajan, and R. Weiner, 1989. "The Dutch Disease in a Developing Country: Oil Reserves in Cameroon." *Journal of Development Economics* 30: 71–92.

Berndt, E. and D. Wood, 1975. "Technology, Prices and the Derived Demand for Energy." *Review of Economics and Statistics* 57: 259–268.

Berry, R., 1992. "Firm (or Plant) Size in the Analysis of Trade and Development." In G. Helleiner, ed., *Trade Policy, Industrialization and Development – New Perspectives* (Clarendon Press, Oxford).

———, 1998a. "Introduction." In A. Berry, ed., *Poverty, Economic Reform and Income Distribution in Latin America* (Lynne Rienner, Boulder, CO).

———, 1998b. "Confronting the Income Distribution Threat in Latin America." In A. Berry, ed., *Poverty, Economic Reform and Income Distribution in Latin America* (Lynne Rienner, Boulder, CO).

Bergman, L., 1988. "Energy Policy Modeling: A Survey of General Equilibrium Approaches." *Journal of Policy Modeling* 10: 377–399.

Bevan, D., P. Collier, and J. Gunning, 1990. *Controlled Open Economies: A Neoclassical Approach to Structuralism* (Clarendon Press, Oxford).

Bhagwati, J., 1965. "On the Equivalence of Tariffs and Quotas." In R. Caves et al., eds., *Trade Growth and the Balance of Payments* (Rand-McNally, Chicago).

———, 1971. "The Generalized Theory of Distortions and Welfare." In J. Bhagwati et al., eds., *Trade, Balance of Payments and Growth* (North-Holland, Amsterdam).

———, 1978. *Anatomy and Consequences of Exchange Control Regimes* (Ballinger Publishing Co., Cambridge, MA).

———, 1987. "Outward Orientation: Trade Issues." In V. Corbo, M. Goldstein, and M. Khan, eds., *Growth-Oriented Adjustment Programs* (International Monetary Fund and The World Bank; Washington, DC)

Bhagwati, J. and T. N. Srinivasan, 1979. "Trade Policy and Development." In R. Dornbusch and J. Frenkel, eds., *International Economic Policy* (Johns Hopkins Press, London).

Bird, R., 1991. "Tax Administration and Tax Reform: Reflections on Experience." In J. Khalizadeh-Shirazi and A. Shah, eds., *Tax Policy in Developing Countries* (The World Bank, Washington, DC).

Blackorby, C., D. Primont, and R. Russel, 1978. *Duality, Separability and Functional Structure: Theory and Applications* (American Elsevier, New York).

Blackorby, C. and R. Russel, 1989. "Will the Real Elasticity of Substitution Please Stand Up?" *American Economic Review* 79: 882–888.

Bliss, C., 1989. "Trade and Development: Theoretical Issues and Policy Implications." In H. Chenery and T. N. Srinivasan, eds., *Handbook of Development Economics, Vol. 2* (North-Holland, Amsterdam).

Blomstrom, M. and H. Persson, 1983. "Foreign Investment and Spillover Efficiency in an Underdeveloped Economy: Evidence from the Mexican Manufacturing Industry." *World Development* 11: 493–501.

Blundell, R., 1988. "Consumer Behavior: Theory and Evidence – A Survey." *Economic Journal* 98: 16–65.

Blundell, R., P. Pashardes, and G. Weber, 1993. "What Do We Learn About Consumer Demand Patterns From Micro Data?" *American Economic Review* 83: 570–597.

Boldrin, M. and J. Scheinkman, 1988. "Learning-By-Doing, International Trade and Growth: A Note." In P. Anderseon, K. Arrow, and D. Pines, eds., *The Economy as an Evolving Complex System* (Addison-Wesley, New York).

Brander, J., 1981. "Intra-Industry Trade in Identical Commodities." *Journal of International Economics* 11: 1–14.

Brannon, J., D. James, and G. Lucker, 1994. "Generating and Sustaining Backward Linkages Between Maquiladoras and Local Suppliers in Northern Mexico." *World Development* 22: 1933–1945.

Brecher, R. and C. Diaz Alejandro, 1977. "Tariffs, Foreign Capital and Immiserizing Growth." *Journal of International Economics* 7: 317–322.

Brown, D., 1991. "Tariffs and Capacity Utilization by Monopolistically Competitive Firms." *Journal of International Economics* 30: 371–381.

Bruno, M., 1988. "Opening Up: Liberalization with Stabilization." In R. Dornbusch and F. Helmers, eds., *The Open Economy: Tools for Policymakers in Developing Countries* (Oxford University Press, New York).

Buffie, E., 1984. "The Macroeconomics of Trade Liberalization." *Journal of International Economics* 17: 121–137.

———, 1985. "Quantitative Restrictions and Welfare Effects of Capital Inflows." *Journal of International Economics* 19: 291–303.

———, 1992. "Commercial Policy, Growth and the Distribution of Income in a Dynamic Trade Model." *Journal of Development Economics* 37: 1–30.

———, 1993. "Direct Foreign Investment, Crowding Out, and Underemployment in the Dualistic Economy." *Oxford Economic Papers* 45: 639–667.

———, 1995. "Trade Liberalization, Credibility and Self-Fulfilling Failures." *Journal of International Economics* 38: 51–73.

———, 1999. "Optimal Trade Liberalization and the Welfare Costs of Imperfect Credibility." *Journal of International Economics.* 47: 371–398.

Buffie, E. and P. Spiller, 1986. "Trade Liberalization in Oligopolistic Industries: The Quota Case." *Journal of International Economics* 20: 65–81.

Calvo, G., 1987. "On the Costs of Temporary Policy." *Journal of Development Economics* 27: 245–261.

———, 1988. "Costly Trade Liberalization: Durable Goods and Capital Mobility." *IMF Staff Papers* 35: 461–473.

———, 1989. "Incredible Reforms." In G. Calvo et al., eds., *Debt, Stabilization and Development* (Blackwell, Cambridge, MA).

Calvo, G. and E. Mendoza, 1994. "Trade Reforms of Uncertain Duration and Real Uncertainty: A First Approximation." *IMF Staff Papers* 41: 555–586.

Casson, M. and R. Pearce, 1987. "Multinational Enterprises in LDCs." In N. Gemmell, ed., *Surveys in Development Economics* (Blackwell, New York).

Celasun, M., 1994. "Trade and Industrialization in Turkey: Initial Conditions, Policy and Performance in the 1980s." In G. Helleiner, ed., *Trade Policy and Industrialization in Turbulent Times* (Routledge, New York).

Chambers, R., 1988. *Applied Production Analysis* (Cambridge University Press, New York).

Cheru, F., 1989. *The Silent Revolution in Africa* (Zed Books, London).

Chiang, A., 1992. *Elements of Dynamic Optimization* (McGraw-Hill, New York).

Chibber, A. and J. Khalizadeh-Shirazi, 1991. "Public Finance." In V. Thomas et al., eds., *Restructuring Economies in Distress: Policy Reform and the World Bank* (Oxford University Press, New York).

Chiwele, D., 1996. "Mining Sector and Real Wages in Zambia." In C. Harvey, ed., *Constraints on the Success of Structural Adjustment Programs in Africa* (St. Martin's Press, New York).

Clarette, R. and J. Whalley, 1987. "Comparing the Marginal Welfare Costs of Commodity and Trade Taxes." *Journal of Public Economics* 33: 357–362.

Clerides, S., S. Lach, and J. Tybout, 1998. "Is Learning by Exporting Important? Microdynamic Evidence from Colombia, Mexico, and Morocco." *Quarterly Journal of Economics* 113: 903–947.

Cnossen, S., 1991. "Design of the Value Added Tax: Lessons from Experience." In J. Khalizadeh-Shirazi and A. Shah, eds., *Tax Policy in Developing Countries* (The World Bank, Washington, DC).

Collier, P., 1991. "Africa's External Economic Relations: 1960–90." *African Affairs* 90: 339–356.

———, 1993. "Higgledy-Piggledy Liberalisation." *World Economy* 16: 503–513.

Collier, P., D. Greenaway, and J. Gunning, 1997. "Evaluating Trade Liberalization: A Methodological Framework." In A. Oyejide, I. Elbadawi, and P. Collier, eds., *Regional Integration and Trade Liberalization in SubSaharan Africa, Volume 1* (St. Martin's Press, New York).

Corbo, V. and P. Meller, 1982. "The Substitution of Labor, Skill and Capital: Its Implications for Trade and Employment." In A. Krueger, ed., *Trade and Employment in Developing Countries, Vol. 2: Factor Supply and Substitution* (University of Chicago Press for the National Bureau of Economic Research, Chicago).

Corden, M., 1974. *Trade Policy and Economic Welfare* (Clarendon Press, Oxford).

Cornes, R., 1992. *Duality and Modern Economics* (Cambridge University Press, New York).

Cornia, G., R. van der Hoeven, and T. Mkandawire, 1992. "Overview of an Alternative Long-term Development Strategy." In G. Cornia, R. van der Hoeven, and T. Mkandawire, eds., *Africa's Recovery in the 1990s* (St. Martin's Press, New York).

Deaton, A. and D. Muellbauer, 1980. *Economics and Consumer Behavior* (Cambridge University Press, New York).

De Gregorio, J., 1992. "Economic Growth in Latin America." *Journal of Development Economics* 39: 59–84.

De La Cuesta, J., 1990. "IS-FM Macroeconomics: General Equilibrium Linkages of the Food Market in Colombia." In L. Taylor, ed., *Socially Relevant Policy Analysis: Structuralist Computable General Equilibrium Models for the Developing World* (MIT Press, Cambridge, MA).

De Melo, J., 1977. "Distortions in the Factor Markets: Some General Equilibrium Estimates." *Review of Economics and Statistics* 59: 398–405.

De Melo, J. and D. Roland-Holst, 1994. "Economy wide Costs of Protection and Labor Market Rigidities." In M. Connolly and J. de Melo, eds., *The Effects of Protectionism on a Small Country* (The World Bank, Washington, DC).

Dervis, K., J. de Melo, and S. Robinson, 1982. *General Equilibrium Models for Development Policy* (Cambridge University Press, New York).

Devarajan, S., 1988. "Natural Resources and Taxation in Computable General Equilibrium Models of Developing Countries." *Journal of Policy Modeling* 10: 505–528.

———, 1991. "Comments." In V. Thomas et al., eds., *Restructuring Economies in Distress: Policy Reform and the World Bank* (Oxford University Press, New York).

Devarajan, S. and J. De Melo, 1987. "Adjustment with a Fixed Exchange Rate: Cameroon, Cote d'Ivoire and Senegal." *World Bank Economic Review* 1: 447–487.

Devarajan, S., J. Lewis, and S. Robinson, 1990. "Lessons from Trade-Focused, Two-Sector Models." *Journal of Policy Modeling* 12: 625–658.

Devarajan, S. and D. Rodrik, 1991. "Do the Benefits of Fixed Exchange Rates Outweight Their Costs? The Franc Zone in Africa." *National Bureau of Economic Research Working Paper No. 3727.*

Devarajan, S. and C. Sussangkarn, 1992. "Effective Rates of Protection When Domestic and Foreign Goods are Imperfect Substitutes: The Case of Thailand." *Review of Economics and Statistics* 74: 701–711.

Diaz Alejandro, C., 1975. "Trade Policies and Economic Development." In P. Kenen, ed., *International Trade and Finance: Frontiers for Research* (Cambridge University Press, New York).

Diewert, W., 1978. "Duality Approaches to Microeconomic Theory." In K. Arrow and M. Intriligator, eds., *Handbook of Mathematical Economics* (North-Holland, Amsterdam).

Dixit, A. and V. Norman, 1980. *Theory of International Trade: A Dual, General Equilibrium Approach* (Cambridge University Press, London).

Dollar, D., 1992. "Outward-Oriented Developing Countries Really Do Grow More Rapidly: Evidence from 95 LDCs, 1976–1985." *Economic Development and Cultural Change* 40: 523–544.

Dollar, D. and K. Sokoloff, 1990. "Patterns of Productivity Growth in South Korean Manufacturing Industries." *Journal of Development Economics* 33: 309–327.

Dornbusch, R., 1992. "The Case for Trade Liberalization in Developing Countries." *Journal of Economic Perspectives* 6: 69–86.

Dutz, M., 1996. "Oligopolistic Firms' Adjustment to Quota Liberalization: Theory and Evidence." In M. Roberts and J. Tybout, eds., *Industrial Evolution in Developing Countries: Micro Patterns of Turnover, Productivity, and Market Structure* (Oxford University Press, New York).

Ethier, W., 1982. "National and International Returns to Scale in the Modern Theory of International Trade." *American Economic Review* 72: 389–405.

Edwards, S., 1984. "The Order of Liberalization of the External Sector in Developing Countries." *Princeton Essays in International Finance*, No. 156.

———, 1992. "Trade Orientation, Distortions and Growth in Developing Countries." *Journal of Development Economics* 39: 31–57.

———, 1998. "Openness, Productivity and Growth: What Do We Really Know?" *Economic Journal* 108: 383–398.

Engel, C. and K. Kletzer, 1991. "Trade Policy Under Endogenous Credibility." *Journal of Development Economics* 36: 213–228.

Engel, R. and D. Foley, 1975. "An Asset Price Model of Aggregate Investment." *International Economic Review* 16: 625–647.

Esfahani, H., 1991. "Exports, Imports and Economic Growth in Semi-Industrialized Countries." *Journal of Development Economics* 35: 93–116.

Falvey, R. and C. Kim, 1992. "Timing and Sequencing Issues in Trade Liberalization." *The Economic Journal* 102: 908–924.

Faini, R., 1994. "Morocco: Reconciling Stabilization and Growth." In W. Easterly, C. Rodriguez, and K. Schmidt-Hebbel, eds., *Public Sector Deficits and Macroeconomic Performance* (Oxford University Press, New York).

Farrell, T., 1987. "Direct Foreign Investment, the Transnational Corporation and the Prospects for LDC Transformation in Today's World: Lessons from the Trinidad-Tobago Experience." In V. Cable and B. Persaud, eds., *Developing with Foreign Investment* (Croom Helm, New York).

Feder, G., 1983. "On Exports and Economic Growth." *Journal of Development Economics* 12: 62–73.

Feenstra, R., 1986. "Functional Equivalence Between Liquidity Costs and the Utility of Money." *Journal of Monetary Economics* 17: 271–291.

———, 1996. "Trade and Uneven Growth." *Journal of Development Economics* 49: 229–256.

Feenstra, R. and G. Hanson, 1996. "Foreign Investment, Outsourcing and Relative Wages." In R. Feenstra, G. Grossman, and D. Irwin, eds., *Political Economy of Trade Policy: Essays in Honor of Jagdish Bhagwati* (MIT Press, Cambridge, MA).

———, 1997. "Foreign Direct Investment and Relative Wages: Evidence from Mexico's Maquiladoras." *Journal of International Economics* 42: 371–393.

Feldstein, M., 1964. "The Social Time Preference Discount Rate in Cost Benefit Analysis." *Economic Journal* 74: 360–379.

Fields, G., 1990. "Labour Market Modelling and the Urban Informal Sector: Theory and Evidence." In D. Turnham et al., eds., *The Informal Sector Revisited* (Organization for Economic Cooperation and Development, Paris).

Flam, H. and E. Helpman, 1987. "Industrial Policy Under Monopolistic Competition." *Journal of International Economics* 22: 79–102.

Flam, H. and R. Staiger, 1991. "Adverse Selection in Credit Markets and Infant Industry Protection." In E. Helpman and A. Razin, eds., *International Trade and Trade Policy* (MIT Press, Cambridge, MA).

Foxley, A., 1983. *Latin American Experiments in Neo-Conservative Economics* (University of California Press, Los Angeles).

Fried, H. and R. Falvey, 1986. "National Ownership Requirements and Transfer Pricing." *Journal of Development Economics* 24: 249–254.

Friesen, J., 1992. "Testing Dynamic Specification of Factor Demand Equations for U.S. Manufacturing." *Review of Economics and Statistics* 74: 240–250.

Galeoti, M. and F. Schiantarelli, 1991. "Generalized Q Models for Investment." *Review of Economics and Statistics* 73: 383–392.

Gaude, J., 1975. "Capital-Labour Substitution Possibilities: A Review of Empirical Evidence." In A. Bhalla, ed., *Technology and Employment in Industry* (International Labour Organization, Geneva).

Geske Dijkstra, A., 1996. "The Impact of Structural Adjustment Programs on Manufacturing: Lessons from Nicaragua." *World Development* 24: 535–547.

Gibbons, P., 1996. "Zimbabwe 1991–94." In P. Engberg-Pedersen et al., eds., *Limits of Adjustment in Africa* (Centre for Development Research, Copenhagen and Heinemann Press, Portsmouth, NH).

Gibson, B., 1990. "A CGE Model for Nicaragua." In L. Taylor, ed., *Socially Relevant Policy Analysis: Structuralist Computable General Equilibrium Models for the Developing World* (MIT Press, Cambridge, MA).

Gindling, T., 1991. "Labor Market Segmentation and the Determination of Wages in the Public, Private-Formal and Informal Sectors in San Jose, Costa Rica." *Economic Development and Cultural Change* 39: 589–605.

Goldberger, A. and T. Gamaletsos, 1970. "A Cross-Country Comparison of Consumer Expenditure Patterns." *European Economic Review* 1: 357–400.

Gorman, W., 1953. "Community Preference Fields." *Econometrica* 21: 63–80.

Greenaway, D., 1992. "Trade Related Investment Measures and Development Strategy." *Kyklos* 45: 139–159.

——, 1993. "Liberalizing Foreign Trade through Rose-Tinted Glasses." *Economic Journal* 103: 208–222.

Greenaway, D. and C. Milner, 1993. "The Fiscal Implications of Trade Policy Reform: Theory and Evidence." *UNDP/World Bank Trade Expansion Program Occasional Paper No. 9* (The World Bank, Washington, DC).

Greenaway, D. and O. Morrissey, 1993. "Trade Policy Reform in Developing Countries: Problems and Prospects." In S. Mansoob Murshed and K. Rutter, eds., *Trade, Transfers and Development* (Edward Elgar, Cambridge, England).

Gregory, P., 1986. *The Myth of Market Failure: Employment and the Labor Market in Mexico* (Johns Hopkins Press, Baltimore, MD).

Griffin, J. and P. Gregory, 1976. "An Intercountry Translog Model of Energy Substitution Responses." *American Economic Review* 66: 845–857.

Grossman, G. and E. Helpman, 1991. *Innovation and Growth in the Global Economy* (MIT Press, Cambridge, MA).

Haddad, M. and A. Harrison, 1993. "Are There Positive Spillovers from Direct Foreign Investment? Evidence from Panel Data for Morocco." *Journal of Development Economics* 42: 51–74.

Handoussa, H., M. Nishimizu, and J. Page, 1986. "Productivity Change in Egyptian Public Sector Industries after the 'Opening'." *Journal of Development Economics* 20: 53–74.

Harris, J. and M. Todaro, 1970. "Migration, Unemployment and Development: A Two-Sector Analysis." *American Economic Review* 60: 126–143.

Harrison, A., "Determinants and Effects of Direct Foreign Investment in Côte d'Ivoire, Morocco and Venezuela." In M. Roberts and J. Tybout, eds., *Industrial Evolution in Developing Countries: Micro Patterns of Turnover, Productivity, and Market Structure* (Oxford University Press, New York).

———, 1996. "Openness and Growth: A Time-Series, Cross-Country Analysis for Developing Countries." *Journal of Development Economics* 48: 419–447.

Harvey, C., 1996. "Constraints on Sustained Recovery from Economic Disaster in Africa." In C. Harvey, ed., *Constraints on the Success of Structural Adjustment Programmes in Africa* (St. Martin's Press, New York).

Havrylyshyn, O., 1990. "Trade Policy and Productivity Gains in Developing Countries: A Survey of the Literature." *World Bank Research Observer* 5: 1–24.

Hayashi, F., 1982. "Tobin's Marginal q and Average q: A Neoclassical Interpretation." *Econometrica* 50: 213–224.

Helleiner, G., 1989. "Transnational Corporations and Direct Foreign Investment." In H. Chenery and T. N. Srinivasan, eds., *Handbook of Development Economics, Vol. 2* (North-Holland, New York).

Helleiner, G., 1990. "Trade Strategy in Medium-Term Adjustment." *World Development* 18: 879–897.

———, 1991. Remarks in panel discussion. In V. Thomas et al., eds., *Restructuring Economies in Distress: Policy Reform and the World Bank* (Oxford University Press, New York).

———, 1994. "Introduction." In G. Helleiner, ed., *Trade Policy and Industrialization in Turbulent Times* (Routledge, New York).

Helpman, E. and P. Krugman, 1985. *Market Structure and Foreign Trade* (MIT Press, Cambridge, MA).

Hertel, T., 1994. "The 'Procompetitive' Effects of Trade Policy Reform in a Small, Open Economy." *Journal of International Economics* 36: 391–411.

Hong, W., 1981. "Export Promotion and Employment Growth in South Korea." In A. Krueger, ed., *Trade and Employment in Developing Countries: Individual Studies, Vol. I* (University of Chicago Press for the National Bureau of Economic Research, Chicago).

———, 1991. "Import Restriction and Liberalization." In L. Krause and K. Kihwan, eds., *Liberalization in the Process of Economic Development* (University of California Press, Berkeley).

Horstmann, I. and J. Markusen, 1986. "Up the Average Cost Curve: Inefficient Entry and the New Protectionism." *Journal of International Economics* 20: 225–247.

Hsiao, M., 1987. "Tests of Causality and Exogeneity Between Exports and Economic Growth: The Case of Asian NICs." *Journal of Economic Development* 12: 143–159.

Hughes, H. and G. Dorrance, 1987. "Foreign Investment in East Asia." In V. Cable and B. Persaud, eds., *Developing with Foreign Investment* (Croom Helm, New York).

Jebuni, C., 1997. "Trade Liberalization and Regional Integration in Africa." In A. Oyejide, I. Elbadawi, and P. Collier, eds., *Regional Integration and Trade Liberalization in SubSaharan Africa, Volume 1* (St. Martin's Press, New York).

Joshi, V. and I. M. D. Little, 1995. "Future Trade and Exchange Rate Policy in India." In V. Joshi and I. M. D. Little, eds., *India: The Future of Economic Reform* (Oxford University Press, New Delhi).

Kamien, M. and N. Schwarz, 1981. *Dynamic Optimization: The Calculus of Variations and Optimal Control in Economics and Management* (North-Holland, New York).

Khalizadeh-Shirazi, J. and A. Shah, 1991. "Introduction and Overview." In J. Khalizadeh-Shirazi and A. Shah, eds., *Tax Policy in Developing Countries* (The World Bank, Washington, DC).

Kohli, I. and N. Singh, 1989. "Exports and Growth: Critical Minimum Effort and Diminishing Returns." *Journal of Development Economics* 30: 391–400.

Kolstad, C. and J. Lee, 1993. "The Specification of Dynamics in Cost Function and Factor Demand Estimation." *Review of Economics and Statistics* 75: 721–726.

Krueger, A., 1978. *Liberalization Attempts and Consequences* (Ballinger, Cambridge, MA).

———, 1981a. "Alternative Trade Strategies and Employment in LDCs: An Overview." *Pakistan Development Review* 20: 277–301.

———, 1983. *Trade and Employment in Developing Countries, Vol. 3: Synthesis and Conclusions* (University of Chicago Press, Chicago).

———, 1991. "Industrial Development and Liberalization." In L. Krause and K. Kihwan, eds., *Liberalization in the Process of Economic Development* (University of California Press, Berkeley).

Krueger, A., et al., 1981. *Trade and Employment in Developing Countries: Individual Studies* (University of Chicago Press, Chicago).

Krueger, A. and B. Tuncer, 1982. "An Empirical Test of the Infant-Industry Argument." *American Economic Review* 72: 1142–1152.

Krugman, P., 1987. "The Narrow Moving Band, the Dutch Disease, and the Consequences of Mrs. Thatcher." *Journal of Development Economics* 27: 41–55.

———, 1993. "Protection in Developing Countries." In R. Dornbusch, ed., *Policymaking in the Open Economy* (Oxford University Press, New York).

Krumm, K., 1993. "A Medium-Term Framework for Analyzing the Real Exchange Rate with Applications to the Philippines and Tanzania." *World Bank Economic Review* 7: 219–245.

Kwan, J. and H. Paik, 1995. "Price Distortions, Resource Allocation, and Growth." *Review of Economics and Statistics* 77: 664–676.

Langhammer, R., 1987. "Effects of Preferential Tariff Reductions Among Developing Countries." In, O. Havrylyshyn, ed., *Exports of Developing Countries* (The World Bank, Washington, DC).

Larrea, C., 1998. "Structural Adjustment, Income Distribution, and Employment in Ecuador." In A. Berry, ed., *Poverty, Economic Reform and Income Distribution in Latin America* (Lynne Rienner, Boulder, CO).

Lee, J., 1997. "The Maturation and Growth of Infant Industries: The Case of Korea." *World Development* 25: 1271–1281.

Levine, R. and D. Renelt, 1992. "A Sensitivity Analysis of Cross-Country Growth Regressions." *American Economic Review* 82: 942–963.

Levine, R. and S. Zervos, 1993. "What Have We Learned About Policy and Growth from Cross-Country Regressions?" *American Economic Review* (May) 83: 426–430.

Lewis, S., 1989. "Primary Exporting Countries." In H. Chenery and T. N. Srinivasan, eds., *Handbook of Development Economics, Vol. 2* (North-Holland, New York).

Little, I. et al., 1993. *Boom, Crisis and Adjustment: The Macroeconomic Experience of Developing Countries* (Oxford University Press, New York).

Little, I., T. Scitovsky, and M. Scott, 1970. *Industry and Trade in Some Developing Countries* (Oxford University Press, London).

Lluch, C., A. Powell, and R. Williams, 1977. *Patterns in Household Demand and Saving* (Oxford University Press, London).

Loxley, J., 1989. "The IMF, the World Bank and Reconstruction in Uganda." In B. Campbell and J. Loxley, eds., *Structural Adjustment in Africa* (St. Martin's Press, New York).

Lucas, R., 1967. "Optimal Investment Policy and the Flexible Accelerator." *International Economic Review* 75: 78–85.

———, 1976. "Econometric Policy Evaluation: A Critique." In K. Brunner and A. Meltzer, eds., *The Phillips Curve and Labor Markets* (North-Holland, Amsterdam).

———, 1980. "Rules, Discretion and the Role of the Economic Advisor." In, S. Fischer, ed., *Rational Expectations and Economic Policy* (University of Chicago Press, Chicago).

Maasland, A., 1990. "Continuing the Tradition of Equity in Sri Lanka: Policy Options in a CGE Model." In L. Taylor, ed., *Socially Relevant Policy Analysis: Structuralist Computable General Equilibrium Models for the Developing World* (MIT Press, Cambridge, MA).

Malkiel, B. et al., 1979. "Expectations, Tobin's q and Industry Investment." *Journal of Finance* 34: 549–561.

Marcouiller, D., V. Ruiz de Castilla, and C. Woodruff, 1993. "Gulf or Gully: The Informal Sector Wage Gap in Mexico, El Salvador and Peru." Mimeo.

Mansur, A. and J. Whalley, 1984. "Numerical Specification of Applied General Equilibrium Models: Estimation, Calibration and Data." In H. Scarf and J. Shoven, eds., *Applied General Equilibrium Analysis* (Cambridge University Press, New York).

Marglin, S., 1963. "The Social Rate of Discount and the Optimal Rate of Investment." *Quarterly Journal of Economics* 77: 95–111.

Markusen, J. and A. Venables, 1988. "Trade Policy with Increasing Returns and Imperfect Competition: Contradictory Results from Competing Assumptions." *Journal of International Economics* 24: 299–316.

Marquette, C., 1997. "Current Poverty, Structural Adjustment, and Drought in Zimbabwe." *World Development* 25: 1141–1150.

Martin, J., 1978. "X-inefficiency, Managerial Effort and Protection." *Economica* 45: 273–286.

Matsuyama, K., 1990. "Perfect Equilibria in a Trade Liberalization Game." *American Economic Review* 80: 480–492.

Mazumdar, D., 1976. "The Urban Informal Sector." *World Development* 4: 655–679.

——, 1984. "The Rural-Urban Wage Gap, Migration and the Working of Urban Labor Markets: An Interpretation Based on a Study of the Workers in Bombay City." *Indian Economic Review* 18/2: 1969–1998.

McCleary, W., 1991. "Pakistan: Structural Adjustment and Economic Growth." In V. Thomas et al., eds., *Restructuring Economies in Distress: Policy Reform and the World Bank* (Oxford University Press, New York).

McFadden, D., 1978. "Cost, Revenue and Profit Functions." In M. Fuss and D. McFadden, eds., *Production Economics: A Dual Approach to Theory and Applications, Vol. I* (North-Holland, Amsterdam).

McKinnon, R., 1979. "Foreign Trade Regimes and Economic Development." *Journal of International Economics* 9: 429–452.

——, 1982. "The Order of Economic Liberalization: Lessons from Chile and Argentina." In K. Brunner and A. Meltzer, eds., *Economic Policy in a World of Change* (North-Holland, Amsterdam).

Meier, G., "Trade Policy, Development, and the New Political Economy." In R. Jones and A. Krueger, eds., *The Political Economy of International Trade* (Blackwell, Cambridge, MA).

Meller, P., 1994. "The Chilean Trade Liberalization and Export Expansion Process, 1974–1990." In G. Helleiner, ed., *Trade Policy and Industrialization in Turbulent Times* (Routledge, New York).

Merrick, T., 1976. "Employment and Earnings in the Informal Sector in Brazil." *Journal of Developing Areas* 10: 337–354.

Michaely, M., D. Papageorgiou, and A. Choksi, 1992. *Liberalizing Foreign Trade: Lessons of Experience in the Developing World, Vol. 7* (Blackwell, Oxford).

Ministry of Planning and National Development, 1998. *Economic Survey 1998* (Nairobi, Kenya).

Mitra, P., 1991. "The Coordinated Reform of Tariffs and Indirect Taxes." In J. Khalizadeh-Shirazi and A. Shah, eds., *Tax Policy in Developing Countries* (The World Bank, Washington, DC).

Mommen, A., 1996. "Zaire's Economic Decline and Ill-Fated Liberalization Policies." In A. Jilberto and A. Mommen, eds., *Liberalization in the Developing World* (Routledge, New York).

Monson, T., 1981. "Trade Strategies and Employment in the Ivory Coast." In A. Krueger, ed., *Trade and Employment in Developing Countries: Individual Studies, Vol. I* (University of Chicago Press for the National Bureau of Economic Research, Chicago).

Morrison, A., 1994. "Are Institutions or Economic Rents Responsible for Interindustry Wage Differentials?" *World Development* 22: 355–368.

Moseley, K., 1992. "Seizing the Chance: Economic Crisis and Industrial Restructuring in Nigeria." In J. Nyang'oro and T. Shaw, eds., *Beyond Structural Adjustment in Africa* (Praeger, New York).

Mulaga, G. and J. Weiss, 1996. "Trade Reform in Manufacturing Performance in Malawi 1970–91." *World Development* 24: 1267–1278.

Muller, A. and D. Rawana, 1991. "Tariff-Limit Pricing, Relative Plant Scale, and the Eastman-Stykolt Hypothesis." *Canadian Journal of Economics* 23: 232–231.

Mussa, M., 1986. "The Adjustment Process and the Timing of Trade Liberalizaton." In A. Choksi and D. Papageorgiou, eds., *Economic Liberalization in Developing Countries* (Blackwell, New York).

Nabli, M., 1981. "Alternative Trade Strategies and Employment in Tunisia." In A. Krueger, ed., *Trade and Employment in Developing Countries: Individual Studies, Vol. I* (University of Chicago Press for the National Bureau of Economic Research, Chicago).

Nishimizu, M. and S. Robinson, 1984. "Trade Policies and Productivity Change in Semi-Industrialized Countries." *Journal of Development Economics* 16: 177–206.

Ocampo, J., 1994. "Trade Policy and Industrialization in Colombia, 1967–1991." In G. Helleiner, ed., *Trade Policy and Industrialization in Turbulent Times* (Routledge, New York).

O'Connell, S., 1997. "Macroeconomic Harmonization, Trade Reform and Regional Trade in Sub-Saharan Africa." In A. Oyejide, I. Elbadawi, and P. Collier, eds., *Regional Integration and Trade Liberalization in Sub-Saharan Africa, Volume I: Framework, Issues and Methodological Perspectives* (MacMillan, London).

Ogaki, M., J. Ostry, and C. Reinhart, 1996. "Saving Behavior in Low- and Middle-Income Developing Countries." *IMF Staff Papers* 43: 38–71.

Ostry, J. and C. Reinhart, 1992. "Private Saving and Terms of Trade Shocks." *IMF Staff Papers* 39: 495–417.

Pack, H., 1979. "Technology and Employment: Constraints on Optimal Performance." In S. Rosenblatt, ed., *Technology and Economic Development: A Critical Perspective* (Westview, Boulder, CO).

———, 1988. "Industrialization and Trade." In H. Chenery and T. N. Srinivasan, eds., *Handbook of Development Economics, Vol. 1* (North-Holland, Amsterdam).

———, 1992. "Learning and Productivity Change in Developing Countries." In G. Helleiner, ed., *Trade Policy, Industrialization and Development – New Perspectives* (Clarendon Press, Oxford).

———, 1994. "Endogenous Growth Theory: Intellectual Appeal and Empirical Shortcomings." *Journal of Economic Perspectives* 8: 55–72.

Pack, H. and J. Page, 1994. "Accumulation, Exports and Growth in the High-Performing Asian Economies." *Carnegie Rochester Papers on Public Policy* (Winter).

Page, S., 1987. "Developing Country Attitudes Towards Foreign Investment." In V. Cable and B. Persaud, eds., *Developing with Foreign Investment* (Croom Helm, New York).

Pereira, A. and J. Shoven, 1988. "Survey of Dynamic Conputational General Equilibrium Models for Tax Policy Evaluation." *Journal of Policy Modeling* 10: 401–436.

Pitt, M. and L. Lee, 1981. "The Measurement and Sources of Technical Inefficiency in the Indonesian Weaving Industry." *Journal of Development Economics* 9: 43–64.

Pollak, R., R. Sickles, and T. Wales, 1984. "The CES-Translog: Specification and Estimation of a New Cost Function." *Review of Economics and Statistics* 66: 602–607.

Porter, A., Blitzer, S. and J. Curtis, 1986. "The Urban Informal Sector in Uruguay: Its Internal Structure, Characteristics and Effects." *World Development* 14: 727–741.

Pritchett, L., 1996. "Measuring Outward-Orientation in LDCs: Can it be Done?" *Journal of Development Economics* 49: 307–336.

Rader, T., 1968. "Normally, Factors Are Never Gross Substitutes." *Journal of Political Economy* 76: 38–43.

Ram, R., 1987. "Exports and Economic Growth in Developing Countries: Evidence from Time Series and Cross-Section Data." *Economic Development and Cultural Change* 24: 51–70.

Rama, M., 1994. "The Labor Market and Trade Reform in Manufacturing." In M. Connolly and J. de Melo, eds., *The Effects of Protectionism on a Small Country* (The World Bank, Washington, DC).

Ravenga, A., 1994. "Employment and Wage Effects of Trade Liberalization: The Case of Mexican Manufacturing." Mimeo (The World Bank).

Reinikka, R., 1994. "How to Identify Trade Liberalization Episodes: An Empirical Study of Kenya." Working Paper Series 94.10 (Centre for the Study of African Economies, University of Oxford).

———, 1996. "The Credibility Problem in Trade Liberalisation: Empirical Evidence from Kenya," *Journal of African Economies* 5: 444–468.

Riddell, R., 1987. "Zimbabwe's Experience of Foreign Investment Policy." In V. Cable and B. Persaud, eds., *Developing with Foreign Investment* (Croom Helm, New York).

Rivera-Batiz, F., 1997. "Trade Liberalization and the International Distribution of the Gains from Growth." In S. Gupta and N. Choudhry, eds., *Globalization, Growth and Sustainability* (Kluwer, Boston).

Roberts, M. and J. Tybout, 1991. "Size Rationalization and Trade Exposure in Developing Countries." In R. Baldwin, ed., *Empirical Studies of Commercial Policy* (University of Chicago Press for the National Bureau of Economic Research, Chicago).

———, 1996. "A Preview of the Country Studies." In M. Roberts and J. Tybout, eds., *Industrial Evolution in Developing Countries: Micro Patterns of Turnover, Productivity, and Market Structure* (Oxford University Press, New York).

Robertson, J., 1992. "The Process of Trade Reform in Nigeria and the Pursuit of Structural Adjustment." In C. Milner and A. Rayner, eds., *Policy Adjustment in Africa* (St. Martin's Press, New York).

Rodriguez, F. and D. Rodrik, 1999. "Trade Policy and Economic Growth: A Skeptic's Guide to the Cross-National Evidence." Mimeo (University of Maryland and Harvard University).

Rodrik, D., 1987. "The Economics of Export-Performance Requirements." *Quarterly Journal of Economics* 102: 533–650.

———, 1988. "Imperfect Competition, Scale Economies, and Trade Policy in Developing Countries." In R. Baldwin, ed., *Trade Policy Issues and Empirical Analysis* (University of Chicago Press, Chicago).

———, 1989. "Promises, Promises: Credible Policy Reform via Signaling." *The Economic Journal* 99: 756–772.

———, 1991. "Policy Uncertainty and Private Investment in Developing Countries." *Journal of Development Economics* 36: 229–242.

————, 1992a. "Conceptual Issues in the Design of Trade Policy for Industrialization." *World Development* 20: 309–320.

————, 1992b. "The Limits of Trade Policy Reform in Developing Countries." *Journal of Economic Perspectives* 6: 87–105.

————, 1992c. "Closing the Productivity Gap: Does Trade Liberalization Really Help?" In G. Helleiner, ed., *Trade Policy, Industrialization and Development – New Perspectives* (Clarendon Press, Oxford).

Roemer, M. and S. Radelet, 1991. "Macroeconomic Reform in Developing Countries." In D. Perkins and M. Roemer, eds., *Reforming Economic Systems in Developing Countries* (Harvard University Press, Cambridge).

Romer, P., 1990. "Endogenous Technical Change." *Journal of Political Economy* 98: S71-S102.

Ros, J., 1994. "Mexico's Trade and Industrialization Experience Since 1960." In G. Helleiner, ed., *Trade Policy and Industrialization in Turbulent Times* (Routledge, New York).

Sachs, J. and A. Warner, 1995. "Economic Reform and the Process of Global Integration." *Brookings Papers on Economic Activity* (No. 1): 1–118.

Samy, J., 1987. "Foreign Investment in the Fiji Economy: A Brief Survey." In V. Cable and B. Persaud, eds., *Developing with Foreign Investment* (Croom Helm, New York).

Seierstad, A. and K. Sydsaeter, *Optimal Control Theory with Economic Applications* (North-Holland, New York).

Sen, A., 1967. "Isolation, Assurance and the Social Rate of Discount." *Quarterly Journal of Economics* 81: 112–124.

Sepehri, A., 1993. "Uganda." In L. Taylor, ed., *The Rocky Road to Reform* (MIT Press, Cambridge, MA).

Serra-Puche, J., 1984. "A General Equilibrium Model for the Mexican Economy." In H. Scarf and J. Shoven, eds., *Applied General Equilibrium Analysis* (Cambridge University Press, New York).

Shafik, N. 1990. "Modeling Investment Behavior in Developing Countries." *PRE Working Paper 452* (The World Bank, Washington, DC)

Shapiro, H. and Taylor, L., 1990. "The State and Industrial Strategy." *World Development* 18: 861–878.

Sheahan, J., 1994. "Peru's Return Toward an Open Economy: Macroeconomic Complications and Structural Questions." *World Development* 22: 911–923.

Sheehey, E., 1990. "Exports and Growth: A Flawed Framework." *Journal of Development Studies* 27: 111–116.

———, 1993. "Exports as a Factor of Production: A Consistency Test." *World Development* 21: 155–160.

Stein, H., 1992. "Deindustrialization, Adjustment and the World Bank and the IMF in Africa." *World Development* 20: 83–95.

Stewart, F., 1994. "Are Short-Term Policies Consistent with Long-Term Development Needs in Africa?" In G. Cornia and G. Helleiner, eds., *From Adjustment to Development in Africa* (St. Martin's Press, New York).

Summers, L., 1981. "Taxation and Corporate Investment: A q-theory Approach." *Brookings Papers on Economic Activity* 1: 67–127.

Summers, L. and L. Pritchett, 1993. "The Structural-Adjustment Debate." *American Economic Review* 83 (May): 383–389.

Svejnar, J., 1989. "Models of Modern-Sector Labor Market Institutions in Developing Countries." *World Development* 17: 1409–1415.

Syrquin, M. and H. Chenery, 1989. "Three Decades of Industrialization." *World Bank Economic Review* 3: 145–182.

Taylor, L., 1990. "Structuralist CGE Models." In L. Taylor, ed., *Socially Relevant Policy Analysis: Structuralist Computable General Equilibrium Models for the Developing World* (MIT Press, Cambridge, MA).

———, 1993. "Stabilization, Adjustment and Reform." In L. Taylor, ed., *The Rocky Road to Reform* (MIT Press, Cambridge, MA).

Thirsk, W., 1991. "Lessons from Tax Reform: An Overview." In J. Khalizadeh-Shirazi and A. Shah, eds., *Tax Policy in Developing Countries* (The World Bank, Washington, DC).

Thomas, V., 1991. "Trade Policy Reform." In V. Thomas et al., eds., *Restructuring Economies in Distress: Policy Reform and the World Bank* (Oxford University Press, New York).

Thoumi, F., 1981. "International Trade Strategies, Employment and Income Distribution in Colombia." In A. Krueger, ed., *Trade and Employment in Developing Countries: Individual Studies, Vol. I* (University of Chicago Press for the National Bureau of Economic Research, Chicago).

Tornell, A., 1991. "On the Ineffectiveness of Made-to-Measure Protectionist Programs." In E. Helpman and A. Razin, eds., *International Trade and Trade Policy* (MIT Press, Cambridge, MA).

Truong, D. and C. Gates, 1996. "Vietnam's Gradualist Economic Reforms." In A. Jilberto and A. Mommen, eds., *Liberalization in the Developing World* (Routledge, New York).

Turnham, D., 1993. *Employment and Development: A New Review of the Evidence* (Organization for Economic Cooperation and Development, Paris).

Tybout, J., 1996. "Heterogeneity and Productivity Growth: Assessing the Evidence." In M. Roberts and J. Tybout, eds., *Industrial Evolution in Developing Countries: Micro Patterns of Turnover, Productivity and Market Structure* (Oxford University Press, New York).

———, 1996. "Scale Economies as a Source of Efficiency Gains." In M. Roberts and J. Tybout, eds., *Industrial Evolution in Developing Countries: Micro Patterns of Turnover, Productivity, and Market Structure* (Oxford University Press, New York).

Tybout, J., J. de Melo, and V. Corbo, 1991. "The Effects of Trade Reforms on Scale and Technical Efficiency: New Evidence from Chile." *Journal of International Economics* 31: 231–250.

Tybout, J. and D. Westbrook, 1995. "Trade Liberalization and the Dimensions of Efficiency Change in Mexican Manufacturing Industries." *Journal of International Economics* 39: 53–78.

Uzawa, H., 1962. "Production Functions with Constant Elasticities of Substitution." *Review of Economic Studies* 29: 291–299.

Vera-Vasallo, A., 1996. "Foreign Investment and Competitive Development in Latin America and the Carribean." *CEPAL Review* 60: 133–141.

Vousden, N. and N. Campbell, 1994. "The Organizational Cost of Protection." *Journal of International Economics* 37: 219–238.

Wagao, J., 1992. "Adjustment Policies in Tanzania, 1981–89: The Impact on Growth, Structure and Human Welfare." In G. Cornia, R. van der Hoeven, and T. Mkandawire, eds., *Africa's Recovery in the 1990s* (St. Martin's Press, New York).

Wanigatunga, R., 1987. "Direct Private Overseas Investment in Export-Oriented Ventures: Recent Developments in Sri Lanka." In V. Cable and B. Persaud, eds., *Developing with Foreign Investment* (Croom Helm, New York).

Weissman, S., 1990. "Structural Adjustment in Africa: Insights from the Experiences of Ghana and Senegal." *World Development* 18: 1621–1634.

Westbrook, D. and J. Tybout, 1993. "Estimating Returns to Scale with Large, Imperfect Panels: An Application to Chilean Manufacturing Industries." *World Bank Economic Review* 7: 85–112.

Wilcoxen, P., 1993. "Supply Elasticities in the Presence of Adjustment Costs." *Journal of Policy Modeling* 15: 91–97.

Williamson, J., 1988. "Migration and Urbanization." In H. Chenery and T. N. Srinivasan, eds., *Handbook of Development Economics, Vol. 1* (North-Holland, Amsterdam).

World Bank, 1993. *The East Asian Miracle: Economic Growth and Public Policy* (Oxford University Press, New York).

Worrell, D. et al., 1987. "Private Foreign Investment in Barbados." In V. Cable and B. Persaud, eds., *Developing with Foreign Investment* (Croom Helm, New York).

Yaghmaian, B., 1994. "An Empirical Investigation of Exports, Development and Growth in Developing Countries: Challenging the Neoclassical Theory of Export-Led Growth." *World Development* 22: 1977–1995.

Young, A., 1991. Learning by Doing and the Dynamic Effects of International Trade." *Quarterly Journal of Economics* 106: 369–406.

Zack-Williams, A., 1992. "Sierre Leone: The Deepening Crisis and Survival Strategies." In J. Nyang'oro and T. Shaw, eds., *Beyond Structural Adjustment in Africa* (Praeger, New York).

Zhang, L., 1994. "Location-Specific Advantages and Manufacturing Direct Foreign Investment in South China." *World Development* 22: 45–53.

Index

For EU product safety concerns, contact us at Calle de José Abascal, 56–1°, 28003 Madrid, Spain or eugpsr@cambridge.org.

 www.ingramcontent.com/pod-product-compliance
Ingram Content Group UK Ltd.
Pitfield, Milton Keynes, MK11 3LW, UK
UKHW012158180425
457623UK00018B/262